"This is an original and welcome theoretical and comparative contribution. Professor Baykan's volume shows the advantages of focusing on the deeds and performative practices of populist micro politics that seek immediacy, responsiveness, and short-term effectiveness. *Populism as Governmental Practice* weaves together how day-to-day interactions between populist political machines and deprived constituencies are based on personalism and clientelism. The volume illustrates how populist policies in Turkey, Venezuela, Greece, India, the Philippines, Egypt, and the U.S. offer immediate material and symbolic rewards over long term solutions".

Carlos de la Torre, *University of Florida Center for Latin American Studies, U.S.*

"The study of populism often centers on its role as an oppositional political force. In this book, Toygar Sinan Baykan makes important contributions to our understanding of populism in power, as a form of government practice. The book sheds new light on the distinctive features of populist governing practices, and the tools adopted by populists to administer their authority. This is a most welcome addition to scholarly debates regarding populism's political style and its implications for democratic governance".

Kenneth Roberts, *Cornell University, U.S.*

POPULISM AS GOVERNMENTAL PRACTICE

Populism as Governmental Practice illustrates how populism functions as a phenomenon of power and draws attention to the brighter and darker consequences of populist rule for ordinary people across the world via bottom-up analyses of populist experiences of government in remarkably different national contexts including Turkey, Venezuela, Greece, India, Philippines, Egypt, and the United States.

By proposing an understanding of politics that is broader than the one embraced in current populism research, it focuses on a realm stretching beyond the electoral high politics of ideas/ideologies, discourses, public performances/styles, and mobilization efforts. The book theorizes populism as a responsive political/governmental practice in congruence with the material and symbolic expectations of populist audiences and analyses it as a rich praxis of governing people and things that is blurring the boundaries between public and the private as well as formal and the informal while embracing swiftness in temporal terms.

Through an interpretive perspective focusing on the bounded rationalities and moral economies embedded in the populist rule and popular obeyance to it, this book would appeal to researchers and students of politics and its sub-disciplines as well as to the non-expert audience curious about the micro dynamics of populist rule.

Toygar Sinan Baykan is an Assistant Professor of Politics at Kırklareli University in Turkey. His main areas of expertise are populism, party politics, party-voter linkages, and Turkish politics. He published reviews and articles in journals such as *Party Politics*, *Democratization*, *Mediterranean Politics*, and *Third World Quarterly*. He is the author of the monograph *Justice and Development Party in Turkey: Populism, Personalism, Organization* (Cambridge University Press, 2018) and he contributed to the volume *Populism in Global Perspective* (Routledge, 2021) with an analysis of contemporary populism in Turkey.

Routledge Studies in Social and Political Thought

Against the Background of Social Reality
Defaults, Commonplaces, and the Sociology of the Unmarked
Carmelo Lombardo and Lorenzo Sabetta

The Cognitive Foundations of Classical Sociological Theory
Ryan McVeigh

Social Theory and the Political Imaginary
Practice, Critique, and History
Craig Browne

Being a (Lived) Body
Aesthesiological and Phenomenological Paths
Tonino Griffero

Revisiting Social Theory
Challenges and Possibilities
Edited by D.V. Kumar

Alfred Schutz, Phenomenology, and the Renewal of Interpretive Social Science
Besnik Pula

Populism as Governmental Practice
Spatial, Operational and Temporal Dynamics
Toygar Sinan Baykan

For a full list of titles in this series, please visit www.routledge.com/series/RSSPT

POPULISM AS GOVERNMENTAL PRACTICE

Spatial, Operational and Temporal Dynamics

Toygar Sinan Baykan

LONDON AND NEW YORK

Designed cover image: Toygar Sinan Baykan

First published 2024
by Routledge
4 Park Square, Milton Park, Abingdon, Oxon OX14 4RN

and by Routledge
605 Third Avenue, New York, NY 10158

Routledge is an imprint of the Taylor & Francis Group, an informa business

© 2024 Toygar Sinan Baykan

The right of Toygar Sinan Baykan to be identified as author of this work has
been asserted in accordance with sections 77 and 78 of the Copyright, Designs
and Patents Act 1988.

All rights reserved. No part of this book may be reprinted or reproduced or
utilised in any form or by any electronic, mechanical, or other means, now
known or hereafter invented, including photocopying and recording, or in any
information storage or retrieval system, without permission in writing from
the publishers.

Trademark notice: Product or corporate names may be trademarks or registered
trademarks, and are used only for identification and explanation without intent
to infringe.

British Library Cataloguing-in-Publication Data
A catalogue record for this book is available from the British Library

Library of Congress Cataloging-in-Publication Data
Names: Baykan, Toygar Sinan, author.
Title: Populism as governmental practice : spatial, operational and
temporal dynamics / Toygar Sinan Baykan.
Description: New York : Routledge, 2024. | Series: Routledge Studies in
Social and Political Thought | Includes bibliographical references and index.
Identifiers: LCCN 2024005508 (print) | LCCN 2024005509 (ebook) | ISBN
9781032279145 (hbk) | ISBN 9781032279107 (pbk) | ISBN 9781003294627 (ebk)
Subjects: LCSH: Populism--Cross-cultural studies.
Classification: LCC JC423 .B2738 2024 (print) | LCC JC423 (ebook) |
DDC 320.56/62--dc23/eng/20240315
LC record available at https://lccn.loc.gov/2024005508
LC ebook record available at https://lccn.loc.gov/2024005509

ISBN: 978-1-032-27914-5 (hbk)
ISBN: 978-1-032-27910-7 (pbk)
ISBN: 978-1-003-29462-7 (ebk)

DOI: 10.4324/9781003294627

Typeset in Sabon
by KnowledgeWorks Global Ltd.

In memory of my grandfathers,
Ali Şükrü Baykan (1923–2007) and Hüseyin
Çağlayan (1931–2017):
Unprivileged men with extraordinary dexterity.

CONTENTS

List of illustrations   *xi*
Preface and acknowledgements   *xii*

SECTION I
Exploring everyday administration by populists   **1**

1 Introduction: Populism as governmental practice   3

SECTION II
**Theory: Uncovering populist undercurrents in
everyday politics and government**   **29**

2 Contemporary theories of populism: Shifting the
focus from the stage of electoral politics to mundane
governmental practice   31

3 Understanding populism as governmental practice:
Colonization of modern governmentalities from below   55

SECTION III
Case studies   **85**

4 Responsive political practice in Turkey in historical
perspective: From "politics of expediency" to "populism"   87

x Contents

5 Populism as public administration and policy in the
AKP years in Turkey: A multi-domain analysis   103

6 The populist economic conduct under Chavez rule
in Venezuela   138

7 Bureaucracy during Greece's populist democracy:
The PASOK practice   153

8 Populist judicial practice in India under BJP rule:
Challenging secularism via judicial tactics   171

9 Duterte's penal populism in Philippines   190

10 Nasser's socio-economic and education policies in
Egypt: Virtues and ills of "populist social contract" 207

11 The populist foreign policy conduct during Trump's
presidency in the United States   222

SECTION IV
Conclusion   **245**

12 Enlarging the scope of "politics": Dynamics and
consequences of populist governmental practice and
some methodological and theoretical implications   247

Index   *271*

LIST OF ILLUSTRATIONS

Tables

2.1	Dimensions of "politics proper" and "micro politics"	36
2.2	Varieties of patron-client relations and their affinity to populism	42
3.1	Non-political, non-populism, and different instances of populism in spatial, operational, and temporal dimensions	63

Figure

3.1	Positive feedback loop among the spatial, operational, and temporal dynamics of populism as governmental practice	64

PREFACE AND ACKNOWLEDGEMENTS

This book, intellectually, has been a journey to the past and, then, to the present for me. With this book, I feel that, I arrived at a synthesis between the intellectual orientation that I acquired on politics at a period stretching back to my undergraduate and early postgraduate years in Turkey thanks to teachers and mentors like Alev Özkazanç, Tülin Öngen, Fethi Açıkel, Galip Yalman, and Necmi Erdoğan and perspectives I acquired during my postgraduate studies thanks to scholars and advisors such as Eric Jan Zürcher, John Breuilly, Aleks Szczerbiak, and Paul Taggart. All of these names, and many other very devoted and talented teachers and mentors that I encountered throughout my undergraduate and postgraduate studies whose names are impossible to fully mention here, left a lasting impact on my understanding of research and teaching. Some of these names were probably not fully aware of how decisive their influence on how their students see things, and they were in the opinion that they were simply doing what they had to do in their relations with their students. The relationships they established with their students were, in fact, excellent exemplary conduct of teaching and mentoring in terms of substance and style. I owe all these people a huge intellectual debt for the perspective that I developed in this book. I hope they accept this as a belated expression of personal and intellectual gratitude.

This also means that the idea in this book has a story that is going back in years to a period before my postgraduate studies had started. As someone who was born and raised in Turkey and who had his undergraduate degree in politics in a "developing" country, it is hard to miss informal aspects of politics and how conventional party politics penetrates into everyday lives of citizens via ways and channels that are surpassing formal implementations of official policy decisions. In contexts like Turkey, it becomes hard to see key concepts of politics like power, policy, democracy, etc., from the perspective of restricted formal meanings attributed to these concepts and from the point of view of approaches exclusively focusing on legal and official realms. Thus, I, in fact, never saw populism from a restricted perspective and only as a phenomenon of electoral politics and its public and official ramifications. No doubt that populism is mainly pertaining to the realm of electoral politics but from the perspective developed in this book, populism, as a governmental practice, always surpasses the domain of electoral politics and shapes official policy formation and implementation as well as non-official and informal measures and practices undertaken by populist incumbents.

But it had not been possible to grasp and present the phenomenon in the way I proposed in this book until very recently, without the long and formative experience I have had in Turkey as a lecturer in a recently founded public university after my postgraduate studies in the United Kingdom. As a student of political science in Turkey, I have been witnessing the rise of the *Adalet ve Kalkınma Partisi* (AKP – the Justice and Development Party), and consolidation of its hold on power, pretty closely, personally, from the very beginning. Later on, I also witnessed this story as a researcher, except for the five-year period I had in the United Kingdom for my postgraduate studies. My witness to the phenomenon of the AKP was, therefore, twofold: I had the chance to observe the dynamics of Turkish politics not only as a citizen and a student of political science but also as a researcher with "boots on the ground". For my PhD degree as well as for a broader research project that I conducted with Murat Somer after I got back to Turkey on the completion of my PhD, I have had an almost "immersive" experience in a series of long field works including hundreds of in-depth interviews with members of Erdoğan's AKP as well as with members and activists of other main parties of the Turkish political system. Although I do not use empirical data obtained in these research projects in this book, the experience and observations in these research projects, and especially in the second longer and more comprehensive project I conducted after my PhD in the United Kingdom, fundamentally altered how I see politics, and especially its practical unfolding in localities, which are in fact, can only be "populist practices", as termed in this book. While I had the chance to transform the outcome of the first research project for my PhD into a monograph (Baykan 2018a), we hope to transform the data and insights acquired in the second one into a comprehensive account of Turkish party politics based on a holistic, relational, and a dynamic understanding in the coming years.[1] Yet, I would like to reassert that these research projects based on in-depth interviews and long hours spent in the field and party

xiv Preface and acknowledgements

offices profoundly modified the way I see the phenomenon of politics and populism and pushed me to adopt a more interpretive, comprehensive, and diffuse understandings of both phenomena with the risk of disciplinary and methodological syncretism. I do think that, it is really important to strive to see the practices populist actors and audiences engaged in from the perspective of these very actors taking part in relations of populist governmental conduct and demonstrate the meanings and rationalities they embrace in these governmental practices. Abovementioned fieldworks were invaluable in this respect and deeply shaped the particular perspective of populism I have developed in this book.

Apart from these fieldworks, however, as a citizen, I believe that colleagues living and working in similar contexts in which populist incumbents are at the helm would agree with me that our personal lives under the impact of these highly politicized regimes turn into a constant fieldwork and provide ample evidence regarding the diffuse everyday impact of politics and populism. Such evidence could also emerge in unexpected encounters and observations while personally navigating the allegedly formal and public affairs of our own. In short, writing on populism under populist rule turns inevitably into personal. And from exactly this personal point of view, I started to think that populism is a phenomenon of politics that is distinguished by surpassing and blurring the boundaries between public and private, local and national, in spatial terms, informal and formal in operational terms, and continuities and ruptures in temporal terms while inclined to be swift and responsive in addressing majority demands. These are interrelated dynamics of populism in three aspects of politics that I am making, hopefully, clear in the following pages of this book.

I actually wanted to pull together this work under more convenient circumstances on a research leave but this could not be possible. I applied for two research grants for this project and they were rejected. In addition, initially, the proposal for this book was rejected by a reviewer and accepted only by two other reviewers. I am in fact indebted to all of these reviewers, yet for such a long-term scholarly commitment, these were hardly supportive incidents for me. I am not mentioning these failures during the process of writing because I actually think that these were exceptional hurdles. Such rejections are part and parcel of the academic vocation and I am sure many colleagues experience such difficulties – and perhaps the worse – and need to endure them. But I wanted to write about these rejections and difficulties to highlight a couple of points: The first point in this regard is that, despite the initial disappointment, I was inclined to interpret these rejections as signs of a "controversy" more than evidence demonstrating the "total failure" of the idea developed in this account since these rejections were accompanied by very encouraging feedbacks from other colleagues. The second point that led me to highlight these failures during the process is that they actually rendered

Preface and acknowledgements **xv**

the support of the colleagues, institutions – in which I undertook this research – and the publisher much more valuable and critical in the production of this account.

As I mentioned, the idea developed in this book was supported by two reviewers with very useful feedbacks. I am certainly indebted to them. In the later exchange of ideas, I was also encouraged by Pierre Ostiguy for the completion of this book. Since my postgraduate studies in the United Kingdom has started, he has been very generous towards me with his time and we had the chance to produce other works together. His support has always been very valuable to me. Yaprak Gürsoy was also by my side during the initial process of writing and responding to review reports regarding the proposal for this book. Her suggestions were immensely beneficial. She also provided me with a publication on Greek politics that I did not have access. I am indebted to her for this particular support too. In a later time during the writing process, I also had the privilege to have the thoughts of Artemis Papatheodorou on a couple of strategic issues regarding the writing process of this book. I would like to especially thank her for the helpful and realistic interpretation in a crisis situation. Her presence in İstanbul during the writing process was a blessing. In order to access Guy Hermet's ideas on populism I needed the help of French colleagues since I do not know French. For this, Elise Massicard came to rescue by providing me with translations of relevant parts of Hermet's work (2001). Since my postgraduate studies in the United Kingdom, Elise Massicard has been very supportive and this time, too, this did not change. She is a colleague who deeply affected the way I see party politics in Turkey through her profoundly innovative analyses of Turkish party politics.

I also would like to acknowledge the contribution of a couple of conferences I attended with the theoretical parts of this book project. In *21st International Public Administration Forum* in 2022 in Eskişehir, Turkey and *The European Union's External Relations and the Perspectives of the Global Order (EUXGLOB) International Conference* in 2022 in Cluj-Napoca, Romania, I had the chance to present and receive feedback regarding some of the ideas included in this book.[2] An original version of the theoretical Chapter 2 was published in Turkish years ago by the *Birikim* (Baykan 2018b). I would like to thank Tanıl Bora and *Birikim* for providing me with the opportunity to publicly express my ideas regarding populism as a practice at that time and now for allowing me to reuse a revised and expanded English version of this article in this book.

After the completion of the first draft of this book, in order to compensate the expert feedback that I was not able to receive in person from the colleagues during the writing process in Turkey, I started to get in touch with experts on the theoretical and empirical parts of this book via email. Carlos de la Torre was one of the first to get back to me with some very useful

xvi Preface and acknowledgements

recommendations for the theoretical parts and he reviewed the chapter on Venezuela. He also drew my attention to a few very important and relevant works for the perspective I developed in this book. I am truly indebted to him for his willingness to help a colleague that he does not know in person. Similarly, it was very kind of Kenneth Roberts who accepted to read parts of this book and eventually suggested a couple of very important clarifications for the theoretical arguments in the book. I am really indebted to him for his time and support. Dimitri Sotiropoulos read theoretical parts of the book as well as the chapter on Greece and provided me with a detailed critical feedback. He was very generous with his time and I am really indebted to him for his constructive criticism. Narendra Subramanian too provided some very critical feedback on the chapter on India which led me to rethink and refine some of the theoretical arguments in the book. I also want to mention Kurt Weyland's help. Unfortunately, he could not find the time to read the book in a very busy period of year. But he was so patient towards my queries, and I was able to find the opportunity to exchange ideas with him regarding a couple of central arguments proposed in this book in a series of email exchanges. This was very kind of him. For the case studies included in the book, I also had the privilege to get very useful and constructive feedback from a series of colleagues and friends. Adele Webb provided important comments and criticisms for the chapter on the Philippines. Özge Özkoç had some crucial suggestions for the chapter on Egypt under Nasser's rule. Thanks to Sarah Holz I was able to get in touch with Faisal Chaudhry, a legal historian focusing on the Indian sub-continent. I benefitted very much from his recommendations in the chapter on India. My friend Nikos Christofis read the chapter on Panhellenic Socialist Movement (PASOK), drew my attention to some critical lacunas and recommended to me a few crucial reads on the topic. I am really indebted to him for his very detailed comments and criticisms. I appreciate the "responsiveness" of all of these colleagues despite their extremely tight schedules.

I would also like to extend my gratitude to my current institution: Kırklareli Üniversitesi (KLU). As an institution, it is, in fact, a product of the populist expansion of higher education in Turkey under the AKP rule. It has many problems like similar institutions across Turkey which I elaborate in Chapter 5 from a generalizing point of view on the impact of populist governmental practice in the realm of higher education. Yet, the KLU, like other similar new higher education institutions, is also home to some really bright and hardworking academics and administrative staff. Especially the Faculty of Economic and Administrative Sciences, and the Department of Politics, in which I am located, has created an environment that is conducive towards opening room and providing flexibility to its members to pursue their own academic goals. While these recently founded institutions may not be that supportive in terms of financing and providing the required logistics (such as adequate collections in libraries, generous travel and conference grants, academic staff with expertise in cases other than Turkey, etc.) for research projects such as this one, with right people at right positions, these institutions may render the production process of projects demanding long-term scholarly commitments much easier with providing their academic staff the required time and flexibility. So, the environment of "negative freedom" at the KLU with regards to the use of time by its academic personnel is much appreciated.

In addition, in this or that way, the perspective I developed in this account has been enriched by numerous encounters across the faculty with colleagues with profoundly different views on politics and society in my department and in other departments. I cannot state every single one of them here but I want to thank all of them, who helped me to develop my perspective in unexpected ways. I, however, especially want to thank Erhan Özşeker and İhsan Ömer Atagenç. In numerous conversations with them, I have benefitted from their thoughts on matters that are relevant to the current account. I would also like to thank the library staff of our university too. They were very helpful and responsive in providing books via interlibrary loan that I needed to read but that were not existing in our library. I had to apply this service pretty frequently.

But probably the most critical contribution made by the institution to this research project was done by my students. Some of my students were, in fact, engaged in politics of the populist AKP, and the rest knew the realities of politics in impoverished Turkish localities in the peripheries of İstanbul and provinces of Turkey very well from their own experiences. In many different courses I taught at the KLU, our discussions revolved around the themes of this book, and in many instances, we exchanged roles since I learned a lot of very interesting details regarding the conduct of politics in Turkey's distinct localities from my undergraduate and postgraduate students. Hence, in my courses at the KLU, teaching has never been a one-way relationship. I thank my students for the contributions they made to the perspective that I developed in this book.

I have already mentioned the rejections and hurdles in the process of writing this book. In this respect, I have this feeling that I owe to express a special acknowledgement for the publisher and editors of this book, most notably Emily Briggs and Lakshita Joshi. They certainly took a risk in their support for this idea since there were counterarguments in one of the reviews regarding the substance of the book proposal and the credentials of the author. Thus, in terms of current international academic hierarchies and conventions,[3] editors and Routledge, in my point of view, took a risky decision to support a work by an early career researcher located in a relatively less established institution in a developing country. This open-mindedness and critical perspective, I think, deserves recognition and I know I am not

xviii Preface and acknowledgements

the only one benefitting from this very merit of Routledge as an institution which always supports the work by established as well as emerging researchers. I am also indebted to the Routledge for more practical support. They also provided me with a critical recent volume on the theme of this book, *Complexity of Populism*, by Diehl and Bargetz (2024a).

The very nature of the interpretive and interdisciplinary approach I embraced in this book also led me to trespass many disciplinary boundaries and areas of expertise. This book is not really only a political science account of populism in Turkish politics but I am also stepping into the domains of several other disciplines of social science and sub-disciplines of political science and writing about several other cases of populism. I cannot at all argue that I am an expert on all of these disciplines and cases included in this book. As a pre-emptive note, I should assert here that, for understanding Greek, Venezuelan, or Indian populism and politics, this book may not be the best starting point at all. But I do think that reading and writing on these remarkably different cases have provided ample evidence to this account to demonstrate some universal proclivities of populism in power at a theoretical level. While doing research on these cases, I was amazed to see many curious parallels between Turkey and other nations in remarkably different corners of the world. It has been a very formative intellectual journey for me. But still, I know, I take the risk of failing in my examinations of these nations in certain respects in this book with standards set by experts of these cases. But this was a risk I wanted to take for such an endeavour that, I believe, especially in the Global South, may provide us with new tools to understand the praxis of populism, which is one of the fundamental aspects of contemporary mass politics. Needless to say, all the errors in the text are mine.

Finally, I would like to apologize to my wife Nigar and my son Ali Tuna for the times that I stole from them for this book and thank them for their patience against my constant excuse of "I have to work".

Kırklareli, Turkey
31.8.2023

Notes

1 For an initial outcome of this second research project, see Baykan and Somer (2022). For further reflection on the process of fieldwork in these research projects, see Baykan (2023).
2 These are accessible in proceedings volumes by these conferences. See Baykan (2022a, 2022b).
3 For a recent demonstration of these academic hierarchies and structural factors underlying them, see Norris (2021).

References

Baykan, T. S. (2018a). *The Justice and Development Party in Turkey – Populism, Personalism, Organization*. Cambridge: Cambridge University Press.

Baykan, T. S. (2018b). "İdare-i maslahatçılık"tan "popülizm"e Türkiye'de duyarlı siyasal pratik: "Popülizm yapıyorsun!". *Birikim*, *353*, 15–36.

Baykan, T. S. (2022a). Popülizm ve Kamu Yönetimi: İçsel Bir Çelişki mi? Research Paper presented in "21. Uluslararası Kamu Yönetimi Forumu", Anadolu Üniversitesi, Eskişehir, Turkey, on March 24–26, 2022.

Baykan, T. S. (2022b). Populism as policy practice: The case of Turkish foreign policy practice. Research Paper presented in "EUXGLOB II, The EU and NATO approaches to the Black Sea region", Babes Bolyai University, Cluj-Napoca, Romania, on May 5–6, 2022.

Baykan, T. S. (2023). Power negotiations in the field: Ethical and practical challenges of field research on party politics in hybrid regime settings. *International Quarterly for Asian Studies*, *54*(1), 59–89.

Baykan, T. S. & M. Somer (2022). Politics of notables versus national machine: Social, political and state transformations, party organizations and clientelism during AKP governments. *European Journal of Turkish Studies*, *34*. https://journals.openedition.org/ejts/8111, accessed: 18.8.2023.

Diehl, P. & B. Bargetz (Eds.). (2024a). *The Complexity of Populism – New Approaches and Methods*. London: Routledge.

Hermet, G. (2001). *Les Populismes dans le Monde*. Paris: Fayard.

Norris, P. (2021). What maximizes productivity and impact in political science research? *European Political Science*, *20*(1), 34–57.

SECTION I

Exploring everyday administration by populists

1

INTRODUCTION

Populism as governmental practice

The catastrophe (by good intentions)

On February 6, 2023, Southeast Turkey was hit by two devastating earthquakes on the same day. The earthquakes affected ten provinces with sizeable urban areas such as Maraş, Hatay, and Adıyaman. While official records state that the disaster took more than 50,000 lives,[1] there are reasons to believe that the number of victims was much higher given the inability of the state to keep such records during the chaos that had prevailed after the earthquakes and the control over the relevant state institutions and mainstream media by the AKP (*Adalet ve Kalkınma Partisi* – The Justice and Development Party).[2] In some cases, such as Hatay and Adıyaman, city centres home to tens of thousands of people were almost completely devastated. The earthquakes and their impact have been subject to extensive discussions in the Turkish media. Throughout long hours and in numerous pages, reasons behind the catastrophe emerged after the earthquakes were scrutinized. The magnitude of the earthquakes (Mw 7.8 and Mw 7.7) was one of the factors many pundits – especially those close to the AKP – pointed out as the main reason behind the catastrophe. Indeed, the magnitude of the February 2023 earthquakes was some of the greatest that the world has experienced in recent decades, although they were not classified as "great" earthquakes. But they were the biggest earthquakes Turkey ever experienced in its modern history.[3]

Geologists and civil engineers discussed the technical dynamics of the earthquakes in length. While there were defensive arguments that no building would survive such a disaster, there were also compelling counterarguments

DOI: 10.4324/9781003294627-2

4 Exploring everyday administration by populists

in the public discussion that much bigger earthquakes caused less suffering in other cases and other parts of the world. As one of the civil engineers who took part in these discussions pointed out, even in such a major earthquake, the residential buildings were expected to keep the inhabitants safe.[4] Indeed, ultimately, the discussion regarding the reasons behind the catastrophe focused on the "human made" factors, such as the choice of land for the construction of residential areas and the quality of buildings.[5] In numerous cases in the areas hit hard by the earthquakes, it was possible to find buildings with no harm at all alongside buildings that turned into rubbles on the ground. The public discussion, therefore, turned into furious debates regarding the responsibility of petty contractors who built these flimsy residential structures. Many investigations were initiated after the earthquake regarding their responsibility in the catastrophe and there were numerous arrests of contractors whose buildings collapsed in the earthquake.[6]

Nevertheless, as some law experts pointed out, investigations about contractors were blatantly missing the "joint liability" in the catastrophe that was based on the informal consensuses/complicities among mayors, local politicians, and a local stratum of entrepreneurs – most notably, petty contractors.[7] Thanks to some up-to-date qualitative research on Turkish party politics and clientelism,[8] we know pretty well that sources unofficially and informally extracted from local as well as national businesses, in general, and the construction sector, in particular, are one of the major methods of financing widespread clientelistic practices in Turkey. Local politicians, and especially mayors, who want to deliver services to their constituencies and need to engage in particularistic and clientelistic relations with the urban poor, in the absence of other financial means, usually exchange their authority to authorize constructions in return of sumptuous "donations" and other, more confidential, kickbacks from the local and national business classes across Turkey. This certainly causes many negligences including the proper controls regarding whether these buildings are built according to safety standards by contractors. Practices like authorizing really high-rise apartment buildings in earthquake zones in return for confidential kickbacks (partly distributed to the urban poor as clientelistic benefits and partly enrich local political elites in corrupt forms) and also the incremental legalization of the slumhouses (*gecekondular*) constructed on the public land by the urban poor – without any expertise and consideration to safety regulations – throughout electoral cycles, have been part and parcel of Turkish urban politics. This is also to say that "joint liability" in the construction sector in Turkey is not confined to the relationships between national and local political elites and national and petty local contractors but also extends to large, poor populations in urban Turkey.

When the picture is complemented with the responsibility of ordinary and underprivileged citizens, it becomes clear that it was remarkably more diffuse

Introduction **5**

and widespread cooperations/complicities and informal practices of government, or what is called "populist governmental practice" in this account, and the "good intentions" behind these practices (the urge to quickly help the urban poor, for example), that paved the road to the terrible outcome on February 6, 2023, and that turned a natural disaster into a "human made" catastrophe. While "populist governmental practice" by populist elites solves problems in the short-term for populist constituencies and majorities by conscious negligences and admirable dexterity (including "petty corruption"), it inevitably paves the way to remarkable problems in the long run. This book strives to problematize such tendencies and informal and unofficial practices of government, or the "populist governmentality", that is shaped under the impact of electoral democracies especially in the developing world. From a more theoretical and methodological point of view, this study proposes to understand populism as a key "practice" in the establishment of diffuse and comprehensive power relations with concrete effects on citizens' life in contemporary mass politics. This also requires a holistic, relational, and interpretive approach to populism, in particular, and, politics, in general. This account is such an endeavour.

The rationale of the book

We are living in an era of populism. Not just in academic debates but in everyday political vocabulary populism has become a reference word for describing unconventional views, discourses, styles, and electoral strategies of media-savvy politicians of our age. But is populism really only about worldviews/ideologies, public discourses, styles, and electoral strategies of parties and leaders? In fact, populism has concrete policy implications. Populism, however one would like to define it, changes our lives for good or bad. Populism is about the distinction between elite and the people, about constructing socio-political identities and new conflict axes, and about mobilizing supporters around controversial leaders. But populism, especially in power, is also about how public policy is designed and implemented, how wealth is distributed, how institutions and bureaucracy are constructed, reconstructed, reformed, and run, and how very mundane day-to-day affairs of national and local government are handled. Populism not only impacts lives of millions today through how it shapes national and macro level political discourses and styles, but it also profoundly changes local and micro level relations in neighbourhoods, institutions, and communities which have immediate impact on our daily lives. The example I chose for beginning this book is not unique. Perhaps not as bitter as this one, but readers of this account can recall many similar incidents in contexts they know well.

Current research on populism, however, has usually been based on a conventional understanding of the "political" and focused on ideologies,

6 Exploring everyday administration by populists

strategies, political discourses, or political styles as the realm of the phenomenon. In this book, first, by focusing on a series of political actors of the multi-party era in Turkey, I explore another realm that may entail implications for studies on populism: More mundane, day-to-day practices of government and administration by populists in local and national offices. I also put Turkey in comparative perspective in this regard and focus on a few important cases of populist governmental practice with remarkably different regional characteristics including the United States, Venezuela, Greece, India, Egypt, and the Philippines.

One of the questions of this inquiry would be as follows: Can we define (a) distinctive way(s) of populist administration of people and things? This question will lead to a broader theoretical discussion focusing on the nature of populism: Is populism something necessarily "redemptive" as Margaret Canovan (1999) argues? Is it, as politics *par excellence*, in full contradistinction with administration as Laclau (2005) argues? Or is it possible to talk about the "dirty institutionality" of populism in power as asserted by Pierre Ostiguy (2016)? Can we understand populism as the colonization of "modern governmentalities" from below? Thus, this book is also an attempt to relate studies on populism with the literature on governmentality and power and resistance in everyday life stretching from Foucault (2000) to Michel de Certeau (2002) and James C. Scott (1990, 1999). Additionally, this account also aims to put theories of populism into dialogue with the literature on public administration and policy.

The relevant literatures

Current theoretical-conceptual discussions on populism

When the pioneering Ionescu and Gellner (1969) volume was published at the end of the 1960s, the consensus around populism was much weaker. The volume was full of distinct empirical reflections of the phenomenon and theoretical propositions based on these partial empirical evidences. At least since the beginning of the 2000s, however, the disagreements regarding the nature of populism gradually diminished and a sort of convention started to emerge around a few conceptual and theoretical approaches to the phenomenon, emphasizing some common features. Of course, it is hard to argue that the conceptual and theoretical problems regarding the nature of populism are completely solved, as Carlos de la Torre recently asserted (2024, 36). But it would not be an exaggeration to say that, now, the phenomenon is gaining a conceptual clarity with the rise of – and improvements in – four main theoretical approaches to populism.

First of these theoretical approaches is the ideational perspective developed by Cas Mudde based on his work on radical right in Western Europe, which defines populism as "an ideology that considers society to be ultimately separated into two homogeneous and antagonistic groups, 'the pure people' versus 'the corrupt elite', and which argues that politics should be an expression of the *volonté générale* (general will) of the people" (2004, 543). Researchers following an ideational approach to populism improved the definition proposed by Mudde in ways that rendered the concept more capable in operational terms and expanded the opportunities for cross-national comparative analyses (Hawkins *et al.* 2018).

The second prominent approach in the study of populism today belongs to Kurt Weyland. Based on his expertise in Latin American politics, Weyland defined populism "as a political strategy through which a personalistic leader seeks or exercises government power based on direct, unmediated, uninstitutionalized support from large numbers of mostly unorganized followers" (2001, 14) in a now classical article. Weyland's work inspired other researchers and shaped their analysis of non-Latin American cases. Most notably, Paul Kenny deployed the political-strategic approach and explained a series of South Asian cases of populism from this perspective (2017, 2018). Kenny locates the phenomenon of populism based on a national personalistic leadership in contradistinction to a politics based on powerful local notables and their local patronage networks or programmatic and institutionalized parties.

Laclau's discourse-theoretical approach has been immensely influential in the literature too and tend to underline the importance of the conflict between the "people" and the "elite" in the phenomenon of populism. According to Laclau (2005) – and researchers following the tradition of discourse-theoretical approach – populism is not a specific idea or ideology but a political logic (in fact, it is the political logic *par excellence* for Laclau) that articulates heterogenous social demands and constructs the "people" against an exclusionary and oppressive "power bloc". Researchers following this approach revised some of the presumptions of Laclau and, for example, interrogated the implication of his work that conflates politics with populism (Stavrakakis 2004; de Cleen & Glynos 2021). Others following a discourse-theoretical approach, for example, emphasized the vertical relationship established between the "people" and the "elite" in populist discourse and tried to distinguish this from more horizontal "us" and "them" distinction that is central to nationalist discourses (de Cleen *et al.* 2018).

Finally, another contemporary conceptual agreement emerged around the performative and socio-cultural approach proposed by Benjamin Moffit (2016) and Pierre Ostiguy (2017). Quite similarly, both these scholars proposed to understand populism as a political style that is appealing to the popular/plebeian culture and taste of ordinary people. Ostiguy, for example, defines populism "as the antagonistic, mobilizational flaunting in politics of the culturally popular and native, and of personalism as a mode

8 Exploring everyday administration by populists

of decision-making" (2017, 84). One of the merits of performative and socio-cultural approach is that it has drawn researcher's attention, at least partially, to a realm that is stretching beyond conventional electoral politics. In a recent volume embracing performative and discourse-theoretical approaches, researchers demonstrate the impact of an allegedly "trivial" socio-cultural dimension in the real practices of populists in our age (Panizza *et al.* 2021). The current book on populist governmental practice should be considered as a further step towards the direction pointed out by performative and socio-cultural approach. But this book also enters into a qualitatively different realm of politics – that is, the realm of public administration and policy in its diffused formal and informal forms – compared to the focus of socio-cultural and performative approach on the "stage" of electoral politics.

Until this day, there was a mood in the scholarly community that all of these different approaches to populism were, at least to a certain extent, mutually exclusive. For example, while Mudde (2017, 40) criticized Weyland's approach on empirical grounds that populism can exist without personalistic leadership, Weyland criticized ideational approach for the importance it attached to ideational aspects of the phenomenon of populism, which is, in fact, inclined to be profoundly opportunistic (2017, 68). In a similar way, Katsambekis (2022) and de Cleen *et al.* (2018) criticized the ideational approach due to its static emphasis on the ideational content of populism and its disregard for the pluralistic reality of the phenomenon. From a discourse-theoretical perspective, populism is, in fact, an enterprise of hegemonic coalition building that is essentially pluralist. On the other hand, Ostiguy criticized ideational and political-strategic approaches. According to him, while ideational approach's emphasis on the "purity" and "homogeneity" of the people does not correspond to the reality, especially in Latin America, Weyland was wrong in assuming that populism is in contradistinction to a strong organization (Ostiguy 2017, 90–92). As I have already noted, discourse-theoretical approach of Laclau (2005) was already problematized by his own followers. As Stavrakakis (2004) and de Cleen and Glynos (2021) argued, it was a mistake to conflate populism with politics.

Among recent endeavours devoted to the conceptual clarification of the concept of populism, the attempt in the volume *The Complexity of Populism* (Diehl & Bargetz 2024a) and theoretical contributions to it by Diehl and Bargetz (2024b), Diehl (2024), and Carlos de la Torre (2024) are worth mentioning. This volume represents an approach that is similar to the endeavour undertaken in this book in terms of its synthetical, interdisciplinary, and non-positivistic perspective. In their theoretical contribution to *The Complexity of Populism* Diehl and Bargetz (2024b) and Diehl (2024) propose a "complex understanding of populism" that is combining three distinct realms of populism. These are ideology, communication style, and organization (Diehl 2024, 18). One of the contentions of these authors is that populism pertains to all of these domains and should be seen as a gradual phenomenon instead of a binary (Diehl 2024, 24). In other words, populism is always an issue of degree and can be seen in fuller or lesser intensity in the realms of ideology, communication, and organization. Thus, a single case can be deeply populist at an ideational level while being less populist in the realm of communication style and organization.

One of the important implications of this volume, as expressed by Carlos de la Torre (2024), is that, currently, there are positivistic and non-positivistic approaches to populism and, especially the positivistic and behaviouralist approaches have their limits. While the positivistic-behaviouralistic approaches are inclined to observe disciplinary boundaries and try to provide researchers with minimal definitions, such as the conceptual-theoretical endeavours by Mudde (2004) and Weyland (2001), non-positivistic approaches adopt a broader lens in their analysis of politics and draw attention to the implications and reflections of populism in other realms of social relations. As de la Torre notes, "non-positivist scholars argue that populism is a heuristic of the scholarly community, and that theory co-constitutes empirical reality. They refuse to reduce the complexity of populism to a definition of one or two sentences, and contend that, because the term is used to make normative arguments about democracy, citizenship, or national belonging, it will continue to be contested" (2024, 37). This non-positivistic perspective also entails interdisciplinarity and enlarges the scope of relevant domains for populism research, as noted by Diehl and Bargetz (2024b, 5).

While the contributions in Diehl and Bargetz's edition problematize the impact of populism on social and cultural domains, it still sees the phenomenon as strongly tied to electoral politics. In other words, they still consider the phenomenon as something that emerges first in the electoral realm and then diffuses to other realms. This book, in contrast, also argues that populism is not only a phenomenon of electoral politics and its socio-cultural and psychological context but is also a phenomenon of diffuse power relations that penetrates into localities and even individual households through concrete, material means as a governmental practice. It is not a phenomenon that is necessarily transmitting from the top electoral politics to the bottom and shapes cultural and social practices. In contrast, populism can also be understood as the culmination of widespread and already existing plebeian practices in the social, cultural, and administrative spheres on the ground at the top of electoral politics in the form of a particular discursive, stylistic, and organizational phenomenon. Thus, while sharing the contention in Diehl's (2024) and de la Torre's (2024) emphases that populism should be understood as a phenomenon pertaining to very different realms such as ideology, communication, and organization, I also add the domain of "governmental practice", or populism's unfolding in the

10 Exploring everyday administration by populists

realm of public administration and policy as a particular form of political praxis with its distinctive spatial, operational and temporal dynamics to this "complexity".

Studies on populism in power

No doubt that the kind of perspective proposed in this book also requires to engage with discussions on populism in power. Nevertheless, with the exception of Albertazzi and McDonnell's (2015) crucial and pioneering study, the phenomenon of populism in power has not been subject to widespread scholarly attention until very recently.[9] When scholars, and particularly political theorists such as Müller (2016) and Urbinati (2019a), focused on populism as a governmental phenomenon, their focus has been on populism's impact on conventional political institutions and realms, such as constitutions, parties, party systems, regime types (democracy or authoritarianism), state apparatuses, electoral systems, media, and civil society. All these excellent theoretical takes on populism, however, lack robust contact with (and an ethnographic grasp of) the reality on the ground regarding the implications of populism in the daily lives of millions of people across the world. While these scholars put forward a sophisticated account of how populism in power effects conventional political institutions at the macro level, they barely touch upon how populists shape and implement policies at the local level and how these leaders are distinguished from non-populist or anti-populist actors on the ground when it comes to public policies that have concrete implications for citizens' lives. The outstanding recent volumes edited by Kaltwasser *et al.* (2017), de la Torre (2019), Stockemer (2019), and Oswald (2022) mainly focus on phenomena in the realm of what I call in Chapter 2, "politics proper", such as populism's impacts on political institutions and actors (e.g., parties, party systems, social movements, and political discourses) in the political systems of polities in very different parts of the world; whereas, these scholars only partially touch upon the broader governmental performance of populism. Ultimately, their interest in populism's impact on office and policy remains within the boundaries of questions regarding how populists shape macro political institutions and discourses.

In recent years, however, we witness that a body of theoretical literature emerged on populism in power with a careful attention to its impact on state institutions and regimes. In this respect, studies by Pappas (2019), Muno and Pfeiffer (2022), Caiani and Graziano (2022), de la Torre and Peruzzotti (2018), and Enyedi and Whitefield (2020) are important. It is, however, crucial to note that more than how populism functions in various realms of administration and policy, these studies are concerned more with populism's impact on major constitutional institutions and the regime. More recently, Dieckhoff *et al.*'s (2022) volume focuses on the phenomenon of populism in power including several in-depth case studies. But this volume too, like previous accounts on the phenomenon of populism in power, is mainly concerned with questions around the impact of populism on democracy. In short, the existing literature on populism in power tend to see the phenomenon from the perspective of a conventional understanding of politics and focus on electoral and institutional politics, which are, no doubt, very important dimensions related to the phenomenon of populism in power. But, these studies are hardly concerned with more diffused impacts of populism in the realm of public administration and policy, except marking its tendency to clientelism (especially Pappas 2019 and Muno & Pfeiffer 2022).

Here, Albertazzi and McDonnell's (2015) account deserves a closer attention within the body of literature on the experience of populism in power since it systematically tests the governmental performance of populists. In an in-depth, comparative account of the experiences of three European populist parties in power (the People of Freedom and the Northern League in Italy and the Swiss People's Party in Switzerland), Albertazzi and McDonnell compellingly test what can be called the "administrative incapacity" hypothesis regarding populists in power, and they demonstrate that, in fact, populists can rule effectively when in office. However, the method Albertazzi and McDonnell employ in their study is more empirical/comparative than ethnographic/historical/comparative. In fact, they overwhelmingly focus on policy and governance outcomes instead of the policy processes and practices embraced by populists. In other words, Albertazzi and McDonnell's otherwise excellent account devoted to the analysis of "populism in power" focuses on exploring the "outcomes" of populism in power in terms of governmental performance instead of the characteristics/qualities/dynamics of the governmental and administrative practices carried out by populists when they come into power. In addition, Albertazzi and McDonnell's account only focuses on European cases of populism in power, where populists must function within more restrictive liberal governmental and institutional frameworks than in some of the cases that will be examined in this book, such as Turkey, Venezuela, and the Philippines.

Here, it should also be noted that all these accounts more or less embrace a similar theoretical/methodological approach to the phenomenon of populism (with the partial exception of some contributors to Kaltwasser *et al.*'s [2017] volume, most notably Ostiguy [2017] and Frank [2017]). All of these accounts consider populism first and foremost as an ideational/discursive phenomenon,[10] and this very ideational/discursive core of the phenomenon, according to the established literature, defines the political practice of populism in power. In other words, all of these studies encourage researchers to focus on populism from a top-down perspective or from the vantage point of the interaction at the elite level between "populist storytellers" and their enemies. This book, in contrast, proposes to understand populism from a

12 Exploring everyday administration by populists

bottom-up perspective, from the standpoint of its actors and audiences[11] on the ground and from the angle of the mundane interactions of – and exchanges between – populists and their supporters. Although such ethnographically oriented studies are by no means missing in the field of populism studies (see especially Auyero [2001]), the main body of literature is far from adopting a bottom-up perspective that focuses on the rich governmental/administrative/ political praxis of populism around the world. This is understandable since the realm of interest in ideational/discursive approaches to the phenomenon is the discursive aspect of populism. However, such macro and top-down perspectives are not very helpful in understanding what is going on "behind the stage" of electoral and institutional politics at the national and local levels because they focus mainly on the elite-driven dimensions of the broader phenomenon of populism. Populism, in fact, can be seen as a linkage strategy, political praxis, and bodily experience.

The recent literature on the nexus between populism and bureaucracy

This account is also directly related to a recently emerging cluster of works which directly focuses on the nexus between populism and bureaucracy, mostly written by researchers specialized in the field of public administration and policy. One of the pioneering accounts in this respect, alongside the case-specific analysis of Sotiropoulos (1996), is Peters and Pierre's article "Populism and Public Administration" (2019). In their article, Peters and Pierre rightly point out that the literature on populism have not paid sufficient attention to the impact of populism on public administration (2019, 1524). Following the ideational perspective to populism, one of the main contentions in Peters and Pierre's article is that anti-elitism of populism also targets bureaucracy, and, as a result, bureaucratic state (2019, 1522). Peters and Pierre define four main consequences to expect from populist rule in the realm of public administration and policy. These are diminishing role of experts, politicization of administration, increasing patronage, and centralization of power in the hands of executive branch, and most notably, in the hands of the president (2019, 1528–1529).

In this respect, Bauer and Becker's article titled "Democratic backsliding, populism and public administration" (2020) is worth mentioning, too, since it is one of the pioneering contemporary works focusing on the relationship between populism and public administration. According to Bauer and Becker, depending on the ideology of populists and the degree of robustness of the administrative state they challenge, the outcome of the encounter between populist rulers and the administrative state changes. Like Peters and Pierre (2019), Bauer and Becker embrace an ideational perspective regarding populism and argue that populism's anti-pluralism shapes its public administration policies and contributes to democratic backsliding (2020, 20–21). Developing a more nuanced perspective than Peters and Pierre, Bauer and Becker argue that populists may also see the administrative state as an instrument of realization of their anti-pluralist ideological proclivities.

Another study that is worth mentioning in this part belongs to Bartha *et al.* (2020). In this article, the authors do not only look at the impact of populism's alleged ideational content on administration and policy-making but also problematize its procedural propensities. According to Bartha *et al.*, "populist leaders tend to downplay the role of technocratic expertise, sideline veto players and implement fast and unpredictable policy changes" (2020, 71). As they note, the field of social policy and welfare is key to populism (Bartha *et al.* 2020, 71).[12] According to these authors, "populist majoritarianism is potentially incompatible with policy expertise: in the case of a marked gap between popular beliefs and area-specific policy evidence, the populist stance is by definition against expert positions shaped by mainstream policy paradigms" (Bartha *et al.* 2020, 74). More importantly, Bartha *et al.* note that "policy making under populist governance tends to have a significantly faster tempo and a shorter duration with frequent episodes of accelerations and an unpredictable timing" (Bartha *et al.* 2020, 74). In sum, according to the authors, "populist governance" in procedural terms depend on "circumventing established institutions, downplaying veto players, limiting participation of technocratic policy experts, opposition parties and civil society actors" and on "direct communication with the electorate" (Bartha *et al.* 2020, 75-Table 2). Another point that is crucial to highlight in the work of Bartha *et al.* is that they convincingly demonstrate that, in terms of policy content, populism has no particular ideological proclivity and can be really flexible and pragmatic (Bartha *et al.* 2020, 75-Table 2). Thus, what explains populism's success in power is its ideological flexibility (Bartha *et al.* 2020, 780).

All of these studies underline the diminishing impact of expertise under populist rule, anti-institutionalist proclivities of populist incumbents and their tendency to patronage. But, these studies are far from providing researchers with a dynamic understanding of populism as a governmental practice, as I try to provide with the current study. In order to do this, researchers need to pay more attention to the spatial, procedural, and temporal dynamics of "populist governance" more than its ideological and discursive dimensions. With the partial exception of Bartha *et al.*'s (2020) work, it is hard to say that current work on the nexus between populism and public administration puts a special emphasis on temporal and procedural/operational dynamics of populism in power. These works on populist governance are more on

14 Exploring everyday administration by populists

the outcomes of populist rule for public administration than its functioning in practice, which generates concrete consequences for the daily lives of ordinary people.

Studies on populism in Turkey

Turkey is a key case in this book. This is why I want to briefly touch upon the literature on populism in Turkish politics. Economists such as Korkut Boratav (1983) and Çağlar Keyder (1987) had defined the political economy of Turkey in 1970s as a regime of "populism" in their work in 1980s.[13] In 1980s, scholars like İlkay Sunar (1985) proposed to understand populism as a phenomenon that is tightly connected to patronage and pork-barrel politics which emerged with the transition to multi-party politics in Turkey in the mid-20th century. Although their understanding of populism was limited with the then available literature on the concept, which was mainly produced for the analysis of Latin American cases, one of the merits of these early studies on populism in Turkey was their emphasis on the centrality of material exchange and a kind of consensual framework between governments and large and unprivileged majorities that populism was based upon.

Following the developments in the general theoretical literature on the phenomenon, it was only in the late 2000s, works on Turkish populism with theoretically more precise approaches started to appear. Some of these studies deployed the notion of neoliberal populism in order to explain the rise of the AKP and its electoral dominance (Yıldırım 2009; Bozkurt 2013). Following these studies, works depending on more "political" understandings of the phenomenon started to appear, largely following the definitions proposed by Cas Mudde and Kurt Weyland. Works by Aytaç and Öniş (2014), Aytaç and Elçi (2019), Selçuk (2016), Dinçşahin (2012), Yabanci (2020), Çelik and Balta (2020), and Çarkoğlu *et al.* (2022) are examples of these theoretically more well-located works. More recently, a series of studies problematizing the relationship between populism and specific policy fields in Turkish politics also started to emerge. The studies by Özpek and Park (2020), Yavuz and Öztürk (2020), and Kaya (2019) are worth mentioning in this respect. And the emergence of a few studies embracing the socio-cultural and performative approach to populism is another significant development in the literature on populism in Turkey. Studies by Aslan (2021) and Karaosmanoğlu (2020) are worth mentioning in this regard.

All these studies, including my previous work (Baykan 2018a, 2019a, 2019b),[14] although contributed to the development of theoretical-conceptual accuracy in the study of populism with reference to the case of Turkey, they share a common conventional view on politics and populism. They mainly focus on parties, politicians, movements and their ideologies, discourses, electoral and mobilization strategies, and political styles/performances. In other words, they focus on electoral politics – and its representation in the cultural realm, and especially in the media – as the realm of the phenomenon of populism. In this account, I propose a much wider lens to see populism in order to understand the intrinsic relationship between populism and political/governmental practice. In this respect, this account can be considered a partial acknowledgement of the early political economy scholarship on the concept of populism in Turkey by focusing on concrete policy implications. Nevertheless, this account, with an interpretivist perspective, also proposes to understand the informal and symbolic dimensions of material exchange in populism as governmental practice based on a "virtual consensus" between populist elites and populist audiences.

Populism as governmental practice: An initial demonstration

I would like to demonstrate the approach embraced in this study with an example. The example that I would like to use in this part comes from the domain of public order and security. In a discussion regarding the demolition of abandoned buildings in provincial Turkey, the Minister of the Interior in a previous AKP government, Süleymen Soylu (who was a populist in his own right) urged the governors (who are not elected but appointed to high-ranking bureaucratic positions in the Turkish administrative system) of those districts to demolish abandoned buildings during the night, without waiting for court verdicts:

> We have achieved considerable progress in the struggle with drugs. I kindly ask you to be courageous. It is a nightmare for us to watch our children poison themselves in these [abandoned buildings]. (…) There were 110.000 abandoned buildings, and we demolished more than 75.000 and restored 15.000 of these. I visited those provinces a couple of days ago and saw our neighbourhood headmen (*muhtarlar*) in Diyarbakır, Adana and İstanbul. They said to me, 'Sir, there are abandoned buildings all over, but we cannot demolish them'. My friend, you demolish them during the night, and the court decisions come later because as long as those buildings remain there, youngsters will use drugs in those buildings. Our citizens ask the neighbourhood headmen about the measures regarding these buildings, and the headmen say, 'There is no court decision, we cannot demolish them'. And I tell them to bring bulldozers in the middle of night and demolish these buildings. Who demolished them? How can we know?[15]

After this call by the minister from the AKP, governors in different provinces across Turkey started ordering the demolition of abandoned buildings.[16] What we see in this incident is not simply the reflection or implication of populist "ideas" or "worldviews" in a concrete policy issue. In fact, this

16 Exploring everyday administration by populists

incident is just an individual illustrative example of populist governmentality that is combining immediacy, responsiveness, and effectiveness while circumventing procedures and principles. From a broader theoretical perspective, populist governmentality is about the colonization of modern rational–legal governmentalities from below by populist politics that embrace the majoritarian, pragmatic/tactical, and ocular-centric orientations of common people.

At this very point, I would like to reiterate that this book is an attempt to interpret diffuse relations of power, resistance, and micro politics from the vantage point of populism studies. As such, this work will also complement analyses of modern governmentalities by focusing on the different modes of articulations between democratic and/or populist politics and modern schemes of "governing people and things" (rational public management and policy). Ultimately, this account is not really about the effect of populist ideas on policy content but about "*what empirically constitutes a populist (foreign, environmental, economic etc.) policy*".[17] Thus, the book, in general, and the central theoretical argument in particular, is not really about the relationship between populist parties/leaders and public administration/policy but about inherently populist practices in the administrative/policy sphere. From the perspective of the view developed in this book, populism is more about the implementation, and it is more about procedures and practices than policy content in terms of what populism embodies in the realm of public administration and policy.

The approach and case selection

As I have briefly demonstrated at the beginning of the literature review, today, there are fundamental differences among various schools of thought in populism studies, and these differences direct researchers' attention to very different domains of politics. Moreover, these different approaches substantially define what researchers think regarding the fundamental nature of politics and power. From an ideational perspective or from a perspective that attaches paramount importance to the discourses generated by populist actors, for example, it is inevitable to focus first and foremost on party politics, electoral competition, and elites generating discursive frameworks for the power struggles at the macro-political level. However, a rather more performative approach that takes the praxis of populism – albeit at the stage of electoral competition – seriously into account has the potential to draw scholars' attention to the broader political/governmental practice of populism. By pointing out the importance of unconventional dimensions of modern mass politics, such as the public image and "stage performance" of populists, such approaches have considerably enlarged our view of what is politics and political power today (Moffitt 2016; Ostiguy, 2017).[18] There is only one more step to be taken in this direction – and presumably also for moving beyond socio-cultural and performative approaches – which is required to reach a more diffuse and comprehensive understanding of politics and power. This step can be taken by connecting the theoretical discussions on populism to the political and social theory problematizing themes of governmentality and everyday forms of power and resistance that deploy a more comprehensive view of politics which is markedly more capable of demonstrating the diffuse impacts of power relations in modern societies to researchers (this is the endeavour that I mainly undertake in Chapter 3).

Here, I also would like to draw attention to the fact that my theoretical, historical, and comparative approaches to the phenomenon of populism have also been informed by my past and current field research experience in Turkey, which includes in person and in-depth interviews with more than 300 people in more than 250 interview meetings with party activists and closely related actors in local and national political fields as well as many hours spent in the offices of the ruling AKP – and other parties in the political system – across Turkey.[19] Although these research projects focused more on conventional dimensions of politics such as parties, mobilization, party–voter linkages, organizations, and electoral competition, these field studies, which I conducted for my PhD dissertation and for a subsequent research project, deeply shaped my understanding of populism. These experiences led me to understand populism as a broader phenomenon that surpasses political discourses, performances, and institutions. In fact, populist discourses and ideas are, to a considerable extent, consequences of populist practices and lived experiences on the ground, not the other way around.

This also brings me to another lacuna in the current conventional ideational/discursive approaches to populism: Many scholars in the field embracing ideational/discursive approaches to populism are inclined to examine elite discourses at the macro-political level. Particularly those in the field of political theory, such as Müller (2016) and Urbinati (2019a, 2019b), have an overwhelmingly top-down (and, as a consequence, restricted) view regarding the political practice of populists on the ground as well as the operations populist parties and actors undertake in neighbourhoods, on the streets and in distant localities of national territories. For political theorists, this is all too understandable, but such top-down views need to be complemented with bottom-up perspectives sensitive to the reality on the ground. This book, therefore, is an attempt to contribute to the established literature on populism (which embraces an overwhelmingly macro-political, institutional, and discursive orientation) with a bottom-up perspective informed by empirical and ethnographic experience in the field.

I understand populist governmental practice as a fundamentally relational phenomenon that connects populist actors and audiences/supporters/voters as well as non-populist or anti-populist political/bureaucratic actors at the national and local and macro and micro levels. This certainly requires a

18 Exploring everyday administration by populists

qualitative approach to the phenomenon. From a more abstract epistemological standpoint, the approach in the book leads me towards a rather more interpretivist perspective. This is to say that this account is also an attempt to unravel the schemes of meaning attributed to their practice by the actors taking part in populist interactions. Therefore, although the research for this book is by no means a full-scale ethnographic study, it nevertheless relied upon a certain "ethnographic sensibility", as Schatz (2009) termed it. This book strives to understand the phenomenon of populism from the perspective of its powerful and subordinate actors.

In addition, and in complementarity to the broader "ethnographic sensibility", the research in this book rely upon a historical–contextual analysis elaborating the processes that create populist governmentalities as a particular consequence of the interaction between bureaucracy formation, the development of competitive party politics and the broader state–society relationships in the cases examined. Nonetheless, this comparative dimension of the study may not be considered a full-scale systematic comparison that relies on conventional methods of comparative causal inference (such as Mills' methods). Instead, I will try to corroborate the theoretical arguments produced from an ethnographically sensitive perspective and historical–contextual analysis of the populist governmental practice in very different policy domains in Turkey, along with the analyses of specific policy domains in other cases, while also placing them into a historical perspective. For the analyses of these cases, this book largely relies upon the interpretation of already existing political–historical accounts on these cases. Furthermore, where possible, I also analyse some key incidents published in the media.

In this book, Turkey should be seen as a crucial representative case which, in several respects, provide researchers with rich empirical material in an analysis of populist governmentality. Since 2002, Turkey has been ruled by a clearly populist government, and throughout this period, the AKP deeply transformed administrative practices and policy implementation in almost every domain of policy in line with a populist logic. While some of these transformations have been positive, some of them have had devastating consequences. In other words, the case of Turkey under AKP represents a "full populism" by not only revealing discursive, ideational, and strategic features in the realm of electoral–political competition but also by embracing a populist governmental practice that attaches enormous importance to responsiveness while being repeatedly unsuccessful at responsible government. I support this argument with comprehensive empirical evidence, especially in Chapter 5. This is why this book also contains a "thick description" (Geertz 1993) of the populist governmental practice in the case of Turkey, which was the inspiration for the entire theoretical proposition in the book. It should also be mentioned here that, before the emergence of populist politics in the realm of conventional politics and macro level electoral competition, populism was a constant dimension behind the scenes of Turkish electoral politics at the national level. A brief analysis of the development of Turkish public administration and policy and urban politics reveals that responsiveness and immediacy are key aspects of Turkey's political practice on the ground. Thus, the analysis in the book also has a historical orientation.

Yet, while focusing on many domains of policy in Turkey, the book will enlarge this "analyses of multiple policy domains" in Turkey and draw attention to the unfolding of populist governmental practices in specific policy domains (such as economy, bureaucracy formation, public order and security, education, and foreign policy) in very different corners of the world and in very different cases of populism in power. Here, the case selection is not arbitrary but aims to reveal the centrality of populist practice in very different parts of the world since populist governmental practice is an integral part of contemporary populism in power. Thus, the case selection in this book is not completely random but instead is made on the basis of an approach akin to the "most different systems design".[20] This is why I preferred to include cases from very different parts of the world.

As I have already highlighted, in this book, I am proposing a new theoretical approach to the phenomenon of populism. This approach was not evident to me when I was writing my first book which was mainly based on my PhD dissertation (Baykan 2018a). In that account, I, to a great extent, took the phenomenon of populism as a political style/performance that is congruent with concrete socio-cultural divides (in line with Ostiguy [2017] and Moffitt [2016]). However, since the time I published that book, my views on the phenomenon have changed as a result of the time I spent in Turkey and a long process of field research – which gradually gained a clear ethnographic dimension – which allowed me to see more clearly the functioning of political parties on the ground, most notably the populist AKP, and how they articulate political discourse and style with concrete administrative practice and policymaking. In short, in my previous book, I focused largely on empirical evidence pertaining to the domain of electoral politics and competition. In this book, however, as the brief example above has demonstrated, I will focus on a remarkably different empirical realm that surpasses words and the stage performance of populists devoted to electoral mobilization. In this regard, too, I contend that the populist "deeds" that I will focus on in this book will shed fresh light on the nature of populism today. I think it is even possible to argue that these "deeds" or the "practices" – beyond the words, performance, and impact of populist parties on political institutions – constitute the core of the phenomenon of populism in power.

Considering the current state of the literature on populism – and the broader field of comparative politics as well – I do think that what we are missing are interpretations and comparative perspectives from scholars with

20 Exploring everyday administration by populists

ethnographic sensibilities in the Global South, who are, in fact, directly exposed to the consequences of the current global wave of populism in power. I am also of the opinion that in the field of comparative politics, comparative accounts with interpretivist sensibilities have an enormous potential to contribute to, and complement – and perhaps interrogate – some predominant positivistic proclivities in the comparative politics literature. Thus, one of the goals of this book is to demonstrate the potentials of the interpretive and historical approaches to the phenomenon of populism for the literature on populism in particular, and, comparative politics in general.

Structure of the book

The introductory theoretical chapters of the book have a twofold aim. On the one hand, they evaluate and categorize various predominant approaches to the phenomenon of populism in a concise and accessible way. Chapter 2 focuses on four commonly used approaches to populism. This chapter demonstrates specific domains/realms that these different approaches focus on for the study of populism. While pointing out differences between these approaches and the domains they focused on, the chapter asserts that predominant approaches see the phenomenon of populism as something strongly tied to the electoral party politics and its actors that are mostly visible at the national scale. In this chapter, I call this realm of politics, in other words, electoral politics – with cultural ramifications – examined by currently predominant approaches to populism as the "politics proper" and propose a more diffused understanding of politics that is capable of seeing "micro politics", a realm of politics penetrating into the everyday lives of citizens via official policies as well as non-official, informal and tactical practices and interactions between authorities and citizens.

By moving beyond this kind of conventional understanding of politics as the business of movements, parties, and leaders and by formulating a "diffused" comprehension of what is political (or not) in a theoretical dialogue with works by Michel de Certeau (2002), James C. Scott (1990, 1999) and Michel Foucault (2000), Chapter 3 proposes to focus on more mundane, day-to-day impact of populist politicians and parties in office on citizen's lives through political/governmental/administrative practices in micro and macro levels. In conclusion, the chapter proposes to understand populism as a *responsive political/governmental practice* that attaches utmost importance to immediacy in the design and conduct of public policy in the local, national, and international levels. In congruence with the expectations and socio-cultural proclivities of its audience, populist parties and politicians tend to design public policy and investments around short-term targets and achievements. The motto for the populists is "now and here for the supporters". Hence, populist parties, leaders, and movements prefer particularistic and clientelistic solutions to well-planned universal frameworks, short-term benefits to long-term credibility and investment, quantity over quality, immediate material gains over long-term preservation and prudence in economy, foreign policy, culture, local government, and urban politics. While this tendency makes populists "heroes" of low-income constituencies with a restricted cultural capital, it costs the societies under populist governments in the long run in economic and cultural terms. Thus, this chapter, with reference to Foucault's work on governmentality, proposes to understand populism in power as the disruption and stealth and incremental colonization of modern governmental rationalities from below.

In this chapter, I also try to demonstrate how populism as a governmental practice is distinguished in spatial, operational, and temporal terms from non-populist liberal institutional politics as well as predominant understandings of populism today based on a restricted view of politics. The chapter highlights the fact that populism as a mode of governmental practice, especially under the circumstances of material and organizational deprivation, blurs the boundaries between public and private and encompasses local and national in spatial terms, deploys informality and tactics alongside official and procedural modes of action in operational terms and attaches utmost importance to responsiveness and immediacy in temporal terms. In this chapter, therefore, populism as a mode of governmental conduct has been defined as *the practical proclivity of weak authorities and political contenders to informality, pragmatism, tactics and responsiveness that is appealing to the short-term material and symbolic expectations, interests and tastes of supporting unprivileged majorities.* Populism is a sort of *metis* aiming predominance in "politics proper" or electoral politics through responsiveness, flexibility, and cunning in the realm of "micro politics".

Based on the theoretical understanding of populism developed in Chapters 2 and 3 (which has also been briefly demonstrated in this introduction so far), Chapter 4 focuses on the roots of populist governmental practice in Turkey that can be found in the drastic modernization process of Ottoman-Turkish polities. The chapter elaborates on the adaptation of modern governmental rationalities in the late Ottoman and early Republican periods and discusses how Ottoman-Turkish political elites handled this process amidst the rising importance of urban public opinion. The chapter highlights the fact that modern governmental rationalities in Ottoman-Turkish polities, due to financial and organizational incapacities of these states, took the form of a "politics of expediency" sensitive towards rising public opinion and popular expectations but unsuccessful at maintaining effective development and institutionalization in the long-term. With the transition to multi-party politics in the mid-20th century and rising importance of "citizens as voters", "politics of expediency" evolved into a "populist political/governmental

22 Exploring everyday administration by populists

practice" that does not only contain a popular communication style but also the articulation of particularistic demands from a heterogeneous constituency by the governmental practices and formation of public policies by populist ruling parties and elites in accordance with a short-term, clientelistic rationale.

In Chapter 5, the AKP era would be under special scrutiny since Erdoğan's party embraced a full-scale populist logic in ideational, discursive, strategic respects as well as with regards to governmental practice. From economy to bureaucracy, judiciary to order and security, social policy to education and foreign policy, the AKP era embraced a particularistic and responsive political/governmental practice and hastily satisfied its constituency with the cost of long-term institutional decay and incapacity. The examination of the AKP era also helps to grasp ties between populism (as a worldview, discourse, and style), personalism, clientelism, and corruption. Based on an empirical approach and factual examples from Turkey, this chapter of the book reiterates the importance of seeing populism as something beyond words and stage performance of parties, politicians, and leaders and, instead, proposes to understand the phenomenon as a political/governmental practice that has implications for the daily lives of millions of people across the world today.

Through Chapters 6 to 11, via brief analyses of six cases of populist rule across time and space in remarkably different contexts, the book demonstrates the implications of populist political/governmental practice in the domain of policy. These concise case studies are by no means comprehensive analyses of populism or policymaking and implementation in these examples. Instead, after briefly introducing the populist qualities of these cases by relying on existing literatures, these chapters on different cases of populism only focus on a specific political/governmental realm and demonstrate the impact of populist governmental practice in this particular realm of policymaking and implementation. Chapter 6 elaborates on the performance of Chavez administrations in the economic realm in Venezuela and demonstrates how redistribution for poor constituencies intermingled with favouritism towards selected supporters and other short-sighted policies ultimately drove Venezuela to economic devastation. Chapter 7 examines the long period of populist democracy in Greece and how populist governmental practice shaped the public sector in general and the public bureaucracy in particular with favouritism and particularism that penetrated into every level of government, from local to national, micro to macro. Chapter 8 focuses on Modi's BJP (Bharatiya Janata Party) and how it affected the judicial establishment of the country, particularly in relation to its stance towards ethnic and religious minorities in India, largely as a response to bottom-up demands from the Hindu majority. Chapter 9 delves into Duterte's controversial methods and measures in his "war on drugs" in the Philippines which perfectly reflects the virtues and

Introduction **23**

vices of populist political/governmental practice in the sphere of law, order, and security. Chapter 10 focuses on Egypt under the rule of Gamal Abd-al Nasser and specifically draws attention to the populist perspectives and practices shaping the reform in educational realm in the country as well as the domain of social policy according to a "populist social contract". With regards to the United States, and the Trump era, the emphasis is on the conduct of foreign policy and how the populist practice of the Trump administration altered the foreign policy establishment and methods of foreign policy making and implementation in an advanced bureaucratic setting in Chapter 11.

The concluding chapter (Chapter 12) summarizes the main theoretical propositions of the book in Section II and the essential empirical evidence demonstrated in Section III. In this chapter, it is reiterated that populism is not only an idea/view/ideology, discourse, strategy, or style/performance, but it is a particular way of governing people and things, a specific political/governmental praxis. Hence, the chapter argues that the understanding of populism should be extended in a way that covers the domain of policymaking and implementation, and more mundane, day-to-day issues of politics and administration. This kind of understanding of the phenomenon of populism certainly requires a much broader understanding of politics. Politics is certainly about parties, elections, campaigns, political leaders, social movements, and struggles for office and power (including conflictual and consensual relations) and the kind of ideologies, discourses, strategies, and styles the actors of party politics and electoral competition generate and embrace for this struggle. But this chapter, based on the theoretical and empirical evidence demonstrated in the previous chapters, proposes to adopt a much wider lens to see the phenomenon of populism as a particular political/governmental practice. The chapter reasserts that politics is also about the relations of grassroots functionaries with the electorate for solving day-to-day problems, the way local government is run, the approach to local and national policymaking and implementation, and so on and so forth. In all these rather more diffused, mundane aspects of politics behind the stage of much more spectacular electoral processes and struggles for office and power, populists tend to prefer concrete over abstract, they tend to be responsive, majoritarian, and ocular-centric in congruence with popular tastes and expectations but they are also short-sighted, personalistic, particularistic and clientelistic. The chapter emphasizes that, in order to understand "populism at work" as a dynamic political/governmental practice always in function, researchers should focus on national as well as local, macro as well as micro, the stage of electoral politics as well as less spectacular political/governmental/administrative practices behind the scene. Only such a broad understanding of politics helps us to achieve a better account of how populism has shaped our world and politics, for good and bad, in the last decades.

24 Exploring everyday administration by populists

Notes

1 https://www.bbc.com/turkce/articles/c51kdv8d15jo#:~:text=%C4%B0%
C3%A7i%C5%9Fleri%20Bakan%C4%B1%20S%C3%BCleyman%20
Soylu%2C%206,bin%20969'unun%20enkaz%C4%B1n%C4%B1n%20
kald%C4%B1r%C4%B1ld%C4%B1, accessed: 24.8.2023.

2 When one considers the fact that more than 12,000 buildings, largely apartment buildings containing multiple flats (usually over three storeys), collapsed during the earthquake, it becomes plausible to argue that the official figures of causality are understating the real catastrophe. See the news on the figure of collapsed buildings after the earthquake: https://www.haberturk.com/depremde-kac-bina-coktu-resmi-rakam-aciklandi-2023-depremde-kac-bina-hasar-gordu-3564717/3, accessed: 24.8.2023.

3 https://edition.cnn.com/2023/02/07/middleeast/earthquake-turkey-syria-why-deadly-intl/index.html, accessed: 24.8.2023.

4 https://www.youtube.com/watch?v=r4WbwW7ookY&ab_channel=FluTV; https://www.hurriyet.com.tr/kelebek/hurriyet-pazar/binanin-eski-ya-da-yeni-olmasi-onemli-degil-uygun-projelendirilip-dogru-denetlenen-her-yapi-saglam-dir-42218325, accessed: 24.8.2023.

5 https://www.hurriyet.com.tr/kelebek/hurriyet-pazar/yonetmelik-ve-standartlara-uygunsa-o-yapi-depremde-yikilmaz-42221807, accessed: 24.8.2023.

6 https://www.cumhuriyet.com.tr/turkiye/kahramanmaras-depremi-sonrasinda-kac-muteahhit-tutuklandi-hangi-binalarin-muteahhidi-yakalandi-2052491, accessed: 24.8.2023.

7 https://www.cumhuriyet.com.tr/turkiye/hukukcu-sozuer-muteahhit-yetkili-ki-silerin-goz-yummasi-olmadan-kurallara-aykiri-bina-yapamaz-2053378, accessed: 24.8.2023.

8 Especially see Ark-Yıldırım (2017), Esen and Gümüşçü (2018), and Arslantaş and Arslantaş (2022). For a detailed analysis of the earthquake and problematization of the relationship between clientelistic practices and populism around this particular incident, see Baykan (2023).

9 Also see my review of this study: Baykan (2016).

10 For a comprehensive discussion on the ideational approach used in studies on populism, see Hawkins *et al.* (2018).

11 In the particular understanding of populism developed in this book I do not refer to passive spectators by the term "audience". In line with de Certeau (2002), I see the "populist audience" as people who are into a sort of "productive consumption" that is capable of agency. This agency, as many examples in this book will reveal, modifies the actions of powerful populist elites.

12 In this respect, I do not see the differences in the modes of economic conduct only through the prism of distinction between, on the one hand, a left-wing redistributive and egalitarian one, and, on the other hand, a right-wing non-egalitarian one that is in favour of the protection of private wealth. As experiences of populist governments today have shown, on the one hand, egalitarian redistributive strategies may intermingle with crony arrangements, corruption, and clientelism, and, on the other hand, neoliberal economic policies may be counter-balanced by various redistributive mechanisms. These hybrid forms are usually generated by populist governmental practices.

13 For an analysis of these studies, see Baykan (2014, 2017).

14 Only in the works after the publication of my book on the AKP I started to see and propose populism as a responsive governmental practice. See Baykan (2018b, 2021).

15 https://www.yenicaggazetesi.com.tr/soyludan-muhtarlara-dozer-metruk-binalari-yiksin-kim-yikti-nereden-bilelim-483027h.htm, accessed 23.11.2021.

Introduction **25**

16 https://www.karar.com/guncel-haberler/birak-yargiyi-yik-binayi-1637387, accessed 23.11.2021.
17 I would like to thank one of the anonymous reviewers of the book proposal that I had submitted for this book for highlighting this particular point.
18 Here, I would like to draw attention to an important recent work by Chou *et al.* (2021), which demonstrates the emerging interest in local politics and "localism" in populism studies.
19 For the outcome of first of these research projects, see Baykan (2018a). The last of these research projects was conducted with Murat Somer and focused on party organizations and party systems in Turkey. The outcomes of this research will be the subject of another monograph focusing on political institutions and the party systems in contemporary Turkey. For an initial outcome of this project, see Baykan and Somer (2022).
20 It should be noted here that this book is not a hypothesis testing endeavour at all. This account should be considered rather a "theory generating" enterprise.

References

Albertazzi, D. & D. McDonnell (2015). *Populists in Power*. London: Routledge.
Ark-Yıldırım, C. (2017). Political parties and grassroots clientelist strategies in urban Turkey: One neighbourhood at a time. *South European Society and Politics*, 22(4), 473–490.
Arslantaş, D. & Ş. Arslantaş (2022). How does clientelism foster electoral dominance? Evidence from Turkey. *Asian Journal of Comparative Politics*, 7(3), 559–575.
Aslan, S. (2021). Public tears: Populism and the politics of emotion in AKP's Turkey. *International Journal of Middle East Studies*, 53(1), 1–17.
Auyero, J. (2001). *Poor People's Politics*. Durham, NC, and London: Duke University Press.
Aytaç, S. E. & E. Elçi (2019). Populism in Turkey. In D. Stockemer (Ed.), *Populism Around the World* (pp. 89–108). Cham: Springer.
Aytaç, S. E. & Z. Öniş (2014). Varieties of populism in a changing global context: The divergent paths of Erdoğan and Kirchnerismo. *Comparative Politics*, 47(1), 41–59.
Bartha, A., Z. Boda & D. Szikra (2020). When populist leaders govern – conceptualising populism in policy making. *Politics and Governance*, 8(3), 71–81.
Bauer, M. W. & S. Becker (2020). Democratic backsliding, populism, and public administration. *Perspectives on Public Management and Governance*, 3(1), 19–31.
Baykan, T. S. (2014). Halkçılık and Popülizm: "official-rational" versus "popular" in the context of "Turkish exceptionalism". Sussex European Institute Working Paper, no. 137.
Baykan, T. S. (2016). *Populists in Power*, by M. McDonnell and D. Albertazzi. *Political Studies Review*, 14(4), 588–589.
Baykan, T. S. (2017). Halkçılık ve Popülizm: Türkiye Vakası ve Bir Kavramın Kullanımları. *Mülkiye Dergisi*, 41(1), 157–194.
Baykan, T. S. (2018a). *The Justice and Development Party in Turkey – Populism, Personalism, Organization*. Cambridge: Cambridge University Press.
Baykan, T. S. (2018b). "İdare-i maslahatçılık"tan "popülizm"e Türkiye'de duyarlı siyasal pratik: "Popülizm yapıyorsun!". *Birikim*, 353, 15–36.
Baykan, T. S. (2019a). Populism and the bourgeoisie: The role of intra-elite factionalism in the growth of populism in Turkey. *New Diversities*, 21(2), 9–22.

26 Exploring everyday administration by populists

Baykan, T. S. (2019b). Türkiye'de ideolojik ve programatik olmayan parti-seçmen bağları üzerine kavramsal bir tartışma: popülizm, personalizm, patronaj. *Toplum ve Bilim*, *147*, 10–44.

Baykan, T. S. (2021). *Islamic Populism in Indonesia and the Middle East*, by Vedi R. Hadiz & *Populism and Crisis Politics in Greece*, by Takis Pappas. *Mediterranean Politics*, *26*(4), 530–534.

Baykan, T. S. (2023). Deprem, "partiler düzeni" ve "bilimsel çözüm" söylemi üzerine: "popülist muvazaa"nın sınırlarına yaklaşırken. *Birikim*, *408*, 10–27.

Baykan, T. S. & M. Somer (2022). Politics of notables versus national machine: Social, political and state transformations, party organizations and clientelism during AKP governments. *European Journal of Turkish Studies*, *34*. https://journals.openedition.org/ejts/8111, accessed: 18.8.2023.

Boratav, K. (1983). Türkiye'de popülizm: 1962–76 dönemi üzerine bazı notlar. *Yapıt*, *1*, 7–18.

Bozkurt, U. (2013). Neoliberalism with a human face: Making sense of the justice and development party's neoliberal populism in Turkey. *Science & Society*, *77*(3), 372–396.

Caiani, M. & Graziano, P. (2022). The three faces of populism in power: Polity, policies and politics. *Government and Opposition*, *57*(4), 569–588.

Canovan, M. (1999). Trust the people! Populism and the two faces of democracy. *Political Studies*, *47*(1), 2–16.

Çarkoğlu, A., E. Elçi, F. Erol & C. Paksoy (2022). Popülizm teorileri işığında Türkiye'de popülizmin Tarihsel gelişimi: Siyasi Partiler üzerine bir inceleme. *Anadolu Üniversitesi Sosyal Bilimler Dergisi*, *22*(1), 323–348.

Çelik, A. B. & E. Balta (2020). Explaining the micro dynamics of the populist cleavage in the "new Turkey". *Mediterranean Politics*, *25*(2), 160–181.

Chou, M., B. Moffitt & R. Busbridge (2021). The localist turn in populism studies. *Swiss Political Science Review*, *28*, 129–141. https://doi.org/10.1111/spsr.12490, accessed: 27.11.2021.

de Certeau, M. (2002). *The Practice of Everyday Life* (S. Rendall, Trans.). Berkeley, CA: University of California Press.

de Cleen, B. & J. Glynos (2021). Beyond populism studies. *Journal of Language and Politics*, *20*(1), 178–195.

de Cleen, B., J. Glynos & A. Mondon (2018). Critical research on populism: Nine rules of engagement. *Organization*, *25*(5), 649–661.

de la Torre, C. (Ed.). (2019). *Routledge Handbook of Global Populism*. London: Routledge.

de la Torre, C. (2024). Differentiating populism – the complex constructions of the leader and the people. In P. Diehl & B. Bargetz (Eds.), *The Complexity of Populism* (pp. 36–52). London: Routledge.

de la Torre, C. & E. Peruzzotti (2018). Populism in power: Between inclusion and autocracy. *Populism*, *1*(1), 38–58.

Dieckhoff, A. *et al.* (Eds.). (2022). *Contemporary Populists in Power*. New York: Palgrave MacMillan.

Diehl, P. (2024). Rethinking populism in complex terms. In P. Diehl & B. Bargetz (Eds.), *The Complexity of Populism* (pp. 18–36). London: Routledge.

Diehl, P. & B. Bargetz (Eds.). (2024a). *The Complexity of Populism – New Approaches and Methods*. London: Routledge.

Diehl, P. & B. Bargetz (2024b). The complexity of populism new approaches and methods. An introduction. In P. Diehl & B. Bargetz (Eds.), *The Complexity of Populism* (pp. 1–15). London: Routledge.

Dinçşahin, Ş. (2012). A symptomatic analysis of the Justice and Development Party's populism in Turkey, 2007–2010. *Government and Opposition*, 47(4), 618–640.

Enyedi, Z. & S. Whitefield (2020). Populists in power: Populism and representation in illiberal democracies. In R. Rohrschneider & J. Thomassen (Eds.), *The Oxford Handbook of Political Representation in Liberal Democracies* (pp. 582–598). Oxford: Oxford University Press.

Esen, B. & Gümüşçü, S. (2018). Building a competitive authoritarian regime: State–business relations in the AKP's Turkey. *Journal of Balkan and Near Eastern Studies*, 20(4), 349–372.

Foucault, M. (2000). *Power – Essential Works of Foucault 1954–1984 – Volume 3* (R. Hurley and others, Trans.). London: Penguin Books.

Frank, J. (2017). Populism and praxis. In C. R. Kaltwasser, P. Taggart, P. O. Espejo & P. Ostiguy (Eds.), *The Oxford Handbook of Populism* (pp. 629–643). Oxford: Oxford University Press.

Geertz, C. (1993). *Interpretation of Cultures*. London: Fontana Press.

Hawkins, K. A., R. E. Carlin, L. Littvay & C. R. Kaltwasser (Eds.). (2018). *The Ideational Approach to Populism: Concept, Theory, and Analysis*. London: Routledge.

Ionescu, G. & E. Gellner (Eds.). (1969). *Populism: Its Meaning and National Characteristics*. London: Weidenfeld & Nicolson.

Kaltwasser, C. R., P. Taggart, P. O. Espejo & P. Ostiguy (Eds.). (2017). *The Oxford Handbook of Populism*. Oxford: Oxford University Press.

Karaosmanoğlu, D. (2020). From Ayran to dragon fruit smoothie: Populism, polarization and social engineering in Turkey. *International Journal of Communication*, 14, 1253–1274.

Katsambekis, G. (2022). Constructing "the people" of populism: A critique of the ideational approach from a discursive perspective. *Journal of Political Ideologies*, 27(1), 53–74.

Kaya, A. (2019). *Populism and Heritage in Europe*. London: Routledge.

Kenny, P. (2017). *Populism and Patronage – Why Populists Win Elections in India, Asia and Beyond*. Cambridge: Cambridge University Press.

Kenny, P. (2018). *Populism in Southeast Asia*. Cambridge: Cambridge University Press.

Keyder, Ç. (1987). *State and Class in Turkey – a Study in Capitalist Development*. London: Verso.

Laclau, E. (2005). *On Populist Reason*. London and New York: Verso.

Moffitt, B. (2016). *The Global Rise of Populism*. Stanford, CA: Stanford University Press.

Mudde, C. (2004). The populist zeitgeist. *Government and Opposition*, 39(4), 542–563.

Mudde, C. (2017). Populism – an ideational approach. In C. R. Kaltwasser, P. Taggart, P. O. Espejo & P. Ostiguy (Eds.), *The Oxford Handbook of Populism* (pp. 27–47). Oxford: Oxford University Press.

Müller, J. W. (2016). *What Is Populism?*. Philadelphia, PA: University of Pennsylvania Press.

28 Exploring everyday administration by populists

Muno, W. & C. Pfeiffer (2022). Populism in power – a comparative analysis of populist governance. *International Area Studies Review*, 25(4), 261–279.

Ostiguy, P. (2016). *Populism in Power: "Dirty Institutionality", Shifting Frontiers, Plebeian Ways, and the Incorporation of Excess*. Paper presented at the APSA Annual Conference, 1–4 September 2016, Philadelphia.

Ostiguy, P. (2017). Populism: A socio-cultural approach. In C. R. Kaltwasser, P. Taggart, P. O. Espejo & P. Ostiguy (Eds.), *The Oxford Handbook of Populism* (pp. 73–97). Oxford: Oxford University Press.

Panizza, F., P. Ostiguy & B. Moffitt (Eds.). (2021). *Populism in Global Perspective: A Performative and Discursive Approach*. London: Routledge.

Oswald, M. (Ed.). (2022). *Palgrave Handbook of Populism*. New York: Palgrave.

Özpek, B. B. & B. Park (2020). *Islamism, Populism, and Turkish Foreign Policy*. London: Routledge.

Pappas, T. S. (2019). Populists in power. *Journal of Democracy*, 30(2), 70–84.

Peters, B. G. & J. Pierre (2019). Populism and public administration: Confronting the administrative state. *Administration & Society*, 51(10), 1521–1545.

Schatz, E. (Ed.). (2009). *Political Ethnography*. Chicago and London: The University of Chicago Press.

Scott, J. C. (1990). *Domination and the Arts of Resistance*. New Haven, CT and London: Yale University Press.

Scott, J. C. (1999). *Seeing Like a State: How Certain Schemes to Improve the Human Condition Have Failed*. New Haven, CT and London: Yale University Press.

Selçuk, O. (2016). Strong presidents and weak institutions: Populism in Turkey, Venezuela and Ecuador. *Southeast European and Black Sea Studies*, 16(4), 571–589.

Sotiropoulos, D. A. (1996). *Populism and Bureaucracy: The Case of Greece under PASOK, 1981–1989*. Notre Dame, IN and London: University of Notre Dame Press.

Stavrakakis, Y. (2004). Antinomies of formalism: Laclau's theory of populism and the lessons from religious populism in Greece. *Journal of Political Ideologies*, 9(3), 253–267.

Stavrakakis, Y. (2018). Populism, anti-populism and democracy. *Political Insight*, 9(3), 33–35.

Stockemer, D. (Ed.). (2019). *Populism around the World*. Cham: Springer.

Sunar, İ. (1985). Demokrat Parti ve popülizm. In M. Belge (Ed.), *Cumhuriyet Dönemi Türkiye Ansiklopedisi Cilt 8* (pp. 2076–2086). İstanbul: İletişim.

Urbinati, N. (2019a). *Me the People*. Cambridge and London: Harvard University Press.

Urbinati, N. (2019b). Liquid parties, dense populism. *Philosophy & Social Criticism*, 45(9–10), 1069–1083.

Weyland, K. (2001). Clarifying a contested concept: Populism in the study of Latin American politics. *Comparative Politics*, 34(1), 1–22.

Weyland, K. (2017). Populism: A political-strategic approach. In C. R. Kaltwasser, P. Taggart, P. O. Espejo & P. Ostiguy (Eds.), *The Oxford Handbook of Populism* (pp. 48–72). Oxford: Oxford University Press.

Yabanci, B. (2020). Fuzzy borders between populism and sacralized politics: Mission, leader, community and performance in "new" Turkey. *Politics, Religion & Ideology*, 21(1), 92–112.

Yavuz, M. H. & A. E. Öztürk (2020). *Islam, Populism and Regime Change in Turkey*. London: Routledge.

Yıldırım, D. (2009). AKP ve Neo-liberal popülizm. In İ. Uzgel & B. Duru (Eds.), *AKP Kitabı: Bir Dönüşümün Bilançosu* (pp. 66–107). Ankara: Phoenix Yayınevi.

SECTION II

Theory

Uncovering populist undercurrents
in everyday politics and government

2

CONTEMPORARY THEORIES OF POPULISM

Shifting the focus from the stage of electoral politics to mundane governmental practice

Introduction[1]

This initial chapter of the theoretical section focuses on predominant contemporary approaches to populism and demonstrates their common tendency to focus on what is called "politics proper" as the realm of their examinations. In this review of current theoretical discussions, I underline the necessity of a much more bottom-up, comprehensive, and relational understanding of the phenomenon of politics as well as populism that does not only pertain to the domain of electoral politics but also to a realm I call "micro politics" consisting of various informal political relations including personalism, clientelism, and tactics. In this chapter, I also underline the "family resemblance" between populism and particular forms of clientelism and problematize the convergences and divergences between these two practices, which have usually been considered different phenomena in mass politics by scholars of comparative politics.

Current theoretical debates: What lies beyond ideology, strategy, discourse, and style?

The question of "what is populism" is one of the fundamental questions in political science today. The scholarship on populism increasingly revolves around four predominant answers that deeply shape the literature. These answers stem from the contributions of Mudde (2004), Weyland (2001), Laclau (2005), Ostiguy (2017), and Moffitt (2016), examined initially in the previous introductory chapter. Mudde (2004) defines populism as an "ideology" that systematically separates people and elite. Weyland (2001)

DOI: 10.4324/9781003294627-4

32 Theory

thinks that populism is a "strategy" in which a personalistic leadership organizes the support of the masses in order to come – or hold on – to power through an unmediated and uninstitutionalized relationship. Laclau (2005) implies a "political logic" by the term populism, which constructs the *people* and locates them against a hostile *other* in an antagonistic mode. Ostiguy (2017) proposes to understand populism as a political appeal/style which is in resonance with values and tastes of popular sectors and which mobilizes widespread and deeply rooted socio-cultural hierarchies in a given society. Moffitt (2016) has a similar perspective too attaching particular importance to the public performance of populists, especially in the media.

The importance of these authors within the literature does not only stem from the convincing answers they proposed for the question of "what is populism" but also from their coherent approach to another fundamental question: "which realm of political activity do we need to focus for the phenomenon of populism?" All of the scholars mentioned so far have searched for populism in different realms of politics. For example, Mudde (2004) and other scholars who understand populism as an "ideology" (Albertazzi & McDonnell 2015) or worldview (Hawkins 2010; Hawkins *et al.* 2018) and who embrace the "ideational" approach put a strong emphasis on whether there is – or there is not – an ideology or worldview systematically revealed in written party materials or official public discourses of party leaders and elites that shapes the party programme and discourse. On the other hand, Weyland (2001) points out the direct relationship between a personalistic leader and masses and, therefore, focuses on the mobilizational/organizational aspects of politics. Similarly, Kenneth Roberts (2006), who focuses on organizations, thinks that rather more conventional aspects of politics such as organization and mobilization is the main realm that researchers should focus on for the analysis of populism. In a similar vein, the works of Barr (2009, 2019) and Kenny (2017, 2018, 2023), who embrace versions of political-strategic approach to populism, propose to focus on the – usually national – "personalistic leadership" and his/her efforts to mobilize masses without intermediaries for political dominance. Similarly, Jansen (2011) too, in his political approach to populism, focuses on the "mobilizational" dynamics in the study of the phenomenon. Laclau (2005), too, focuses on the form of political conflict in the public realm, which usually reveals itself as an antagonism or a strategic divide that is visible in the public space.

In short, even in critical analyses outside the positivistic mainstream, the kind of realms that understood as political are, in this or that way, more "serious", "proper", and "conventional" subjects such as ideology, organization/mobilization and the form of political conflict and divisions. Not surprisingly, therefore, Margaret Canovan (1999), who had major contributions to the literature on populism, relates the phenomenon of populism to the "redemptive" aspect of modern mass politics. Thus, for many researchers, populism is a phenomenon that is closely related to the conventional realms of politics, but, at the same time, it is a "redemptive" diversion from politics as "business as usual", it is a form of "hyper politics". Not surprisingly, current academic discourses on populism also frequently deploy the concept of "charisma" too (Kenny 2018; Pappas 2019) and draw attention to the polarising impact and "transformative" intentions of populism in power (especially Pappas 2019).

Among the scholars I have mentioned so far, the approach that understands populism as a style – embraced by scholars such as Ostiguy (2017), Moffitt (2016), and, in a less systematic fashion, Knight (1998) – has the potential to lead researchers to a new realm that can enrich our understanding of populist praxis in opposition as well as in government by focusing on the "non-proper" and informal aspects of politics. Nevertheless, scholars understanding populism as a political style, and particularly Ostiguy, are inclined to consider the phenomenon as a vivid, time to time entertaining public reflection of a much more serious socio-political conflict and divide (the "high-low divide") underlying the political system. Therefore, these scholars, too, tend to relate their analysis to more conventional aspects of politics such as cleavage structures and mobilization of social divides (especially Ostiguy 2017). However, understanding populism as a political style draws our attention to a realm of politics that is widely underemphasized in the literature but which makes the phenomenon a resilient historical dimension of modern mass politics: It is the *responsive, flexible and pragmatic political and governmental practice* which usually accompanies a populist style and public performance, which is skilfully examined by scholars such as Ostiguy (2017), Moffitt (2016) and, in a different way, by de la Torre (1992).

Especially Ostiguy's work in this respect has a particular merit that can lead researchers' attention to the praxis of populism. Because while his approach has been influential through his analysis of the socio-cultural dimension of populism, in fact, in his definition of the concept, Ostiguy attaches equal importance to the "political cultural" dimension of the phenomenon and defines "informality" and "personalism" as fundamental aspects of populism *vis-à-vis*, what he calls, "proceduralism" and "legalism" (2017, 79). In recent generalizing analyses of the phenomenon too, one can notice a new awareness regarding this particular praxis of populism. For example, Oswald *et al.* (2022), in the introductory chapter they wrote for *The Palgrave Handbook of Populism* (Oswald 2022), while embracing a largely ideational and discursive perspective regarding populism, also pointed out the tendency to "simplification" of problems and solutions as a fundamental feature of the phenomenon of populism. According to Oswald *et al.*, "this often results in policies that resonate with the population but often are only geared toward

34 Theory

short-term gains" (2022, 18). Yet, this practical dimension of populism, or its praxis as a whole, has drawn far less attention in the relevant theoretical literature on populism so far. But this less "bookish" and, in a sense, less "spectacular" dimension of politics comprised of acts and specific modes of governmental practices is central to the establishment of populist linkages on the ground and in localities.

Understanding populism as a form of political-governmental practice requires the examination of the relationship between modern mass politics and archaic and mundane forms of power relations and governmental practice. Therefore, the literature on populism should also be put in a dialogue with a body of literature that stretches from the works of Foucault (1998, 2000, 2006, 2007) on "governmentality", "biopolitics" and "discipline technologies" to the studies of scholars such as Michel de Certeau (2002) and Scott (1990, 1999) that focuses on the repertoires of actions and tactics in everyday forms of power and resistance. No doubt that the abovementioned scholars' views can hardly be located within the sphere of the conventional understanding of politics. Before moving on to the analysis of the nexus between populism as governmental practice and modern governmentalities and contemporary theories of power and resistance in detail in the next chapter, I would like to further problematize two main assumptions in the current literature on populism regarding the nature of politics and the relationship between populism and particularistic party-voter linkages (such as clientelism and patronage) in this chapter.

While waiting for the "politics proper": Taking micro politics into account

The approach that evaluates populism as an ideology (Hawkins *et al.* 2018; Mudde 2004) implies that politics is mainly a civilized electoral endeavour – which is time to time interrupted by populism – in which more or less systematic ideologies are in an orderly competition, especially in Western Europe. In Weyland's (2001, 2017, 2021) understanding, politics is a struggle among contending elite groups for seizing political power through mass mobilization and in this understanding populism emerges as one of the main strategies in the power struggles (Kenny 2023), especially in Latin America. Both of these approaches see populism as an extension of – more or less – democratic electoral competition and focus on parties or on the electoral and mobilizational struggle to seize or manipulate the political-institutional power by leaders who use/deploy these parties. Laclau (2005), however, by surpassing these analyses regarding struggles only between political parties and leaders, considers politics as the practical and discursive struggle among every kind of political actor for establishing "hegemony". Although Laclau's approach has shifted our focus outside of a realm that can be called conventionally "political" consisting of party politics and strategies of personalistic leaderships, it still remains within the boundaries of a realm of political "hegemony", "conflict", and "institutional power" which I would like to call "politics proper".

Hitherto, approaches that see populism as an ideology or strategy or, as in Laclau's approach, as a discourse that is politics itself, ultimately focus on the realm of "politics proper" in which parties, political leaders, social movements, mass mobilization, and political discourses occupy the centre stage. The other side of the coin is that these approaches underestimate rather more non-official, informal, everyday, and "mundane" forms of politics. Understanding populism as a political style, a specific form of public communication that connects politicians and leaders to their constituencies and other political parties within the party systems, draws our attention exactly to these day-to-day, repetitive, non-official, informal and, in a sense, "banal" but very effective dimensions of modern mass politics. As such, understanding populism as a political style indeed sheds some light on the less conventional dimensions of modern mass politics, but it is still far from illuminating the broader realm containing all of these everyday, mundane, formal, and informal practices in politics. I am going to call this broader dimension of modern mass politics "micro politics", which, in fact, largely overlaps with rather less spectacular domains of public administration and policy, such as social assistance, education policies, policies of law and order, etc. as well as many informal political relationships and practices such as clientelism, patronage, and tactics.

While acknowledging the merits of socio-cultural and performative approaches, it should be noted here that this approach still focuses on the stage of "politics proper" and the – usually sensational – "performances"[2] of leaders, parties, and political and social movements in the realm of electoral and/ or contentious politics. Nevertheless, both before and after the spectacular appearance of populism in the stage of "politics proper" in particular historical moments, especially in "developing" contexts like Turkey, populism keeps living as a persistence undercurrent, as a "dirty institutionality" (Ostiguy 2016)[3] or as a responsive political "praxis" (Frank 2017)[4] in which clientelism, personalism, patronage, major and minor tactics, and – occasionally beneficial – "petty corruption" occupy a central position. This kind of approach to populism necessitates to focus on formal as well as non-official and informal political practices that lie beyond the realm of "conventional politics" as the public and official struggle between political parties, movements, and leaders for institutional power.

The approach developed in this book also requires researchers to interrogate some of the presumptions in the conventional literature such as the implicit belief that characteristics of populism unfolds mainly in the opposition and when populist actors come to power they are destined to quickly

36 Theory

fall. In fact, populism can manage quite well – and for remarkably prolonged periods of time – in power despite long-term structural failures it generates. Especially under circumstances of financial and organizational incapacity in the developing world, populist leaders and parties are usually trusted as cunning ruling forces that are capable of solving the grave problems of these nations since they are more likely to deploy formal as well as informal methods and resources. When they are voting for populists in opposition, populist constituencies usually make this under the impression that these are the "guys" that have the "stomach" to play dirty in order to correct what the majorities deemed wrong and unjust. And when populists come to power, such traits and "vices" are seen as part of the competency of populists by ordinary majorities, as the popular Turkish expression asserts: "They steal but they get things done!" ("*Çalıyorlar ama çalışıyorlar!*"). The approach in this book, therefore, puts a special emphasis on the features of populism as a ruling force in order to understand its appeal to broad segments of national electorates and its resilience as a governing force.

Thus, understanding populism as a governmental practice also requires researchers to focus on non-official and informal dimensions of modern mass politics. In this respect what I understand from informality is really similar to the way McFarlane (2012) proposes. Informality, in fact, surpasses the territorial and social class boundaries, as well as the frontier separating governing authorities and the governed. As McFarlane notes, "framing informality and formality as practices means dispensing with both the idea that informality belongs to the poor and formality to the better off, and the associated idea that informality and formality necessarily belong to different kinds of urban spaces" (2012, 105). I elaborate on the boundaries of the "political" in the next chapter with reference to the work of prominent political theorists and in a dialogue with the contemporary literature on governmentality as well as everyday forms of power and resistance. In Table 2.1, however, I would like to briefly and schematically demonstrate the distinction I proposed in this chapter between "politics proper" and "micro politics"

TABLE 2.1 Dimensions of "politics proper" and "micro politics"

Dimensions of "politics proper"	Dimensions of "micro politics"
Politics as electoral and contentious politics	Politics as "diffused power relations" with interpersonal implications
Ideas, ideologies, programmes	Mundane administration and formal policy implementation, informal practices, clientelistic linkages and tactics
Leaders, parties, movements, institutions, and mobilization	Personalism (as a mode of representation and execution)
Official and public discourses	Socio-cultural performances and proclivities

While mainstream approaches to populism today, particularly ideational, discourse-theoretical, and political-strategic approaches, focus on "politics proper", the socio-cultural/performative approach partly focuses on "micro politics". The perspective developed in this book, however, proposes to understand populism not only as a phenomenon pertaining to the domain of "politics proper" and in relation to dimensions of electoral politics but, equally, as a phenomenon of "micro politics" and all of its dimensions. Thus, going a further step beyond socio-cultural and performative approach, the perspective developed in this book proposes to problematize the relationship of populism with public administration and policy, informal practices, clientelistic linkages, tactics, and personalism at the local and national levels.

Clientelism and personalism as responsive governmental practices

Especially the discussions over populism during the 1960s and 1970s, by relating the concept to distributive policies and patronage (Baykan 2017),[5] may help to relocate populism into the framework of "micro politics". Although current literature on populism asserts that populism has nothing to do with an economic regime based on import substitution or a set of redistributive tactics or techniques (Weyland 2001), there is a "family resemblance"[6] between populism (as a political style and practice) and formal and informal redistributive practices, and especially patronage and clientelism. I neither argue that patronage and clientelism are the defining features of populism nor propose that they are the same phenomenon. Both phenomena have their own dynamics and boundaries. While, for example, patronage and clientelism largely pertain to the domain of material exchange, populism – as a governmental practice – contains a marked symbolic dimension. But there are commonalities, and, in fact, large "overlaps" and "criss-crossings" – as Wittgenstein would say – between populism in power and certain forms of clientelism which causes these distinct phenomena to appear usually alongside each other. It is precisely these overlaps and criss-crossings between these distinct phenomena that vitalize populism as a governmental practice.

There is a large literature on patronage and clientelism. In order to demonstrate the family resemblance that I have highlighted above, I would like to briefly draw attention to a few basic works on the subject. Since the 1960s, the phenomenon of patronage has drawn attention of the scholars working on especially rural developing contexts. In fact, patronage has not been a phenomenon that was unknown to Western scholars since the beginning of mass politics in the cradles of liberal democracy, such as the United States and United Kingdom, was based on a certain type of patronage or regional-local machine politics.[7] However, with the modernization of political institutions, at least the mass dimension of the phenomenon of clientelism began to

38 Theory

dissolve as robust welfare and administrative states emerged in the developed West (Kitschelt & Wilkinson 2007).

However, even today, patronage and clientelism have been part and parcel of modern mass politics in large parts of the globe, especially in the developing world. One of the pioneering works on contemporary patronage in this respect belongs to Wolf, in which he defines the concept as offerings of an inferior party in the form of loyalty and political support in a relationship with a patron providing critical needs and services (1969, 16–17). In another oft-cited study, for example, Scott demonstrates the importance of material exchange between a powerful patron and his clientele for rural politics in Southeast Asia (1972, 92). Weingrod (1968) too defines patronage similarly as an asymmetrical relationship between a patron and his subordinate client. But he also introduces the concept of "party-directed patronage" in order to differentiate traditional/classical forms of patronage from modern types of patron-client relations (1968, 381). In a similar vein, Scott differentiates the patron-client relations in democratic politics and calls this "machine politics" in a slightly earlier work. According to Scott, for machine politics to arise, there should be at least the existence of three factors: "1-the selection of political leaders through elections; 2-mass (usually universal) adult suffrage; 3-a relatively high degree of electoral competition over time - usually between parties, but occasionally within a dominant party" (1969, 1143). Thus, Scott sees "machine politics" as a phenomenon tightly connected to party and electoral competition (1969, 1143–1144).

In more recent works, scholars also problematized the relationship between clientelism and democracy. Morlino (1998), for example, highlights the fact that, in democracies of Southern Europe, clientelistic relations incorporated masses into political systems and facilitated democracies under pretty inconvenient circumstances (i.e. widespread lack of conviction to democratic principles and relative economic underdevelopment). Hilgers's (2012a) crucial edition in this respect requires a special attention, too, in which the authors of the volume provide a rather more nuanced analyses of the problematic relationship between clientelism and democracy. Hilgers (2012b) and Shefner (2012), for example, note that clientelism, under specific conditions, can substantiate democracy by providing an instrument to politicians for the incorporation of the poor and materially excluded populations into the political systems, usually more effectively than the formal programmatic methods. In this respect, clientelism can be a part of democratic politics and in a competitive political system, there would be inevitable overlaps between clientelism and populism.

In more recent works on the phenomenon, some scholars tend to distinguish different forms of patron-client ties more clearly, most notably the "rural personal forms" and "the urban, and, more anonymous forms". Because, while there was a form of patronage based on the individual influence and economic resources of the traditional social elites before the modernization/urbanization process, as a result of these processes, political parties gained a critical importance in patron-client relations. Although there is a consensus in the literature about what these two forms of patronage are, it seems that there is a confusion concerning the naming of these forms. As already noted, Weingrod (1968), for example, called the traditional form of patronage as "patron-client relation" and the more contemporary form as the "party-directed patronage". Hopkin defines the first of these two different forms of patron-client relations, namely the form in which the traditional patrons are personally in the centre, as "old clientelism", while he calls the modern form in which the parties are in the centre as "new clientelism" (2006, 407). In other studies, too, researchers propose distinctions to underline the basic differences between the largely personal and largely anonymous forms of patron-client ties. This particular difference is highlighted with terms such as "rural clientelism" vs. "urban clientelism" (Çınar 2016), "clientelism" vs. "populism" (Mouzelis 1985), "old/classical patronage" vs. "new patronage" (Baykan 2018a), "patronage" vs. "mediation" (Ayata 2010), and "relational clientelism" vs. "retail clientelism" (Berenschot & Aspinall 2020). Following Ayata (2010), it is possible to emphasize the difference between the concepts of "patronage" and "clientelism" in order to explain these two different types of patron-client relations.

Patronage, as the etymology of the word indicates, is an asymmetrical power relationship in which a powerful "boss/patron" is at the centre. This boss/patron mobilizes his personal resources for political power in a – usually – face-to-face relation with its clientele. However, as the origin of the word indicates, the emphasis in clientelism has shifted to the "client" (the "customer-voter"), and it is the party – usually under the control of a populist leader – that provides the protection, resources, benefits and the social capital created by the party to its clientele. Especially in cases of populism, this sort of clientelism is run by local functionaries/brokers on behalf of the populist and personalistic leadership. (This is a point that I will turn in the following part.) The decline of traditional, rural economies and the rise of new capitalist urban economies have created a shift from patronage to clientelistic relations, in which "brokers" rely more on the resources and authority of the parties (especially in power) than their own (Ayata 2010; Baykan 2019). That is, in the "new clientelism", the power of the "bosses" has decreased and the power of well-educated, party bureaucrat-type intermediaries has increased (Hopkin 2006, 409). Even in cases in which the traditional patrons somehow managed to maintain their power in an urbanizing context, this resulted in the formation of very weak parties. These weak parties keep opening room for the traditional patrons to retain their power.

Since the seminal work of Mouzelis (1985) on the politics in "semi-periphery", the impact of powerful national leaders on democratic mass

40 Theory

politics has been problematized in studies on populism. In this work, Mouzelis distinguished old forms of patronage exercised by powerful local oligarchies from the domination of powerful national leaders in a comparative study. But, somewhat confusingly, he calls the domination of local oligarchical families "clientelism" and the predominance of national leaders "populism". In fact, with the terminology proposed above, the control exercised by powerful local oligarchies should be considered reflections of "classical patronage". But when Mouzelis points out the important role of national leaders and the direct relationship between the leader and the masses, without any institutionalized intermediation, he actually set the precursor of an influential approach to populism, namely the political-strategic approach.[8] However, it is important to note that, unlike Weyland, Mouzelis noticed the importance of a kind of governmental performance in the phenomenon of populism personified by a populist leader resembling "the traditional patron-protectors" (1985, 340–341). One should note here that these paternalistic authority patterns take clearly clientelistic forms in populism under the control of a loyal class of brokers, or the "new men", created by populist parties and movements in the course of modernization or, in the course of a transition from an "oligarchic society" to a "post-oligarchic order", as termed by Mouzelis. In this sense, populism in power has a strong proclivity to depend on modern forms of clientelism based on brokers loyal to national populist leaderships.[9]

Paul Kenny elaborates exactly on this point, and, like Weyland, he draws attention to the importance of the distinction between clientelistic exchange and populism as a political strategy. In his various accounts (especially 2017 and 2023), Kenny distinguishes two forms of political strategy: (a) politics based on powerful local patrons and (b) unmediated relationship between national personalistic leaderships and the masses. He calls the latter "populism". But, as many cases demonstrate, stretching from PASOK rule to Erdoğan's *Adalet ve Kalkınma Partisi* (AKP – the Justice and Development Party), populism as a governmental practice involves a peculiar form of material exchange between the incumbents and the supporters based on modern forms of clientelism functioning through loyal brokers instead of powerful patrons. In other words, observations arguing that populism excludes clientelism are only partly true and mostly valid for cases of populism in opposition. Populism, especially in power, in fact, usually excludes more traditional forms of patronage, but as a responsive governmental practice, it usually develops forms of "systematic mass clientelism" and pork-barrel politics that is appealing to poor constituencies in material as well as symbolic respects. While emphasizing the role of personalistic leadership in populism is a merit of political-strategic approach, their straightforward exclusion of all forms of patron-client relations from their definition is a misleading one, simply due to the family resemblance between these two phenomena and the elective affinity between them under specific conditions (more precisely, populism in power

Contemporary theories of populism **41**

under the circumstances of acute poverty). Yet, as the political-strategic approach asserts, populism and (classical) patronage are different phenomena. Nevertheless, systematic mass clientelism, with its reliance on brokers loyal to the populist leader (instead of autonomous "patrons"), should be seen as a component of populism in power and its propensity to personalistic leadership at the national level.

In a relatively neglected study titled "A Case of Bureaucratic Clientelism?", another Greek scholar, Christos Lyrintzis, highlights the indications of a change from classical oligarchic patronage to a more systematic clientelism in competitive Greek politics:

> Bureaucratic clientelism is a distinct form of clientelism and consists of systematic infiltration of the state machine by party devotees and the allocation of favours through it. It is characterised by an organised expansion of existing posts and departments in the public sector and the addition of new ones in an attempt to secure power and maintain a party's electoral base. When the state has always played a central role in both economic and political development, it is very likely that the parties in government turn to the state as the only means for consolidating their power, and this further weakens their organisation and ideology. Such a political party becomes a collective patron, with the clientelistic networks based on and directed through an intricate combination of party mechanisms and the state apparatus. In a system such as this the public bureaucracy is orientated less towards the effective performance of public service than towards the provision of parasitic jobs for the political clientele of the ruling sectors, in exchange for their political support.
>
> *(Lyrintzis 1984, 103–104)[10]*

Although he calls this dynamic "bureaucratic clientelism", it would be better to call it "systematic mass clientelism" since the latter term allows us to differentiate clientelistic operations under the rule of populists in competitive political contexts from the remarkably impersonal and unresponsive implementation of clientelism under autocratic hegemonic party rules. While in systematic mass clientelism, clientelism serves democracy and intermingles with populism, "bureaucratic clientelism" in hegemonic party rules blurs the boundary between clientelism and coercion (Trantidis 2015, 126), serves autocratic rule and drifts the party-voter linkages away from populism.

In this regard, however, a diverging phenomenon in this context is the rise of "new men" in rapidly urbanizing societies that are being incorporated into capitalist market relations with deeply personalized and fragmented competitive political systems. Under these circumstances, powerful "new men" emerged in rapidly urbanizing contexts have a marked propensity to populism. Here, the primary example is the Philippines as can be seen in local

42 Theory

populist political practice this political system has generated so far. While challenging the authority of traditional large landholders and notables, as Machado (1974) notes, these "new men" emerged as heroes of the ordinary people since they shared the plebeian culture of their supporters more deeply than former elites (Machado 1974, 536).

However, as already noted, patronage based on the autonomy of dispersed local power holders and their individual economic and symbolic resources is in contradistinction to populism, especially when these local power holders rely on traditional symbolic resources (such as coming from established notable families and local oligarchies). In addition, rather more bureaucratized forms of clientelism under the control of hegemonic parties and populist practices should be considered mutually exclusive, too, since the degree of authoritarianism in hegemonic party systems barely requires political elites to engage in "niceties" of populism. Thus, "clientelism", as a modern form of patron-client relations, can also be observed independently from populism in a rather more bureaucratized way, as can be seen in hegemonic party autocracies (Greene 2007; Magaloni 2006). But a different form of systematic clientelism that is conducted via loyal functionaries/brokers in localities under the control of national personalistic leadership – as described by scholars like Lyrintzis (1984) and Mavrogordatos (1997) – is a phenomenon that is highly likely to be seen accompanying the phenomenon of populism in power. This is the case, for example, that we clearly see in Turkey under Erdoğan's rule: The rise of a clientelistic "national machine" based on relatively powerless functionaries at the local level who are deeply loyal to Erdoğan's personal rule (Baykan & Somer 2022). Table 2.2 demonstrates the relationship between these different forms of patron-client relations and their affinity to populism described so far.

TABLE 2.2 Varieties of patron-client relations and their affinity to populism

Main locus	Forms of patron-client relations	Degree of congruence with populism
Local	*Classical patronage* exercised by nobles, local notables, local oligarchies	Low
	Personal patronage by "new men" in fragmented, personalized, and competitive local political systems	High
National	*Bureaucratic clientelism* exercised by hegemonic parties	Low
	Systematic mass clientelism or *"patrimonial clientelism"* run by loyal local brokers under the control of personalistic national leadership	High

In sum, in the absence of a national level personalism, it is highly likely that patron-client relations exclude a populist orientation-only with the exception of "new men" in local urban politics with populist proclivities in fragmented, personalized, and competitive political systems. When a personalistic leader with a clearly populist orientation comes to power, sooner or later, s/he engages in clientelistic practices in such a way that undermines local power holders and strengthens the personalistic leadership. Thus, systematic mass clientelism under the control of – not a party but – a powerful national personalistic leadership is part and parcel of populist governmental practice.

As Garrido (2017) notes in a very important ethnographic study of the appeal of populism for the poor, genuine populist styles of the national popular leaders – such as Joseph Estrada in the Philippines – amplify the effects of even very limited clientelistic benefits provided to supporters by these leaders. In fact, populism transforms a particular form of clientelism into the logical material extension of the largely symbolic orientation of populism. Populism, as a form of contemporary "patrimonial domination" that can be seen in very different socio-economic and socio-cultural contexts (Hanson & Kopstein 2022) combines a performance of strong leadership with sincerity. It facilitates trust and creates the perception among the populist audiences that only the strong populist leader can deliver benefits and services to the poor under the conditions of chronic material deprivation. This perception and trust is largely the outcome of the specific social policy orientation of populism which is delineated in a relatively neglected study of Kurt Weyland (2013). In his chapter "Populism and social policy in Latin America" Weyland (2013) draws attention to the pretty hasty implementation of poorly planned new redistributive social policies by populist leaders as soon as they rise to power. Weyland (2013) also notes that these leaders combine formal and informal methods and ways to implement these policies, which, especially in the short term, improve the conditions of the most underprivileged segments of their societies. Thus, the quick implementation of such redistributive measures that usually surpasses the boundaries of a well-planned universal social policy implementation and satisfies the immediate needs of populist constituencies facilitate the impression among the popular sectors that such benefits can only be provided by a strong national populist leader – nor by a collective leadership or programmatic party neither by local bosses. Therefore, not every form of clientelism but what I call "systematic mass clientelism" or "patrimonial clientelism" that blurs the boundary between formal and informal redistribution initiated and controlled by national populist leaders is part and parcel of populist way of doing politics. And under the contexts of chronic material deprivation, such as we see in Latin America (Vilas 2003), it is not simply the fact that the leader delivers material benefits to a constituency under poverty but *the populist way* that he delivers these benefits, his/her "will", "swiftness" and "disregard for procedures",

44 Theory

that tends to be appealing symbolically for the popular sectors long excluded from the political and economic system and denied the privileges of better off segments of their society. (I elaborate these spatial, operational, and temporal dynamics of populist governmental practice in the following chapter.)

While it is pretty easy to distinguish populist governmental practice from liberal democratic procedural rule since the former tends to disregard legal and bureaucratic frameworks in power, it is remarkably more difficult to distinguish some of the informal governmental practices of populism from those in relatively more authoritarian systems under the control of non-populist incumbents since both of these systems surpasses legal-formal means and realms. For, practices such as personalism, clientelism, and tactics that undermine the positions of political rivals are not unique to populism and they are usually part and parcel of authoritarian systems too. Thus, this discussion also turns into a debate regarding the relationships among populism-democracy-authoritarianism. In the absence of a meaningful political competition, political actors do not really need populist practices since the domination of ruling elites in dictatorships mostly depends on coercion and security instruments more than the support of numbers. Thus, the other distinguishing feature of informal practices in populism from those in dictatorships is that they are not targeting only the elite supporters of the regime and deploy security apparatuses for domination but rely on numbers and work in the benefit of widest possible majorities at local and national levels. Even when such redistributive informal practices target masses in authoritarian systems, they are done in remarkably more irresponsive and humiliating ways that are missing the symbolic paternalistic aspect of populist forms of clientelism and tactics. Autocratic rule, therefore, deploys personalism, clientelism, and tactics in a very cold and calculating way and dismisses all the "niceties" of populist informality and arbitrarily empowers the leadership *vis-à-vis* the ruled. This is especially clear in the deeply autocratic personal rule in the 20th century which was called as "sultanistic" by the seminal work of Stephan Linz (2000, 152–153). Thus, there should also be some competitive pressure on the incumbents if they are going to embrace populist practices (even in Nasser's Egypt, an authoritarian regime, the incumbents had this competitive pressure stemming from the real risk of effective violent mass mobilization and grievances of former traditional elites in the absence of a robust security apparatus). This was why there is a lot of corruption and crony relations in hegemonic party autocracies or sultanistic rule (which ultimately become cleptocracies as we see in, for example, Haiti under Duvalier) that mostly benefit elite minorities, but there is no full-fledged populist practice alongside that is benefitting majorities in the short-run. As a result, populism has usually been associated with hybrid regimes (i.e. "electoral democracies" or "competitive authoritarian regimes") (Levitsky & Loxton 2013) and incentives for populist practices in full-fledged dictatorships are extremely small.

As Trantidis notes, when clientelism intensifies to greater extents and starts to deprive a) opposition parties of effectively challenging the incumbent (2015, 118) and b) electoral majorities of capability of choosing from among different political alternatives, it actually approximates to coercion (2015, 126) and becomes an instrument of autocratic rule. Thus, the form of clientelism as a dimension of populist rule is paternalistic, usually systematic and leader-centred, but performed and organized in such a way that do not – or cannot – kill political competition. Populism, as a practice, eventually, is the child of competitive mass politics.

In addition to this organizational dimension, however, one should also highlight the symbolic dimension regarding the divergences and convergences between the phenomenon of patron-client relations and populism. Patron-client relations under populism have never been solely transactional. In fact, patron-client relations always contain a symbolic and cultural dimension (Auyero 2001). However, this symbolic dimension is remarkably stronger in the practice of clientelism under populist rule. In a very illuminating example, Dasgupta highlights this symbolic dimension unique to populist governmental practice that separates it from other forms of patron-client relations such as classical patronage and rather more bureaucratized forms of clientelism. In an analysis of gentrification/beautification of some peripheral neighbourhoods in Indian metropoles, Dasgupta (2021) underlines the fragile and cosmetic orientation of these urban development projects and their lack of sufficient infrastructural investment. Dasgupta also highlights the fact that how these urban development projects and "beautification of the leisure spaces, appear to involve a regularized chain of petty corruption involving members of the local club, the ruling party cadres, and the traders they choose to favour" (Dasgupta 2021, 192). Yet, Dasgupta also underlines the important impact of these "beautifications" of the peripheral neighbourhoods on the popular sectors in India. A substantial portion of visitors of these newly gentrified neighbourhoods consists of young people from middle and lower-middle classes with various religious, gender, and caste backgrounds, and they appear content to be in spaces that make them feel part of the contemporary urban lifestyle, all within their financial means (Dasgupta 2021, 189). As Dasgupta notes, such fragile "pork-barrel" arrangements targeting certain underprivileged constituencies create a symbolic identification between the provided benefits and the populist leadership (Dasgupta 2021, 193).

In this example, in fact, one can see a double – and largely illusionary – identification process typical in the populist exercise of clientelistic practices. On the one hand, especially contemporary populists – under the constraints of neoliberalism – tend to target the ocular-centric orientations of their constituencies with cosmetic changes and usually without "time-consuming" substantive infrastructural investments and long-term developmental

46 Theory

projects. But these cosmetic changes mean a lot to underprivileged local constituencies. On the other hand, populist leaders strongly tie these clientelistic benefits to their persona to an extent that the constituencies start to think that, without the populist leadership and their cunning and dexterity, these benefits would disappear. Thus, without personalistic leadership and symbolic dimension that is transforming clientelistic exchange into populist practice (a practice that is consolidating the impression that unprivileged masses are protected by the populist leader and offered privileges that they were strictly denied previously), patron-client relations take a purely transactional form, which is, usually unsuccessful in relatively competitive political systems.[11]

From a more general perspective, with its contemporary forms that are not based on status honour, patron-client relations require a close relationship between poor masses in need and politicians who possess economic and other resources and brokers who are able to distribute these resources. Research on patronage and clientelism in Latin America demonstrates that, for more or less competitive systems, when clientelistic linkages between parties/ leaders and voters are successful, they tend to rely on a populist cultural framework (Auyero 2001). The central role of a populist communication style in the transformation of the material exchange between political leaders and clients in notoriously clientelistic political traditions such as Peronism has already been highlighted in the literature (Auyero 2001). Therefore, it is plausible to argue that the most important feature of populist parties and leaders that are close to office or that are in power is to establish and maintain linkages based on systematic mass clientelism circumventing or subjugating local powerholders that emerges in a context of culturally and performatively populist framework. This is a point confirmed recently by scholars such as Pappas (2019) and Müller (2016) as well as a series of recent works on the relationship between populist incumbents and public administration and policy (Bauer & Becker 2020; Bartha *et al.* 2020; Peters & Pierre 2019).

Hence, despite the existence of cases of populism which are not into patronage and clientelism (or which could not find the opportunity to engage in such practices) it is not surprising that electorally successful cases of populism (such as Erdoğanism, Peronism and Chavismo as well as PASOK rule in Greece) have been very successful practitioners of clientelism. For, the way populism is engaged with – what I have called – "micro politics" and its penetration into the ordinary, face-to-face, repetitive practices of daily life, its grim reality – which is usually full of poverty and difficulties for underprivileged majorities – clientelism is an almost unavoidable key practice that can lighten the burden for large segments of populist constituencies. The clientelistic linkages with the masses occupy a central place in the everyday practice of "doing populism" in many developing national contexts and

Contemporary theories of populism **47**

represent a natural extension of the populist style. These practices also help populist leaders and parties to reach beyond the media-oriented public stage.

This family resemblance between populism and what I call here "systematic mass clientelism" or "patrimonial clientelism" stems from the fact that both of these methods to get in touch with the masses are in contradistinction to what is a "proper", serious, procedural institutionality. Instead, they represent a "dirty institutionality" as termed by Ostiguy (2016) or "informal institutions" as called by O'Donnell (1996). Political agents who embrace these methods usually opt for fast and personalized solutions to problems. The combination of "responsiveness", "immediacy" (Arditi 2005), and "personalism" emerge as the basis of populism as a responsive micro politics and governmental practice. The responsive and accessible image of populist leaderships in national scale, the sense that the populist leader is similar to the masses s/he represents and close to them, the sense that s/he is *the embodiment of power, "here and now", in front of our eyes* without institutional mediation is complemented by the clientelistic practices of the lower level loyal party/movement functionaries in populist politics. Those are these actors who complement the "immediacy" and personalism of populist performance on the national scale through locating themselves in the heart of local power networks and *finding solutions to the problems of underprivileged constituencies "here and now"*. It is even possible to take a further step and argue that a populist leadership at a national scale is, in fact, the reproduction of these power relations evident to low-income constituencies at the grass-roots on a larger scale. When there is no supply of populist leaders on a national scale, what ensures the survival of populism as a persistent undercurrent, especially in the Global South, is the continuous practices of actors engaged in clientelism at the local level as local populist heroes (in contradistinction to powerful traditional patrons). It should be asserted here that, sometimes, what is appreciated by the constituency is not the solution itself and its durability but the "attempt to solve", "the concern" with the clients' problem, the transformation of the clientelistic relationship into a "sweet gesture of populism".[12] In this context, functionaries and brokers at the local levels have a critical role in populist governmental practice, too, since they are the key actors persuading poor populist constituencies through their activities that the populist party and the leader are here – in the neighbourhood, on the streets and even in the household – to help and that the populist constituencies are not alone.

Nevertheless, the "sweet gestures of populism" should not distort the view of researchers from focusing on the dark side of "micro politics" or responsive political practice. Populist and responsive political practice and its horizon confined to the boundaries of "micro politics" may do harm to general public interests in the long run and inhibit the imagining of a rather more egalitarian and just order. The immediacy and responsiveness of "micro

48 Theory

politics", its urge to respond quickly to popular demands and expectations does not only cause dangerous mistakes in the conduct of public policy,[13] services, and administration but it may also take such forms that confirm established hierarchies and power asymmetries. There is certainly a demand for justice in populism.[14] But one should not miss the fact that this demand of justice usually does not (or cannot) evolve into a sort of progressive, egalitarian and transformative project that pushes for the arrangement of a rather more horizontal forms of power relations and hierarchies. Popular sectors, through populist leaders, loudly demand the return of their dignity in the stage of "politics proper". Nevertheless, this reclamation does not contain the abolition of the power asymmetries intrinsic to populist political relations and practices. Populist political practices – and other related responsive forms of political relationships – are based on the power asymmetries between populist leaders and supporters, brokers and clients. For, from the perspective of popular sectors and their "common sense"[15] – which has been developed throughout the ages under the conditions of state and class-based societies – inequalities regarding wealth, power, and status are part and parcel of social relations. The dominant figures in populist political practice are reluctant to solve unequal relations, but the dominated participants of populist practice too usually do not expect the transformation of these relationships towards a more egalitarian direction either – despite temporary moments of suspension (Ostiguy 2018). Instead, expectations of dominated segments from the populist leader and the party are characterized by a rather "right-wing" content: "speak with a language that I can understand, do not belittle me, do not step over my dignity, help me materially, protect me and I support you by confirming your superiority and by respecting you". No doubt that, in populist political practice, even this demand of dignity may not be responded properly and inequalities may inflict injury.[16] Therefore, when approaching populist practice, particularly in the developing world, avoiding romanticizing the populist relationship is at least as important as trying to understand the positive components inherent to the phenomenon.

Concluding remarks

This chapter was an attempt to have an initial look behind the stage of "politics proper", which is characterized by the struggle between different discourses, strategies, and styles in the realm of electoral politics from a theoretical perspective. I have tried to demonstrate that understanding populism simply and only as a strategy [of organization and mobilization], discourse or ideology may inhibit seeing a much richer body of practices that is behind the stage of "politics proper" that are fundamentally populist in character. I have defined a realm of political practice (termed "micro politics" in this chapter) consisting of various informal practices, most

Contemporary theories of populism **49**

notably clientelism and personalism as well as other sorts of tactics and pragmatic political-governmental inclinations, and argued that populism has a close relation with these other minor practices in the realm of politics. The close relationship between populism and other practices of micro politics that takes responsiveness and immediacy seriously into account and that aim to find prompt and usually personal solutions to the problems of "voters, supporters, people, and citizens" demonstrate that populism cannot be confined into the realm of "discourse" or "organizational strategy" or political communication based on "stage performance". Populism, as a responsive way of doing politics, is deeply related to the realm of political-governmental practice as well as linguistic and style-based features. In sum, a "full populism" must contain the personalistic, particularistic but always responsive and accessible style and predispositions of "micro politics" alongside an antagonistic language, discourse, and political logic required by the realm of "politics proper". In short, populism is not only something spoken but also something *done*. And it is done in a manner that surpasses the performative stage acts and reaches the everyday struggles of populist constituencies with material implications. In this respect, Peronism, Chavismo, and Erdoğanism, for example, are cases of populism *par excellence* combining discursive, strategic, and stylistic features with political-governmental practice. In the next chapter, I will provide the reader with a more comprehensive view regarding the rich praxis of populism in power with a theoretical discussion putting political theory, studies on governmentality, and contemporary theories on everyday forms of power and resistance as well as the recently emerging literature on populism and public administration into dialogue.

Notes

1 This chapter is a substantially revised, expanded, and improved version of an essay previously published in Turkish. See Baykan (2018b).
2 For the concept of performance in the context of discussions over populism, see Moffitt (2016).
3 Ostiguy (2016) conceptualizes the political practice of populism in power that goes forth and back between formal and informal spheres as "dirty institutionality". In this book, what I am trying to do is taking another step in the direction pointed out by Ostiguy that emphasizes the practice and inclinations of populist leaders in power by focusing on the populist political-governmental practice that is effective in the everyday relationships of power and administration on the ground.
4 In a study titled "Populism and praxis", Jason Frank (2017) stresses how political theorists ignored the very rich political praxis of populism while focusing on its antagonistic qualities.
5 I point out these associations between populism and patron-client relations in the literature produced before the 1980s in Baykan (2017).
6 For the concept of "family resemblance", see Wittgenstein (1986, 31–32).

50 Theory

7 See Ostrogorski's (1964) classic text in this respect which testifies the role of powerful patronage networks of notables in the rise of political parties in the West.
8 Also see Di Tella (2001).
9 This is a pattern that we demonstrated in a recent work on the transformation of patron-client relations in Turkey and the position of Erdoğan's AKP *vis-à-vis* these transformations. See Baykan and Somer (2022).
10 Also, see Mavrogordatos (1997) for a very similar diagnosis regarding the change of patron-client relations in Greece.
11 See Stokes' (2007, 622) work in which she notes that clientelism run by non-populist political parties in Argentina fail electorally. In addition, for example, hegemonic parties that are based on more coercive means and located in only nominally competitive systems may not involve in such niceties in clientelistic exchange that can be observed in regimes with predominant populist incumbents located in relatively competitive electoral politics.
12 This is a dynamic that I have observed during my fieldwork on Turkish party politics for my PhD research and for a subsequent research project on party-voter linkages. For an initial outcome of this subsequent research project, see Baykan and Somer (2022). Many grass-root activists that I interviewed in fieldworks for these research projects, and especially those from the AKP, repeatedly emphasized to me that the most important thing for the constituency is the local politicians and functionaries' (in the case of the AKP these are mainly the neighbourhood representatives-*mahalle temsilcileri*) attention to their problems. Evidently, even in the case populist brokers cannot solve the immediate and material problems of their constituency, the populist constituency values the attempt by local populists to solve these problems.
13 The long-term insufficiency of populist social policies in Latin America is compellingly demonstrated by Weyland (2013).
14 Both in Argentina and Turkey, there is the term "justice" in the names of parties that are known with their profoundly populist proclivities: The Justice and Development Party (*Adalet ve Kalkınma Partisi* – AKP) of Erdoğan in Turkey and the Peronist Justicialist Party in Argentina.
15 In this context, I use the term "common sense" as it is used by Gramsci in order to describe spontaneous world view of unprivileged masses which contains progressive as well as archaic and reactionary elements. See Gramsci (1992, 173). With regards to populist political practice, I see "common sense" in close relation to a cognitive state characterized by "oral culture" that is prone to think in context-depended, empirical, and concrete ways. See Ong (2002).
16 See the self-evaluation of people receiving social aid under the AKP rule related by Kutlu (2018, 369) for the social pain and suffering experienced in the receiving end of the clientelistic exchanges: "I belittle myself, it is very embarrassing ... I tell myself that I need even this little help. I am angry with myself".

References

Albertazzi, D. & D. McDonnell (2015). *Populists in Power*. London: Routledge.
Arditi, B. (2005). Populism as an internal periphery of democratic politics. In F. Panizza (Ed.), *The Mirror of Democracy* (pp. 72–98). London and New York: Verso.
Auyero, J. (2001). *Poor People's Politics*. Durham, NC and London: Duke University Press.
Ayata, A. G. (2010). *CHP-Örgüt ve İdeoloji* (B. Tarhan & N. Tarhan, Trans.). Ankara: Gündoğan.

Barr, R. R. (2009). Populists, outsiders and anti-establishment politics. *Party Politics*, 15(1), 29–48.

Barr, R. R. (2019). Populism as a political strategy. In C. de la Torre (Ed.), *Routledge Handbook of Global Populism* (pp. 44–56). London: Routledge.

Bartha, A., Z. Boda & D. Szikra (2020). When populist leaders govern – conceptualising populism in policy making. *Politics and Governance*, 8(3), 71–81.

Bauer, M. W. & S. Becker (2020). Democratic backsliding, populism, and public administration. *Perspectives on Public Management and Governance*, 3(1), 19–31.

Baykan, T. S. (2017). Halkçılık ve popülizm: Türkiye vakası ve bir kavramın kullanımları. *Mülkiye Dergisi*, 41(1), 157–194.

Baykan, T. S. (2018a). *The Justice and Development Party in Turkey – Populism, Personalism, Organization*. Cambridge: Cambridge University Press.

Baykan, T. S. (2018b). "İdare-i maslahatçılık"tan "popülizm"e Türkiye'de duyarlı siyasal pratik: "Popülizm yapıyorsun!". *Birikim*, 353, 15–36.

Baykan, T. S. (2019). Türkiye'de ideolojik ve programatik olmayan parti-seçmen bağları üstüne kavramsal bir tartışma: Popülizm, personalizm, patronaj. *Toplum ve Bilim*, 147, 10–45.

Baykan, T. S. & M. Somer (2022). Politics of notables versus national machine: social, political and state transformations, party organizations and clientelism during AKP governments. *European Journal of Turkish Studies*, 34. https://journals.openedition.org/ejts/8111, accessed: 18.8.2023.

Berenschot, W. & E. Aspinall (2020). How clientelism varies: Comparing patronage democracies. *Democratization*, 27(1), 1–19.

Canovan, M. (1999). Trust the people! Populism and the two faces of democracy. *Political Studies*, 47(1), 2–16.

Çınar, K. (2016). A comparative analysis of clientelism in Greece, Spain, and Turkey: The rural–urban divide. *Contemporary Politics*, 22(1), 77–94.

Dasgupta, R. (2021). The borrowed geographies of neoliberal neighbourhoods: Populist governance in India. In P. Chakravarty (Ed.), *Populism and its Limits – After Articulation* (pp. 187–198). London: Bloomsbury.

de Certeau, M. (2002). *The Practice of Everyday Life* (S. Rendall, Trans.). Berkeley, CA: University of California Press.

de la Torre, C. (1992). The ambiguous meanings of Latin American populisms. *Social Research*, 59(2), 385–414.

Di Tella, T. (2001). *Latin American Politics – a Theoretical Approach*. Austin, TX: University of Texas Press.

Foucault, M. (1998). *The History of Sexuality-1 – The Will to Knowledge* (R. Hurley, Trans.). London: Penguin Books.

Foucault, M. (2000). *Power – Essential Works of Foucault 1954–1984-Volume 3* (R. Hurley and others, Trans.). London: Penguin Books.

Foucault, M. (2006). *Hapishanenin Doğuşu* [The Birth of Prison] (M. A. Kılıçbay, Trans.). Ankara: İmge Kitabevi.

Foucault, M. (2007). *Security, Territory, Population – Lectures at the College de France 1977–1978* (G. Burchell, Trans.). New York: Palgrave MacMillan.

Frank, J. (2017). Populism and praxis. In C. R. Kaltwasser, P. Taggart, P. Ochoa Espejo & P. Ostiguy (Eds.), *The Oxford Handbook of Populism* (pp. 629–643). Oxford: Oxford University Press.

Garrido, M. (2017). Why the poor support populism: The politics of sincerity in Metro Manila. *American Journal of Sociology, 123*(3), 647–685.

Gramsci, A. (1992). *Prison Notebooks – Volume I* (J. A. Buttigieg, Trans. & Ed.). New York: Columbia University Press.

Greene, K. F. (2007). *Why Dominant Parties Lose: Mexico's Democratization in Comparative Perspective*. Cambridge: Cambridge University Press.

Hanson, S. E. & J. S. Kopstein (2022). Understanding the global patrimonial wave. *Perspectives on Politics, 20*(1), 237–249.

Hawkins, K. A. (2010). *Venezuela's Chavismo and Populism in Comparative Perspective*. Cambridge: Cambridge University Press.

Hawkins, K. A., R. E. Carlin, L. Littvay & C. Rovira Kaltwasser (Eds.). (2018). *The Ideational Approach to Populism: Concept, Theory, and Analysis*. London: Routledge.

Hilgers, T. (Ed.). (2012a). *Clientelism in Everyday Latin American Politics*. New York: Palgrave.

Hilgers, T. (2012b). Democratic processes, clientelistic relationships, and the material goods problem. In T. Hilgers (Ed.), *Clientelism in Everyday Latin American Politics* (pp. 3–22). New York: Palgrave.

Hopkin, J. (2006). Clientelism and party politics. In R. Katz & W. Crotty (Eds.), *Handbook of Party Politics* (pp. 406–412). London: Sage.

Jansen, R. S. (2011). Populist mobilization: A new theoretical approach to populism. *Sociological Theory, 29*(2), 75–96.

Kenny, P. (2017). *Populism and Patronage – Why Populists Win Elections in India, Asia and Beyond*. Cambridge: Cambridge University Press.

Kenny, P. (2018). *Populism in Southeast Asia*. Cambridge: Cambridge University Press.

Kenny, P. (2023). *Why Populism – Political Strategy from Ancient Greece to the Present*. Cambridge: Cambridge University Press.

Kitschelt, H. & S. Wilkinson (Eds.) (2007). *Patrons, Clients and Policies: Patterns of Democratic Accountability and Political Competition*. Cambridge: Cambridge University Press.

Knight, A. (1998). Populism and neo-populism in Latin America, especially Mexico. *Journal of Latin American Studies, 30*(2), 223–248.

Kutlu, D. (Ed.) (2018). *Sosyal Yardım Alanlar - Emek, Geçim, Siyaset ve Toplumsal Cinsiyet*. İstanbul: İletişim.

Laclau, E. (2005). *On Populist Reason*. London and New York: Verso.

Levitsky, S. and J. Loxton (2013). Populism and competitive authoritarianism in the Andes. *Democratization, 20*(1), 107–136.

Linz, S. (2000). *Totalitarian and Authoritarian Regimes*. London: Lynne Riener Publishers.

Lyrintzis, C. (1984) Political parties in post-junta Greece: A case of "bureaucratic clientelism"?. *West European Politics, 7*(2), 99–118.

Machado, K. G. (1974). From traditional faction to machine: Changing patterns of political leadership and organization in the rural Philippines. *The Journal of Asian Studies, 33*(4), 523–547.

Magaloni, B. (2006). *Voting for Autocracy: Hegemonic Party Survival and Its Demise in Mexico*. Cambridge: Cambridge University Press.

Mavrogordatos, G. T. (1997). From traditional clientelism to machine politics: The impact of PASOK populism in Greece. *South European Society and Politics*, 2(3), 1–26.

McFarlane, C. (2012). Rethinking informality: Politics, crisis, and the city. *Planning Theory & Practice*, 13(1), 89–108.

Moffitt, B. (2016). *The Global Rise of Populism*. Stanford, CA: Stanford University Press.

Morlino, L. (1998). *Democracy between Consolidation and Crisis: Parties, Groups, and Citizens in Southern Europe*. Oxford: Oxford University Press.

Mouzelis, N. (1985). On the concept of populism: populist and clientelist modes of incorporation in semiperipheral polities. *Politics & Society*, 14(3), 329–348.

Mudde, C. (2004). The populist zeitgeist. *Government and Opposition*, 39(4), 542–563.

Müller, J. W. (2016). *What Is Populism?*. Philadelphia, PA: University of Pennsylvania Press.

O'Donnell, G. A. (1996). *Another Institutionalization: Latin America and Elsewhere*. Kellogg Institute Working Paper No. 222. Notre Dame: University of Notre Dame. https://kellogg.nd.edu/sites/default/files/old_files/documents/222_0.pdf, accessed: 28.2.2024.

Ong, W. J. (2002). *Orality and Literacy*. London: Routledge.

Ostiguy, P. (2016). *Populism in Power: "Dirty Institutionality", Shifting Frontiers, Plebeian Ways, and the Incorporation of Excess*. Paper presented at the APSA Annual Conference, Philadelphia, 1–4 September 2016.

Ostiguy, P. (2017). Populism: A socio-cultural approach. In C. R. Kaltwasser, P. Taggart, P. O. Espejo & P. Ostiguy (Eds.), *The Oxford Handbook of Populism* (pp. 73–97). Oxford: Oxford University Press.

Ostiguy, P. (2018). Pierre Ostiguy ile Söyleşi [Interview with Pierre Ostiguy by T. S. Baykan]. *Birikim*, 354, 57–67.

Ostrogorski, M. (1964). *Democracy and the Organization of Political Parties – Vol. I–II*. New York: Anchor Books.

Oswald, M. (Ed.). (2022). *Palgrave Handbook of Populism*. New York: Palgrave.

Oswald, M., M. Schäfer, & E. Broda (2022). The new age of populism: Reapproaching a diffuse concept. In M. Oswald (Ed.), *The Palgrave Handbook of Populism* (pp. 3–27). New York: Palgrave.

Pappas, T. S. (2019). Populists in power. *Journal of Democracy*, 30(2), 70–84.

Peters, B. G. & J. Pierre (2019). Populism and public administration: Confronting the administrative state. *Administration & Society*, 51(10), 1521–1545.

Roberts, K. (2006). Populism, political conflict, and grass-roots organization in Latin America. *Comparative Politics*, 38(2), 127–148.

Scott, J. C. (1969). Corruption, machine politics, and political change. *American Political Science Review*, 63(4), 1142–1158.

Scott, J. C. (1972). Patron-client politics and political change in Southeast Asia. *American Political Science Review*, 66(1), 91–113.

Scott, J. C. (1990). *Domination and the Arts of Resistance*. New Haven, CT and London: Yale University Press.

Scott, J. C. (1999). *Seeing Like a State: How Certain Schemes to Improve the Human Condition Have Failed*. New Haven, CT and London: Yale University Press.

54 Theory

Shefner, J. (2012). What is politics for? Inequality, representation, and needs satisfaction under clientelism and democracy. In T. Hilgers (Ed.), *Clientelism in Everyday Latin American Politics* (pp. 41–59). New York: Palgrave.

Stokes, Susan C. (2007). Political clientelism. In C. Boix & S. C. Stokes (Eds.), *The Oxford Handbook of Comparative Politics* (pp. 604–627). Oxford: Oxford University Press.

Trantidis, A. (2015). Clientelism and the classification of dominant party systems. *Democratization, 22*(1), 113–133.

Vilas, C. (2003). Participation, inequality, and the whereabouts of democracy. In D. A. Chalmers, C. M. Vilas, K. Hite, S. B. Martin, K. Piester & M. Segarra (Eds.), *The New Politics of Inequality in Latin America – Rethinking Participation and Representation* (pp. 3–42). Oxford: Oxford University Press.

Weingrod, A. (1968). Patrons, patronage, and political parties. *Comparative Studies in Society and History, 10*(4), 377–400.

Weyland, K. (2001). Clarifying a contested concept: Populism in the study of Latin American politics. *Comparative Politics, 34*(1), 1–22.

Weyland, K. (2013). Populism and social policy in Latin America. In C. J. Arnson & C. de la Torre (Eds.), *Latin American Populism in the Twenty First Century* (pp. 117–145). Washington: Woodrow Wilson Center Press/Johns Hopkins University Press.

Weyland, K. (2017). Populism: A political-strategic approach. In C. R. Kaltwasser, P. Taggart, P. O. Espejo & P. Ostiguy (Eds.), *The Oxford Handbook of Populism* (pp. 48–72). Oxford: Oxford University Press.

Weyland, K. (2021). Populism as a political strategy: An approach's enduring – and increasing advantages. *Political Studies, 69*(2), 185–189.

Wittgenstein, L. (1986). *Philosophical Investigations* (G. E. M. Anscombe, Trans.). Oxford: Basic Blackwell.

Wolf, E. R. (1969). Kinship, friendship and patron-client relations in complex societies. In M. Banton (Ed.), *The Social Anthropology of Complex Societies* (pp. 1–22). London: Tavistock Publications.

3

UNDERSTANDING POPULISM AS GOVERNMENTAL PRACTICE

Colonization of modern governmentalities from below

Introduction

This second chapter of the theoretical section aims to clarify the conceptualization of populism as a particular mode of "political and governmental practice" *vis-à-vis* other forms of politics and other conceptualizations of populism. The chapter also locates populism as governmental practice into the framework of modern governmental rationalities under the impact of electoral mass politics. In order to do this, the chapter first locates "populist governmental practice" into the context of a broader question regarding the nature of modern mass politics and distinguishes populism from other liberal, procedural, or authoritarian forms of politics as well as from more conventional understandings of populism with restricted perspectives focusing on electoral politics. As a result, I argue that, even throughout the periods that populism does not dominate the public stage of politics with populist leaders and parties, it keeps effecting everyday affairs of politics and social life as a resilient undercurrent and as a particular mode of political conduct. In this chapter, in line with a broader understanding of politics inspired by contemporary theories on power and resistance, I also argue that the resilience of populism in political life stems from the fact that populism, as a governmental practice, in fact, surpasses the realm of public electoral politics and penetrates into the daily lives of populist constituencies as a sort of *metis* applied by "weak authorities" at the level of public administration and policy. This also requires to locate populism as a governmental practice in the context of the discussions over the development of modern governmental rationalities

DOI: 10.4324/9781003294627-5

56 Theory

as well as works problematizing the relationship between populism and public administration and bureaucracy.

The nature of modern mass politics: Moving beyond electoral politics

The discussion around the concept of populism, especially as a phenomenon of power, invites a discussion about a fundamental question of political theory: "what is political?" While more mainstream approaches to the concept do not problematize this basic question about the nature of politics, especially discourse-theoretical understandings of the concept do reflect on such ontological questions. For example, in their work, scholars like Mudde (2004), Mudde and Kaltwasser (2017), or Weyland (2001, 2017, 2021) do not reflect on the question of what is the fundamental nature of politics. And neither the followers of these ideational (Hawkins 2010; Hawkins *et al.* 2018) and political-strategic approaches (Barr 2009, 2019; Jansen 2011; Kenny 2017, 2023) reflect upon the question of "what is political?". In fact, for these mainstream approaches, the answer to this fundamental question of ontology is usually taken for granted: What can be inferred from these authors' work is that politics for mainstream approaches to populism is usually understood as a public and – mostly – official-formal activity, which, sooner or later, generates consequences in electoral politics. Thus, subjects of enquiry in these approaches have been parties, party leaders, and, to a lesser extent, social movements. The realm of policy and administration usually falls outside the considerations of the works on populism by scholars adhering to ideational and political-strategic approaches. While the socio-cultural and performative approach (Moffitt 2016; Ostiguy 2017), to a certain extent, relies upon an enlarged understanding of politics, it does not really systematically reflect on the nature of modern mass politics too. Surprisingly, prominent scholars embracing a political theory perspective on the concept of populism too do not comprehensively reflect upon the nature of politics. Ultimately, in the works of Urbinati (2019a, 2019b), Pappas (2019), and Müller (2016), for example, populism is understood as a phenomenon pertaining to the realm of conventional politics. For these scholars of populism, the realm of populism is political leadership, mass mobilization, electoral politics, and the public struggle to seize and control the executive authority through electoral or other means.

The discourse-theoretical approaches to populism should be seen as an exception in this regard with their careful consideration on the nature of politics. Laclau (1977, 1990, 2005) has always considered politics as the realm of "conflict", "antagonism", and "contingency". Mouffe too, in her various works (1993, 2005), emphasized the importance of conflictual relations as a fundamental part of politics. In this respect, she suggests an "agonistic" approach in politics that can tame conflict but never tries to fully expel it

Understanding populism as governmental practice **57**

from the public sphere. Because, confirming scholars like Schmitt (2018), Laclau (2005), and Ranciere (1998), Mouffe thinks that, without conflict and dissensus, there is no politics. Laclau clearly demonstrates the centrality of conflict and dissent to politics through his distinction between "politics" and "administration" (2005, 18). Laclau asserts that since it is only populism that represents the construction of antagonistic frontiers between two poles of aggregated differences, populism is, in fact, politics *par excellence* as opposed to "administration". To Laclau, "populist reason—which amounts [...] to *political* reason *tout court*—breaks with two forms of rationality which herald the end of politics: a total revolutionary event that, bringing about the full reconciliation of society with itself, would make the political moment superfluous, or a mere gradualist practice that reduces politics to administration" (2005, 225). Here, it is not difficult to grasp the parallels between Schmitt's and Laclau's understanding of the political. While Schmitt proposes to understand politics as the distinction between "friend" and "enemy" under circumstances of a state of exception (Schmitt 2018), Laclau see the political as the reflection of the conflict between "people" and the "elite" under circumstances of "dislocation" (Laclau 2005, 121–122).

While the consideration on the nature of politics is one of the fundamental merits of the discourse-theoretical approach today, one should, however, emphasize the common ground that the discourse-theoretical approach shares with mainstream ideational and political-strategic approaches. For both of these approaches, ultimately, populism is something related to the conflict at the public stage in ideational, mobilizational, or discursive terms. Thus, for these approaches, populism and politics are ultimately confined to conventional politics based on actors such as political leaders, parties, and social or grassroots movements.

However – as demonstrated so far with reference to the socio-cultural and performative approaches to populism – today, populism and politics cannot be seen within the limited framework of conventional electoral politics consisting of mobilization by parties, social movements, and leaders and their discourses. It is also about the bodily socio-cultural performances of populists appealing to large, underprivileged constituencies and their cultural expectations. But ultimately, socio-cultural and performative approaches to populism too give priority to the conflictual cultural dimension of populism and its impact at the elite public electoral stage. Performative and socio-cultural approaches to populism do not provide researchers with a perspective regarding the construction of populist rapports between politicians and citizens at the lower, less "spectacular" echelons of politics. For example, socio-cultural and performative approaches to populism provide little insight regarding the functioning of populism in localities, which usually surpasses the public realm and penetrates into the private lives of populist constituencies. In order to understand the impact and penetration of populism into

58 Theory

these infinitesimal dimensions of modern social relations, one requires a more comprehensive understanding of politics with regard to spatial, operational, and temporal dynamics.[1]

Spatial, operational and temporal dynamics: "Comprehensiveness", "informality", and "responsiveness" as basic features of populism as governmental practice

Before talking about what is populist in politics in spatial, operational, and temporal dimensions, it is necessary to talk about the "non-populist" in politics for a better understanding of the populist governmental practice. Leaving aside Laclau's contention that the non-populist would be "administrative" or profoundly "revolutionary", it is possible to think of a kind of "politics" containing an administrative and consensual propensity possible. At its extreme ends, the administrative and consensual modes of politics can indeed transform into something non-political by ruling out every possibility of dissent and contingency. Examples of this may be the authoritarian-totalitarian arrangements in the 20th century and a fully unfolded surveillance capitalism aimed by contemporary tech corporations (Zuboff 2018). But today, still, a partially consensual and administrative mode of politics is predominant and define liberal democracies that are opening the public space for orderly competitive electoral politics while minimizing the role of radical forces. In spatial terms, however, this non-populist politics tends to confine itself to the local and national public realm and conventional electoral politics that is minimizing dissent and rendering the entire system conducive towards consensus. This administrative and consensual mode of politics is also based on well-functioning bureaucracies and procedures in operational terms and attaches great importance to the "formal" and the "official". The temporal consequence of the proclivities of non-populist liberal politics in spatial and operational dimensions is bringing continuity and stability to the fore while disregarding the importance of being responsive and swift in reactions to social demands.

This tendency of non-populist democratic politics of our age has ultimately amounted to, as Peter Mair (2013) termed it, "hollowing of Western democracy" and facilitated the rise of populist forces as a reaction to the representation crisis this generated. In terms of spatial, operational and temporal dimensions of modern mass politics, therefore, populism – especially as a governmental practice – is largely the opposite of this liberal democratic institutional politics. Populism as a governmental practice, spatially, usually blurs the boundaries between the public and the private and functions at national as well as local levels. Operationally, or as a mode of action, it puts an emphasis on conflict in politics and usually takes an informal and tactical form in its everyday unfoldings. In temporal terms, it usually tends to

Understanding populism as governmental practice 59

emphasize the ruptures in time and try to be responsive and swift in its reaction to social demands.

Nevertheless, predominant understandings of populism today have more restricted views regarding the spatial, operational, and temporal dynamics of populism. In spatial terms, ideational, discursive, political-strategic, and – to a lesser extent – socio-cultural/performative conceptualizations of populism are inclined to see the phenomenon as a mode of politics that largely takes place in the public realm, like non-populist liberal institutional politics. Moreover, with the partial exception of the socio-cultural and performative approach, the public realm in populist politics has been usually conceived as the "national public realm" and, more precisely, the national electoral politics.[2] This is especially the case in the ideational and political-strategic approaches. More particularly, the recent interpretations of political-strategic approaches tend to conflate populism with personalistic and opportunistic national leaderships (Kenny 2017, 2023; Weyland 2017, 2021). In operational terms, too, regardless of their differences, contemporary theoretical perspectives tend to highlight the conflictual nature of populist politics. The temporal consequence of understanding populism only as a conflictual public activity mainly taking place in electoral politics and around the office of executive is that scholars of current approaches to populism are inclined to highlight the discontinuous and episodic character of populism in temporal terms. In addition, by understanding it as a specific mode of public electoral-conventional politics, scholars of populism today usually highlight the role of the formal political struggles over policy in populism, which only very *slowly* produces administrative outcomes.

By diverging from these approaches, the perspective developed in this book deploys a more comprehensive view of "the political" in spatial, operational, and temporal dimensions. Inspired by the advances in contemporary social and political theory (especially on governmentality and everyday forms of power and resistance) and, to a lesser extent, by the views of feminist political theory highlighting the importance of the "personal" and "the private" in politics (Okin 1989, especially ch. 6),[3] the contention in this book is that populism, as a political and governmental practice, blurs the boundaries between public and the private. It also emerges at the local as well as at the national levels. As a practice, populism is not necessarily the occupation of national political leaders, but local politicians, grassroots functionaries, local brokers, and activists have roles in populists politics, too, when they show certain discursive, performative, and practical propensities. This is the consequence of the operational ("mode of action and interaction") dynamics of populism that contains vital informal aspects requiring populist actors to be in direct touch with their constituencies for the swift exchange of symbolic and material benefits. In order to respond to the expectation of populist constituencies *politicians should be accessible and responsive*. This is why populists usually

60 Theory

tend to be active in localities for being ready to help their constituencies "here and now". It is also very important to respond quickly to particularistic material demands of the constituency in populist governmental practice. This usually leads populists to move beyond the public realm and step symbolically and physically into the private spaces of their constituencies. For example, take a visit by local populist politician/functionary to a poor voter in order to deliver good wishes for the sick child in the household as an example. If possible, the populists also help the family for the treatment of the child. This example is a populist practice *par excellence* including symbolic and material dimensions, and requires populist politicians to effectively cross the boundary between private and public at the local level.[4]

While these exchanges sometimes exclude parties/constituencies that are enemies of populist power holders and reveal conflictual characteristics, they usually depend on the complicity/cooperation between populists and their followers. However, frequently, even the reluctant parties/constituencies in a political system dominated by populists can benefit from the "virtual consensuses" or the "informal social contracts" created by populist incumbents and become complicit to the populist governmental practice. Here, the example can be the non-populist constituencies benefitting from generous populist redistribution or taking advantage of populists turning a blind eye to the common irregularities such as tax evasion and trespasses in residential construction activities – not only for their constituency but for the entire population. In return, informality and complicity implicit in populist governmental practice further blur the boundaries between the public and the private and render populism as a diffused practice with solid implications at local and national levels. These "informal social contracts" encompassing non-populist constituencies are essential to the resilience of contemporary populism in different corners of the globe today.

All these spatial and operational dynamics in populist practice entail concrete consequences for the perception of time by populists and their pace of action as a reaction to social demands.[5] At times, populists indeed highlight the "crisis" (Moffitt 2016) and ruptures in their discursive engagement with the temporality. In fact, however, populism as a governmental practice also functions on the basis of a perception of a continuous, uninterrupted time full with the endless flow of minor and major demands by the populist constituency. Thus, populists' perception of time may be based on crisis, ruptures, discontinuity as well as continuity and permanence of social problems and demands. But, the emphasis on crisis and ruptures in broader politics of populism tends to be more about populist ideas, discourses, and stage performances than populist governmental practice. Regardless of the broader perception of time by populists, the "pace of action" they embrace in the governmental practice is characterized by swiftness and responsiveness towards the expectations of "immediacy" and "responsiveness" widespread among the populist constituency.[6]

This tendency is certainly surpassing the electoral and non-electoral moments/ruptures of "high" politics. Thus, responsiveness and swiftness characterize populism as a governmental practice.[7] Even in cases in which populists can't solve problems or can't deliver to their constituencies in a time frame shaped by popular expectations, they strive hard to give the image that they are working quickly and diligently to solve the problem. And this "impression management" is usually the case for populists given the contextual impediments to swift solutions most populist incumbents experience during their executive activities. These contextual impediments could be tight financial means and organizational incapacity as well as lack of adequate human resources under the control of populist incumbents. Hence, one of the fundamental outcomes of populist practice at the operational level is a tendency to "acting as if" (Wedeen 1998) due to the temporal pressure. When populists can't solve the problems in the short run, they either pretend that they are working fast and hard to solve the problem or they frequently engage in palliative, make-shift solutions. The aim here is usually "impression management" through pretentious governmental practice.

At this point, it is really crucial to acknowledge the exceptional grasp of the essential temporal proclivity of populism towards short-cuts and swiftness by Guy Hermet in his seminal *Les Populismes dans le Monde*.[8] According to Hermet (2001), populism depends upon a short-cut between governing and the governed. Populism, in Hermet's understanding, is a desire to eliminate the barrier that separates people's immediate personal or collective desires from their realization due to the complexities of political and governmental processes. To Hermet, this fundamental proclivity to short-cuts and speed sets populism apart and serves as the core of the definition of the concept. More precisely, for Hermet, populism is characterized by a temporal orientation that stands in stark contrast to the standard timeframe of politics, which is defined by long-term considerations, the necessity of prioritizing and reconciling diverse demands, and the careful, gradual management of their inclusion on the agenda. Hermet notes that the essence of politics mainly revolves around arranging this agenda while adhering to an ethics more rooted in responsibility than conviction. In contrast, for Hermet, populists maintain a relationship with time that is distant to the fundamental principles of politics. Hermet contends that populists refuse to acknowledge the extended timeframes required to address popular demands imposed by the intricate nature of governance. For Hermet, populism is primarily defined by an anti-political temporality, promising an instantaneous response to problems or aspirations that, in reality, cannot be addressed or fulfilled so swiftly by any government action. Thus, in Hermet's analysis, what distinguishes democracy from

62 Theory

populism as a mode of governance is not its claim to "represent" popular sovereignty – this is perhaps done more convincingly by populism – but its procedural orientation towards deliberation, legitimate conflict of interests, and, ultimately, the management of conflicts that spread over time.

In this part of the chapter, to a great extent, I share the views of Hermet on the temporal proclivities of populism, except the fact that he sees this as essentially anti-political. In fact, the temporal proclivities of populism do not render it anti-political unless we conflate politics with liberal democratic proceduralism. As long as one accepts non-liberal ways of "doing politics" and governing things and people, the particular relationship of populism with time distinguishes it from liberal institutional proceduralism in governmental and executive respects as a form of politics. In Table 3.1, I schematically summarize the discussion in this part and demonstrate the specific understanding of the political and the populism embraced in this book – with reference to main approaches to populism and in comparison with other modes of political and non-political conduct.

It should be noted that there is also a positive feedback loop among the spatial, operational, and temporal dynamics of populist governmental practice. As Hermet implies, this positive feedback loop usually stems from populism's distinctive temporal proclivity to swiftness and short-cuts. This temporal tendency reinforces informality, use of tactics, and reliance on "mass complicity/ cooperation" in populist practice, blurs the boundaries between the public and the private, and renders it important to implement populism at the local as well as national levels. In turn, the tendency of populist governmental practice towards "comprehensiveness" in spatial terms leads to surpass the distinction between formal and informal. The blurring of the boundaries between the public and the private, national and the local as well as formal and informal reinforces the tendency in populist practice to swiftness in temporal terms in order to cope with the continuous flow of endless particular and collective demands from the populist constituency. In Figure 3.1, I demonstrate the positive feedback relationship among the spatial, operational, and temporal dynamics of populism.

Thus, current research on populism usually underexamined a large realm of politics that is lying beyond the formal, public, and national electoral domains as well as the temporal dynamics of modern mass politics. Studies on governmentality, on the other hand, missed the impact of modern mass politics and democracy/populism on the very formation of governmental rationalities penetrating into the lives of populations and individuals - especially in contexts where modern mass democracy had a strong proclivity to populist governmental practice. In the next part of this chapter, I will briefly focus on contemporary studies on governmentality as well as public administration and policy in order to define populist governmental practice as a mode of distinct governmental rationality.

Understanding populism as governmental practice **63**

TABLE 3.1 Non-political, non-populism, and different instances of populism in spatial, operational, and temporal dimensions

Forms of non-political and political	Dynamics and dimensions		
	Spatiality: Private or public, national or local	Operationality (mode of action and interaction): Conflictual or consensual, formal or informal	Temporality (perception of time, pace of action): Intermittent or continuous, swift/ responsive or slow/responsible/ unresponsive
Non-political domination (totalitarian control; fully realized surveillance capitalism)	Spatial distinctions disappear	Formal and consensual suffocate the political and social	Continuous/cyclical and unresponsive
The non-populist political (liberal institutional proceduralism)	Public and local, public and national	Formal/procedural and consensual opening room for tamed dissent and conflict	Continuous, responsible, and slow
Populism as ideology	Public and national	Formal and conflictual	Intermittent/ focusing on critical moments, slow (due to its ideational concerns)
Populism as strategy	Public and national	Largely formal and conflictual	Intermittent/ focusing on critical moments, responsive
Populism as performance and socio-cultural appeal	Public and private, local and national	Formal, informal, and conflictual	Intermittent based on cultural continuities, responsive
Populism as governmental practice	Blurred boundaries between public and private, national as well as local	Conflictual as well as consensual, formal as well as informal: Informality, "acting as if", tactics, and complicity/ cooperations ("the informal social contract") playing key roles	Intermittent/ focusing on crisis, but as well as continuous based on routinized material and symbolic reciprocity, responsive and swift

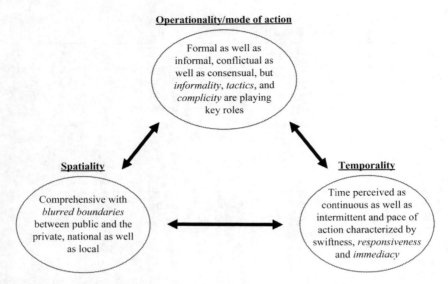

FIGURE 3.1 Positive feedback loop among the spatial, operational, and temporal dynamics of populism as governmental practice

Populism as governmentality: Colonization of modern governmentalities from below

Foucault's work on governmentality has been immensely influential in modern social and political theory. Even before he coined the term "governmentality", however, his views on power had already provided scholars with a critical perspective. In contrast to largely legal and state-centred analyses of politics and power that were overemphasizing the coercive and punitive dimensions, Foucault inclined to emphasize its empowering aspects as a relationship rendering dominated actors productive and capable of carrying out desired actions. In his *History of Sexuality*, therefore, Foucault noted that "in political thought and analysis, we still have not cut off the head of the king" (1998, 88–89) and proposed to move beyond the analysis of legal and formal domains as well as the coercive and punitive capacities in relations of domination (2005, 105–110). Thus, following the *History of Sexuality* and based on theoretical and methodological premises developed in this work (especially in volume I), Foucault delved into the details of various structures of discipline and government developed in Western Europe, which unfolded in the Western thought on politics and administration (2007b, especially the Lecture 4 on "governmentality").

Foucault has defined various different levels of power relations in his work. For example, according to Foucault, "sovereignty" based on coercion and a "right to kill" preceded more modern forms of domination such as disciplines, biopolitics, and governmentality. One of the basic features of sovereign power is that it really is not interested in the welfare of the ruled (Foucault 1998, part five). As Foucault asserts in his seminal work titled "Governmentality", the main aim of "sovereign power" has been sustaining itself, protecting its privileged position *vis-à-vis* the ruled with minimum effort (2007b). This usually resulted in the embodiment of power in relations of sovereignty as a sort of "coercive" force forbidding actions, containing and punishing the ruled. Nevertheless, in "Governmentality", Foucault also points out the birth of a line of thought which he calls the "arts of government" in the 16th century, in the post-Machiavellian era in Western political thought. In this lecture, Foucault explores a series of underexamined works in Western political thought which asserts the responsibilities of rulers towards the ruled. At a certain moment in the development of Western polities and societies, and largely based on a genealogy of what Foucault called "pastoral power" (2005, 211) based on Christian thought, rulers started to take "administration" of "people and things" more seriously into account. Gradually, responsibilities of rulers started to surpass basic coercive and security-related obligations and enlarged in spatial and temporal dimensions. The legitimacy of rulers was no longer based on their coercive capacity and their ability to impose rules (and forbid certain kinds of acts) at certain moments of crisis or trespasses. Instead, now rulers were expected to deliver more complex services and goods to populations on a continuous basis (Foucault 2007b). Foucault defines "governmentality" in his seminal work as follows:

> By this word "governmentality" I mean three things. First, by "governmentality" I understand the ensemble formed by institutions, procedures, analyses and reflections, calculations, and tactics that allow the exercise of this very specific, albeit very complex, power that has the population as its target, political economy as its major form of knowledge, and apparatuses of security as its essential technical instrument. Second, by "governmentality" I understand the tendency, the line of force, that for a long time, and throughout the West, has constantly led towards the pre-eminence over all other types of power – sovereignty, discipline, and so on – of the type of power that we can call "government" and which has led to the development of a series of specific governmental apparatuses (*appareils*) on the one hand, [and, on the other] to the development of a series of knowledges (*savoirs*). Finally, by "governmentality" I think we should understand the process, or rather, the result of the process by which the state of justice of the Middle Ages became the administrative state in the fifteenth and sixteenth centuries and was gradually "governmentalized."
>
> *(Foucault 2007b, 108–109)*

66 Theory

In his other works, Foucault elaborated further on modern methods and dynamics of government such as "disciplines" and "biopolitics". In *The Birth of Prison*, Foucault demonstrates the rise of various new practices and institutions of domination in Western Europe from the 18th century onwards, including, most notably modern prisons, but also many other modern institutions of "confinement" such as asylums, hospitals and schools. In *The Birth of Prison*, ironically, Foucault asserts the "productive" dimension of these practices and institutions of "great confinement" which produced docile but empowered subjects. The aim of the "disciplinary power", therefore, has not been only punishment and isolation but also shaping individuals in mental and physical terms and make them capable subjects playing productive roles in a broader political economy of power (Foucault 2006).

In *History of Sexuality* (1998) and the lecture on "Governmentality" (2007 b), Foucault also asserted that this modern rationality of government does not only target individuals, but through various means and mechanisms, it started to target "populations" as an object of government. At some point, governments started to rule their populations according to various statistical indicators pertaining to the domains of health, reproduction, crime, education, unemployment, etc.: "such a power has to qualify, measure, appraise, and hierarchize, rather than display itself in its murderous splendour" (Foucault 1998, 144). What Foucault calls "biopolitics" is, in fact, in contradistinction with "sovereignty". While "bio-power" strives to protect and support "life" at the level of "species", the "sovereign power" refers to itself and is based on the "capacity to kill" and "forbid" to sustain itself.

After defining the realms of discipline and biopolitics in the *Birth of Prison* (2006) and *History of Sexuality* (1998), Foucault reflected on the rise of "governmentality" and examined the role of modern states in the functioning of disciplinary and biopolitical modes of power relations. Foucault draws attention to the fact that, gradually, more autonomous and local mechanisms of discipline and biopolitics started to being subjugated to central states – in contrast to the view that modern central states created these technologies (Rose *et al.* 2006). And this process – in this or that form – diffused from Western Europe to other parts of the world. Hence, the relationship between rulers and ruled started to become "governmentalized" at a global scale. Other researchers following Foucault have focused on the "governmentalization" processes in different periods and parts of the world than Foucault had focused (i.e., the continental Europe). For example, Nikolas Rose focused on similar themes, and being inspired by Foucault's discussion on "neoliberal governmentality" (Foucault 2008), he started to assert the shift from a "modern welfare state-centred rule" to "market-centred neoliberal rule" that is delegating more and more responsibility on individuals by rendering them imagine themselves as "enterprises" (1990, 1999).

Understanding populism as governmental practice **67**

One of the major problems of the Foucauldian approaches to the study of modern governmental rationalities, however, has been their disengagement with the impact of electoral politics and mass democracy on rather more structural dimensions of "government". This is, of course, understandable given the initial caution of Foucault towards any state-centred, legal, and institutional analysis of modern power he set in the *History of Sexuality* (1998). While this has been a lesser issue for Western democracies based on robust liberal democratic institutions and financially and organizationally capable bureaucratic administrations, in the non-Western developing world, modern governmental rationalities have been comprehensively and effectively shaped by electoral or contentious politics. And, populism has been one of the very important dimensions of modern mass democracies since the rise of mass politics in the developing world, generating serious implications for the development of modern governmental rationalities in these parts of the globe.

Partha Chatterjee's work, in this respect, is crucial and proposes a reinterpretation of the notion of "governmentality" for non-Western contexts. In a recent contribution to a volume titled *South Asian Governmentalities,* Chatterjee (2018) demonstrates the development of a governmental mode of power under the impact of colonial rule in India as a way to better exploit the sub-continent with uneven consequences for different regions/areas and sectors of population (Chatterjee 2018, 42). However, as Chatterjee notes, even before the end of British rule, the Indian middle classes started to take important roles in the governmentalization processes in India (2018, 45). But, just like the colonial governmentalization, the native urge in India to governmentalize the state encountered concrete obstacles, such as the immensity of the country as well as its dramatic poverty. These obstacles kept defining governmentalization processes in India after the independence. As Chatterjee notes, "most of the time, the poor in the city were not property owners, nor did they always observe the duties of proper urban citizens. What were the terms on which they might be recognised as parties to governmental negotiation? It was difficult to find purely technical, depoliticised tactics of power that could serve the purpose" (2018, 49). Under these circumstances, what Chatterjee termed "political society" and the constant political negotiations between urban poor and authorities started to shape governmental practices in India. Most of the time, these practices diverged from the formal governmental schemes and rationalities. Chatterjee's examples, in this respect, are typical and vividly represent an instance of what I call "populist governmental practice":

> The urban poor, for instance, frequently occupy land that does not belong to them and use water, electricity, public transport and other services without paying for them. But governmental authorities do not necessarily punish or evict them because of the political recognition that these

68 Theory

populations serve certain necessary functions in the urban economy and that to forcibly remove them would involve huge political costs. On the other hand, they cannot also be treated as legitimate members of civil society who abide by the law. As a result, municipal authorities or the police deal with these people not as rights-bearing citizens but as urban populations who have specific characteristics and needs, and who must be appropriately governed. On their side, these groups of urban poor negotiate with the authorities through political mobilisation and alliances with other groups.

(Chatterjee 2018, 49–50)

Not unexpectedly, in the following part of his work, Chatterjee calls these governmental practices as "populist governmentality" (2018, 54) but does not elaborate on the term. Yet, this particular example given by Chatterjee and his entire consideration on the transformations and articulations of governmentality in the "developing" East provides crucial points of access for a historical understanding of "populism as a governmental practice". Especially in non-Western developing contexts, governmental schemes have always been subject to "political" negotiations imposed by electoral and mass mobilizational activity as well as clientelistic bargains. Chatterjee's example demonstrates how "populist governmentality" turns into an "informal social contract" between authorities and the governed by circumventing legal procedures and formal policy implementations according to the needs of the urban poor and convenience of bureaucratic authorities. While populist audiences impose their agenda on authorities through various formal and informal means, populist authorities rationally give in to these demands and compromise "grand governmental schemes" and "principles" lest electoral-political costs arise. This is certainly a "governmental rationality" but not exactly in the Foucauldian sense which requires effectively imposing a technocratic administrative rationality upon a population. This is a governmentality that is shaped by electoral and political pressures in a poor developing context, a context which is not really exceptional but pretty widespread, feeding populism as a governmental practice on a global scale, especially as mass-suffrage and democracy expand globally. Hence, in contexts like India, while politics turn into populism for the masses, governmentality also reveals itself in the real practices of government that is shaped by informality and political resistance of diverse populations and individuals. Thus, in such contexts, governmentality does not necessarily and really fully unfolds in the formal mental and discursive schemes of authorities and intellectuals.

In fact, Foucault's work on power and governmentality has received various interrelated criticisms which draw attention to the fact that his work mainly focused on intellectual schemes and formal programmes of government and did not pay attention to factual reality and practical implementations

Understanding populism as governmental practice **69**

(Rose *et al.* 2006, 99) and "real history" (Lemke 2016, 214). As Foucault himself noted however, as a scholar of intellectual history and social theory, his aim was to demonstrate the rationalities behind the implementations of various techniques of government more than demonstrating these techniques themselves (Lemke 2016, 214–215). The other interrelated criticism has been that Foucault's work has underestimated the role of resistance against governmental schemes and programmes (Rose *et al.* 2006, 100). However, as students of governmentality themselves note, "governmental analysis does not aspire to be such a sociology [focusing on real implementations of techniques and programmes of government]. But there is no reason why it could not be articulated with such work" (Rose *et al.* 2006, 100).

A series of scholars, in fact, has been more attentive to the role and resistance of "subjugated" actors in diffused and everyday relations of domination that Foucault had analysed in his work. Michel de Certeau, in this respect, demonstrates the mundane practices of especially the subjugated segments in power relations in his influential work, *The Practice of Everyday Life*. He defines the aim of his work as demonstrating "an operational logic [...] which has in any case been concealed by the form of rationality currently dominant in Western culture" (de Certeau 2002, xi–xii). Two main concepts in de Certeau's work are "strategy" and "tactics". De Certeau defines strategy in such a way that it can only belong to dominant actors in power relations. To de Certeau, strategy is "the calculation (or manipulation) of power relationships that becomes possible as soon as a subject with will and power (a business, an army, a city, a scientific institution) can be isolated. It postulates a place that can be delimited as its own and serve as the base from which relations with an exteriority composed of targets or threats (customers or competitors, enemies, the country surrounding the city, objectives and objects of research, etc.) can be managed" (2002, 35–36). In contrast, de Certeau defines "tactics" as "a calculated action determined by the absence of a proper locus. No delimitation of an exteriority, then, provides it with the condition necessary for autonomy. The space of a tactic is the space of the other. Thus it must play on and with a terrain imposed on it and organized by the law of a foreign power. It does not have the means to keep to itself, at a distance, in a position of withdrawal, foresight, and self-collection" (2002, 37). Thus, tactics are pure improvisation and innovation without any concrete programme that strictly strive to control and order space, action, and time (de Certeau 2002, 37).

Although de Certeau contends that "tactic is an art of the weak" (2002, 37), it is not necessarily the mode of action pursued only by the absolutely subjugated actors. Keeping in mind the radically relational approach of de Certeau, tactics can well be the instruments of powerful actors in a context of general deprivation and lack of resources. Thus, especially for "weak authorities", tactics can play a major role in the conduct of everyday

70 Theory

government and administration. From the perspective of electoral politics, populist incumbents can be considered "weak authorities" in front of the demands of populist constituencies and anti-populist institutional and social opposition, especially in a context of electoral democracy under the circumstances of economic, financial, and organizational deprivation. In addition, in most cases, populist ruling cadres deeply share the ordinary socio-cultural orientations of their constituencies – their "oral culture" (Ong 2002) – and their proclivity towards tactics. Thus, populist governmentality tends to be profoundly tactical with a limited horizon of time and poor control over the space that cannot, for example, demarcate the public realm from the influences of the private.

As such, "populist governmentality" emerges as the practical colonization of modern rational governmental schemes and programmess from below by populist leaderships embracing the tactical, informal, and opportunistic propensities of their populist constituencies. This colonization of modern governmentalities also amounts to a mass complicity between the populist leaderships/governments and masses, which benefits the populist audiences in ways that are clearly contradictory to the formal schemes and programmes of modern governmental rationalities in return of their bottom-up support for populist incumbents. On the other side of the coin, the populist audience turns a blind eye to the governmental failures, and especially populist governments' inability to provide effective conduct of public administration and services, as long as their immediate needs are satisfied. Such complicities may range from populist governments turning a blind eye to the construction of slums on public land and work of poor populations as street vendors without proper permissions to the impunity for tax evasion and local petty crime critical to the survival of the poor, etc. At the symmetrical opposite, populist audiences turn a blind eye to the incapacities of the government, for example, in properly controlling and policing public life and activities as long as these incapacities secure the survival of the urban poor and the populist constituencies in general. Thus, as long as the livelihood of populist constituencies is not threatened, they tend to ignore the apparent inability of populist governments to check, for example, whether the residential buildings are safe, whether local crime is dealt properly and legally or whether public transportation is comfortable, humane and secure, etc.

It was not only Michel de Certeau but also James C. Scott who had crucial works (1990, 1999) which continued the tradition of focusing on the actions and mentalities of the subjugated actors in diffused everyday power relations surpassing the formal public realm. Especially in *Seeing like a State*, Scott fully focused on the "practice" itself in various power relations without overfocusing on discourses, ideologies, symbols, and rituals.[9] In *Seeing Like a State*, Scott highlights the importance of what he calls "*metis*" that emerge in the web of diffused and complex power relations that counter-balances

Understanding populism as governmental practice **71**

top-down and ambitious projects of modern governments. In fact, many projects that have been devoted to "improve the human condition" failed due to the complexities of physical reality on the ground as well as the complexity of power relations in human societies. Scott reveals the discrepancy between these "high-modernist-rationalist" programmes of government and the local and social reality with various compelling examples pertaining to domains as different as agriculture, architecture, and urbanization. There have always been some informal aspects that were not possible to calculate in the "rational plans" and frequently unexpected consequences which were not planned at all by the actors designing and implementing plans to "improve the conditions of the people". One such example discussed by Scott in this regard is the highly planned and strictly managed forests by German agricultural experts, which, ultimately, deprived the forest of bio-diversity that can protect it from the invasion of harmful species and diseases (Scott 1999, 20–22). Such "rational" interventions to human relations and societies, however, as Scott notes in this work, have usually been absorbed and corrected by the informal practices on the ground and in localities. According to Scott, these practices can be called *"metis"* which denotes comprehensive practical abilities and understandings acquired in an everchanging natural and social environment (Scott 1999, 313). As such, like "tactics" of de Certeau, *metis* works through improvisations addressing local, immediate, and practical needs. It also targets practical outcomes and achievements (Scott 1999, 323–324) with a very loose attention to the rational, ethical, or aesthetic unfolding of the practice. *Metis* becomes perfect by trial and error (Scott 1999, 330):

> Metis, far from being rigid and monolithic, is plastic, local, and divergent. It is in fact the idiosyncracies of metis, its contextualness, and its fragmentation that make it so permeable, so open to new ideas. Metis has no doctrine or centralized training; each practitioner has his or her own angle. In economic terms, the market for metis is often one of nearly perfect competition, and local monopolies are likely to be broken by innovation from below and outside. If a new technique works, it is likely to find a clientele.
>
> *(Scott 1999, 332)*

In this respect, what is called populist governmental practice in this book is a form of *metis* in the realm of politics and administration that usually depends on improvisations, informal practices, and tactics oriented towards concrete political and administrative outcomes instead of unfolding of a pregiven ideology, idea or plan in the form of a specific policy in the realm of government and administration.[10] Populism as *metis* also emerges under the circumstances of various political, economic, and social constraints that renders rational administration based on long-term

72 Theory

goals ineffective. These constraining contexts are usually fragile electoral democracies with incapable bureaucratic institutions, widespread poverty, and relatively low levels of education. Especially under such circumstances, populism (as a governmental practice), for many incumbents, becomes the only viable and credible mode of government and it usually rules out highly programmatic and ideologically rigid public administration and policy orientations as alternative options and modes of government. But even in relatively better off contexts, like the United States examined in this book, "weak populist incumbents" with a sense of urgency and under the pressures of strong institutional opposition hastily embraces *metis* in their political struggles against established institutions. In this respect, populism, as a mode of governmental conduct, can be defined as *the practical proclivity of weak authorities and political contenders to personalism, informality, tactics and responsiveness (in spatial, operational and temporal terms) that is appealing to the short-term material and symbolic expectations, interests and tastes of supporting unprivileged majorities.* In short, as a praxis, *populism is a practical and pragmatic majoritarianism.*

Populism in power and public administration

While mainstream scholarship on populism has usually underexamined the relationship between populism and bureaucracy and makes only passing reference to the anti-institutional propensity of populist parties and leaders, more recently, a series of works directly focusing on the impact of populist incumbents on bureaucracies emerged. In this respect, Peters and Pierre's (2019) account could be considered a pioneering work problematizing the impact of contemporary populism on bureaucracies. According to Peters and Pierre, the "elite" in the populist discourse usually includes the bureaucrats as well (2019, 1522). This is why populism in power usually turns against the "administrative state". Peters and Pierre also note that populism in power usually entails the disappearance of expertise, politicization of the administrations, patronage, and the concentration of power in the hands of the top executive authority (the President or the PM) and ministers (2019, 1528). Thus, populists in office usually push for personalization and centralization of administrative power.

In another important recent scrutiny of the impact of populism on bureaucracy Bauer and Becker (2020) too highlight the importance of the ideological/discursive "core" of populism shaping populist incumbents' approach to bureaucracies. According to Bauer and Becker, there is a "common anti-pluralist core of populist public administration policies" (2020, 20). With a rather more nuanced view, Bauer and Becker argue that populists may see the state from a positive perspective (for example, as a vehicle of redistribution

Understanding populism as governmental practice **73**

and a robust instrument of "law and order") as well and this may transform the strategies pursued by populists in their dealings with bureaucracies. Some populists may want to capture the state like Orban in Hungary, some of them may want to dismantle it like Fujimori in Peru (Bauer & Becker 2020, 25). Or in the case of Trump, for example, in which a weak incumbent facing a set of robust administrative institutions, populists opt for "sabotage" (Bauer & Becker 2020, 26).

In a couple of other recent works on populism in power, researchers tend to put greater emphasis on the impact of populists in power on state institutions. In this respect, Pappas's work (2019) is worth mentioning in which he identifies four proclivities of populists in power. These are overwhelming reliance on personalistic leadership, polarization, state control, and systematic patronage (Pappas 2019, 70). Pappas identifies these proclivities of populist incumbents based on the analysis of several crucial cases of populism including Greece during the PASOK rule and Venezuela under Chavismo. Pappas contends that his account refuted "the groundless idea that ruling populism may be a 'corrective' to the shortcomings of democracy" (2019, 82). In a similar vein, and following Pappas' definition and approach to the phenomenon of "populism in power", Muno and Pfeiffer highlight the democracy eroding impact of populism, especially if they "encounter insufficient opposition" (2022, 2). One of the contentions in Muno and Pfeiffer's work is that the ideological core of populism, its alleged "anti-pluralism", defines its practice. Besides elements pertaining to political communication, this substance creates proclivities towards state capture through patronage and mass clientelism and unfair measures/instruments against opposition forces through methods such as "discriminatory legalism", avoidance of intermediary institutions, media capture, and repression of civil society (Muno & Pfeiffer 2022, 7).

Parallel to all of these discussions, a recent volume exclusively focusing on "populism in power" focuses more on the impact of populism on democracy than its praxis in government and how populism "functions". In *Contemporary Populists in Power*, Dieckhoff *et al.* underline that populism's record when it comes to its impact on democracy "is mixed: while in office, some populists of the left do try to renew patterns or forms of political participation, or try to improve the political representation of otherwise marginalised social groups. On the contrary, some national-populists, once in power, claim to represent a 'people' they define in restrictive (ethnical, religious, political …) terms and tend to limit pluralism" (2022, 4). Thus, like Albertazzi and McDonnell's (2015) pioneering work, *Contemporary Populists in Power* too focuses more on regime and policy outcomes than the way populist rule functions.

One of the inadequacies of all of these recent works problematizing populism in power and the relationship between populist incumbents and

74 Theory

bureaucracies is their focus on the impact of the alleged "ideational core" of the phenomenon of populism in power. But as argued in the previous parts, when the issue is "populism in government", this book defends the position that researchers should attach more importance to deeds than ideas/ideologies. This also brings us to another lacuna in the existing works on populism in power and studies on populism's impact on state and bureaucracy. The works analysed so far have an overwhelmingly top-down perspective to the phenomenon of populism in power and mostly problematize the impact of national populist leaderships on national administrations. But populism as a governmental practice, as it is understood in this book, is a diffused phenomenon of power that can have local and even personal impacts, which penetrates into the everyday lives of populist (and non-populist) constituencies. Thus, any scrutiny regarding populism in power should take its practical and procedural dimensions more seriously into account and should also notice populism's impact on local, and, even interpersonal, relations of power and resistance.

In this respect, Bartha *et al.*'s analysis of what they call "populist governance" (2020), deserves a serious acknowledgement in which the authors put a special emphasis on the procedural dimensions of populism in power as a dynamic phenomenon. Like other researchers focusing on the definition of populism Bartha *et al.* too point out the substantive/ideational/ideological features of populism as well as its discursive propensities (2020, 72). But Bartha *et al.* (2020) also problematize the procedural aspects of populist governance in contradistinction to procedural inclinations of conventional liberal public administration and policy implementation. According to this particular study, liberal public administration tends to rely on ideas and tends to be orthodox in content, and is inclined to formalism and institutionalism in procedural terms and pluralism in discursive-ideational respects (2020, 73). In contrast, "populist governance", according to the authors, in terms of content, embraces "policy heterodoxy, strong willingness to adopt paradigmatic reforms and an excessive responsiveness to majoritarian preferences" (Bartha *et al.* 2020, 71). Bartha *et al.* also note that "regarding the procedural features, populist leaders tend to downplay the role of technocratic expertise, sideline veto players and implement fast and unpredictable policy changes. Discursively, populist leaders tend to extensively use crisis frames and discursive governance instruments with a Manichean language and a saliently emotional manner that reinforces polarisation in policy positions" (Bartha *et al.* 2020, 71).

One of the important merits of Bartha *et al.*'s study is that they clearly notice the temporal dimension of populism. Bartha *et al.* draw attention to the fact that "policy making under populist governance tends to have a significantly faster tempo and a shorter duration with frequent episodes of accelerations and a unpredictable timing" (2020, 74). Yet, despite all of these merits,

Bartha *et al.*'s study take "populist governance" as an overwhelmingly top-down phenomenon pertaining to the domain of national bureaucracies and decision-makers. This book, in contrast, proposes to take populism's practical orientation more seriously into account as well as its diffuse impacts on the governed and the interaction between populist incumbents and populist audiences in localities. Only such a bottom-up and relational perspective on populism as a phenomenon of governance can help grasp the essential practical orientation of populism as the "colonization of modern governmental rationalities from below".

Finally, I would like to note here that the populist colonization of modern governmentalities, and more particularly the colonization of modern governmental institutions (in the form of Weberian bureaucracies) in liberal democratic contexts, could be facilitated by the rise of "neoliberal governmentalities" (Miller & Rose 2008, especially ch. 8). Especially the unfolding of "neoliberal governmentalities" as the New Public Management (NPM) attaching importance to techniques such as privatization, increasing reliance on contracts in public employment, performance management in personnel administration, etc. (Dean 1999, especially ch. 8) are prone to articulation by populist governmental practice. For example, as Bauer and Becker note (2020, 24), Orban controls the bureaucracy in Hungary with means such as introducing short-term employment contracts, performance measures, etc.. As a result, career bureaucrats lost ground in Hungary (Bauer & Becker 2020, 24). In fact, all these measures recommended by the NPM perspective become the instruments of a populist government in the case of Hungary. In other parts of the world too, especially right-wing populist governments can take advantage of the ideas espoused by the advocates of NPM in order to subjugate public bureaucracy. Hence, legal-rational Weberian bureaucratic conventions, their proceduralism, and the importance they attach to expertise and science are anathema to populist governmental practice. Whereas the NPM, its emphasis on "flexibility and responsiveness" and its recommendation to "curbing down bureaucracy" is, in many respects, in congruence with populist rule and its practical orientation.[11]

Populism and the popular legitimacy

From the perspective of political theory, all of these discussions have implications regarding the nature of political legitimacy in an age of populism. In his classic discussion, Weber (1978, 941–955) defines three types of legitimate domination: Traditional, charismatic, and legal-rational. While traditional domination is getting increasingly out of date in modern politics with the fall of traditional power holders such as monarchs, aristocrats, and local notables, charismatic authority, time to time, unfolds in politics, usually with devastating consequences, as we have seen especially in the interwar period

76 Theory

in the 20th century. In fact, what we have been witnessing in the last couple of centuries – if we need to define it with Weberian terms – is the increasing prevalence of the legal-rational authority structures, albeit with frequent interruptions by the rise of "big man" and their visions of a "new order and society". Yet, it is hard to see the phenomenon of populism today, especially as a governmental practice, as a phenomenon of charismatic leadership, in contrast to the arguments by scholars such as Pappas (2019) and Kenny (2023). In fact, populism today tends to be highly personalistic, but personalistic leadership is not necessarily always charismatic. It could or could not be. Charisma, as I have argued in a previous work, in line with Weber, should be seen as a very exceptional phenomenon.[12] On the other hand, I have already pointed out that populism is in contradistinction with legal-rational authority.

Hence, from where do populists, in fact, derive their legitimacy today? Especially in opposition, of course, they derive this legitimacy from the legal-rational frameworks of the electoral and political systems in which they challenge the authorities and from their ethical claims to end the "corruption" and irresponsiveness of these systems. And in power, of course – at least, initially – the legitimacy still derives from populists' electoral success and their legal-rational standing. But, populists in power, as discussed so far, usually tend to transgress this very legal-rational framework granting them an electoral and political legitimacy when they try to colonize the state, when they try to satisfy the demands of their constituencies swiftly through particularistic means and when they try to undermine the standing of their opponents. Even in such cases (in which populism tends to transform into something semi-democratic, i.e., "hybrid regimes" or "competitive authoritarianisms"), populist incumbents still tend to be perceived as legitimate authorities by the majority of citizens.[13]

Here, I think it is possible to talk about a different type of legitimacy that was not perhaps that obvious in the time of Weber, simply because his was a time frame that modern mass democracies were still in their infancy. But modern mass democracies – and especially their populist variants in the developing world – generated a new phenomenon of legitimacy based on the congruence between governmental practice by elected officials and popular common sense and expectations. In other words, it is not simply the leader or their persona and the populist discourse emphasizing the superiority of popular sovereignty and people *vis-à-vis* elite, but the practice of populism, its responsiveness, its urge to "deliver" to its constituencies hastily, and its proclivity to short-cuts, tactics, and *metis* – which appeals to popular astuteness – that generates the "popular legitimacy" that populists enjoy in power.[14] It is also the "informal social contracts" that are established by populist rule among populist elites, populist constituencies, as well as non-populist parts of the population (who mostly and privately tend to free-ride the benefits of

Understanding populism as governmental practice   **77**

the populist governmental practice with publicly espoused opposition to it) that is consolidating the popular obeyance to populist rule. This is why one of the frequently used expressions in Turkey regarding the populist incumbents is as follows: "they steal but they get things done!" (*"Çalıyorlar ama çalışıyorlar!"*). Thus, what legitimizes populists in power is not a universal morality and propriety but a sort of "moral economy" based upon the virtual consensus established between populist incumbents and their supporters.

Concluding remarks

In this chapter, I tried to further clarify the location of populism as a governmental practice *vis-à-vis* other forms of politics as well as more visible dimensions of populism, namely its discursive, ideational, and strategic faces. More importantly, this chapter also scrutinized the impact of mass politics, and specifically its populist form, that is pretty widespread, especially in the developing world, on modern governmentalities. The chapter also reviewed the recent literature problematizing populism in power as well as the relationship between populist incumbents and bureaucracies. The initial point that is asserted in this chapter with a political theory discussion is that researchers of populism need to see politics with a broader perspective to notice the realms stretching beyond the electoral sphere and encompassing issues of everyday administration and policy. By relying on this broader perspective on politics, one of the contentions in this chapter has been that populism is a comprehensive form of politics in spatial terms generating implications for both private and the public realm and local and national levels. In fact, populism as a diffuse practice of government blurs the boundaries between the public and the private and creates immediate and particularistic consequences, especially for its supporters, in the form of social relations. Populist constituencies enjoy material and symbolic benefits that these social relations potentially deliver. These blurred spatial boundaries in the practice of populism also entail a certain mode of action. In operational terms, populism usually tends to be informal and tactical. This informality and tacticalness to circumvent procedures usually require the complicity between populist incumbents and their supporters, a "complicity" that makes both sides of the populist rapport to turn a blind eye to, from a proceduralist/legalist perspective, what is considered "petty corruption". This is also tied to the temporality of populism. In this chapter, I highlighted the fact that what distinguishes populism from non-populist forms of politics is its urge to act quickly and immediately as a reaction to the social demands of its constituency. Populism, in temporal terms, characterized by responsiveness and immediacy. This is in contradistinction to the proceduralism and caution of Weberian administrations.

All these propensities of populism with regard to the spatial, operational, and temporal dynamics of modern mass politics usually put populist

78 Theory

governmental practice in conflict with modern governmentalities. Thus, in this chapter, I also highlight the importance of taking into account the impact of electoral democracy on the practical development of modern governmentalities, especially in the developing world. I argue that electoral democracy, and especially its populist propensity in a context of material deprivation, deeply transforms the modern rationalities of government and especially its Weberian legal-rational form. Populist politics, and especially populist governmental practice, creates a kind of "populist governmentality" based on informality, tactics, *metis,* and complicities/cooperations (or "the informal social contract") between populist incumbents and populist constituencies, and undermine legal-rational administrative state and its claim to legal order based on ideals, laws, plans, regulations, programmes, etc.. In fact, populism, as a form of rule, colonizes modern governmentalities from below in line with the expectations of populist constituencies. This is exactly the practice of populism that I tried to explore theoretically in this chapter. Through a dynamic and bottom-up view of populism, I also tried to contribute to the recent literatures focusing on populism in power and the relationship between populist incumbents and public administration, which tend to have a very static and top-down view of the phenomenon (focusing on the outcomes of populist rule in the realm of national public administration and policy more than the diffuse functioning of populism). I also argued in this chapter that this praxis of populism provided populist incumbents with a new kind of legitimacy, a "popular legitimacy", based not on traditional, legal-rational, or charismatic sources but on the practical and short-term efficiency of populist governmental practice under the circumstances of mass electoral politics despite ruling populists' proclivity to "corruption" and intolerance to opposition.

Notes

1 In this chapter, I, to a great extent, agree with Leftwich's suggestion to understand politics in a remarkably comprehensive way, which is related to "all the activities of conflict, negotiation and cooperation over the use of resources [...] involving two or more people" (2004, 15). I, nevertheless, unlike Leftwich, think that certain kinds of violent confrontations such as civil conflicts and wars should be distinguished from politics. Conflicts of politics, however violent they may be, should avoid the physical elimination of opponents if they want to remain as meaningful relations of power between parties with conflicting interests. A war or civil conflict usually marks the end of a meaningful power relationship that contains some sort of potential for deliberation.

2 Recently, Chou *et al.* (2021) drew attention to the importance of populism in the local politics. And as a whole, I think performative and socio-cultural approaches to populism have the merit to provide researchers with a perspective that can be useful in understanding how populism blurs the boundaries between the public and the private.

3 For the increasing importance of the personal and the intimate in modern electoral mass politics also see Stanyer (2013).

4 I should note here that this example is not fictional at all and I heard many similar stories from my interlocutors, especially from the AKP in Turkey, during my previous fieldwork experiences on party politics.

5 For two crucial works highlighting the importance of the temporality in politics, see Grzymala-Busse (2011) and Esposito and Becker (2023). Although temporality has many dimensions such as duration, tempo, acceleration, and timing as Grzymala-Busse notes (2011, 1268), the most important dimension for the analysis developed here is related to the "tempo" of populism as a political practice which distinguishes it from other forms of political-governmental practice. Following the categorization of the various relationships between time and politics proposed by Esposito and Becker (2023), I should also note here that for the current analysis it is the "time of politics" that is more important and "politics of time" and "politicized time", in other words, institutional and discursive-intellectual power struggles and domination efforts around the perception of time are less important.

6 For a recent work empirically demonstrating the marked "impatience" of populist constituencies compared to supporters of non-populist parties, see Aronsson *et al.* (2023).

7 The tendency of populism as a form of policy implementation to be swift and poorly organized as well as its positive consequences for the short-term benefits of popular sectors and long-term hazards for the collective interest have been convincingly demonstrated by Weyland (2013) in the context of Latin America, although he did not pay attention to this dynamic of populist policy implementation in a more systematic and theoretical fashion. In fact, as I try to show in this chapter, this temporal dynamic is part and parcel of "populism as a governmental practice".

8 I would like to thank one of the reviewers of the book proposal for drawing my attention to Hermet's work. I am also indebted to Elise Massicard for providing me with a copy of Hermet's main account on populism and spotting the relevant parts of his work with reference to the temporality of populism in this account stretching from page 45 to the end of Chapter 1 (Hermet 2001). This was very kind of her. In my interpretation of Hermet's work, I relied on translations by *Google Translate* and *DeepL* since I do not know French.

9 Scott's emphasis on the ideological content of the hidden transcripts of the poor and dominated almost amounts to attributing a coherent ideology to the dominated in his seminal *Domination and the Arts of Resistance* (1990). In fact, the content of the ideologies of subjugated segments in diffused power relations is always deeply incoherent and inconsistent. For a very compelling critique in this regard, see Erdoğan (2000). This is why the more important aspect of these relations is not the discursive content but the "deeds" of the subjugated/dominated segments, or, as de Certeau calls, their "tactics" more than their discourses.

10 I would like to acknowledge here that, although focusing heavily on more conventional dimensions of party politics, Betz perfectly captured this essential proclivity of populism in his seminal *Radical Right-Wing Populism in Western Europe*: "In the 'postmodern' present, where the ideological foundations of the modern age are fundamentally questioned, and where idealism has largely been displaced by skepticism, ideology appears to have given way to a pragmatism of common sense. Populist parties are generally held to lack grand visions or comprehensive ideological projects. Instead, they are presumed to appeal to the common sense of the common people, seek to divine the mood swings of an increasingly volatile electorate, and shape their political programs accordingly" (1994, 107).

11 For further information on NPM, see Hughes (2003).

80 Theory

12 See my discussion on the relationship between populism and charisma (Baykan 2018, ch. 4). In this work, I draw attention to the fact that, with such shallow intellectual and ideological convictions and with an excessively practical orientation, populist leaderships usually lack the transformative capacities of thoroughly charismatic leaderships of the 20th century. Also, see Taggart (2019), Mudde and Kaltwasser (2014), and McDonnell (2016, 2017) for nuanced discussions of this particular issue. All of these scholars agree upon the fact that charisma is not a defining feature of populism.
13 Pierre Ostiguy draws attention to such a paradox and proposes to define a new type of legitimacy. See Ostiguy (2018). My discussion in this part is in accord with his approach to this particular problem.
14 This kind of legitimacy that populists enjoy approximates to what Beetham calls "performance" legitimacy (1991, 136–142). But in the case of populism it contains a markedly theatrical aspect manipulating public opinion regarding the real capacity of populists in "delivering" services and goods.

References

Albertazzi, D. & D. McDonnell (2015). *Populists in Power*. London: Routledge.

Aronsson, T., C. Hetschko, & R. Schöb (2023). Populism and impatience. *Umeå Economic Studies*, no. 1019. http://www.usbe.umu.se/ues/ues1019.pdf, accessed: 27.12.2023.

Barr, R. R. (2009). Populists, outsiders and anti-establishment politics. *Party Politics*, 15(1), 29–48.

Barr, R. R. (2019). Populism as a political strategy. In C. de la Torre (Ed.), *Routledge Handbook of Global Populism* (pp. 44–56). London: Routledge.

Bartha, A., Z. Boda & D. Szikra (2020). When populist leaders govern – conceptualising populism in policy making. *Politics and Governance*, 8(3), 71–81.

Bauer, M. W. & S. Becker (2020). Democratic backsliding, populism, and public administration. *Perspectives on Public Management and Governance*, 3(1), 19–31.

Baykan, T. S. (2018). *The Justice and Development Party in Turkey – Populism, Personalism, Organization*. Cambridge: Cambridge University Press.

Beetham, D. (1991). *The Legitimation of Power*. New York: Palgrave Macmillan.

Betz, H-G. (1994). *Radical Right-Wing Populism in Western Europe*. New York: Palgrave Macmillan.

Chatterjee, P. (2018). Governmentality in the East. In S. Legg & D. Heath (Eds.), *South Asian Governmentalities – Michel Foucault and the Question of Postcolonial Orderings* (pp. 37–57). Cambridge: Cambridge University Press.

Chou, M., B. Moffitt & R. Busbridge (2021). The localist turn in populism studies. *Swiss Political Science Review*, 00, 1–13. https://doi.org/10.1111/spsr.12490, accessed: 27.11.2021.

de Certeau, M. (2002). *The Practice of Everyday Life* (S. Rendall, Trans.). Berkeley, CA: University of California Press.

Dean, M. (1999). *Governmentality – Power and Rule in Modern Society*. London: Sage.

Dieckhoff, A., C. Jaffrelot & E. Massicard (Eds.) (2022). *Contemporary Populists in Power*. New York: Palgrave MacMillan.

Erdoğan, N. (2000). Devleti idare etmek: maduniyet ve düzenbazlık. *Toplum ve Bilim*, 83, 8–31.

Esposito, F. & T. Becker (2023). The time of politics, the politics of time, and politicized time: An introduction to chronopolitics. *History and Theory*, 62(4), 3–23.

Foucault, M. (1998). *The History of Sexuality-I – The Will to Knowledge* (R. Hurley, Trans.). London: Penguin Books.

Foucault, M. (2005). *Entelektüelin Siyasi İşlevi* (I. Ergüden, O. Akınhay & F. Keskin, Trans.). İstanbul: Ayrıntı Yayınları.

Foucault, M. (2006). *Hapishanenin Doğuşu [The Birth of Prison]* (M. A. Kılıçbay, Trans.). Ankara: İmge Kitabevi.

Foucault, M. (2007a). *Cinselliğin Tarihi [History of Sexuality]* (H. U. Tanrıöver, Trans.). İstanbul: Ayrıntı Yayınları.

Foucault, M. (2007b). *Security, Territory, Population – Lectures at the College de France 1977–1978* (G. Burchell, Trans.). New York: Palgrave MacMillan.

Foucault, M. (2008). *The Birth of Biopolitics – Lectures at the College de France 1978–1979* (G. Burchell, Trans.). New Yor: Palgrave MacMillan.

Grzymala-Busse, A. (2011). Time will tell? Temporality and the analysis of causal mechanisms and processes. *Comparative Political Studies*, 44(9), 1267–1297.

Hawkins, K. A. (2010). *Venezuela's Chavismo and Populism in Comparative Perspective*. Cambridge: Cambridge University Press.

Hawkins, K. A., R. E. Carlin, L. Littvay & C. Rovira Kaltwasser (Eds.). (2018). *The Ideational Approach to Populism: Concept, Theory, and Analysis*. London: Routledge.

Hermet, G. (2001). *Les Populismes dans le Monde*. Paris: Fayard.

Hughes, O. E. (2003). *Public Management and Administration*. New York: Palgrave Macmillan.

Jansen, R. S. (2011). Populist mobilization: A new theoretical approach to populism. *Sociological Theory*, 29(2), 75–96.

Kenny, P. (2017). *Populism and Patronage – Why Populists Win Elections in India, Asia and Beyond*. Cambridge: Cambridge University Press.

Kenny, P. (2023). *Why Populism – Political Strategy from Ancient Greece to the Present*. Cambridge: Cambridge University Press.

Laclau, E. (1977). *Politics and Ideology in Marxist Theory: Capitalism, Fascism, Populism*. London: New Left Books.

Laclau, E. (1990). *New Reflections on the Revolution of Our Time*. London: Verso.

Laclau, E. (2005). *On Populist Reason*. London and New York: Verso.

Leftwich, A. (2004). Thinking politically: On the politics of politics. In A. Leftwich (Ed.), *What Is Politics?* (pp. 1–22). Cambridge: Polity.

Lemke, T. (2016). *Politik Aklın Eleştirisi – Foucault'nun Modern Yönetimsellik Çözümlemesi* (Ö. Karlık, Trans.). Ankara: Phoenix.

Mair, P. (2013). *Ruling the Void – The Hollowing of Western Democracy*. London: Verso.

McDonnell, D. (2016). Populist leaders and coterie charisma. *Political Studies*, 64(3), 719–733.

McDonnell, D. (2017). Populist leadership. *Social Alternatives*, 36(3), 26–30.

Miller, P. & N. Rose (2008). *Governing the Present – Administering Economic, Social and Personal Life*. Cambridge: Polity.

Moffitt, B. (2016). *The Global Rise of Populism*. Stanford, CA: Stanford University Press.

Mouffe, C. (1993). *The Return of the Political*. London: Verso.

82 Theory

Mouffe, C. (2005). *On the Political.* London: Routledge.

Mudde, C. (2004). The populist zeitgeist. *Government and Opposition,* 39(4), 542–563.

Mudde, C. & C. R. Kaltwasser (2014). Populism and political leadership. In R. A. W. Rhodes & P. 'T Hart (Eds.), *The Oxford Handbook of Political Leadership* (pp. 376–388). Oxford: Oxford University Press.

Mudde, C. & C. R. Kaltwasser (2017). *Populism – A Very Short Introduction.* Oxford: Oxford University Press.

Müller, J. W. (2016). *What Is Populism?.* Philadelphia, PA: University of Pennsylvania Press.

Muno, W. & C. Pfeiffer (2022). Populism in power – a comparative analysis of populist governance. *International Area Studies Review,* 25(4), 261–279.

Okin, S. M. (1989). *Justice, Gender and the Family.* New York: Basic Books.

Ong, W. J. (2002). *Orality and Literacy.* London: Routledge.

Ostiguy, P. (2017). Populism: A socio-cultural approach. In C. R. Kaltwasser, P. Taggart, P. O. Espejo & P. Ostiguy (Eds.), *The Oxford Handbook of Populism* (pp. 73–97). Oxford: Oxford University Press.

Ostiguy, P. (2018). Pierre Ostiguy ile Söyleşi [Interview with Pierre Ostiguy by T. S. Baykan]. *Birikim,* 354, 57–67.

Pappas, T. S. (2019). Populists in power. *Journal of Democracy,* 30(2), 70–84.

Peters, B. G. & J. Pierre (2019). Populism and public administration: Confronting the administrative state. *Administration & Society,* 51(10), 1521–1545.

Ranciere, J. (1998). *Disagreement – Politics & Philosophy.* Minneapolis, MS: University of Minnesota Press.

Rose, N. (1990). *Governing the Soul: The Shaping of the Private Self.* London: Routledge.

Rose, N. (1999). *Powers of Freedom: Reframing Political Thought.* Cambridge: Cambridge University Press.

Rose, N., P. O'malley & M. Valverde (2006). Governmentality. *Annual Review of Law and Social Science,* 2, 83–104.

Schmitt, C. (2018). *Siyasal Kavramı* (E. Göztepe, Trans.). İstanbul: Metis.

Scott, J. C. (1990). *Domination and the Arts of Resistance.* New Haven, CT and London: Yale University Press.

Scott, J. C. (1999). *Seeing Like a State: How Certain Schemes to Improve the Human Condition Have Failed.* New Haven, CT and London: Yale University Press.

Stanyer, J. (2013). *Intimate Politics – Publicity, Privacy and the Personal Lives of Politicians in Media-Saturated Democracies.* Cambridge: Polity.

Taggart, P. (2019). Populism and "unpolitics". In G. Fitzi, J. Mackert & B. Turner (Eds.), *Populism and the Crisis of Democracy – Volume 1: Concept and Theory* (pp. 79–87). London: Routledge.

Urbinati, N. (2019a). *Me the People.* Cambridge and London: Harvard University Press.

Urbinati, N. (2019b). Liquid parties, dense populism. *Philosophy & Social Criticism,* 45(9–10), 1069–1083.

Weber M. (1978). *Economy and Society* (E. Fischoff and others, Trans.). Berkeley, CA: University of California Press.

Wedeen, L. (1998). Acting "as if": symbolic politics and social control in Syria. *Comparative Studies in Society and History,* 40(3), 503–523.

Weyland, K. (2001). Clarifying a contested concept: Populism in the study of Latin American politics. *Comparative Politics*, *34*(1), 1–22.

Weyland, K. (2013). Populism and social policy in Latin America. In C. J. Arnson & C. de la Torre (Eds.), *Latin American Populism in the Twenty First Century* (pp. 117–145). Washington, DC: Woodrow Wilson Center Press/Johns Hopkins University Press.

Weyland, K. (2017). Populism: A political-strategic approach. In C. R. Kaltwasser, P. Taggart, P. O. Espejo & P. Ostiguy (Eds.), *The Oxford Handbook of Populism* (pp. 48–72). Oxford: Oxford University Press.

Weyland, K. (2021). Populism as a political strategy: An approach's enduring – and increasing advantages. *Political Studies*, *69*(2), 185–189.

Zuboff, S. (2018). *The Age of Surveillance Capitalism*. New York: Public Affairs.

SECTION III
Case studies

4

RESPONSIVE POLITICAL PRACTICE IN TURKEY IN HISTORICAL PERSPECTIVE

From "politics of expediency" to "populism"

Introduction

Even before the rise of the *Adalet ve Kalkınma Partisi* (AKP – the Justice and Development Party), populism was a concept that Turkish elites and intellectuals were deploying in their analysis of politics and discursive struggles for hegemony. Especially in the 1980s and 1990s, the concept of populism was frequently used in parliamentary discussions, as evidenced by the records of the conventions in the Grand National Assembly of Turkey (*Türkiye Büyük Millet Meclisi* – TBMM). With this term, the Turkish political elite were describing something that is akin to the definition of populism as governmental practice embraced in this book: A pragmatism in the realm of policy that is aiming to appeal to majority expectations without any consideration of long-term consequences. In this chapter, I explore this longer history of populism as political-governmental practice in post-1980 Turkey through some examples from the parliamentary discussions. But this chapter also highlights that the "geneology" of populism as a governmental practice in Turkey goes back to the pre-1980 period. The chapter reveals that populist political-governmental practice was in place in the 1960s and 1970s for different political traditions in Turkey, independent from the left-right distinction. This chapter also problematizes the roots of populist governmental practice in Turkey that goes back to much earlier times, to the late Ottoman period. Through the use of memoirs and some theoretically informed historical accounts of the period, I demonstrate the roots of populist practice in Turkey in the form of "politics of expediency" in the modernization attempts of Ottoman-Turkish polities. As a way to cope with the increasing governmental and biopolitical responsibilities of becoming a modern state,

DOI: 10.4324/9781003294627-7

88 Case studies

Ottoman political elites embraced "politics of expediency", and, with the transition to competitive mass politics, "populism" as a governmental practice has become an essential component of contemporary Turkish administrative culture and rationality. Thus, this chapter also argues that, in countries like Turkey with a legacy of late modernization, the rise of the principle of national sovereignty, growth of the urban public opinion, responsibilities of becoming a modern Western-style state, and the financial and organizational incapacity inherited from pre-modern polities have caused widespread implementation of "politics of expediency". The Ottoman political elite engaged in practices that was in congruence with modern governmental and biopolitical legitimacy (such as providing the citizenry with some basic state services in cities that improve their capacities as individuals and provide better conditions to the "population") and that is appealing for urban public opinion while they concealed the unsustainable and palliative nature of their measures.

Politics of expediency

In this part of the chapter, before focusing on the perception of media and politicians on populism in the 1980s, I would like to elaborate on the deeply rooted history of what I have called "micro politics" in the history of Ottoman-Turkish polities through the phenomenon of "politics of expediency" (*idare-i maslahat*), which lies at the roots of the responsive political practice in Turkey.[1] Since the modernization process of the Ottoman Empire has started, the concept of "politics of expediency" has been used by Ottoman-Turkish political elites and intellectuals to critically denounce palliative solutions to the country's fundamental problems. Yet, governmental and political practices since the beginning of modernization in Ottoman-Turkish history have always been in congruence with public tastes and expectations. The relatively well-educated social segments that have enlarged throughout the modernization process which embraced a "high-pedagogical" attitude regarding the social and political processes frequently criticized the political and governmental practice in Turkey with the concept of "politics of expediency". The concept of "politics of expediency" has had such wide circulation in the discussions of the parliament that *The Dictionary of Official Meeting Record Terms* (*Tutanak Terimleri Sözlüğü*), which was published by the Grand National Assembly of Turkey included this particular definition for the term: "To accomplish a duty not properly but according to the present conditions; to let things slide, to loosely carry out responsibilities" (Aydın & Çakır 2015, 74).

Use of "politics of expediency" as a pejorative concept, and more precisely, as a way of accomplishing things in a substandard way also raises the question of what has been the "standard" for critical Turkish elites and intellectuals during the late Ottoman and early Republican periods. Since the late Ottoman period, these standards were deeply "Western" in character. And not only in the domain of political and judicial institutions, the very "biopolitical" and "governmental" transformation of Western polities – that was penetrating into the daily lives of individuals and populations – embraced as "standards" by the elites of the modernizing Ottoman-Turkish polities. Not only modern Republican principles of national sovereignty and rule of law, but also modern "disciplinary", "biopolitical", and "governmental"[2] developments in the West were embraced as the "standard" by parts of the Turkish elite and intellectuals (Baykan 2015, 78–81). It should also be noted that such discussions gained remarkable visibility with the rise of public opinion and urban politics based on constitutional and parliamentarian ideals in the Empire, especially after the 1908 Revolution. This led some of the elites and intellectuals to criticize so-called "pretentious" and "deficient" attempts to modernize public administration and policy for appealing to newly rising urban public opinion and taste. Nevertheless, these critics, in fact, underlined some evident inadequacies and real problems in the administrative practices of the modernizing Ottoman-Turkish polities.

Especially in municipal practices, "politics of expediency" became clearly visible in the late Ottoman period. Not surprisingly, a solid example here comes from the domain of "biopolitics" and, more precisely, from the domain of urban planning and hygiene targeting the general welfare of the population. In his memoirs, an important Ottoman artist and intellectual, Celal Esad Arseven, related an incident in which, how due to a lack of adequate financial and organizational resources, the municipal administration in İstanbul during the late Ottoman period substituted a cheap and easy landscaping project instead of a costly and time consuming but necessary infrastructural development:

After establishing the organization [in the municipality], Cemil Paşa first tendered İstanbul's plan to a foreign company. Now the streets were swept and watered every day and new roads were built. On the other hand, plans were prepared to transform the Topkapı Palace into a park. This scientist, who loved consultation, always asked our opinion and attached great importance to expertise. I objected to the idea of constructing a park. Although it was difficult, it was the right thing to start from the sewers and streets of İstanbul and to achieve improvements on that front with our tight budget. I proposed not to spend money on the park and leave it for later. He was not in this opinion. He said: "If we start from the sewers of İstanbul, all the streets will be dug, pits will be dug, and the people who cannot walk in heaps of soil and mud will begin to complain, the newspapers will cry out, and the government will not leave us in our place. In contrast, the pleasure of a park that they have not seen before will please

90 Case studies

the people and strengthen our position, so we will be able to develop the city". In fact, it unfolded as he expected. The park increased the fame and prestige of the Cemil Paşa in the eyes of the government, and allowed him to do other works.

(Arseven 1993, 117)

One of the important points that should be asserted here is that "politics of expediency" is a way to postpone dealing with real problems and gain time while avoiding a confrontation that can stem from radical and drastic measures. Even in the early Republican period, which was, in fact, a substantially authoritarian episode, the Turkish elite avoided confrontations with the masses when the issue at stake was secularizing measures. As Faroz Ahmad noted, Mustafa Kemal Atatürk was well aware of the fact that if he pushed secularising measures to greater extents, for example, that require unveiling all Turkish women, he could incite upheaval (Ahmad 2002, 86–87). Moreover, the Kemalist regime always looked for consensuses with a plethora of local elites despite its centralizing and modernizing ideology and fervour even in a period in which it established a single party authoritarian regime (Meeker 2001). Thus, even the most revolutionary periods in Ottoman-Turkish history have been tamed by a kind of "passive revolutionary" (Gramsci 1996, 232) attitude avoiding direct political confrontation and conflict due to a strong proclivity to "politics of expediency". No doubt that these attitudes were largely a result of financial and organizational incapacity of Ottoman-Turkish polities.

The proclivity towards "politics of expediency" did not disappear with the transition to multi-party politics either. Even a quick search in the National Assembly Meeting Records reveals the frequent use of the term "politics of expediency" and demonstrates the strong proclivity to populist governmental practice during the multi-party era in Turkey too. I am not going to demonstrate many examples here but discuss a couple of important instances which show the relationship between populism (as a governmental and political practice) and "politics of expediency". One of these examples comes from a discussion in the TBMM in 1967 over education policies of the period. In this meeting, Senator Tahsin Banguoğlu from the Republican People's Party (*Cumhuriyet Halk Partisi* – CHP) raised the issue of education policies of this period (*Cumhuriyet Senatosu Tutanak Dergisi* 1967, February 4, 675). The republican senator actually criticized the dramatic increase in the number of secondary schools under the auspices of the populist Democratic Party (*Demokrat Parti* – DP) of the 1950s and the populist Justice Party (*Adalet Partisi* – AP) of the 1960s. Both of these parties tried to enlarge opportunities for education for underprivileged segments of Turkish society. Yet, as Banguoğlu stressed, it was not clear whether the organizational and financial capacity of the Turkish state was adequate to provide a high quality education to large segments of population in these new institutions. Nevertheless, populist actors in Turkish politics in the 1950s and 1960s opted for enlarging the number of secondary schools in order to respond to the demands and expectations of poor masses immigrated to urban centres despite the inevitable mediocrity of these new institutions.[3] Hence, although they increased the number of education institutions their quality remained poor and the populist governments of the era preferred to pretend as if things were going well by praising themselves through the quantitative change.

When Turkey made a transition to multi-party politics in the mid-20th century, and industrialization and urbanization accelerated, "politics of expediency" in Turkey started to transform into a "populist governmental practice" under the conditions of an electoral democracy. One of the major developments in Turkey in the 1950s and 1960s was the mushrooming of slumhouses (*gecekondular*) as a result of rapid industrialization. With regards to this problem, "politics of expediency" was the mode of "policy response" embraced by the Turkish political elite of the time. As Ayşe Buğra notes, the state did not find a solution to the housing problem in the 1950s and 1960s, and the social policy gap in this area was filled by slums based on a tacit agreement between the state and the electorate (Buğra 2010, 183). This "informal social contract" was based on two populist practices: While citizens were building their own modest slumhouses, the state was turning a blind eye. And, especially before elections, the ruling parties were providing these slumhouses with official recognition and bringing municipal services to the illegally occupied areas. As Buğra highlights from the parliamentary records of the mid-1960s, the deputies of the era were prone to confirm the efficiency of this solution, as a quote from one of the deputies of the era testifies: "The Turkish nation has found a dwelling type by trial and error that suits its destiny" (Buğra 2010, 184). As a whole, it is possible to see the entire social welfare realm in Turkey as a product of "politics of expediency". As Buğra asserted, the consequence of the financial and organizational insufficiency of the modern Turkish state resulted in the construction of a "traditional welfare regime" (Buğra 2001), which relied on a tacit consensus between authorities and the governed. This consensus required the governed segments to undertake many social policy responsibilities. According to Buğra, family solidarity has been at the centre of this "welfare regime" (2001, 24). This model created a framework in which the regime expected maximum cooperation from citizens in all areas in which the state formally claims to provide social security, and as a result of this "cooperation/complicity", the state largely ignored informality working for the benefit of majorities. Especially in the realm of social policy, the consequence of populist practice has been the persistence of widespread inequality and poverty in Turkey due to short-term and palliative solutions.

In both of these examples, populism and politics of expediency intermingles. While populist politics responds to the expectations and desires

92 Case studies

of underprivileged supporters of populist politics, populist politicians are inclined to conceal deficiencies in populist governmental practices (the long-term damage done by the populist political practice to the general interest) through "politics of expediency" that is prone to deny, ignore and under-estimate problems, and manipulate the public opinion. In these examples, just like the janus faced relationship between populism and democracy, the darker and brighter sides of populism as a governmental practice can be seen together: While populist practices quickly respond to the expectations and demands of low-income, underprivileged constituencies and undertake a highly inclusionary function, especially in material respects (Mudde & Kaltwasser 2013), these democratizing accomplishments are usually achieved at the cost of long-term negative consequences. Especially after the transition to multi-party politics in Turkey, the term "politics of expediency" has gained markedly pejorative meanings. In other examples, where the term was used by politicians to criticize governmental practices of a series of populist centre-right actors in Turkey, the main issues of discussion remained in the realm of "policy" and "public administration" such as health, education, and security. All of these were domains in which politicians and government officials needed to be in constant and close touch with citizens and their everyday problems and demands.

It should be underlined here that what makes this close relation among populism, mass clientelism (for example, in the form of recognizing and authorizing slumhouses of the supportive poor) and politics of expediency on the basis of micro politics is a – from time to time tactical, and perhaps pretentious – "responsiveness" that aims to "quickly" respond, in this or that way, to the tastes, demands and expectations of public, citizens, voters or supporters. In many examples of "politics of expediency", one can notice the desperate attempts of political and bureaucratic elite in striking a balance between the pressures of public expectations, a modern and rational form of "governmentalization", insufficiency of the financial and organizational capacity of the state and the voter demands as Turkey made a transition to multi-party politics. "Doing politics" in Turkey for the dominant and dominated actors, therefore, is based on a "moral economy" (Carrier 2018), which is related to "politics of expediency", patronage, and populism more than deliberation regarding – and conflict between – ideologies, parties, identities, and values. One of the brilliant descriptions of this way of doing politics based on promptness and being attentive towards expectations of the citizens –usually with a limited horizon of time – comes from Süleyman Demirel and his AP in the 1960s, a tradition of politics which had always been notoriously successful at clientelism in particular, and, micro politics in general (Bora 2000):

> In the election campaigns for the 1965 general elections, the leading issue raised by the CHP was "planning". The chair of the party, İsmet İnönü,

was arguing that "development is only possible through planning" and the election manifesto of the CHP was proposing the establishment of planning units in every ministry and an extra institution that may assist State Planning Organization. ...The chair of the AP, Süleymen Demirel, in response, was claiming that they were not against planning but they were suspicious of exaggerating the functions of planning: "A plan is not a dam. It is not a bridge. It is not a road, a seaport, silo, factory. It cannot be eaten or drunken. As long as it is left as it is, it may not affect the daily lives of the nation. In this form, a plan is a pile of paper". The slogan of the AP in this election was summarizing this approach: "plan or *pilav* (rice)?"

(Aslandaş & Bıçakçı 2006, 186–187)

In this attitude of Demirel and his AP, we see the reflection of the insufficiencies of state capacity in an underdeveloped country, the mentality of populist right-wing political elite, and the pressures stemming from an electoral democracy for political elites altogether. But we also see a genuine concern regarding the deprivation and urgent needs of people which led the populist political elite to populism as a governmental practice.

In sum, from a broader theoretical perspective, in terms of modes of operation in the administrative realm, we see a shift from "politics of expediency" to "populist governmental practice" in the history of modernization of the Ottoman-Turkish polities. At the very beginning of the modernization process in the late Ottoman period, the flexibility imposed on the Ottoman elite by the deficiencies emerged throughout the adaptation of Western forms of governmental practice required to deploy "politics of expediency" that is targeting the "Western gaze" through largely pretentious performative acts of administration and short-term, short-cut and palliative solutions to many substantial problems (Baykan 2015). However, when a sort of public opinion emerged and the idea of national sovereignty started to grow in domestic politics, the "politics of expediency" also started to target a domestic gaze, the gaze of the literate urban classes, and has started to shape practices of Ottoman-Turkish governing elites.[4] The governmental needs of a society that is rapidly modernizing and urbanizing in Western lines, however, did not lead to a Western type of "governmentality" or "biopolitics" but to "politics of expediency" that strikes a balance between "positive technocratic governmental results and policy outputs" and "public opinion and expectations of a broad, non-expert audience". With the transition to multi-party politics, the "domestic gaze" that Ottoman-Turkish political elites wanted to satisfy started to change and enlarged in such a way that it began to contain the majority of the voters. At this very moment of the introduction of meaningful mass suffrage, politics of expediency turned into populist governmental practice in Turkey.

94 Case studies

Populism and right-wing incumbency in Turkey

Especially after the 1980s, another concept has been included in the vocabulary of Turkish political elites and popular analysts in order to criticize very similar governmental problems that had been criticized with the concept of "politics of expediency" in the previous periods. This concept is, not surprisingly, "populism". Starting with the 1980s, and especially in discussions over the government budget, the use of the term populism has started to dominate the critiques of government and opposition.[5] For instance, law drafts frequently proposed by the AKP regarding tax amnesties were criticized by the CHP deputies as "the instrument of populism and electoral economy" (TBMM Genel Kurul Tutanağı 2014). But in some instances, particularly the centre-right tradition in Turkey had proudly embraced the accusations regarding populism. For example, at the beginning of the 2000s, the centre-right True Path Party (*Doğru Yol Partisi* – DYP) fiercely defended its policies which were labelled as "populist" by their opponents and proudly embraced the accusations of "doing populism" as a practical response to majority demands:

> You have devastated the nation, you led the nation to an awful situation. Now, a tobacco producer is completely deprived of capabilities to help his child receive education. As if these mistakes are not enough you cut the credits of Ziraat Bankası too. Now, in the middle of winter, tobacco producing regions... You can go and see dear deputies; but you cannot, you have no touch with the people, you are not among them anymore. The reason of this suffering is the unresponsive policies of this government. And when we defend the rights of the nation they argue that we are "doing populism". If this is your understanding, then, we consider doing populism as an honourable duty for serving to the nation.
>
> *(TBMM Tutanak Dergisi 2001)*

In another example, which emerges in the criticism of a CHP deputy, the relationship between populism, clientelism, and micro politics in the politics of AKP becomes evident.

> In the budget meeting Mr. Prime Minister argued that "Turkey has got rid of electoral economy in the AKP years". I think Mr. Prime Minister does not know the refrigerators his party's members have distributed in the winter months. Or he does not know the fact that [his party's members] have delivered trucks and machines to the Ovaazatlı district of Bursa Mustafakemalpaşa -which was stripped of its municipality status by the government- with notes on them: "The present of Minister and Prime Minister". ... In another occasion, the Prime Minister argues that

"yesterday there was a Turkey which was not able to extend roads to the villages of Ankara. Today there is a government in Turkey which brings roads and water to every village of Turkey". Dear friends, currently there is no running water in the eighty residential areas in Balıkesir because the electric pumps of these water networks are not working. ... In the last referendum process, the AKP representatives go to the Nergiz Village of Balıkesir and tell them that "vote for us in the referendum if you want your water network working". ... The second example is from Kocasinan Village of Sındırgı sub-province. A former AKP deputy goes to this village and say the following: "If you vote for us in 2004 local elections you will get electricity". They get the desired vote and the electricity technicians climb the electric tower and release the stream. Is not this populism? Is not this electoral politics?

(TBMM Genel Kurul Tutanağı 2008)

It is, however, common to see that, despite criticism from the opposition, some of the pro-AKP journalists and columnists explicitly defended populism in governmental terms. A columnist writing for the pro-AKP newspaper *Sabah*, for example, in his comments on the discussions regarding the idea of a third bridge that crosses the Bosphorus Strait, argued that those who objected the construction of the bridge did not have a concern about environment that may be affected by this project. According to Babaoğlu, "these segments who get annoyed when they hear the word 'nation', the word 'people'", "who wants a genocide for ignorant masses in Turkey", actually do not pay any attention to the interests and problems of the nation. To Babaoğlu, "populism ... is much better than these people's liberalism, socialism and their costive ideologies" and the "good aspects of populism are evident".[6] Here the question becomes "what is populism", and "what is good politics" for the AKP elite. It is certainly not only a discourse that exalts people versus elite but also a political performance as well as a governmental practice that concretely appeals to popular sectors. The following quotation from one of Erdoğan's public speeches is a flawless reflection of this understanding:

I could live in İstanbul in a very different luxury... But I know the slums of İstanbul. I visit these households. I know how a Gypsy lives. I spend time with these people. Or I spend time with one of my Kurdish, Zaza or Bosnian brother in the periphery of İstanbul, I chatted with these people, I had food with them. I have done all of these. I did these when I was a mayor and I did this when I was the Prime Minister. Because if I need to know these people, if I need to understand these people I have to see, understand their lifestyles. I had to live with them. I recommend this to all of my friends [in the party]. We have to do these [kinds of activities] wherever

96 Case studies

we are. Now they argue that "they distribute handouts (*sadaka*)". … This is not handout; this is not charity. We act as a social state. … It is not our concern if the previous governments did not do the same thing. What am I supposed to do if I cannot find jobs to everybody? We will bring something to these people for their living. We will bring them food and coal. This is our duty. This is not handout. This is the fundamental right of my citizen. [If I do not do this] there is no point for me and for my friends to occupy these posts.[7]

These quotes from Erdoğan's speech, in fact, represent the core of the AKP cadres' approach to politics: It is the fusion of a populist communication style in the national public stage and grassroots communication (visits to ordinary citizens, having food together with voters, etc.) with a populist political/governmental practice. In this approach, "micro politics" becomes the main ground of political activity.

The mastery of the AKP governments in "politics of expediency", clientelism, and populism, in short, in "micro politics" throughout its 20 years of rule, however, left a heavy burden to Turkey. This is a point that I will turn to in the following chapter with greater detail. But I would like to give a specific example in this chapter too in order to demonstrate the darker side of populist governmental practice. A train accident which resulted in the death of tens of people in a sub-province in Turkey can be seen as a tragedy stemming from populist governmental practice. In this particular case, it was evident that the "politics of expediency" caused fatal mistakes in the construction of railways and resulted in this tragic accident. Considering the news published in the media regarding the construction of this particular railway, it becomes clear that, in order to quickly respond to the demands of citizens[8] and back the discourse of "service delivery", the construction of the railway was persistently rushed[9] and this led to overlook many preventive measures that needed to be taken for such a construction. The other impact of responsive political practice in this particular accident was that, in order to finish the construction as quickly as possible, the populist government closed down the entire construction process to the control of experts that may extend the construction time.[10] Ultimately, the responsive political practice and its short-term horizon led to a typical prospect in which the populist government simply ignored the warnings of experts and politicians from the opposition.

Turkish left and populism

I have elaborated the relationship between responsive political practice consisting of politics of expediency, populism, and clientelism on the basis of micro politics mostly exerted by Turkish right-wing political traditions so far. In this part of the chapter, however, I would like to briefly discuss the record of Turkish left-wing politics when it comes to micro politics that is responsive towards demands of "citizens, voters, people and the nation" in order to show that "populist governmental practice", in fact, crosses the ideological boundaries between right and left. I will focus particularly on the left-wing politics of the 1970s.

The experience of Revolutionary Path (*Devrimci Yol – Dev-Yol*) in the 1970s in Turkey, in this regard, diverges from the rest of the Turkish left when it comes to responsive political practice. The Revolutionary Path, a left-wing Marxian socio-political movement which achieved an unprecedented mass support in the 1970s, did not only fight against the fascist aggression of the era but also developed a mode of politics which was extremely responsive towards mass demands and expectations. According to one of the founders of the movement, Oğuzhan Müftüoğlu:

One of the conventional weaknesses of the Turkish left is its distance to the working masses. The conventional left in Turkey has always remained a closed circle of intellectuals because it could never develop a considerable presence within popular sectors and working classes. It is usually accepted that the Revolutionary Path achieved an important success in this respect. ... This achievement is based on various factors ranging from the style of language, to an approach that is based on the concrete interests of people, from a convincing programme of struggle with concrete targets to a line of action that is legitimate and right.

(Müftüoğlu 1988, 2250–2253)

In this achievement, "the resistance committees" organized by the Revolutionary Path in Turkey had a special role. For, as pointed out by Müftüoğlu, these committees were shaping a concrete, simple, and prompt political practice that was based on "micro politics" and never sacrificed this populist political practice to the long-term strategic goals of left-wing "politics proper": "For example, there was a Kurdish village in Tunceli, Çemişgezek, with 2.000 population. There was the organization of a committee in this village which was led by revolutionary teachers. The peasants in the village, who were into livestock farming, did not know agriculture. In order to overcome this, the committee channelled the water from the nearby river to the lands stretching along houses. The purpose was to help these peasants to produce agricultural products. There were many similar developments in similar settings" (Bostancıoğlu 2011, 194).

The political influence of the Revolutionary Path in the 1970s in Turkey was strongly connected to a political practice that took "micro politics" seriously into account. According to Necmi Erdoğan, the Revolutionary Path organization and its political practice in the 1970s overcame the persistent

98 Case studies

problems of the Turkish left and achieved an unprecedented level of mass support. For example, "in the Revolutionary path [...] there was a sensibility lest the dressing of revolutionaries contradict that of the people. The revolutionary woman who were undertaking political roles in slums, for example, wore shalwar and did not put make up. The revolutionaries were even going to Friday prayers with the 'region's people'" (Erdoğan 2007, 266).[11] Not simply in its political style but also in its political practice, the Revolutionary Path experience was a deeply populist movement: "The resistance committees were undertaking responsibilities in order to solve the problems of people such as roads, water, sewage when there were no fascist aggression. They conducted a campaign called 'end to mud' in Fatsa and they engaged in activities against usury and tried to solve the problems of slumhouses (*gecekondular*). All of these were the product of the general approach of the Revolutionary Path that embraced the principle of 'finding concrete solutions to the concrete problems of the people'" (Erdoğan 2007, 270).

Indeed, the political inclination of the "resistance committees" in some local contexts took a particular form that was mainly functioning on the ground of "micro politics" in which the revolutionaries found immediate solutions to the urgent problems of people. The Revolutionary Path activists in different regions provided people in need with land for the construction of slumhouses (*gecekondular*), they occupied bakeries and baked bread in order to protest the price of the bread, distributed coal and wood to the residents of their neighbourhoods as fuel, run grocery stores for selling cheap fruit and vegetables and distributed water to the people (Bozkurt 2008, 88–89). Through these responsive practices, the Revolutionary Path movement diverged from the main body of conventional left and achieved a remarkable hegemonic presence in Turkish and Kurdish metropoles and provinces. This was in stark contrast with the ideologically stricter, more conventional, and unresponsive strategies of other left-wing traditions in Turkey.

A very illustrative example demonstrating the unresponsive "politics proper" in the Turkish left has been related by Bora (2011), which clearly demonstrates the difference between populist and non-populist approaches to politics in practical terms:

It is an example among many other similar examples. Around two years ago, a mass organization has initiated a literacy education in one of the poor neighbourhoods of İstanbul. The women participated in these educations, which was designed in line with adult education models, did not only learn how to read and write but also developed a group dynamic. Meanwhile, they frequently started to visit the place of this mass organization with a left-wing reputation, even outside the time of educations. And then, when May 1 was approaching, the headquarters of this mass organization ordered the branch to bring these women to the May 1 celebrations. When those women were asked their opinion, most of them, perhaps because they were scared, or perhaps, because simply they were not interested in it at all, did not want to attend. The central executives of the mass organization interpreted the reluctance of these women to attend the May 1 meeting as an indication of the uselessness of this activity. They stopped the literacy education and released the participants. So, what is considered 'action' in this particular example? It is evident that the May 1 was considered as a routine, as the most proper form of action – like routine "practices" of Turkish Armed Forces! But the gatherings of a group of 'ignorant' women which allowed them to join public life by teaching them how to read and write, which enhanced their agency, which opened room for new kinds of socialization, new relationships were apparently considered as an instrumental phase that was designed for raising consciousness for the real 'actions' in the future.

(Bora 2011, 54–55)

Today, it is accepted that rather more centrist segments of left in Turkey in the 1970s achieved a remarkable success in adopting a populist style under the leadership of Ecevit too (Erdoğan 2007). This achievement of adopting a populist appeal was a decisive factor in bringing mass support and electoral success to the left during the second half of the 1970s. In fact, examinations of the CHP at that time reveal the fact that, despite its tradition of "high" politics as the main actor behind the secular nation building process, the party has never been disconnected to "micro politics" in which personalistic relations and patronage played major roles (Ayata 2010). Even in the current intra-party politics of the CHP, it can be observed that patronage, personalistic relations, and material exchange keep influencing party's fortunes, especially in the CHP municipalities. Nevertheless, particularly after the 1980s and after the populist impact of Ecevit as the "Black Son" (*Karaoğlan*) of the masses faded away, the CHP moved away from embracing a populist discourse and practice that can mobilize broad, unprivileged masses. The CHP discourse and practice since the 1980s, in fact, has been characterized by a rather more bookish and "high" content and form, which started to put greater stress on issues regarding secularism on the one hand and attempts for transforming the party into a modern social democratic force on the other, despite some unsuccessful endeavours to form a populist discourse.

These examples from the politics of the Turkish left imply that populism, as a political-governmental practice, is not associated strictly with left or right-wing politics – just like populism as a worldview/ideology, discourse, or style cannot be associated exclusively with left or right. But populism as a practice, regardless of the ideologies espoused by political actors, is certainly associated with a practical hegemonic orientation, a hegemony that does not

100 Case studies

only aim to dominate the elite discursive stage but also strives to receive the support and loyalty of unprivileged majorities through grassroots practices among popular sectors.

Concluding remarks

In this chapter, I tried to locate populism as a governmental practice in a historical context pertaining to the modernization of Ottoman-Turkish polities and the development of mass democracy in Turkey since the mid-20th century onwards. In a timeframe stretching from the end of the Ottoman Empire to the AKP rule, "politics of expediency" has been the basis of "populist governmental practice" appealing to the expectations of majorities through short-term, tactical solutions. In this respect, the case of Turkey, and particularly Erdoğan's AKP, represents a "full populism" complete with ideational, discursive, stylistic, and practical governmental dimensions. But this initial historical analysis of the case of Turkey also indicates that there are some darker consequences of "full populism". And these consequences are not simply due to the disregard of populism for liberal democratic institutionality but also because of the damage populism causes in the long run for welfare and security of citizens. It is hard to find a better example than the AKP rule when it comes to the problems created by the vicious circle of responsive political practice, personalized leadership, tactical power relations, and clientelism in the long run. The next chapter, through a closer scrutiny of the AKP period, aims to provide the reader with an empirical understanding of the vices and virtues of populist governmental practice in Turkey.

Notes

1 For a discussion on the concept of "politics of expediency", see Baykan (2015).
2 For these concepts see the work of Foucault (2005, 2006, 2007a, 2007b).
3 There was a dramatic increase in the number of secondary schools and students receiving education in these institutions in the period stretching from the 1950s to the 1970s. In 1950, there were only 406 secondary schools and 88 high schools across Turkey. In 1970 there were 1,842 secondary schools and 518 high schools. While there were only 68,000 students in secondary schools in 1950, the number increased to 783,000 in 1970. The increase in the number of high school students reveals a similar trend by jumping from 22,000 in 1950 to 245,000 in 1970. These rates were far beyond the population increase rates in Turkey. See Tekeli (1983, 666).
4 There is a series of inspiring works that reveal the development of a new sensibility among the Ottoman-Turkish state elites that takes public opinion seriously into account. See Deringil (2007), Aymes et al. (2016), Kırlı (2009), and Metinsoy (2011).
5 For these discussions see TBMM Genel Kurul Tutanağı (2011, 2016, 2018).
6 See https://www.sabah.com.tr/yazarlar/babaoglu/2016/03/08/ucuncu-kopru-populizm-vs, accessed: 15.8.2018.

Responsive political practice in Turkey in historical perspective **101**

7 See http://www.haber7.com/siyaset/haber/696517-erdogan-siparis-usuluyle-gelmedik, accessed: 8.8.2018.
8 http://www.cumhuriyet.com.tr/haber/turkiye/1021437/CHP_li_vekilden_tren_fa-ciasina_iliskin_sok_iddia___Yapilanlar_abartili_sunulup_sorunlar_hasiralti_edil-iyor_.html, accessed: 8.8.2018.
9 https://www.birgun.net/haber-detay/demiryollari-yeni-facialara-davetiye-cikariyor-demiryolu-aginda-yuzde-85-lik-kisim-yenilenmedi-222747.html, accessed: 8.8.2018.
10 https://www.birgun.net/haber-detay/insaat-muhendisleri-odasi-felaketlerin-nedeni-muhendislik-ve-muhendislerin-yok-sayilmasidir-222484.html, accessed: 8.8.2018.
11 In her account, Doğan (2016, 75) indicates that better-off activists of the AKP refrain using sun glasses (which is considered an upper class luxury by the poor) when they are working for the party in poor neighbourhoods.

References

Ahmad, F. (2002). *The Making of Modern Turkey*. London: Routledge.

Arseven, C. E. (1993). *Sanat ve Siyaset Hatıralarım*. İstanbul: İletişim.

Aslandaş, A. S. & B. Bıçakçı (2006). *Popüler Siyasi Deyimler Sözlüğü*. İstanbul: İletişim.

Ayata, A. (2010). *CHP: Örgüt ve İdeoloji*. İstanbul: Gündoğan Yayınları.

Aydın, H. F. & Ö. Çakır (2015). *Meclis-i Mebusan ve Meclis-i Ayan Tutanak Terimleri Sözlüğü*. Ankara: TBMM Basımevi.

Aymes, M., B. Gourisse & E. Massicard (Eds.). (2016). *Devlet Olma Zanaatı – Osmanlı'dan Bugüne Kamu İcraatı* (A. Berktay, Trans.). İstanbul: İletişim.

Baykan, T. S. (2015). Türkiye siyasetinde iki anlayış: 'İdare-i maslahatçılık' ve 'otoriter iradecilik'. *Birikim, 313*, 76–93.

Bora, T. (2000). Demirel. *Birikim, 132*, 3–6.

Bora, T. (2011). *Sol, Sinizm, Pragmatizm*. İstanbul: Birikim Yayınları.

Bostancıoğlu, A. (2011). *Bitmeyen Yolculuk – Oğuzhan Müftüoğlu Kitabı*. İstanbul: Ayrıntı.

Bozkurt, S. (2008). *The Resistance Committees: Devrimci Yol and the Question of Revolutionary Organization in Turkey in the late 1970s* [Unpublished MA thesis]. Ankara: METU.

Bugra, A. (2001). Ekonomik kriz karşısında Türkiye'nin geleneksel refah rejimi. *Toplum ve Bilim, 89*, 22–30.

Buğra, A. (2010). *Kapitalizm, Yoksulluk ve Türkiye'de Sosyal Politika*. İstanbul: İletişim.

Carrier, J. G. (2018). Moral economy: What's in a name. *Anthropological Theory, 18*(1), 18–35.

Cumhuriyet Senatosu Tutanak Dergisi (1967, February 4). Birleşim: 29, Oturum: 1.

Deringil, S. (2007). *Simgeden Millete* (S. Nilüfer, E. Gürbüz & U. Peçe, Trans.). İstanbul: İletişim.

Doğan, M. (2016). *Mahalledeki AKP*. İstanbul: İletişim.

Erdoğan, N. (2007). 1970'lerde sol popülizm üzerine notlar. In T. Bora & M. Gültekingil (Eds.), *Modern Türkiye'de Siyasi Düşünce Vol. 8 – Sol* (p. 266). İstanbul: İletişim.

102 Case studies

Foucault, M. (2005). *Entelektüelin Siyasi İşlevi* (F. Keskin, I. Ergüden & O. Akınhay, Trans.). İstanbul: Ayrıntı.

Foucault, M. (2006). *Hapishanenin Doğuşu* (M. A. Kılıçbay, Trans.). Ankara: İmge.

Foucault, M. (2007a). *Cinselliğin Tarihi* (H. U. Tanrıöver, Trans.). İstanbul: Ayrıntı.

Foucault, M. (2007b). *Security, Territory, Population* (G. Burchell, Trans.). New York: Palgrave Macmillan.

Gramsci, A. (1996). *Prison Notebooks – Volume II* (Joseph A. Buttigieg, Trans. and Ed.). New York: Columbia University Press.

Kırlı, C. (2009). *Sultan ve Kamuoyu – Osmanlı Modernleşme Sürecinde "Havadis Jurnalleri"*. İstanbul: İş Bankası.

Meeker, M. (2001). *A Nation of Empire – the Ottoman Legacy of Turkish Modernity*. Berkeley, CA: University of California Press.

Metinsoy, M. (2011). Fragile hegemony, flexible authoritarianism, and governing from below: Politicians' reports in early Republican Turkey. *International Journal of Middle East Studies, 43*(4), 699–719.

Mudde, C. & Kaltwasser, C. R. (2013). Exclusionary vs. inclusionary populism: Comparing contemporary Europe and Latin America. *Government and Opposition, 48*(2), 147–174.

Müftüoğlu, O. (1988). Devrimci Yol üzerine notlar. In M. Belge (Ed.), *Sosyalizm ve Toplumsal Mücadeleler Ansiklopedisi Vol. – 7* (pp. 2250–2253). İstanbul: İletişim.

TBMM Genel Kurul Tutanağı (2008). 23. Dönem, 3. Yasama Yılı, Birleşim: 39. (Aralık 27, 2008).

TBMM Genel Kurul Tutanağı (2011). 24. Dönem, 2. Yasama Yılı, Birleşim: 31. (December 8, 2011).

TBMM Genel Kurul Tutanağı (2014). 25. Dönem, 4. Yasama Yılı, Birleşim: 119. (July 18, 2014).

TBMM Genel Kurul Tutanağı (2016). 26. Dönem, 1. Yasama Yılı, Birleşim: 105. (June 22, 2016).

TBMM Genel Kurul Tutanağı (2018). 26. Dönem, 3. Yasama Yılı, Birleşim: 60. (February 15, 2018).

TBMM Tutanak Dergisi (2001, December 28). Birleşim: 44, Oturum: 2.

Tekeli, İ. (1983). Osmanlı İmparatorluğu'ndan günümüze eğitim kurumlarının gelişimi. In M. Belge (Ed.), *Cumhuriyet Dönemi Türkiye Ansiklopedisi – Vol. 3* (p. 666). İstanbul: İletişim.

5

POPULISM AS PUBLIC ADMINISTRATION AND POLICY IN THE AKP YEARS IN TURKEY

A multi-domain analysis

Introduction

This chapter focuses on contemporary populism of Erdoğan's *Adalet ve Kalkınma Partisi* (AKP – The Justice and Development Party) and demonstrates the diffuse impact of populism as a governmental practice in remarkably different realms of policy such as economy, education, foreign policy, etc., in Turkey. Before doing this, however, this chapter also provides the reader with a critical review of the existing literature on the AKP's populism and shows the predominance of approaches which mainly see populism as something pertaining to the domain of electoral politics. In the existing scholarship, researchers in their analysis embraced either an ideational, discourse-theoretical, strategic-mobilizational, or performative/socio-cultural approach and confirms the populism of the AKP. But all of these analyses have been far from grasping the diffuse implications of populism, and, more precisely, populism as a praxis in different domains of public administration and policy generating concrete material consequences for citizens in the short and long-term. Based on this review and with a close examination of different domains of administration and policy, the chapter demonstrates that populism, alongside being an ideational, discursive, stylistic and strategic phenomenon, is also a responsive governmental practice attaching importance to immediacy in responding to the expectations of its supporters with a short-term horizon under the circumstances of democratic mass politics.

DOI: 10.4324/9781003294627-8

104 Case studies

The consensus in the mainstream literature: Erdoğan's AKP as an emblematic case of populism

Erdoğan and his AKP have become one of the most important cases of populism across the globe in the last decades. This was not only because of Erdoğan and his party's long tenure but also due to the profoundly populist ideas, discourses, mobilizational methods, and performances revealed by the party. Thus, from a variety of different angles, researchers saw a similar proclivity to populism in the case of AKP. Now, there is an extensive literature on the AKP and Erdoğan and all of these studies confirm the deeply populist nature of the party and Erdoğan.

The ideational approach to the AKP's populism

The ideational approach, as already discussed in the previous theoretical chapters, today dominates the analysis of populism across the globe. The case of Turkey too has been subject to such analysis and theoretical proponents of this particular approach themselves identified Turkey as one of the most emblematic cases of populism in the world in recent decades in their efforts to provide a global, comparative index of populism (Hawkins *et al.* 2019, 7–8). As the ideational approach became more and more powerful, many studies analysing the Turkish case from this perspective appeared too. One of the pioneering studies on contemporary Turkish populism from an ideational perspective is Erçetin and Erdoğan's study, in which the authors show the populist "thin ideology" expressed in AKP leaders' speeches (Erçetin & Erdoğan 2018, 382). In another study, Çelik and Balta (2020) demonstrated the prevalence of populist ideas widespread among the constituency of the AKP from an ideational perspective. Aytaç *et al.* (2021, 37) too deploys an ideational approach and draw attention to the AKP's populism. In another study, Elçi (2022), from an ideational point of view, highlights the correlation between Ottoman nostalgia and populist attitudes among the Turkish public.

The discourse-theoretical approach to the AKP's populism

Alongside the ideational approach, in recent years, a series of studies on contemporary populism from a discourse-theoretical perspective appeared. One of the first studies on AKP's populism deploying the discourse-theoretical approach inspired by Laclau's (2005) work is Dinçşan's analysis of a critical juncture around the "judicial crisis" of presidential election in the parliament in 2007, which demonstrates the antagonistic logic of Erdoğan's discourse that constructs the "people" against an allegedly unresponsive and hostile "elite". In a similar vein, Özçetin (2019) analysed a debate on a TV series and demonstrated the deeply populist discourse in the Turkish public realm generated by pro-AKP journalists. According to Özçetin, populism doesn't adhere to a straightforward dichotomy of "us" versus "them" limited to the realm of political parties and leaders. Media and popular culture serve as significant channels and environments where populist concepts and topics are created, endorsed, and disseminated (Özçetin 2019, 952). Ateş's (2017) work is also another example which embraces a discourse-theoretical approach and shows that the AKP discursively constructed "the people" with reference to majoritarian religious identities, whereas it identified the opponents of the party as "non-people" in an antagonistic fashion.

The populist mobilization by the AKP: Personalism and organization

Relying on works by Weyland (2001) and Barr (2009), Selçuk identified Erdoğan and the AKP as a case of populism in a comparative study by highlighting the central role of Erdoğan and his "anti-institutionalism". According to Selçuk (2016), from a mobilizational perspective, through skilful utilization of television and social media, Erdoğan effectively connected with the masses on an ongoing basis, maintaining a perpetual campaign mode. Consequently, in all nationally televised events, Erdoğan consistently occupied the central stage and received the most significant portion of the airtime (Selçuk 2016, 577). Hence, personalism is a key aspect of AKP's populism in Turkey.

The populist performance of the AKP: Appealing to the "low" in Turkey

In recent years, accompanying the increasing methodological and theoretical accuracy in the general literature on contemporary Turkish populism, a few studies also embraced the socio-cultural and performative definition of populism proposed by Ostiguy (2017) and Moffitt (2016). In this regard, following Ostiguy, Baykan (2021) demonstrates how Erdoğan and the AKP elite appealed to the popular and plebeian tastes, expectations, and values of large and underprivileged masses, not only through their discourse but through their public performance including extra-linguistic elements. Similarly, Gürsoy notes that when it comes to the construction of populist identities, there has always been a broader repertoire that is mobilizing the symbols and meanings embedded in a deeper and broader socio-cultural rift in Turkey (2021, 166). In a joint article, Baykan *et al.* (2021) demonstrate how the socio-cultural rift behind populism in Turkey rendered the populist incumbent so resilient against anti-populist military interventions. In a remarkable recent contribution, Aslan also embraces a performative-stylistic approach to populism and focuses on "public tearfulness" of AKP elites. According

106 Case studies

to Aslan, by displaying genuine emotions through tears, Erdoğan aimed to construct a sense of emotional connection with the people and uphold his anti-elite rhetoric (2021, 1).

Populism as a strategy of cross-class coalition building: The political economy perspective on the AKP

Apart from these studies embracing perspectives focusing more on political, electoral, and socio-cultural dimensions of contemporary Turkish populism, several work by political economists in Turkey highlighted the redistributive proclivities as a fundamental dimension of the AKP politics. Deploying an economistic understanding of populism, these studies highlight that redistributive measures helped the AKP to counter-balance the negative impact of neoliberal policies and keep upper and lower class elements in a cross-class hegemonic coalition that dominated Turkish politics so far. A pioneering work in this regard belongs to Yıldırım (2009), in which the author argues that the AKP's redistributive strategies in the realms of education, to a certain extent, counter-balanced the harmful impact of neoliberal policies on working populations. In a similar vein, Akçay (2019, 57–62) highlights the importance of "compensating mechanisms" such as social assistance spending and cheap credit rendered available for poor households as the basis of the AKP's appeal to the poor while the party was actually embracing neoliberal economic policies and working for the interests of the rich. According to Yalvaç and Joseph (2019) too the AKP's economic strategies were grounded in principles of neoliberal economic governance, which included implementing measures proposed by the International Monetary Fund (IMF) and the World Bank's stand-by agreements and structural adjustment packages. These measures involved liberalizing financial and capital markets, enforcing strict monetary policies, and privatizing state-owned enterprises. The primary outcomes of these policies were unstable working conditions, the emergence of an informal and flexible labour market, and sluggish growth in real wages. However, rather than engaging in direct conflict with the working classes, the AKP pursued a hegemonic approach. They aimed to co-opt working class grievances by implementing various redistributive measures while simultaneously trying to fragment the working class and mitigate class-based conflicts (Yalvaç & Joseph 2019, 12).

In this respect, the approach in this book, to a certain extent, aligns with studies conducted from a political economy perspective, which tend to underline the concrete material implications of populism working in the benefit of poor constituencies. This book, however, also highlights that, populism, as a governmental practice, surpasses the domains of economic and social policy and, as a praxis including informal dynamics, it has implications in a much broader realm of public administration and policy. By diverging from a pure political economy perspective, this account also highlights the spatial, operational, and temporal dynamics of populist governmental practice which are tightly connected to its symbolic dimension as a form of reciprocal relationship between populist elites and audiences.

The AKP rule as populist governmental practice: A multi-domain analysis

In this part of the chapter, I will focus on different domains of public policy and administration in Turkey throughout the AKP rule. Brief analysis of domains as different as economy, bureaucratic formation, judiciary, order and security, social policy as well as foreign policy demonstrates that, in profoundly populist rule by populist incumbents such as the one we see in Turkey, populism transforms into a tactical logic of government under the circumstances of mass politics focusing on responsive, quick and short-term solutions in order to address majority expectations. This part will start with a brief analysis of economy and end with the exploration of foreign policy conduct during the AKP years.

Populist practice in the realm of economy: Unsustainable responsiveness, favouritism and debt

Turkish economy during the AKP years had periods of boom and bust. Nevertheless, it has expanded remarkably until the end of the 2000s when there was optimism regarding the democratizing potential of the AKP rule *vis-à-vis* the Kemalist tutelary institutional order. In 2001, according to World Bank development indicators, the GDP (gross domestic product) per capita was only 3.100$ in Turkey.[1] In 2013, it reached the peak of 12.500$. But since 2012, the GDP per capita in Turkey is in constant decline and almost got back to where it was in the mid-2000s by decreasing to 8.500$. No doubt that such ups and downs in the GDP per capita do not tell about populism *per se*. But the structure of economy, the policies pursued by the populist elite, and how they have created many fragilities during the AKP era have been directly related to their populism as a governmental practice.

In fact, throughout its long tenure, the economic policies officially espoused by the AKP could be considered quite orthodox neoliberal policies. According to the first programme of the AKP the party is "for a functioning free market economy with all of its institutions and rules" (AK Parti 2002, 33). The party programme also asserted that it is "against the involvement of the state into any economic activity" (AK Parti 2002, 33). The AKP also embraced "privatizations" and "globalization" as well as international cooperation for economic growth and welfare (AK Parti 2002, 34). It is ironic to see that, in its initial programme, the AKP also argued that it avoids

108 Case studies

"a daily, populist, short-term understanding" and embraced "a realistic, long-term, reformist and dynamic understanding" in the realm of economy (AK Parti 2002, 36). Yet the party, from the very beginning, also embraced a redistributive role in the realm of social policies and pledged to form "special programmes for poor people, for old people in need of care, for children and for unemployed. The party will not allow citizens in difficult circumstances to feel left behind and alone" (AK Parti 2002, 71). Even today, the AKP officially embraces a capitalist market economy with pretty orthodox principles alongside some extensive redistributive strategies.[2] This was why, perhaps, a few important accounts of the AKP rule called the AKP's strategies as "neoliberal populism" that is mixing pro-free market economics with some relieving redistributive mechanisms (Yıldırım 2009; Bozkurt 2013; Akçay 2019).

It can, however, be argued that not the neoliberal but the populist proclivities of "neoliberal populism" in Turkey have been stronger when populism is understood as a governmental practice that is inclined to quickly respond to the immediate needs of large and underprivileged segments of society. First and foremost, despite its official claim that it had a long-term view, the AKP did not really attempt to fundamentally change the structure of the Turkish economy for the long-term common good of Turkish society. In contrast to the discourse of "structural reform", sectoral composition of the Turkish economy did not change at all for supporting a sustainable long-term development, and the productivity of the economy remained remarkably low by relying largely on commerce, construction, and service (tourism) sectors.[3] Researchers of political economy reveal this fragility of the Turkish economy. For example, Karataşlı and Kumral note that "the AKP's economic growth strategy did not focus on investing in industry, agriculture, or finance but primarily on producing its bourgeoisie through creative destruction of the urban and rural landscape" (2023, 32). To realize this goal, the AKP deployed public-private partnership schemes to undertake grandiose and often overpriced mega-construction ventures, including motorways, bridges, tunnels, airports, shopping centres, and housing projects across the country. These projects were financed through affordable credit, state-guaranteed payments, and non-competitive public tenders awarded to construction companies with exceptionally strong ties to Erdoğan (Karataşlı & Kumral 2023, 32).

One should also note the blatant favouritism in public procurements in Turkey as the primary vehicle of financing politics throughout the AKP era, which is skilfully demonstrated in the accounts of Çeviker-Gürakar (2016) and Gümüşçü (2021). The AKP governments repeatedly changed the public procurement law in order to provide privileges to supporting business people, and this resulted in staggering amounts of public financial loss. As public procurement became less competitive, AKP benefitted from the sources provided by the contributions of a plethora of "rising" businessmen in order to run its widespread clientelistic operations. It is important to note here the role of the proclivity to swiftness and responsiveness inherent to populism, which drove AKP governments to take advantage of the public procurements. In order to respond clientelistic expectations of its poor constituencies in a populist manner – quickly and effectively – the AKP opted for abusing its authority to redistribute public resources. One should also note that, as a result of such "privileged" relations of reciprocity between the AKP and its protected business class (and its indebtedness to the party), the AKP chairs, for example, can easily find employment for the party's unskilled supporters in localities in the enterprises of pro-AKP business people (Arslantaş & Arslantaş 2022). This is why, although they are not the same or identical phenomena, there is a very strong connection between execution of systematic and widespread clientelism and populism. In fact, populist logic in government, sooner or later, leads to "mass clientelism".

Other research on the structure of the industrial sectors also reveals the fragilities within this sector, which significantly lacks innovation and high-tech production. According to Dinçer and Tekin-Koru (2019), the AKP governments provided significant subsidies and actively participated in the construction industry. This approach could have conveyed an unintended message to manufacturers, suggesting that they should not prioritize staying and growing within their own sector. It may have also discouraged potential foreign investors from considering manufacturing investments in Turkey (Dinçer & Tekin-Koru 2019, 9). And the built-in weaknesses of the manufacturing sector in Turkey has remained intact during the AKP period. As Dinçer and Tekin-Koru notes "technological composition of the manufacturing sector in Turkey suggests that the production structure with low technology has not changed" during the period between 2005 and 2015 (2019, 12).

As Akçay and Güngen (2019) note, one should also add to this picture the foreign-debt-based growth of the Turkish economy during the AKP years, which unsustainably raised the living standards of ordinary Turkish citizens, at least initially. Beginning in the early 2000s, Turkey witnessed a significant expansion of credit, which enabled previously marginalized groups in society to access loans. Furthermore, there were growing efforts to enlarge the country's financial markets throughout the AKP era (Akçay & Güngen 2019, 18–19). But with the economic turmoil Turkish society started to experience, at least since the beginning of the pandemic, it has become clear that what many people had during the 2000s and throughout most of the 2010s in terms of purchasing power was not compatible with the real economic potentials of the country. This was, in fact, based on cheap credit.

No doubt that there were many historical-structural and political-strategic variables in play in such a tendency in the realm of economy. But when viewed from the perspective of the definition of populism embraced in this book, the structure and main dynamics of the economic policies during the AKP era in Turkey may well be related to a profoundly populist proclivity

110 Case studies

that embraced a short-term, pragmatic tendency responding quickly to the immediate needs of its constituency mainly comprised of a rising conservative small-scale entrepreneur class and large, underprivileged social segments. Finally, it should also be noted that it was not only due to cynical electoral concerns but because of "short-term horizon" of populist praxis as well as its inherently "tactical tendency" and pragmatism that led the AKP elite to such populist policies in the realm of economy. For, from the perspective of populist elites, it is always more important to provide concrete and fast solutions and respond to the immediate demands of their constituency than investing in future for a more sustainable economy.

Populism and bureaucracy: Responsiveness, informality, and expansion

The neoliberal policies that the AKP embraced in its initial years required the party to approach the problem of "bureaucracy" very seriously. The party indeed explicitly stated that the state should move away from an interventionist role except basic responsibilities such as fulfilling functions in the realms of law, order and security, education, and health (AK Parti 2002, 60). Even today, the AKP pledges its constituencies to "remove unnecessary bureaucracy".[4] The anti-institutional tendencies of populism that can be observed in other cases have also been evident in the AKP's approach to bureaucracy. In numerous speeches in the party's initial years, for example, Erdoğan argued that "there is a bureaucratic oligarchy which manipulates even the politics".[5] In one of his numerous meetings with neighbourhood headmen (*muhtarlar*) Erdoğan made his views on bureaucracy very clear with popular analogies:

> This bureaucratic oligarchy is the calamity of nations. This is not only valid for Turkey. We lived through this. If the governments are not strong, the bureaucratic oligarchy will try to be in power and everything will stop in the country. After that, you cannot expect to leap forward and development in that country. All the work stops. He passes to him, and him to the other. This goes on. They spin the ball in the midfield just like in football. When it comes to score, there is no goal.[6]

Not surprisingly, the AKP introduced some official measures to reduce the bureaucracy in Turkey, and this was compatible with a neoliberal orientation. Especially in their initial years, the AKP elite saw neoliberal reforms as a vehicle to curb the power of the Kemalist institutional order (Atasoy 2009). Thus, the anti-bureaucratic attitude in the AKP has always been very strong as a result of the overlap between their neoliberal economic proclivities, their deeply populist worldview, which viewed the Kemalist institutional elite tutelage before the AKP as the main adversary, and, more importantly, due to their deeply populist practical orientation attaching importance to immediacy and responsiveness.

The AKP governments introduced several reform attempts in order to curb the power of bureaucracy and render it more responsive towards the expectations of ordinary citizens. For example, it introduced extensive "e-governance and e-government" regulations despite some obstacles (Üstüner & Yavuz 2018, 829). The party also established an Ombudsmanship in 2012 with the law no 6382.[7] The aim here was to protect individuals from unjust decisions and acts of public authorities with an easily accessible administrative mechanism alongside the judiciary (Şahin 2018, 128–129). According to the figures provided by Şahin (2018, 131), applications to the institution reached 17,131 in 2017, which testified the fact that this institution became an important instrument for ordinary citizens in their objections to bureaucratic decisions and activities which they deemed unjust. It is pretty easy to apply to this institution online via the Ombudsmanship website.[8]

The more important and widely used instrument by the AKP governments in order to render the public administration more responsive to citizens, however, has been the Presidential Communication Centre (*Cumhurbaşkanlığı İletişim Merkezi* – CİMER; earlier known as the Primeministership Communication Centre/*Başbakanlık İletişim Merkezi* – BİMER). CİMER was established as a call centre and an online website for citizens to enable them to directly convey their problems to the head of the executive in 2012. The forerunner of CİMER was BİMER and it was established by a Primeministership circular (no 2006/3) in 2006.[9] According to this circular, the aim of the BİMER was to "establish a well-working, fast and efficient system for conveying the citizens' complaints, demands, views and suggestions to the administration".[10] In addition, the circular strongly underlined the importance of promptness and care in responses to citizen queries in the functioning of the system and it also envisaged the establishment of a call centre that can be directly reached from anywhere across Turkey and a relevant IT programme.[11] The circular also highlights that these measures would help the administration "convey the oral and written applications by citizens to relevant public institutions and authorities *quickly* for them to address these issues *as soon as possible*, and in case of delays, warn relevant authorities".[12] With the transition to the presidential system in 2018, the BİMER changed its name and became CİMER. As the booklet published by the recently founded Presidential Communication Directorate (*Cumhurbaşkanlığı İletişim Merkezi*) about CİMER highlights, the function of this instrument is contributing "to form a public control over civil servants alongside administrative and legal oversight" (CİMER n.d., 15).

As Boyraz noted, CİMER has been one of the main instruments of AKP's populist hegemony (2018, 438). According to the figures conveyed by Uysal (2021, 75), since the establishment of the communication centres, the

112 Case studies

number of applications to BİMER/CİMER geometrically increased and was around 6,000,000 in 2020. According to a news report, in 2022, this figure reached 6,180,000. This reveals the fact that ordinary citizens embraced CİMER as a kind of populist control mechanism over state institutions. Just like Ombudsmanship, it is very easy to reach CİMER via phone or an online system.[13] Yet, the problems with such short-cuts between the people and the executive political authority are evident. As Uysal notes in an important study, such direct communication channels are abused to such an extent that they may be identified as "espionage" channels contributing to the autocratization dynamics in Turkey. For example, Uysal relates some incidents of CİMER complaints that were publicized in the media testifying the attempts to undermine opposition municipalities (Uysal 2021, 80). In addition, CİMER could also be abused as an instrument of social conservatism, which contributed to authoritarian dimensions of right-wing populism in Turkey. In a news report regarding a particular CİMER application, it has been related that one of the parents of a secondary school student in İzmir complained about the "mini skirts" of teachers that "set a bad example for children in puberty". It seems that this application led to a local interrogation by the sub-provincial national education directorate in this particular secondary school.[14]

All of these efforts to render the public administration more accessible also led the public administration frequently circumvent procedures and engage in many informal practices. But most of the time, these informal practices went hand-in-hand with clientelistic relations between the AKP and its supporters. For, AKP members and supporters with a "reference" from the local or national party leadership have been able to solve their "problems" with the bureaucracy much easily and more quickly. A disturbing example in this context, according to a news report, was how some health professionals in İzmir could avoid responsibilities in teams formed by the local health directorate to track Covid patients with the help of political protection by AKP elites in the province.[15] This is only a single news publicized, but such examples are abundant, especially in the everyday functioning of local bureaucracies. As members of sub-national level local societies, Turkish citizens are frequently exposed to such dynamics, or they take advantage of these informal ways of "solving problems". In fact, this "informality" and "personal relations" has always been part and parcel of the routine functioning of Turkish bureaucracy (Alexander 2002). But the extent of such "informal relations" in Turkey reached to unprecedented levels with the rise of the populist AKP. As one of the leading figures of an opposition party argued jokingly in a TV interview, in recent years, it is not possible to find a "grave space" in the cemetery without the AKP "reference".[16] Thus, populist governmental practice has another dark side stemming from its representational concerns:

Supporters of populist parties benefitted from unfair advantages in the bureaucracy provided by the party.

This is especially evident in the recruitments to state bureaucracy. As Üstüner and Yavuz (2018) note, "over-politicization" of the bureaucracy is one of the major problems of public administration in Turkey. Such direct control and interference have detrimental effects on the expertise within the bureaucracy and the sustainability of the merit-based system. This, in turn, jeopardized the quality, efficiency, and effectiveness of public services, ultimately undermining the strength of the Turkish state. The problem becomes particularly acute when it comes to appointments to higher-level positions, as it erased the distinction between political and administrative leadership and eliminated the competitive selection process that ensured merit-based appointments. Furthermore, the politicization of the Turkish national bureaucracy extended its influence across all levels of public administration (Üstüner & Yavuz 2018, 830). Adar and Seufert too makes a similar point with regards to purges the government engaged in after the failed 2016 coup d'etat (2021, 17–18).

A close view of the news regarding the control exerted by the AKP over local and national bureaucracies, in fact, confirms the concerns of Üstüner and Yavuz (2018). From local to national bureaucracy, the populist control exerted by the AKP has been truly extensive and denied any autonomy to the local and national level bureaucracy to function effectively in line with a technocratic logic. For example, there are lots of reports in the media in recent years addressing the problematic relationships between AKP elites and appointed governors in sub-provinces (*kaymakamlar*) and governors in provinces (*valiler*), demonstrating the disappearing autonomy of high-ranked Turkish bureaucrats.[17] It is also evident that some of the lower-ranked local bureaucrats and personnel too widely benefit from the AKP patronage[18] and those who are not submissive enough can be penalized.

Such uses of the bureaucracy as a source of patronage also resulted in the unnecessary expansion of the public bureaucracy. According to the figures provided by Üstüner and Yavuz, "as of May 2016", "there are 3.390.738 public employees. This reflects more than 40% increase over the last 10 years, corresponding to more than 750.000 new positions" (2018, 824). Today, according to official figures, there are 5,036,795 people employed by public institutions in Turkey.[19] It is ironic to see that the populist logic in the rule of the AKP overweighed the "neoliberal" proclivity the party had in its initial years and, instead of achieving a smaller state and bureaucracy, as a result of populist governmental practice, the AKP ended up with a large bureaucracy and millions depending on the state, similar to the examples that will be analysed below regarding Venezuela, Greece, and Egypt.

114 Case studies

Populist dynamics in the judicial realm: The tight executive control, court packing, judicial tactics, and the majoritarian drift

One of the main tendencies of populist governments across the globe has been their desire to tightly control the judiciary. Most of the time, this desire turns into a mechanism of autocratization guised as the realization of "national will". The AKP too, from the very beginning, saw the judiciary as part of an elite coalition that is against the "national will". Indeed, the judiciary in Turkey, and judicial activism in particular, until the rise of the AKP, have been highly politicized and intervened in politics on highly ideological grounds (Özbudun 2007). Especially the high judiciary and the Turkish Constitutional Court had a largely negative view of the political class, and particularly of right-wing politicians prone to religious conservatism, and they frequently closed down parties and penalized conservative-Islamist politicians. The AKP had its own struggles with the judiciary in its initial years too. In 2007, a former member of the high judiciary in Turkey, on ideological grounds, led campaigns in the parliament to obstruct the nomination of an AKP candidate for presidency through a dubious interpretation of the constitution that the president can only be selected in voting in which 367 MPs are present, more than the MPs the AKP had by that time. In addition, the Turkish Constitutional Court carried out a legal case to close down the AKP in 2008 and the party avoided the worst outcome only due to a lack of qualified unanimity. But the AKP could not get away from receiving a large financial fine.

After overcoming these initial assaults by the high judiciary – in alliance with the Gülen Community[20] – the AKP strived to change the main institutional dynamics of the high judiciary in Turkey through a referendum on a partial change of the constitution in 2010. In this referendum, the AKP won and changed the constitution in such a way that it would consolidate the party's grip on high judiciary. Two major changes in this referendum regarding the composition of the Constitutional Court and the High Council of Judges and Prosecutors (*Hakimler ve Savcılar Yüksek Kurulu* – HSYK) were the initial steps in consolidating the executive grip over the judiciary by granting more room to the president to pick and appoint desired candidates to these expanded critical judicial bodies. As a pro-AKP academic interprets from a populist perspective, these changes had the potential to "reduce the judicial leg of the bureaucratic tutelage" in Turkey (Hakyemez 2010, 405).[21] As an empirical study demonstrates, these changes in the Constitutional Court marked a substantial departure from the Court's previous ideological stance. The Court has moved, and is still moving, towards a more right-wing position. This shift can likely be attributed to alterations in the Court's composition and the process of appointing its members (Varol *et al.* 2017, 213).

But as the AKP consolidated its position in power, its control over the judiciary increased and started to be perceived as beyond the examples that can be seen in liberal democratic settings. As Özbudun (2015), a leading expert on constitutional politics and political parties in Turkey, noted in the mid-2010s, the AKP started to drift away from democracy and towards a "competitive authoritarian regime" by further changing laws regarding the composition and functioning of the Constitutional Court and the HSYK in order to tighten the executive grip over the high judiciary. This process towards a complete grip over the judiciary has been complemented by another referendum for constitutional change in 2017, which transformed Turkey from a parliamentarian regime into a semi-autocratic presidential one. As Yılmaz (2020) noted, the 2017 constitutional change consolidated the position of the executive and the president in an unprecedented manner. With this change, the president started to possess the authority to issue presidential decrees concerning matters pertaining to executive authority. This enabled the president to circumvent legislative processes, which are already subject to significant dependence and constraints. Additionally, the president can return laws to the parliament for reconsideration. Furthermore, as both the head of state and government, the president is responsible for appointing ministers, high-ranking state officials, selecting half of the Council of Judges and Prosecutors, appointing 12 out of the 15 members of the Constitutional Court of Turkey, determining the nation's annual budget, and holds the prerogative to dissolve the parliament (Yılmaz 2020, 276). These processes were also complemented by the "patronage" practices, through which the AKP filled the judicial posts with loyalists from the top to the ground (Soyaltın-Colella 2022, 454). The trend in the high judiciary was followed by evident patronage in the lower ranks of the judiciary in Turkey, especially since the failed coup in 2016. A lot of news was publicized after this process demonstrating the direct links between newly appointed judges and prosecutors and the AKP, which were appointed to fill the places in the judiciary left vacant by the purge of Gülenists.[22]

Yet, the populist inclination in the realm of the judiciary, and especially the tendency towards executive control in Turkey, has much deeper roots, that is perhaps dating back to the late Ottoman Empire and the early Republican Turkey. As Sofos notes in an important analysis of the roots of Turkish populism, the modern Turkish Republic was founded under the circumstances of an imperial demise and a national independence war against irredentism, which inflicted a profound sense of "ontological insecurity" (2022, 125) upon the psyche of Turkish elite. This led the early Republican political elites to see a kind of continuous "state of exception" around them, and hence, they embraced a kind of "state in motion" (Sofos 2022, 149) that is responding to these allegedly continuous crises and threats. A very similar point has been

116 Case studies

made by Parslow in his analysis regarding the use of "exceptional executive powers" in early republican Turkey (2016, 29). Parslow asserts that the AKP itself, especially after the failed 2016 coup, widely used exceptional executive powers to circumvent the regular legal order protecting individual rights and liberties. As Parslow noted, "emergency powers are no accidental, contingent feature of the Turkish legal tradition; they have been intrinsic to it since the very beginning of the republic" (2016, 52). Yılmaz, too, especially with respect to the post-2016 period, highlights the use of exceptional legal powers granted to the executive, or the "executive prerogative" for circumventing the regular legal order and driving the system towards a more autocratic direction. He calls this tendency as "strategic legalism": "The strategic legalism and accompanying multi-layered emergency have provided smooth paths for consolidating Erdoğan's presidential regime and containing any mobilization for democracy by combining subtle strategies of judicial repression, colonization of state institutions, proliferation of liminal judicial venues, and finally, introduction of twilight zones into the legal system" (Yılmaz 2020, 280). It is hard to miss the "tactical orientation" here that is avoiding abrupt ruptures and confrontations and the embrace of stealth, gradual moves that finally amounted to the subjugation of the "rule of law" to the "populist will". On the one hand, the populist government strived hard to protect the image of a kind of legal order. But on the other hand, in fact, by instrumentalizing legal institutions, they undermined the "rule of law".

But one should never miss the specific "majoritarian" tendency here. When it comes to populism, interpreting all of these developments as the cynical pursuit of personal power can be misleading. The change in the judiciary undermining its institutional autonomy should also be seen as the unfolding of the majoritarian inclinations of populism. In fact, the Turkish political system always had a very strong propensity to "majoritarianism" with its legal and political institutional components, as Lord (2012) notes in an important study.

Order, security, and penal policy: The politics of expediency

Like other right-wing populist actors, Erdoğan's AKP time to time strived to appeal to a conservative audience through claiming that how they were successful in the realm of order and security. Especially in its initial years, one of the major achievements of the party had been presented as its combat with "mafia". According to a statement made in 2009 by one of the founders of the AKP, Bülent Arınç, the party destroyed "mafia and gangs in Turkey".[23] More recently, Süleyman Soylu, a long-serving minister of interior in previous AKP governments and a populist in his own right, for example, urged police officers to break the legs of drug dealers wandering around schools.[24] It is important to note here that such approaches to deal with the problems of order and security align really well with the expectations and proclivities of ordinary citizens. With regards to drug dealers, for example, there were numerous news reports on how ordinary citizens beat up suspected drug dealers and turned them into police authorities.[25] There is also no evidence regarding how these attitudes of ordinary citizens were handled by the public authorities. But it seems that there is widespread impunity for such common, bottom-up reactions against suspected criminals.

Yet, apart from informal and extra-legal ways of dealing with problems of order and security, the AKP also empowered the police and, in a pretty populist fashion targeting responsiveness, the AKP rule enlarged room for manoeuvre for the police by granting them new "discretionary" powers. However, these changes also created opportunities for the police to exercise discretion that could potentially infringe upon fundamental rights and freedoms. Some new laws granted the police the authority to use force, including lethal force, when individuals failed to comply with police warnings. Additionally, the AKP era has been marked with efforts to expand the police's authority relative to the judiciary, particularly in matters related to wiretapping and accessing private information from communication companies (Kaygusuz 2018, 9).

Yet, all of these measures to strengthen police and respond to the popular expectations regarding order and security have been accompanied by a very tight political control over police. In an emblematic instance, for example, son of an AKP deputy who had a verbal quarrel with a police officer in a subprovince of Hatay could – through political influence – put the police officers in a very difficult and humiliating position and could also make the chief police officer at the sub-provincial police department removed temporarily from his post.[26] According to another publicized instance, a female police officer working in an AKP sub-provincial branch committed suicide and died after being scolded by the sub-provincial AKP chair in front of the sub-provincial chief police director.[27] Finally, a video recording of an AKP deputy insulting traffic police due to a regular police check on the road caused a sensation. In the leaked video, the AKP deputy insulted the police as "bastards" (şerefsizler).[28] Later on, the police officers who were insulted by the AKP deputy were dismissed from their posts due to recording the incident and the "infringement of the privacy".[29]

Despite AKP's pretensions that the party is being tough on crime, in the realm of order, security, and punishment too, however, the party engaged in a lot of "tactical" measures. While these measures helped the party to circumvent evident financial and organizational incapacities of the Turkish state, they also pleased parts of its constituency. In this respect, politics of amnesty during the AKP years is a major example in which tactical orientations of the populist government became visible. In fact, previous governments too implemented widespread *de facto* amnesties in order to deal with the problem

118 Case studies

of incapacity in the prisons. One of these amnesties was introduced in the 2000s, just before the rise of the AKP, and resulted in the release of around 30,000 prisoners.[30] But this amnesty received a lot of criticism afterwards because it created many problems, including dramatic crimes committed by people released with the *de facto* amnesty.[31] This is why the AKP has been very careful with regard to the term "amnesty". But the AKP government had similar problems with its predecessors in the 1990s with regards to prison overpopulation. Over the years, the number of prisoners in Turkish prisons exceeded well beyond their capacities. One of the measures to tackle this problem has been introducing a probation system: "the ruling party abused the probation system as form of amnesty and pardon to get votes and foster penal populism" (Akgül *et al.* 2019, 12). Also, Yıldırım and Kuyucu noted that, in order to refrain from a general amnesty, the AKP abused the probation system to a considerable extent (2017, 891). And especially during the pandemic, and by using health measures as an excuse, the AKP enlarged and extended the probation to such an extent that it almost amounted to a "general amnesty" without not terming it as such.[32] And these expansions and extensions were done just before a critical national and presidential election in 2023. So, the populist AKP aimed to kill two birds with a single stone through abusing "probation": Relieving the pressures on prisons and getting the support of released prisoners and their families. In this case, the short-term, tactical, pragmatic proclivity of populist practice that is appealing to a large population is crystal clear. Yet, it seems that such short-term solutions did not work and despite the decrease in prison population in 2020 to 266,000 from 291,000 in 2019,[33] it surged over 314,000 in 2022, according to the official figures.[34]

Populist practice in the realm of social policies: Between "universal redistribution" and "clientelistic practices"

Neoliberal proclivities of the AKP governments have always been balanced by some redistributive measures relieving the problem of poverty. When the AKP came to power, poverty was an urgent issue. GDP per capita in 2001 was only slightly over 3,000$ and the economic crises hit worst the most underprivileged segments of society, most notably the urban poor.[35] As an AKP deputy noted in 2004, the problem of poverty with serious consequences for order and security was evident for the AKP cadres (Yörük 2022, 140). Under these circumstances, the AKP introduced some important measures to solve these problems. The AKP raised social spending in its initial years (Bakırezer & Demirer 2009). As Buğra and Keyder (2006) note, the AKP also strived to reform the hierarchical and corporatist welfare regime in Turkey, which did not address the problems of large parts of populations working in the informal sector. The AKP also deployed networks of religious charities for dealing with poverty (Buğra & Keyder 2006, 224).

Even today, in the realm of social policies, the AKP tries to counter-balance its devotion to free market economics with considerable redistribution. According to the party manifesto for the critical 2023 elections: "As the AK Party, although we defend the market economy and free market, we have never embraced wild capitalism. The state is not the main actor of the economy, but the regulator and controller. It has been our basic policy to use the income from private sector-based economic activities to increase the welfare level of our people, and to take care of the poor and all disadvantaged segments".[36] When seen from a long-term perspective, it is clear that the social policy spending in Turkey has increased. According to official records, while in 2004, slightly over 79 billion Turkish Lira (13.8 percent of the GDP) was spent for education, health, and social protection, this figure raised to 550 billion Turkish Lira in 2018 (16 percent of the GDP).[37] More importantly, the amount spent for direct social aid increased remarkably throughout the AKP years. While it was 1.5 billion in 2004 (0.3 percent of the GDP), it increased to almost 30 billion Turkish Lira in 2018 (0.9 percent of the GDP).[38]

As Yörük notes, the AKP significantly expanded social assistance programs, both in terms of in-kind and cash transfers. These initiatives encompassed various aspects such as free healthcare for the impoverished, conditional cash transfers, support programs for orphans, food assistance, housing aid, educational support, and disability assistance for those in need. Over time, the number of beneficiaries and the allocation of government budgets to these programs witnessed substantial growth. For instance, the enrolment in the green card (*yeşil kart*) program, which provided free healthcare to the economically disadvantaged, surged from 4.2 percent to 12.7 percent of the population between 2003 and 2009. In 2012, a universal healthcare system was introduced, encompassing the green card holders as well. In 2004, the AKP proposed changes to the Metropolitan Municipalities Law to enhance the social assistance capabilities of municipalities (Yörük 2022, 139). The central government spending for the social aid in Turkey is complemented by social aid (food and some single time cash transfer) by AKP municipalities across Turkey (Urhan 2018). As Yörük asserts, the populist logic to increase social spending and especially the direct social assistance for the AKP is evident: "From the onset, the AKP relied on poor voters and this reliance has grown ever further over the years" (2022, 139).

It should be noted here, however, that the AKP has not only relied on the state but, in a pretty populist and pragmatic manner, it also deployed the resources generated by "civil society", relatives, and neighbours of people in need. Thus, the AKP, to a certain extent, drifted away from a rights-based social assistance practice (Karagöz 2020, 157–158). The AKP also engaged

120 Case studies

in some populist innovations, for example, in the realm of care for elders, by providing the relatives of old people with cash assistance. Instead of focusing on bolstering the availability of professional social care services from either the public or private sectors, this program places its emphasis on directly supporting these family caregivers (Yılmaz 2018, 111). In fact, the AKP "equated all social policies to family policies in a special way and started to implement comprehensive social transfer policies so as to establish a strong connection between poor/highly indebted families and the party" (Yılmaz 2015, 384). As Göçmen (2014) notes, in recent years, religiously motivated associations (RMAs) have become part and parcel of social assistance practices as a whole too. A major problem, particularly with the distribution of benefits through RMAs, is that they are being subject to tight party control, which "created a feeling of gratitude, indebtedness, and dependency among the recipients" towards the AKP (Özdemir 2020, 14–15).

Thus, one of the main characteristics of the social policies throughout the AKP period has been the blurring of the boundary between programmatic "universal distribution" and "clientelistic" practices. It seems that even the recipients of official social assistance in Turkey feel the pressure to vote for the AKP (Kutlu 2015, 385–395). As Özdemir notes:

> The AKP's neoliberal policies increased unemployment, curbed employee rights and labour organizations, and decreased some aspects of state's social responsibilities. Yet the AKP utilizes poverty alleviation programmes and social protection measures to relieve the hopeless, insecure, unorganized, poor and deprived masses and create dependency and submission. In fact, social policy has become a direct tool of AKP's party patronage, helping AKP expand its political reach and power. AKP's social policy largely benefited the informal and unorganized working classes, while decreasing the benefits of the rest; and although some policies are programmatic and universal, others are particularistic and clientelistic. With social policies AKP successfully conceals its neoliberal and anti-labour agenda. Also, these social policies sustain poverty and deprivation by politically pacifying the poor working classes against the neoliberal policies and authoritarianism.
>
> *(2020, 16–17)*

The realm of health care should be briefly considered in this regard, too, since the improvements in this sphere contributed a lot to the positive perception of the AKP governments and the support it received in elections (Yılmaz 2017, 155–159). In the pre-AKP periods, public health services were characterized by poor quality and unresponsiveness. Long queues, poor infrastructure, miserable material conditions, and extremely busy doctors were part and parcel of public hospitals. Thus, there were serious problems for poor and ordinary citizens to access reasonably good health services. During the AKP years, as a response to these problems, health care expenditures of the public increased considerably (Yılmaz 2017, 91). The health care reform had been one of the priorities of the early AKP years. The populist logic here was evident, as testified by the comments conveyed from the field by Yılmaz:

> A medical doctor who had worked in a public hospital and was a member of the Association for Human Health and Education explained an anecdote about how the poor felt empowered in the hospital setting after the AK Party's healthcare reform: "The lower class feels more integrated into the system ... They did this in health. For instance, we tell people in emergency services that if there are urgent cases, people without bona fide emergency health conditions will be denied services. This is something normal .... But their response to us was, 'we are now in the government, you have to examine us, you can't deny services to us'".
>
> *(2017, 162–163)*

One of the consequences of such extensive accessibility, however, has been the weakening positions of health professionals in public hospitals *vis-a-vis* ordinary citizens. In recent years, violence towards health professionals, and most notably towards doctors, surged dramatically.[39] Some of these instances of violence, unfortunately, resulted in the death of health professionals in several instances.[40] Another problem with the enhanced access to health services for all citizens, and especially to specialist physicians, ironically, has been the lack of dates of appointment to visit doctors within a plausible waiting time (like a few weeks) and dates given to patients for several months in the future.[41] Thus, short-term benefits of easy access for broad segments of citizens to specialists ironically created problems of access and proved to be unsustainable in the long run.

But populism as a governmental practice that is deeply bounded to popular and electoral legitimacy has always been prone to short-term solutions. One of the best examples of this occurred in Turkey, again in the realm of social policy and, more precisely, in the realm of social security system, just before the critical 2023 elections. In the 1980s and 1990s, as a result of populist policies of the era, many Turkish citizens started to retire after 20 years of active employment. Towards the end of the 1990s, this started to create an unsustainable burden on the Turkish social security system. In 1999, the government introduced a new regulation that imposed a certain age limit for retirement – regardless of the number of days the employees worked or the amount of payments for the pensions – in order to lighten the burden on state budget. This drastic change deprived many people of receiving pensions at a very early age.[42] Throughout the last couple of decades, those deprived of pensions due to this drastic change got organized and turned into a kind of

122 Case studies

pretty powerful "pressure group".[43] The problem with the 1999 regulation and those adversely effected by this has repeatedly become a subject of public political discussions throughout the AKP rule. Erdoğan's previous approach to these demands had been, in fact, pretty, prudent.[44] But the wake of critical 2023 elections and the adverse economic conditions surrounding it due to inflation and the fall of the value of Turkish Lira made the AKP reconsider its position on the "early retirement problem". Just a month before the May 2023 elections, on March 1, 2023, the AKP introduced legislation to solve the problems of those who were adversely affected by the 1999 regulation.[45] This "solution" resulted in 2.5 million people that suddenly became eligible for retirement and started to receive pensions. No doubt that this will have some negative consequences on the public budget, inflation, and broader economic indicators as well as the sustainability of the entire social security system in the long run.[46]

From a general perspective with regard to social policies of the AKP, however, it is really difficult to disagree with Yörük's statement: "the party increased the level of pro-poor social assistance programs and used an anti-elite populist discourse. The AKP expanded social assistance programs as the most important platform for providing social inclusion for the vast informal and rural sectors that never had access to welfare benefits enjoyed by workers in the formal sector and by the middle class up until then" (2022, 152). Nevertheless, the extent of social assistance in Turkey has also been reproducing poverty. As experts of the field note, social policies of the AKP are far from grasping the entire experience of poor people and empowering them for other problems related to poverty (Yıldırım & Şahin 2019, 2542–2543). As Buğra demonstrates, the recent direction of social policy in Turkey has not been primarily driven by concerns about class inequality, as seen in certain influential European social policy discussions and labour market regulations found in advanced capitalist nations. Instead, the changes in social policy have not led to increased equality in class relations; in fact, they have often moved in the opposite direction (2018, 10–11). Hence, populism became a very practical phenomenon in Turkey in the realm of social policies, too, with its short-term virtues and long-term ills.

Populism and the education, especially the higher education: Rapid expansion and its ills

Education has been one of the important realms for the AKP to respond to the demands of its low-income constituencies. While Turkey witnessed the expansion of private education institutions throughout the AKP years, the AKP also invested considerably in public education. The party introduced a few specific measures in the realm of education that were highly appealing for its largely low-income constituencies. For example, beginning with the 2003–2004 academic year, the party started to distribute textbooks to primary, secondary, and high school students for free.[47] The party also abolished the fees for public universities in 2012.[48] All of these measures have been received very well by the supporters of the AKP, especially by poor families. But, like every populist policy implementation, all of these measures had their own consequences. For example, distribution of free textbooks, according to some observers, caused waste and environmental damage since the quality of some of the books distributed by the state was so low that some schools did not use them and handed in them to recycle factories.[49] And the abolishment of fees for public universities also made some harm to faculties of medicine by depriving of them from an important financial resource.[50]

During the AKP era, one of the most significant developments in Turkey in the realm of education has been the rapid growth in the number of universities and students in higher education. A study on the key indicators of the higher education sector in Turkey reveals that in 2001, there were only 76 universities in the country. However, by 2011, this number had risen to 165 (Günay & Günay 2011, 7). Similarly, in 2001, the total number of higher education students, including those pursuing associate degrees and distance learning, was approximately 1.5 million. Remarkably, within a decade, this figure nearly tripled, reaching almost 4 million in 2011 (Günay & Günay 2011, 13). As of 2023, these figures continue to increase steadily. According to statistics provided by the Higher Education Institution (*Yüksek Öğretim Kurumu* – YÖK) of Turkey, there are currently 209 universities in the country, with nearly 7 million students enrolled in higher education institutions.[51]

Undoubtedly, there are valid reasons for scepticism when it comes to the quality of these institutions.[52] Many of these universities were established in economically disadvantaged regions of Turkey, where limited economic and cultural opportunities exist. Consequently, these universities face challenges in terms of providing an academic environment that is conducive towards innovative and productive research. Moreover, human resources in these newly established universities generally lack the qualifications and expertise necessary to compete on par with Western academic standards. Additionally, these institutions are susceptible to favouritism and patronage, further compromising their already subpar quality. The rapid growth of these universities has also resulted in significant infrastructure issues, including inadequate libraries, inexperienced administrative units, insufficient research and teaching facilities, and logistical problems such as cleanliness, lack of space, and accommodation for faculty and students. Furthermore, these universities often lack autonomy due to political control and fail to foster an environment conducive to independent and free academic thought, as they tend to be highly bureaucratic in nature.

Nevertheless, these universities have a significant and multifaceted influence on Turkish youth and society. Despite their challenges, the establishment

124 Case studies

of universities in every province of Turkey is driving economic and cultural transformation in these socially conservative cities. For instance, the presence of a new university with 20,000 students in a town of 80,000 residents has a profound transformative effect. Gradually, these cities become economically reliant on these universities. Furthermore, despite the issues faced by these institutions, the expansion of the higher education sector, as evidenced by the increase in the number of university students, has also had a democratizing impact. The lower and lower-middle classes in Turkey have gained unprecedented opportunities for higher education through the growth of these new institutions. However, it should be noted that, in the short-term, due to the ongoing challenges of the Turkish economy, this does not necessarily translate into immediate upwards social mobility opportunities.

As an initial observation, it is notable that some of these universities exhibit a greater diversity in terms of ethnic and social class backgrounds, religious orientations, and political views of their administrative and academic staff, as compared to more established higher education institutions in major metropoles in Turkey. In these new universities, one is more likely to encounter individuals of Turkish or Kurdish descent from lower-class origins and from conservative provincial families. Whereas, it is highly unlikely to find such a social diversity in prestigious established higher education institutions in Turkey that have been operating for decades. Typically, these established institutions are staffed by individuals from more affluent, secular middle and upper-middle-class families with roots in major urban centres in Turkey. However, the rapid expansion of these universities has also attracted individuals with more secular orientations who were unable to find opportunities in İstanbul and Ankara and were compelled to seek opportunities in these peripheral institutions. The trade-offs, however, inherent to populist governmental practice between quantity and quality, short-term gains, and long-term sustainability are evident in the case of rapid expansion in higher education in Turkey.

Populist foreign policy: The bravado and metis in the realm of diplomacy

The relationship between populism and Turkish foreign policy has been subject of scholarly examination in recent years since the case of Erdoğan's AKP is globally one of the major examples of "populism in power" today. Many researchers analysed the impact of populism on Turkish foreign policy throughout the AKP years. Most of these studies, however, embrace the mainstream ideational approach to populism and they mostly focus on the foreign policy discourse (Balta 2018; Özpek & Tanrıverdi-Yaşar 2018; Kaliber & Kaliber 2019; Bulut & Hacıoğlu 2021; İşeri & Ersoy 2021; Destradi *et al.* 2022). These works either emphasize the stress upon the distinction between conspiring international elites and the pure people in the foreign policy-related discourse generated by populists as the hallmark of a populist foreign policy or they point out the anti-Westernism as an important consequence of populism in the realm of foreign policy. This is mainly a consequence of understanding populism as an "ideational phenomenon" (Mudde 2004; Hawkins *et al.* 2018). Nevertheless, even in these studies embracing a mainstream ideational approach to populism, there are clear signs that populism is not really exclusively an ideational phenomenon. It is, in fact, deeply related to a certain kind of political practice defined by pragmatism, personalism, anti-institutionalism, and a taste and orientation that is sensitive to popular common sense and sentiment.

In a concise and informative article, Balta (2018) demonstrates the overall transformation of Turkish foreign policy throughout the AKP years. What Balta emphasizes regarding the Turkish foreign policy under a populist incumbent is its "dramatic shifts and abrupt reorientations", the blurring of the boundaries between domestic and foreign policy, and more precisely, the use of foreign policy to mitigate domestic crises, and the increasing predominance of Erdoğan in the foreign policy realm (Balta 2018, 15–18). Very similarly, Kaliber and Kaliber (2019) highlight the fact that the AKP has deployed foreign policy in order to consolidate its position in power in domestic politics. They also draw attention to the increasing emphasis on anti-Westernism in the foreign policy discourse and the rising prominence of Erdoğan in foreign policy-related issues, and particularly his personal connections with world leaders – especially with those revealing populist attitudes such as Trump (Kaliber & Kaliber 2019, 9). Özpek and Tanrıverdi-Yaşar (2018) too emphasize the pragmatism of the AKP in the foreign policy realm and draw attention to how the party deployed foreign policy discourse to consolidate its power in domestic politics. Destradi *et al.* (2022), too, with reference to Turkish foreign policy, highlight that populists politicize the foreign policy for domestic mobilization to hold on power. İşeri and Ersoy (2021), too, in a very similar vein, argue that the AKP mitigates domestic political failures with a highly populist discourse on foreign affairs. Here, a particularly nuanced analysis belongs to Taş (2022) in which, alongside populisms' impact on foreign policy discourse and content, the author puts a special emphasis on the "procedural" dimensions of a "populist foreign policy". In line with Destradi and Plagemann's (2019) contention, Taş emphasizes that "populism impacts the style and processes rather than the substance of the foreign policy" (2022, 19). According to Taş, "personalization of decision-making along with the centralization of power in the hands of the populist leader", "gradual sidelining of established diplomatic and bureaucratic institutions", "privileging *ad hoc* processes, bilateral one-on-ones, and the direct communication of foreign policy issues on social media while circumventing

126 Case studies

established processes of diplomatic declaration, consensus-seeking, and compromise-building" have become part and parcel of populist foreign policy conduct in Turkey (2022, 6–7).

The taste and expectations of ordinary majorities deeply shape the substance as well as the procedural forms of foreign policy under populist governments, as the following examples demonstrate too. In a foreign policy-related incident in 2016, for example, Erdoğan threatened the EU representatives by "opening the borders" and "sending refugees to Europe". According to the leaked meeting records between Erdoğan and the EU representatives regarding the financial support by the EU to Turkey for containing the refugee flow, Erdoğan threatened the EU representatives in a very direct manner: "We can open the doors to Greece and Bulgaria anytime and we can put the refugees on busses. If you say 3 bn for two years [instead of 3 bn per year], no need to discuss further".[53] While, from a diplomatic point of view, this was an excessively frank way of expressing demands, such a tone in international relations was exactly deeply appealing for the domestic populist audience. As the AKP spokesperson later on commented on a question regarding these leaked meeting records, for the populist audience, "these are words that makes us [them] only feel proud".[54]

In another foreign policy-related incident, Turkish Police detained an American evangelical priest on the accusation of political and military espionage. Later on, the issue turned into a diplomatic crisis between the United States and Turkey. In a meeting with Erdoğan in Washington, Trump requested the release of priest Brunson from Erdoğan. Hastily, Brunson's situation turned into a blackmail opportunity for Erdoğan in order to receive Fethullah Gülen from the United States, the leader of Gülen Community – which involved in a failed coup d'etat after a long process of state colonization in Turkey in a partnership with the AKP. In a public speech in Turkey Erdoğan revealed his take of the issue very clearly, in obvious populist style: "They [the US] say that 'give us the priest'. You [the US] have another priest [Fethullah Gülen]. You give him back to us and we do whatever necessary in the judicial process to give him [Brunson] back to you". While initially, this blackmail diplomacy worked in favour of Erdoğan and resonated very well with his constituency's expectations, it later on turned into a diplomatic failure on the part of the AKP after a wave of serious sanctions by the United States. The priest was ultimately released and turned back to the United States and Turkey received nothing back from the United States in return.[55]

In some cases, populist practice in the foreign policy realm is not that transactional and may well be the reflection of the spontaneous reaction of the populist leader. This was the case when Erdoğan harshly criticized the then president of Israel, Şimon Perez, by accusing Israel of "killing children" in a public panel in the 2009 Davos Economic Forum. When he was not allowed to continue by the moderator of the panel, he protested and left the

Populism in the AKP years in Turkey **127**

panel in the middle of it.[56] While this attitude was criticized by old school diplomats in Turkey from a conventional international relations view,[57] it was, nevertheless, received very well by Erdoğan's audience (Erdoğan 2013). Thousands of Erdoğan's supporters waited for him in the Atatürk Airport for his arrival and he gave them a short speech in the middle of night: "Tonight, with your silent and graceful stance here, you say that 'we do not want politicians who say different things behind closed doors, in the media or at meeting spaces. ...We want politicians who frankly say everywhere the same true things that they believe in'".[58]

Turkish foreign policy throughout the AKP era, therefore, was not only defined by a ruthless pragmatism amounting to blackmail or "hostage" (Taş 2022) diplomacy but also by spontaneous reactions of Erdoğan. But perhaps, more important than these, and in line with theoretical evaluations regarding the relationship between populism and foreign policy, one of the major implications of populist foreign policy in Turkey has been the "personalization" of this deeply technocratic and procedural realm of policy. Erdoğan has come to the forefront of all the major foreign policy issues throughout the AKP rule. His direct relations with presidents of major world powers such as Russia and the United States have increasingly defined Turkish foreign policy. According to a news report relying on information leaked from high-ranked American bureaucrats, Trump had the greatest number of calls with Erdoğan during his tenure.[59]

What we see in these incidents is not simply the reflection or implication of populist "ideas" or "worldviews" in concrete policy issues. In fact, these incidents are illustrative examples of populist governmentality that is combining informality, immediacy, responsiveness, and effectiveness while circumventing procedures and principles. In the foreign policy realm, these orientations, in fact, turn into a kind of "street smart foreign policy", a kind of *"metis"* (Scott 1999) which is extremely pragmatic, flexible, short-term, personalized, and spontaneous – and that is profoundly lacking a longer time horizon.

Concluding remarks

This chapter has focused on contemporary Turkish populism. With the rise of Erdoğan's AKP, students of Turkish politics started to engage with the concept of populism through more rigorous methodological and conceptual tools. From a variety of different perspectives, AKP's politics has been defined as populist by different scholars embracing ideational, discourse-theoretical, political-strategic as well as performative/socio-cultural approaches. Thus, throughout the years, a broad consensus has emerged in the scholarly literature on the populism of Erdoğan's AKP. Yet, all of these approaches to contemporary Turkish politics have focused on the domain of electoral and party politics. In fact, contemporary populism in Turkey, under the rule of

128 Case studies

Erdoğan's AKP, has always extended beyond the realm of electoral party politics. It has had implications for various realms of public administration and policy. The party's populism has become a governmental practice in realms as different as economy, bureaucratic administration and recruitment, order and security, social policy, education, and foreign policy. Only the work on the economic realm and studies inspired by the notion of neoliberal populism, to a certain extent, tried to grasp the material impact of populism on the day-to-day struggles of ordinary citizens in Turkey. But these studies had the major shortcoming of focusing only on a single realm, the economy. In fact, as demonstrated in the relevant parts of this chapter, populism has remarkably diffuse and widespread penetration into very different realms of policy when the concept is defined as a responsive governmental practice relying on short-term considerations and formal and informal short-cuts in order to respond immediately to material and symbolic demands of supportive majorities. In turn, populism depends on the complicity of the masses who take advantage of short-term material and/or symbolic benefits provided by populist governmental practice.

As the relevant parts of this chapter demonstrated, it is possible to see the impact of populism in very different realms of administration and policy. First of all, we see its impact in the realm of economy and how the AKP has always opted for policies that are easy to implement and more beneficial for their upper as well as lower class constituencies. This led the Turkish economy to an overdependence on the construction sector – as well as cheap foreign capital/credit – for growth which benefitted poor as well as rising pro-AKP business sectors in Turkey only in the short term. But the consequence of reliance on growth in unproductive sectors resulted in, especially in recent years, souring inflation and falling living standards for the majority of Turkish people, especially the middle classes. All these measures in the economy have also been complemented by widespread favouritism benefitting pro-AKP business sectors as well as pro-AKP poor. A very similar dynamic can be seen in the realm of bureaucratic formation and recruitment. While the AKP strived to render the public administration more responsive by establishing new "populist" institutions such as Ombudsmanship and CİMER (the Presidential Communication Center), it also expanded and politicized the bureaucracy to such an extent that appointed governors (*valiler* and *kaymakamlar*) in the Turkish administrative system – who has always been seen as the symbol of state neutrality in Turkey – have started to be seen as AKP supporters.[60] In the judicial realm, the AKP also established a tight grip over high as well as lower courts through majoritarian constitutional and legislative change and concentrated the powers in the hands of the executive and, more precisely, in the hands of Erdoğan. Even at the lower courts, populism amounted to "court packing" by the appointment of many former provincial members and executives of the AKP as judges and prosecutors. In the realm of order and security too, populist governmental practice has been key. While the AKP, in a clearly populist fashion in performative terms, claimed to be tough on crime (in contrast to the previous era in the 1990s, which became notorious after a *de facto* amnesty causing widespread problems), in fact, the financial and organizational incapacity of the Turkish criminal justice system led the party subtly abuse "probation" to evacuate the prisons and lighten the prison over-population. But, again, such short-cuts did not work as expected and the prison population soured again in Turkey. In the realm of social policies too, the AKP tried hard to improve the conditions of poor in Turkey since it came to power even though the party embraced neoliberal economic principles to a great extent. The social spending, and especially remarkably the social as-sistance spending, increased considerably throughout the AKP governments. But here again, these measures to improve the lives of underprivileged inter-mingled with informal clientelistic practices. More importantly, the AKP's approach to social assistance reproduced poverty in Turkey since it did not empower the poor in a way that can render them break the cycle of poverty. In the realm of education, too, the populist practice rendered the life easier for the poor and underprivileged in the short term through measures such as free textbooks and the abolition of fees for public universities. More impor-tantly, higher education in the AKP period expanded spectacularly, and this created unprecedented opportunities for the inclusion of the poor. But in all of these measures, responsive practices also entailed problems of quality and sustainability. In the realm of foreign policy, the AKP also appealed to the majoritarian sensitivities in symbolic terms and, time and again, disregarded diplomatic calculus. During the AKP years, Turkish foreign policy got per-sonalized. and the boundaries between domestic and foreign policies disap-peared to a great extent.

In short, in many different realms – and not only directly in the realm of electoral politics – what we see in Turkey in the domain of public administra-tion and public policy has been a "populist governmental practice" appealing to the immediate symbolic and material expectations of the economically and culturally underprivileged segments of the population. Populist governmen-tal practice, as I have demonstrated through a multi-domain analysis of pub-lic administration and policy in Turkey, is defined by responsiveness and, to a certain extent, informality in order to circumvent procedures to immediately respond to the needs of supportive majorities. Especially in cases where the populist practice has gone "informal", it has also generated the complicity of the "populist audience". But, in the long run, it is evident that the populist governmental practice creates problems, possibilities of which are usually "swept under the rug" in the initial stages of policy implementation as a re-sult of the complicity between ruling populist elites and their mass clienteles: The former receives the votes and secures mobilization capacities, and the latter receives the means of psychological and material survival in the short

130 Case studies

run from the populist exchange. In the following parts, I turn to other cases of "populist governmental practice" where we can see the functioning of populism in policy realms as different as the economy in Venezuela, bureaucracy in Greece, the judiciary in India, order and security in the Philippines, economic, social and educational policies in Egypt, and the foreign policy in the United States.

Notes

1 https://data.worldbank.org/indicator/NY.GDP.PCAP.CD?end=2021&locations=TR&start=2001, accessed: 27.6.2023.
2 See the party manifesto for the 2023 elections: https://www.akparti.org.tr/parti/2023-siyasal-vizyon/toplum/, accessed: 27.6.2023.
3 For the change of sectoral distribution of employment in Turkey from 2005 to 2021, see: https://cevreselgostergeler.csb.gov.tr/istihdamin-sektorel-dagilimi-i-85697, accessed: 27.6.2023. The data reveals that no significant change has occurred. Industrial sector remained the same, service sector slightly expanded at the cost of agriculture. Construction sector expanded too.
4 See the party pledge for the 2023 election on the party website: https://www.akparti.org.tr/parti/hedef-2023/diger/gereksiz-burokrasi-ortadan-kalkacak/, accessed: 28.6.2023.
5 For Erdoğan's comments in 2003 see: https://www.hurriyet.com.tr/ekonomi/erdogan-burokratik-oligarsi-bizi-parmaginda-oynatiyor-38471519, accessed: 28.6.2023. For another comment by Erdoğan in 2009 claiming that "the bureaucratic oligarchy impedes concrete achievements such as infrastructural investments", see: https://www.ntv.com.tr/turkiye/erdogan-burokratik-oligarsi-en-buyuk-engel,6gl7qYSfjky5aYBQ6nGfjQ, accessed: 28.6.2023.
6 For the meeting held in 2015 and Erdoğan's speech, see: https://www.tccb.gov.tr/haberler/410/37391/burokratik-oligarsi-ulkelerin-felaketidir.html, accessed: 28.6.2023.
7 See the law on Ombudsmanship: https://www.mevzuat.gov.tr/mevzuatmetin/1.5.6328.pdf, accessed: 28.6.2023.
8 See the e-application page of the Ombudsmanship website: https://ebasvuru.ombudsman.gov.tr/, accessed: 28.6.2023.
9 See the circular on BİMER: https://www.resmigazete.gov.tr/eskiler/2006/01/20060120-5.htm, accessed: 28.6.2023.
10 Ibid.
11 Ibid.
12 Ibid. Italics are mine.
13 See the online application page of CİMER: https://www.cimer.gov.tr/, accessed: 28.6.2023.
14 See the news report of *Sözcü* with a picture of the order from the relevant sub-provincial national education directorate (*ilçe milli eğitim müdürlüğü*) asking an inquiry by the school administration: https://www.sozcu.com.tr/2020/gundem/mersinde-ogretmenlere-mini-etek-incelemesi-6083499/, accessed: 28.6.2023.
15 https://www.cumhuriyet.com.tr/haber/izmirde-akpli-olan-bazi-saglik-calisanlari-ekiplere-girmemek-icin-siyasi-ariyor-1792036, accessed: 28.6.2023.
16 https://www.youtube.com/watch?v=fpOSD8Q_bIE&t=84s&ab_channel=196Sekiz, accessed: 28.6.2023.
17 For a series of news regarding the support lend to AKP election campaigns by governors, see: https://www.sozcu.com.tr/2023/gundem/son-dakika-burokrasi-

tarihine-gececek-manzaralar-valiler-akplilerle-kol-kola-7664881/; https://www.
sozcu.com.tr/2023/gundem/son-dakika-burokrasi-tarihine-gececek-manzaralar-
valiler-akplilerle-kol-kola-7664881/; https://www.birgun.net/haber/mugla-valiligi-
nden-secim-oncesi-akp-propagandasi-klip-paylasildi-417674; accessed: 28.6.
2023. For the removal of a provincial governor from his post after a conflict
with an AKP provincial chair, see: https://www.toplumsal.com.tr/akpli-baskanla-
tartisan-vali-gorevden-alindi, accessed: 28.6.2023. For the news regarding a sub-
provincial governor urging neighbourhood headmen to make the residents of their
neighbourhoods vote for the AKP, see: https://alevinet12.com/guncel-haberler/
kaymakam-muhtari-tehdit-etti-akpye-oy-cikacak/, accessed: 28.6.2023. For a
news report claiming that a provincial governor, a sub-provincial governor and
a sub-provincial police director involved in the AKP campaigns, see: https://arti-
gercek.com/guncel/kaymakam-savci-ve-emniyet-amiri-akp-ye-oy-istiyor-89062h,
accessed: 28.6.2023.

18 For a news regarding the appointment of the wife of an AKP member to the
directorship of a sub-provincial national education directorate, see: https://
artigercek.com/guncel/kaymakam-savci-ve-emniyet-amiri-akp-ye-oy-istiyor-
89062h, accessed: 28.6.2023. For a news report regarding the appointment of
the husband of an AKP deputy to the directorship of a provincial tourism and
culture directorate, see https://www.sozcu.com.tr/2022/gundem/akp-milletvekili-
adayi-turizm-il-muduru-olarak-atandi-7237434/, accessed: 28.6.2023. For the
appointment of the brother (who is also an imam by profession) of an AKP
sub-provincial chair to the directorship of the sub-provincial social service directorate, see: https://t24.com.tr/haber/akp-milletvekili-cemal-tasar-in-kardesi-dev-
let-malzeme-ofisi-genel-mudur-yardimciligina-atandi,1065028, accessed: 28.6.
2023. For the appointment of the "driver" of the minister for national education as a "director" of secretary of the Ministry of National Education (*Milli
Eğitim Bakanlığı*) see: https://www.milligazete.com.tr/haber/10364246/akpde-
bir-atama-skandali-daha-sofor-bakanlikta-mudur-oldu, accessed: 28.6.2023. For
the appointment of the brother of an AKP deputy to vice-directorship of the
State Supply Office (*Devlet Malzeme Ofisi*) see: https://t24.com.tr/haber/akp-
milletvekili-cemal-tasar-in-kardesi-devlet-malzeme-ofisi-genel-mudur-yardimcili-
gina-atandi,1065028; accessed: 28.6.2023. In this respect examples publicized in
local and national media are endless.

19 See the records of Strategy and Budget Unit of the Presidency: https://www.sbb.
gov.tr/kamu-istihdami/, accessed: 28.6.2023.

20 The Gülen Community was a powerful religious community in Turkey based on an
immense patronage network. It colonized the state institutions in Turkey through
its highly educated members with highly dubious and unaccountable ways. In the
AKP's initial years, there was an alliance between the Gülen Community and the
AKP *vis-à-vis* Kemalist elites embedded in critical state institutions. After Kemal-
ists in the state institutions lost their power and influence, the Gülen Community
and the AKP turned against each other. The community's involvement in the failed
2016 coup sealed its faith and members of the community were, to a great extent,
purged from the state institutions.

21 In 2016, Hakyemez was appointed to the Constitutional Court by Erdoğan.
See the news report: https://www.haberturk.com/gundem/haber/1287635-
recai-akyel-ve-yusuf-sevki-hakyemez-anayasa-mahkemesine-uye-olarak-atandi,
accessed: 29.6.2023.

22 For a news report listing 90 judges and prosecutors appointed in 2019 with
clear official links with the AKP, see: https://www.cumhuriyet.com.tr/haber/
hakim-ve-savci-olarak-atanan-akplilerin-listesi-ortaya-cikti-1254227,
accessed: 29.6.2023. Some examples of such affiliations are as follows: Former

132 Case studies

AKP Zonguldak provincial youth branch chair appointed as the Mersin prosecutor. Former AKP Rize provincial administration board member appointed as a judge to the Mersin court. Former AKP Trabzon provincial vice-chair appointed as a judge to Kayseri court.

23 https://www.ntv.com.tr/turkiye/arinc-ergenekonu-tepeledik, qPnLZknkeUKvVr1DgYZOfQ, accessed: 29.6.2023.

24 https://www.cumhuriyet.com.tr/haber/bakan-soyludan-polislere-bacaklarini-kirin-talimati-gerekirse-20-yil-yatariz-897764, accessed: 29.6.2023.

25 See https://www.ensonhaber.com/3-sayfa/sislide-mahalleliden-torbacilara-dayak-suclarini-itiraf-ettiler; https://www.ittifakgazetesi.com/bursada-uyusturucu-saticisina-meydan-dayagi-kamerada; https://www.odatv4.com/guncel/kizina-uyusturucu-satan-kisiyi-doverek-polise-goturdu-246467; accessed: 29.6.2023.

26 https://www.posta.com.tr/gundem/vekil-oglu-polisi-tek-siraya-dizdi-132118, accessed: 29.6.2023.

27 https://www.sozcu.com.tr/2021/gundem/akp-ilce-baskaninin-hakaretlerine-dayanamayan-polis-memuru-intihar-etti-6681843/, accessed: 29.6.2023.

28 https://www.sozcu.com.tr/2021/gundem/polise-hakaret-eden-akpli-vekilden-pes-dedirten-aciklama-6608606/?utm_source=ilgili_haber&utm_medium=free&utm_campaign=ilgilihaber, accessed: 29.6.2023.

29 https://t24.com.tr/haber/akp-li-yilmaz-in-aracini-durdugu-icin-ekibe-tukururum-serefsiz-diyerek-hakaret-ettigi-polis-ihrac-edildi,1115804, accessed: 29.6.2023.

30 https://www.haberturk.com/rahsan-affi-nedir-rahsan-affi-ne-zaman-cikarildi-kimleri-kapsadi-2559953, accessed: 29.6.2023.

31 https://www.yeniakit.com.tr/haber/rahsan-affinin-millete-bedeli-agir-oldu-cezaevinden-cikan-mahkumlarin-buyuk-cogunlugu-tekrar-suc-isledi-522032.html, accessed: 29.6.2023.

32 https://www.trthaber.com/haber/gundem/koronavirus-3-yargi-paketi-calismalari-ini-hizlandirdi-469769.html accessed: 29.6.2023.

33 https://bianet.org/1/19/268468-sayilar-katlaniyor-cezaevi-personel-hukumlu-ve-tutuklu-kisi-sayisi-artiyor, accessed: 29.6.2023.

34 https://cte.adalet.gov.tr/Resimler/Dokuman/istatistik/istatistik-1.pdf, accessed: 29.6.2023.

35 https://data.worldbank.org/country/turkiye?view=chart, accessed: 30.6.2023.

36 https://www.akparti.org.tr/parti/2023-siyasal-vizyon/toplum/, accessed: 30.6.2023.

37 https://sbb.gov.tr/wp-content/uploads/2018/10/Kamu-Kesimi-Sosyal-Harcama-%c4%b0statistikleri.pdf, accessed: 30.6.2023.

38 Ibid.

39 http://www.sagliksen.org.tr/haber/12308/saglik-sen-2022-yili-saglikta-siddet-raporu, accessed: 30.6.2023.

40 For a couple of news reports regarding doctors murdered by relatives of patients, see https://t24.com.tr/haber/hasta-yakini-doktoru-bicaklayarak-oldurdu,201881; https://www.ntv.com.tr/galeri/turkiye/hastanede-oldurulen-doktor-ekrem-kara-kayaya-veda,7pUQfVLE50eLZa5zlf-Gag; accessed: 30.6.2023.

41 https://sputniknews.com.tr/20220216/ttb-baskani-fincanci-anlatti-mhrsde-neden-randevu-bulunamiyor-1053893565.html, accessed: 30.6.2023.

42 https://www.bbc.com/turkce/haberler-turkiye-62612364, accessed: 30.6.2023.

43 For the federation of associations for those effected by 1999 regulation see: https://www.eyt.org.tr/, accessed: 30.6.2023.

44 https://www.bbc.com/turkce/haberler-turkiye-62612364, accessed: 30.6.2023.

45 https://www.sgk.gov.tr/Haber/Detay/Emeklilikte-Yasa-Takilanlar-ile-Ilgili-Duzenlemeyi-Iceren-Kanun-Teklifi-TBMM-Genel-Kurulunda-Kabul-Edilerek-Yasalasti-2023-03-01-01-42-59, accessed: 30.6.2023.

Populism in the AKP years in Turkey **133**

46 https://tr.euronews.com/2022/12/29/yeni-eyt-duzenlemesi-ekonomiyi-nasil-et-kileyecek, accessed: 30.9.2023.
47 http://dhgm.meb.gov.tr/yayimlar/dergiler/milli_egitim_dergisi/165/bayrakci.htm, accessed: 1.7.2023.
48 https://www.trthaber.com/haber/gundem/universite-harclari-kalkti-53495.html, accessed: 1.7.2023.
49 https://www.gazeteduvar.com.tr/tonlarca-ucretsiz-ders-kitabi-hic-kulla-nilmadan-cop-oluyor-haber-1586879#:~:text=DUVAR%20%2D%20 2003%2D2004%20e%C4%9Fitim%20%C3%B6%C4%9Fretim,milyon%20 ders%20kitab%C4%B1%20da%C4%9F%C4%B1t%C4%B1m%C4%B1%20 yap%C4%B1ld%C4%B1, accessed: 1.7.2023.
50 https://www.saglikaktuel.com/haber/acilen-desteklenmezse-tip-fakulteleri-bati-yor-40953.htm, accessed: 1.7.2023.
51 https://istatistik.yok.gov.tr/, accessed: 4.9.2023.
52 Most of the observations related in this part stem directly from my own experience as a lecturer in a recently founded public university in provincial Turkey from 2017 onwards and previous experiences as an undergraduate and graduate student in a couple of more established higher education institutions in Ankara.
53 https://www.cumhuriyet.com.tr/haber/erdoganin-pazarlik-tutanagi-ortaya-cikti-3-milyar-avro-ise-hic-konusmayalim-477710, accessed: 1.7.2023.
54 https://www.bbc.com/turkce/haberler/2016/02/160211_erdogan_omer_celik_multeciler_aciklama, accessed: 1.7.2023.
55 https://tr.euronews.com/2018/10/12/adim-adim-brunson-krizi-abd-turkiye-il-iskilerinde-yaptirimlar-noktasina-nasil-gelindi-, accessed: 1.7.2023.
56 https://www.dw.com/tr/erdo%C4%9Fan-davosu-terk-etti/a-3988806, accessed: 5.5.2022.
57 https://www.denizhaber.com/gundem/diplomatlarin-gozuyle-davos-cikisi-h15539.html, accessed: 1.7.2023.
58 https://www.hurriyet.com.tr/gundem/istanbulda-miting-gibi-karsilama-10887578, accessed: 1.7.2023.
59 https://tr.euronews.com/2020/06/30/trump-n-dunya-liderleriyle-yapt-g-telefon-gorusmeleri-erdogan-onu-trump-soyup-sogana-cevir, accessed: 1.7.2023.
60 In popular political rumour in Turkey – which usually contains a great amount of truth – this dynamic is expressed more bluntly. In my field research on Turkish political parties, I many times heard from my interlocutors that the governors of sub-provinces and provinces (*kaymakamlar* and *valiler*) have turned into "vice chairs" to sub-provincial and provincial AKP chairs.

References

Adar, S. & G. Seufert (2021). *Turkey's Presidential System after Two and a Half Years: An Overview of Institutions and Politics.* (SWP-Studie, 2/2021). Berlin: Stiftung Wissenschaft und Politik – SWP – Deutsches Institut für Internationale Politik und Sicherheit. https://doi.org/10.18449/2021RP02
AK Parti (2002). *Kalkınma ve Demokratikleşme Programı.* Ankara: AK Parti.
Akçay, Ü. (2019). Türkiye'de neoliberal popülizm, otoriterleşme ve kriz. *Toplum ve Bilim, 147,* 46–70.
Akçay, Ü. & A. R. Güngen (2019). *The making of Turkey's 2018–2019 economic crisis.* Institute for International Political Economy (IPE), Berlin, Working Paper, No. 120/2019.

134 Case studies

Akgül, A., H. Akbaş & A. Kule (2019). Probation system in Turkey: An analysis of a public policy formation using multiple streams framework. *International Journal of Comparative and Applied Criminal Justice*, *43*(4), 325–340.

Alexander, C. (2002). *Personal States – Making Connections Between People and Bureaucracy in Turkey*. Oxford: Oxford University Press.

Arslantaş, D. & Ş. Arslantaş (2022). How does clientelism foster electoral dominance? Evidence from Turkey. *Asian Journal of Comparative Politics*, *7*(3), 559–575.

Aslan, S. (2021). Public tears: Populism and the politics of emotion in AKP's Turkey. *International Journal of Middle East Studies*, *53*(1), 1–17.

Atasoy, Y. (2009). *Islam's Marriage with Neo-Liberalism*. New York: Palgrave Macmillan.

Ateş, K. (2017). AKP, dinsel popülizm ve halk-olmayan. *Mülkiye Dergisi*, *41*(1), 105–129.

Aytaç, S. E., A. Çarkoğlu & E. Elçi (2021). Partisanship, elite messages, and support for populism in power. *European Political Science Review*, *13*(1), 23–39.

Bakırezer, G. & Y. Demirer (2009). AK Parti'nin sosyal siyaseti. In İ. Uzgel & B. Duru (Eds.), *AKP Kitabı: Bir Dönüşümün Bilançosu* (pp. 153–178). Ankara: Phoenix Yayınevi.

Balta, E. (2018). The AKP's foreign policy as populist governance. *Middle East Report*, *288*, 14–18.

Barr, R. R. (2009). Populists, outsiders and anti-establishment politics. *Party Politics*, *15*(1), 29–48.

Baykan, T. S. (2021). The high-low divide in Turkish politics and the populist appeal of Erdoğan's justice and development party. In F. Panizza, P. Ostiguy & B. Moffitt (Eds.), *Populism in Global Perspective: A Performative and Discursive Approach* (pp. 199–222). London: Routledge.

Baykan, T. S., Y. Gürsoy & P. Ostiguy (2021). Anti-populist coups d'état in the twenty-first century: Reasons, dynamics and consequences. *Third World Quarterly*, *42*(4), 793–811.

Boyraz, C. (2018). Neoliberal populism and governmentality in Turkey: The foundation of communication centers during the AKP era. *Philosophy & Social Criticism*, *44*(4), 437–452.

Bozkurt, U. (2013). Neoliberalism with a human face: Making sense of the Justice and Development Party's neoliberal populism in Turkey. *Science & Society*, *77*(3), 372–396.

Buğra, A. (2018). Social policy and different dimensions of inequality in Turkey: A historical overview. *Journal of Balkan and Near Eastern Studies*, *20*(4), 318–331.

Buğra, A. & Ç. Keyder (2006). The Turkish welfare regime in transformation. *Journal of European Social Policy*, *16*(3), 211–228.

Bulut, A. T. & N. Hacıoğlu (2021). Religion, foreign policy and populism in Turkish politics: Introducing a new framework. *Democratization*, *28*(4), 762–781.

Çelik, A. B. & E. Balta (2020). Explaining the micro dynamics of the populist cleavage in the "new Turkey". *Mediterranean Politics*, *25*(2), 160–181.

Çeviker-Gürakar, E. (2016). *Politics of Favoritism in Public Procurement in Turkey*. New York: Palgrave Macmillan.

CİMER (n.d.). *50 Soruda Cimer*. Ankara: Cumhurbaşkanlığı İletişim Merkezi.

Destradi, S. & J. Plagemann (2019). Populism and international relations: (Un)predictability, personalisation, and the reinforcement of existing trends in world politics. *Review of International Studies*, 45(5), 711–730.

Destradi, S., J. Plagemann & H. Taş, (2022). Populism and the politicisation of foreign policy. *The British Journal of Politics and International Relations*, 24(3), 475–492.

Dinçer, N. and Tekin-Koru, A. (2019). *An anatomy of productivity in Turkey in the AKP era through a political economy lens*. MPRA paper, No. 96844.

Elçi, E. (2022). Politics of nostalgia and populism: Evidence from Turkey. *British Journal of Political Science*, 52(2), 697–714.

Erçetin, T. & E. Erdoğan (2018). How Turkey's repetitive elections affected the populist tone in the discourses of the Justice and Development Party Leaders. *Philosophy & Social Criticism*, 44(4), 382–398.

Erdoğan, E. (2013). Dış politikada siyasallaşma: Türk kamuoyunun "Davos krizi" ve etkileri hakkındaki değerlendirmeleri. *Uluslararası İlişkiler Dergisi*, 10(37), 37–67.

Göçmen, İ. (2014). Religion, politics and social assistance in Turkey: The rise of religiously motivated associations. *Journal of European Social Policy*, 24(1), 92–103.

Gümüşçü, Ş. (2021). AKP'nin siyasal iktisadı ve patrimonyal rejimin yükselişi. *Toplum ve Bilim*, 158, 53–67.

Günay, D. & A. Günay (2011). 1933'den günümüze Türk yükseköğretiminde niceliksel gelişmeler. *Journal of Higher Education & Science/Yükseköğretim ve Bilim Dergisi*, 1(1), 1–22.

Gürsoy, Y. (2021). Moving beyond European and Latin American typologies: The peculiarities of AKP's populism in Turkey. *Journal of Contemporary Asia*, 51(1), 157–178.

Hakyemez, Y. Ş. (2010). 2010 Anayasa değişiklikleri ve demokratik hukuk devleti. *Ankara Hacı Bayram Veli Üniversitesi Hukuk Fakültesi Dergisi*, 14(2), 387–406.

Hawkins, K. A., R. E. Carlin, L. Littvay & C. R. Kaltwasser (Eds.). (2018). *The Ideational Approach to Populism: Concept, Theory, and Analysis*. London: Routledge.

Hawkins, K. A. *et al.* (2019). *Measuring Populist Discourse: The Global Populism Database*. Paper presented at the 2019 EPSA Annual Conference in Belfast, UK, June 20–22.

İşeri, E. & M. Ersoy (2021). Framing the Syrian operations: populism in foreign policy and the polarized news media of Turkey. *International Journal of Communication*, 15, 24.

Kaliber, A. & E. Kaliber (2019). From de-Europeanisation to anti-Western populism: Turkish foreign policy in flux. *The International Spectator*, 54(4), 1–16.

Karagöz, S. (2020). Türkiye'de sosyal devletin sosyal yardım bağlamında değerlendirilmesi. *Ekonomi İşletme ve Maliye Araştırmaları Dergisi*, 2(2), 146–169.

Karataşlı, Ş. S. & Ş. Kumral (2023). Crisis of capitalism and cycles of right-wing populism in contemporary Turkey: The making and unmaking of Erdoğanist hegemony. *Journal of Agrarian Change*, 23(1), 22–46.

Kaygusuz, Ö. (2018). Authoritarian neoliberalism and regime security in Turkey: Moving to an "exceptional state" under AKP. *South European Society and Politics*, 23(2), 281–302.

136 Case studies

Kutlu, D. (2015). *Türkiye'de Sosyal Yardım Rejiminin Oluşumu – Birikim, Denetim, Disiplin*. Ankara: Notabene.

Lord, C. (2012). The persistence of Turkey's majoritarian system of government. *Government and Opposition*, 47(2), 228–255.

Moffitt, B. (2016). *The Global Rise of Populism*. Stanford, CA: Stanford University Press.

Mudde, C. (2004). The populist zeitgeist. *Government and Opposition*, 39(4), 541–563.

Ostiguy, P. (2017). Populism: A socio-cultural approach. In C. R. Kaltwasser, P. Taggart, P. O. Espejo & P. Ostiguy (Eds.), *The Oxford Handbook of Populism* (pp. 73–97). Oxford: Oxford University Press.

Özbudun, E. (2007). Türk anayasa mahkemesinin yargısal aktivizmi ve siyasal elitlerin tepkisi. *Ankara Üniversitesi SBF Dergisi*, 62(3), 257–268.

Özbudun, E. (2015). Turkey's judiciary and the drift toward competitive authoritarianism. *The International Spectator*, 50(2), 42–55.

Özçetin, B. (2019). 'The show of the people' against the cultural elites: Populism, media and popular culture in Turkey. *European Journal of Cultural Studies*, 22(5–6), 942–957.

Özdemir, Y. (2020). AKP's neoliberal populism and contradictions of new social policies in Turkey. *Contemporary Politics*, 26(3), 245–267.

Özpek, B. B. & N. Tanrıverdi-Yaşar (2018). Populism and foreign policy in Turkey under the AKP rule. *Turkish Studies*, 19(2), 198–216.

Parslow, J. (2016). Theories of exceptional executive powers in Turkey, 1933–1945. *New Perspectives on Turkey*, 55, 29–54.

Şahin, Ü. (2018). İyi yönetişimin Türk kamu yönetiminde uygulanması ve Kamu Denetçiliği Kurumu. *Ombudsman Akademik, Special Issue* (1), 99–139.

Scott, J. C. (1999). *Seeing Like a State – How Certain Schemes to Improve the Human Condition Have Failed*. New Haven, CT and London: Yale University Press.

Selçuk, O. (2016). Strong presidents and weak institutions: Populism in Turkey, Venezuela and Ecuador. *Southeast European and Black Sea Studies*, 16(4), 571–589.

Sofos, S. (2022). *Turkish Politics and "the People" – Mass Mobilisation and Populism*, Edinburgh: Edinburgh University Press.

Soyaltin-Colella, D. (2022). How to capture the judiciary under the guise of EU-led reforms: Domestic strategies of resistance and erosion of rule of law in Turkey. *Southeast European and Black Sea Studies*, 22(3), 441–462.

Taş, H. (2022). The formulation and implementation of populist foreign policy: Turkey in the Eastern Mediterranean. *Mediterranean Politics*, 27(5), 563–587.

Urhan, G. (2018). Yerel refah sisteminin oluşumunda belediye yardımları ve yardım alma deneyimi: işlev ve sonuçları açısından bir değerlendirme. In D. Kutlu (Ed.), *Sosyal Yardım Alanlar – Emek, Geçim, Siyaset ve Toplumsal Cinsiyet* (pp. 171–192). İstanbul: İletişim Yayınları.

Üstüner, Y. & N. Yavuz (2018). Turkey's public administration today: An overview and appraisal. *International Journal of Public Administration*, 41(10), 820–831.

Uysal, A. (2021). Muhbirliğin kurumsallaşması ve korku rejiminin konsolidasyonu. *Toplum ve Bilim*, 158, 68–86.

Varol, O. O., L. Dalla Pellegrina & N. Garoupa (2017). An empirical analysis of judicial transformation in Turkey. *The American Journal of Comparative Law*, 65(1), 187–216.

Weyland, K. (2001). Clarifying a contested concept: Populism in the study of Latin American politics. *Comparative Politics*, *34* (1), 1–22.

Yalvaç, F. & J. Joseph (2019). Understanding populist politics in Turkey: A hegemonic depth approach. *Review of International Studies*, *45*(5), 786–804.

Yıldırım, D. (2009). AKP ve neo-liberal popülizm. In İ. Uzgel & B. Duru (Eds.), *AKP Kitabı: Bir Dönüşümün Bilançosu* (pp. 66–107). Ankara: Phoenix Yayınevi.

Yıldırım, B. & F. Şahin (2019). Esping-Andersen'in refah devleti sınıflandırması ve makro sosyal hizmet uygulamaları temelinde Türkiye'nin konumu. *OPUS International Journal of Society Researches*, *11*(18), 2525–2554.

Yıldırım, İ. & T. Kuyucu (2017). Neoliberal penality and state legitimacy: Politics of amnesty in Turkey during the AKP period. *Law & Society Review*, *51*(4), 859–894.

Yılmaz, V. (2017). *The Politics of Healthcare Reform in Turkey*. New York: Palgrave MacMillan.

Yılmaz, V. (2018). Introduction: Social policies and social inequalities in contemporary Turkey. *Research and Policy on Turkey*, *3*(2), 103–114.

Yılmaz, Z. (2020). Erdoğan's presidential regime and strategic legalism: Turkish democracy in the twilight zone. *Southeast European and Black Sea Studies*, *20*(2), 265–287.

Yılmaz, Z. (2015). "Strengthening the family" policies in Turkey: Managing the social question and armoring conservative–neoliberal populism. *Turkish Studies*, *16*(3), 371–390.

Yörük, E. (2022). *The Politics of the Welfare State in Turkey – How Social Movements and Elite Competition Created a Welfare State*. Ann Arbor, MI: University of Michigan Press.

6

THE POPULIST ECONOMIC CONDUCT UNDER CHAVEZ RULE IN VENEZUELA

Development of populism in Venezuela: The rise of Chavez movement

The socio-political background in Venezuela, which eventually gave rise to the radical populism of the Chavez movement – and later resulted in its predominant position based on a long series of consecutive victories in elections – has been shaped by the dramatic expansion of oil industry in the 1920s (Salas 2015). After this economic transformation, the politics of Venezuela has started to revolve around the question of how to manage, distribute, and use the resources generated by the massive wealth stemming from oil production. The expansion of oil industry has had two major consequences for Venezuela that paved the way to an extremely fertile ground for the socio-cultural "high-low" divide (Ostiguy 2017) and the future rise of populism. On the one hand, it created affluent social segments strongly tied to the oil trade between Venezuela and the United States. These social segments not only benefitted economically from the oil trade but also embraced a highly Americanized way of life. On the other hand, oil production and the changes it created in the traditional and agricultural Venezuelan economy rapidly pushed rural masses to cities and created an urban working class, as well as a large informal sector highly responsive to populist appeals (Salas 2015, 63–64). Between 1958 and 1992, however, Venezuela was ruled within the framework of a liberal party system which relied on an agreement between a couple of centrist political forces. This democratic period termed as the "Punto Fijo era".

When the political frustration caused by the demise of the legitimacy of the political system created by the Punto Fijo agreement was coupled with

DOI: 10.4324/9781003294627-9

economic hardships, the social divides deepened, and a radical brand of populism started to reveal itself, first, in 1992 with a failed coup and, in 1998, by the electoral victory of Chavez. Similar to the support base of the *Adalet ve Kalkınma Partisi* (AKP – The Justice and Development Party), the Chavez movement has been supported by a "broad [cross-class] coalition of the poor, the middle classes and even some wealthy sectors" and "the very rich have opposed [Chavez] disproportionately" (Lupu 2010, 7–32). Chavez, both in style and discourse, presented himself and his movement as the populist defender of underprivileged segments of Venezuelan society. He has been described "as a 'popular caudillo' who knew folklore and popular music by heart, danced the typical 'joropo,' and was a powerful storyteller who became 'the great prophet of the people'" (*Consalvi quoted in* Block & Negrine 2017, 184).

Chavez governments increasingly more decisively supported the poor and the excluded segments of Venezuelan society through poverty alleviation programs and "missions" created for solutions to specific social problems (Hawkins 2010, 195–230). Meanwhile, the project of Chavismo started to encapsulate masses supportive of the Chavez regime in more concrete organizational forms such as local grassroots organizations called "Bolivarian Circles" (Ellner 2008, 175–194; Hawkins 2010, 166–194) and, later, under a much more well-coordinated mass organization, the United Socialist Party of Venezuela (USPV) (Handlin 2016). Chavez governments also effectively weakened the institutional checks and balances in Venezuela by taking judicial and legislative branches, as well as institutions such as the National Electoral Council, under executive control (Roberts 2012). It did not take too long for the Chavez government to trigger a coup which was backed by affluent segments of Venezuelan society (Barracca 2007, 143). The coup in 2002 against Chavez was certainly an anti-populist intervention that aimed for the restoration of the pre-Chavez political order and the privileges of the upper and middle classes and the established business circles (Barracca 2007, 151).

State and bureaucracy in modern Venezuela: The populist proclivity

Oil wealth was decisive both in the formation of the Venezuelan party system as well as the Venezuelan state bureaucracy from the mid-20th century onwards. Despite Venezuelan intellectuals urge towards creating a more productive economy by the strategy of so-called "sowing the oil", the Venezuelan political system has never been successful at transforming the oil wealth into industrial and agricultural productivity. Thus, the Venezuelan politics and state, in some respects, demonstrated the features of a "rentier system" which has deeply shaped the state and bureaucracy formation in Venezuela.

140 Case studies

Since there was oil revenue, "during most of its life the Venezuelan state has not depended on taxes" (Rita 1994, 503). The consequence was that, especially during oil price booms, there was no budgetary pressure on the formation and expansion of the Venezuelan bureaucracy. As Ellner notes with reference to Terry Karl's seminal essay, "oil-derived revenue encouraged the state to create a large, highly unproductive bureaucracy at the same time that it borrowed money from abroad to finance unrealistic, if not quixotic, megaprojects" (Ellner 2003, 13).

As Rita highlights, "a quick profile of Venezuelan bureaucracy can be given through three adjectives: authoritarian, clientelistic, and incompetent" (1994, 501). It seems pretty clear that family and party networks have always impeded the formation of a meritocratic bureaucracy in Venezuela. Since the dictatorship of Jimenez, clientelistic networks have been seen as vital for the formation of bureaucratic institutions. When Venezuela made a transition to a democratic system at the end of the 1950s through the Punto Fijo system, the clientelistic recruitment strategies in the public bureaucracy remained the same, but now, parties have started to play a central role. In 1973 and 1974, the rise of the price of oil worldwide expanded the public bureaucracy even further (Rita 1994, 502–503). It contributed to enormous levels of clientelism in Venezuela and paved the way for unsustainable expansion of the public sector (Brading 2013, 45–46).

During the 1970s, and relying on oil wealth, the Venezuelan state initiated a series of social and economic programs. Some of these programs were reflecting the inherent populist proclivities of the Venezuelan political and bureaucratic system: "Some of these programs were part of a redistributive effort to make oil money available to most of the Venezuelan population through social policies (more health and education services, especially), but others were related to an enhanced presence of the state in the economic sphere" (Rita 1994, 504). Throughout this process Venezuelan bureaucracy were staffed with more personnel with less competence "through the usual means of party patronage and family links" (Rita 1994, 504). The oil revenue has gradually started to shape the mentality of Venezuelan citizens and they increasingly started to see themselves as entitled to the particularistic benefits presented by the Venezuelan oil economy (Rita 1994, 505). As Ellner notes, "the paternalist mentality created by easy oil money induces Venezuelans to look to the central government, which administers the revenue, for quick solutions to their problems" (2003, 15).

In various moments throughout the Punto Fijo era, the Venezuelan political elite tried to reform the bureaucracy, but, ironically, the bureaucracy gradually deteriorated, starting in 1973. The original intentions of laws to reform bureaucracy were twisted, transforming these into mere assurances of employment security for government workers. The primary factor for recruitment became one's political party affiliation, and for the first time, salaries were insufficient to attract skilled individuals into civil service roles. There was almost no assessment of the performance of civil servants, and the training process was completely neglected. In the 1980s, the reform attempts were still highlighting the problems generated by "the spoils system". The system relied on the government utilizing revenue from oil to allocate specific advantages (such as positions, scholarships, contracts, and subsidies) among its supporters. These advantages even extended to securing a stable government job. Instead of meritocracy, the bureaucracy was founded on principles of loyalty and obedience (Monaldi *et al.* 2006, 56–57). It was only PDVSA (*Petróleos de Venezuela, S.A.*) and the Central Bank that remained outside this populist patronage system in Venezuela, at least until the rise of Chavez movement. However, these institutions' bureaucratic autonomy was not similar to the conventional autonomy of bureaucratic institutions that can be observed in more consolidated democracies. Particularly, the PDVSA, in fact, turned into a "state within the state" (Mommer 2003, 144) that was loosely connected to the expectations of Venezuela's poor majority.

In fact, it seems that the sharing of the oil revenue by the political class and citizens under the patronage of the political elite created a kind of complicity in Venezuela among the elite and the citizens that was diverting Venezuelan public's attention from the simple fact that oil is a finite resource and Venezuelan economy remains very fragile as long as it largely relies upon the production of a single commodity. But the culture of "*facilismo*" (Marquez 2003, 204) and paternalism (Marquez 2003, 211) in Venezuela, which emerged throughout decades of oil-based public administration and policy, unfolded itself in the form of "a populist governmental practice" that blinded the long-term horizon of Venezuelan political elite and society. Because, especially in the 1970s, the poor really benefitted from the entire populist redistributive consensus (Marquez 2003, 199).

The long-term consequence of this populist process and practice when there was a transition to neoliberal policies in the 1980s and 1990s was the dramatic decline in the capacity of the Venezuelan state in providing basic services to the citizens. This process culminated in the *Caracazo* events, which "was a spontaneous collective social response to the collapse of 'state responsibility' with the 'people'" (Brading 2013, 47). In the 1990s, the incapacity of the Venezuelan administrations deepened to such an extent that communities started to carry out their own basic services such as "garbage collection [...] security of private property [...] food distribution, personal security, elementary education" (Buxton 2003, 117). However, the rise of Chavismo, despite its initial pledges to save the state from the corruption of the previous era, did change nothing when it came to clientelistic and patronage-based proclivities of Venezuelan public bureaucracy. In contrast, things started to get worse. As Maya (2018) notes, the radical personalism of the Chavez rule effectively undermined the already limited institutional

142 Case studies

capacity of the Venezuelan state. For example, "Chavez's official discourse constantly disqualified the institutions that regulated the executive labeling them as 'bourgeois' and/or 'oligarchic'" (Maya 2018, 68). Even in the Chavez era, nepotistic and patronage-based appointments of people loyal to Chavez to the state bureaucracy were a visible trend, according to Maya's account (2018, 68–70). During the Maduro period, and in the lack of Chavez's charisma, things got worse and nepotism, cronyism, and clientelism reached unprecedented levels that the line between legitimate state activity and criminality blurred to the extent that Venezuelan state started to be seen as an "*estada delincuento*" (Maya 2018, 67).

A brief glance at the economic policies in Venezuela

Oil lies at the heart of the Venezuelan politics and bureaucracy because it lies at the heart of the Venezuelan economy. Since its discovery at the beginning of the 20th century, oil created a kind of "path dependency" for the Venezuelan economy, which amounted to a "resource curse". Various attempts throughout the era of competitive politics after 1958 to redirect the oil revenue towards more productive sectors failed in Venezuela. For example, in the 1970s, Venezuela had failed attempts in developing an endogenous automobile and tractor industry (Coronil 1997, 11). However, Venezuelan political elites did not shy away from deploying oil revenues for clientelistic and redistributive purposes and creating a kind of cartel system in politics during the Punto Fijo era (Monaldi *et al.* 2006, 63).

Especially the rise of global oil prices in the 1970s resulted in the consolidation of redistributive aspects of the Venezuelan economy and social policies. As Coronil highlights, "the circulation of torrents of oil money not only undermined productive activity and stimulated the spread of financial speculation and corruption but also facilitated the concentration of power at the highest levels of government" (1997, 11). But when the oil prices started to fall dramatically towards the end of the 1970s Venezuelan political elite gradually switched to neoliberal policies and austerity in the 1980s. Even in the 1980s, however, the Venezuelan political elite kept the centrality of state intact, courted with popular sectors through clientelistic methods, and kept "further concentrating the wealth at the top, and placing the burden of the debt on the working population for generations to come" (Coronil 1997, 379). However, from the 1980s until the rise of Chavez towards the end of the 1990s, Venezuelan *pueblo* started to see once the democratic model of Latin American politics, the Venezuelan competitive party system and its elite, as the clientelistic "*partidocracia*" under a closed elite rule ("*cogolloracia*") (Coronil 1997, 368–369). As Brading highlights, neoliberal reforms were seen as feeding the clientelistic elite under the conditions of falling oil prices (2013, 51). Towards the end of the 1980s, these economic and political

The abrupt end of the classical redistributive populist economy in Venezuela, the weeks long *Caracazo* protests, which were violently crushed, and, a couple of years later, in 1992, a military coup led by Colonel Hugo Chavez. As Coronil notes, "these events marked a crisis of the populist project that had defined the relationship between state and pueblo since 1936" (1997, 378).

The abrupt end of the classical redistributive populist economy in Venezuela in the 1980s and 1990s (Ellner 2008, 99) resulted in a deeply divided nation consisting of "an internationally connected upperclass and its local associates and an impoverished majority that includes a shrinking middle class" (Coronil 1997, 383). At the end of the 1990s, Venezuelan poor started to embrace an extremely bleak and grim view of the wealthy minority, perceive them as the "enemy" (Ellner 2003, 19). As Roberts notes, Venezuelan political parties have always been cross-class entities and under the conditions of oil wealth, they emerged as "pitting alternative patronage machines" (Roberts 2003, 58). This cross-class nature of Venezuelan politics remained intact during the 1990s because, due to neoliberal reforms, the informal sector and precarity expanded rapidly and confined large parts of populations into subjugated positions in competing patronage parties (Roberts 2003, 60). Such heterogeneous constituencies, once again, undermined the programmatic handling of the problems of Venezuelan constituencies by any political party. While Venezuela's social divisions could not be abated throughout Chavez years, populist policy practice in the economic and social realms made a spectacular come back in the 2000s.

Venezuelan economy under Chavez rule: Populist practice in full swing

Today, Chavez is known with his radical economic policies and as the architect of the so-called "21st century socialism". But surprisingly Chavez embraced a very cautious economic policy in his initial years and retained some of the conservative aspects of the previous government's economic policies (Buxton 2003, 124). Until 2002, Chavez's economic policies remained moderate but his administration, at the same time, was keen to solve the acute problem of poverty emerged throughout the 1980s and 1990s. In order to cope with this major problem, even during those relatively "orthodox" initial years, Chavez administration focused on public welfare provisions. For example, the Chavez government was well aware of the much deeper poverty affecting women and it created credit facilities that directly targeted the poor women through *Banco de la Mujer*. The Chavez government also strived to support small and medium sized businesses and incorporate informal sector workers into the system through improving educational standards and providing the latter with "public pension and health protection rights" (Buxton 2003, 126). Not surprisingly, even these

144 Case studies

modest measures to solve the problem of abject poverty perceived with hostility by the elite in Venezuela. While critics of the government were preoccupied with their worries about how the state would finance public welfare programs, these proposals naturally gained widespread support among Chavez's followers. Even in this more moderate phase of Chavez's economic and social policies, his approach was depicted as "attempts by the government to install an authoritarian, statist model" by his opponents (Buxton 2003, 128).

Reintroducing radical redistribution and "Misiones"

These modest initial redistributive measures of the Chavez government, in a couple of years, drew the hostility of the Venezuelan elite and, first, paved the way to a nationwide strike led by PDVSA and FEDECAMARAS (*Federación de Cámaras y Asociaciones de Comercio y Producción de Venezuela* – Venezuelan Federation of Chambers of Commerce and Production) and, then, to a military coup toppling Chavez for a short duration. After this general strike and the coup in 2002, Chavez government intensified its social policies. These social and economic policies contained micro and macro level measures and innovations and were targeted to lighten the burden on the poor Chavista constituencies. For example, the Chavez government created a "nationwide food supply network (PDVAL) in order to cope with inflation and scarcity" (Schincariol 2020, 48–49) and distributed small pieces of land to peasants, which they occupied for more than three years. But the government also introduced some more encompassing redistributive economic policies such as the nationalization of PDVSA and a new labour law that appeals to Chavista constituencies (Schincariol 2020, 52). With a decree law, the Chavez government provided itself with a much wider margin of intervention to the economy (Schincariol 2020, 57).

In fact, initially, Chavez government, like previous Venezuelan governments, wanted to diversify the economy and continue the idea of "sowing the oil" for a more productive and diversified economy. Yet, Chavez governments, from a macro-economical point of view, kept embracing economic policies prioritizing consumption and import (Schincariol 2020, 50). In order to satisfy the immediate needs of citizens, the Chavez government kept the national currency, Bolivar, overvalued for easily importing consumption goods. Particularly throughout the period between 2003 and 2008, this kind of approach seemed entirely credible since there was a spectacular rise in oil prices. Economic policies of this particular era, As Corrales and Penfold (2011) argue, guided by the enormous rise in oil prices. Despite public pledges highlighting the importance of diversifying the economy, the period of oil price boom has "diminished the incentives to stimulate the growth of other sectors" (Corrales & Penfold 2011, 47–48). Yet, just like in the previous periods, as majorities benefited from the highly redistributive measures, problematic background of these economic policies was largely ignored (Corrales & Penfold 2011, 49).

Since the majority of Chavez's voters were "poor wage owners", it was not surprising to see that Chavez government channelled the increasing oil revenue to social policy expenditures (Hawkins 2010, 199). Beginning in 2003, Chavez governments initiated a series of *"misiones"* to cope with the country's immediate problems. These *misiones* ranged from health care to education, subsidized food to housing, and land redistribution to assistance for marginalized groups and indigent mothers (Hawkins 2010, 203). Especially *misiones* of health care and subsidized food are worth noting since these formed the core of the populist practice of Chavez governments. As Hawkins notes, the *misiones* helped a lot to consolidate the support for Chavez governments among the urban poor (2010, 201–202). Another aspect of the *misiones* making it possible to see them as a reflection of the tactical-innovative proclivity of populist governmental practice is the way they were organized. Chavez governments did not organize them as extensions of already existing bureaucratic institutions but as "parallel institutions" that could circumvent the traditional clientelistic bureaucracy: "Thus the 'Missions,' which have created structures outside of the established ministries, are unique programs designed to enhance living conditions in poor neighborhoods. Approximately 12.000 Cuban doctors live, work and are fully incorporated in poor neighborhoods throughout the country, while the literacy and other educational Missions are also community centered" (Ellner 2005, 184).

Poverty rates started to decline in 2003 during the Chavez era (Weisbrot *et al.* 2006, 815). The poverty rate saw a substantial decline, dropping from its highest point of 55.1 percent in 2003 to 30.4 percent by the end of 2006, which aligns with expectations stemming from the significant economic growth observed during the preceding three years (Weisbrot & Sandoval 2007, 10). *Misiones* certainly improved conditions of the poor in Venezuela beyond these calculations by providing, for example, free health care and education to poor and contributing to their overall welfare, as Weisbrot and Sandoval noted (2007, 10–11). A populist practice was also in effect in the financing of *misiones*, which aimed at circumventing bureaucratic and budgetary procedures. In this sense, tightening the political control over the heart of Venezuelan economy, the PDVSA, in 2003 was key, as documented in detail by Corrales and Penfold (2011, 78–81). As Vera notes, almost all resources required to finance such expanded social programmes acquired through circumventing the budgetary procedures by creating the off budget development fund, FONDEN (*Fondo de Desarrollo Nacional* – The National Development Fund) and defining new responsibilities for the PDVSA such as providing financial resources and managing social programs (2015, 548).

146 Case studies

The consequences of these processes, and the populist policy practice that is targeting short-term solutions to immediate problems, have been typical. As Chavez government tightened its control over the PDVSA, this immediately undermined the institution's productivity and efficiency. Chavez appointed people to the executive positions in the institution who were not coming from within the oil industry and the new administration expelled 18,000 experienced and competent top and middle tier administrators (Corrales & Penfold 2011, 78). The PDVSA, under the control of Chavistas, established an unaccountable social development fund (Fondespa) as well to fund the *misiones* (Corrales & Penfold 2011, 80). Moreover, under the rule of Chavez governments, the PDVSA displaced the relevant ministries and became the foci of social spending. The direct deployment of PDVSA resources, however, as Corrales and Penfold acknowledge, remarkably improved basic social indicators (2011, 83–84).

In addition to this, the PDVSA was also used as a patronage resource for unemployed Chavistas. The number of staff in the PDVSA under Chavez governments skyrocketed from 30,000 to 80,000. It should be noted here that the increase in the number of state personnel was not limited to the PDVSA and there was a general trend of the enlargement of the public bureaucracy. From the start of Chavez rule to 2008, the number of state personnel increased by 53.5 percent (Corrales & Penfold 2011, 64). Not surprisingly, the PDVSA also heavily subsidized the oil throughout the Chavez years (Corrales & Penfold 2011, 87–88). These changes decisively undermined the productivity and efficiency of the petrol industry in Venezuela (Corrales & Penfold 2011, 72, 97). In general, towards 2008, public expenditures were out of control due to the expansion of public sector employment, successive nationalizations, and inefficiencies these nationalizations have created (Corrales & Penfold 2011, 67). Beginning with 2008, oil prices started to decline and the costs of populist policies and practices in the realm of economy became visible in Venezuela.

The problem of fixed currency exchange rates

The structural qualities of the Venezuelan economy, its heavy dependence on the oil industry and the inability of governments (including the Chavez governments) to diversify the economy, decisively kept productive sectors such as agriculture and manufacturing underdeveloped (Schincariol 2020, 71–77). This structural proclivity of the economy was consolidated by the rising oil prices between 2003 and 2008 and the deeply populist proclivities of the Chavez government. These deep-rooted populist proclivities in Venezuela, an essential aspect of which is the culture of *"facilismo"*, constantly led Chavista elite to opt for short-term solutions to immediate problems. For example, the Chavista elite, as noted above, decided to solve the problem of poverty through *Misiones,* but this solution, ironically, consolidated the import-based old food system in Venezuela. Not just the food but for sustaining a level of abundance in consumer goods in the short term, throughout the Chavez years, the Venezuelan economy depended largely on imports. It has become one of the few most import-based economies in Latin America (Schincariol 2020, 82). No doubt that resources for such high levels of imports were coming from the booming oil prices. Throughout this process of relative abundance, Chavista economists opted for an "overvalued currency" to "support low-cost imports, especially food, and this penalized exporters, contributing to worsening of the balance of payments" (Pittaluga *et al.* 2021, 342). In other words, Chavez governments provided Venezuelan citizens with cheap, heavily subsidized dollars backed by oil revenues for their daily needs. But in practice, "the [fixed] exchange-rate regime creates huge incentives for importers to pocket their cheap dollars rather than bring in goods—and that gives rise to lines. Long lines. For all the basics" (Toro & Kronick 2015). As Sutherland explained, through this monetary policy to back the import of basic consumption goods, the Venezuelan state provided importers with dollars in return of so little Bolivars that the importers, in fact, did not even engage in trade and opted to exchange their dollars on the black market to gain excessive profits (2018, 145–146).

This abuse of state resources in Venezuela reached new heights during the Maduro governments and ironically paved the way to the formation of oligarchic rule in Venezuela comprising of a new rich stratum called "boligarchs". The currency exchange control system has paved the way for the accumulation of significant fortunes, particularly by those referred to as "*enchufados*" in Venezuela, who were individuals connected to positions of power and state-supported preferential advantages (Maya 2018, 74). It seems that a scheme started with good intentions to respond to the immediate needs of the supportive poor constituencies by incentivizing easy import of basic consumption goods ended up in massive corruption channelling the wealth of Venezuela into the hands of the few.

Hyperinflation and scarcity

As noted so far, from an economic point of view, Chavismo mainly opted for massive redistributive measures, which were largely financed by oil revenues. As long as oil prices were high, such radical redistribution was possible. Nevertheless, its extent, combined with imprudent fiscal and monetary policies as well as widespread tax evasion (Schincariol 2020, 95), gradually became unsustainable. When the oil prices started to fall in 2008, the Chavista governments decided to support its radical redistributive programs through inflationary financing (Pittaluga *et al.* 2021, 337). During mid-2014, a decrease in the global oil price had a negative impact on government income.

148 Case studies

However, the government did not reduce public expenditures. This combination of reduced revenue and continued high public spending led to a growing budget deficit. To cover this deficit, the government resorted to printing more money, which ultimately culminated in hyperinflation (Pittaluga *et al.* 2021, 341). One should also add the detrimental impact of the policy of fixed currency exchange to the picture since the corruption that emerged around this system created additional inflationary pressures. Because cheap dollars obtained through the state system by *"enfuchados"* or *"bolibourgesia"* usually did not turn into imported goods and instead they were exchanged for illicit gains in the Venezuelan black markets for currency exchange (Toro & Kronick 2015; Bajpai 2018). Since the Venezuelan economy depended on imports for almost everything it needed, except the oil, this system caused shortages of many critical goods and enormous rises in prices in the middle to long run despite (or because of) police measures desperately trying to keep the prices low. The result was, as various accounts dramatically demonstrate, acute shortages of basic needs such as food, hygiene products, medicines, and medical equipment (Naim & Toro 2016; Kurmanaev 2019) culminating in remarkable number of casualties and flight of millions of people from Venezuela to neighbouring countries.[1]

Concluding discussion: "Now and here" for the constituency (at the expense of future)!

In this chapter, I have focused on the economic conduct of the Chavez rule as a crystallized case of "populist governmental practice". This chapter demonstrated that, under the immediate circumstances of dramatic inequalities and acute poverty, Chavez governments opted for redistributive strategies that paved the way to corruption and inefficiency in the economy in the long run. Coupled with Venezuelan economy's long-term structural problems such as the heavy dependence on oil and unsustainable monetary policies such as the fixed currency exchange rate, the populist conduct of economy remained highly vulnerable in the face of global ups and downs of oil prices. Especially towards the end of the Chavez era, the Venezuelan economy entered into a vicious circle: High public expenditures to support Chavez governments electorally created inflationary pressures and inflationary pressures fed poverty and further pressure on government to support the poor through social expenditures. Today, however, it is hard to argue that Venezuela is as successful as it was during the 2000s in alleviating the problems related to poverty. According to a research conducted in 2020–2021, more than three-fourths of the Venezuelan population lives in extreme poverty.[2]

From a broader theoretical point of view, the case of Venezuelan economy under Chavez rule provided evidence to reconsider a contemporary proclivity to confine populism into the realm of electoral party politics. As Hawkins notes in his important account of the phenomenon of Chavismo, today, there is a much larger consensus than there was a few decades ago (Boratav 1983; Dornbusch & Edwards 1991; Keyder 2003) regarding the relationship between economic policy and populism: Now, unlike 1980s and 1990s, mainstream approaches to the phenomenon of populism are inclined to see populism and economic policy, and especially redistributive variants of economic policy, as completely different phenomena. In this respect, the contribution of seminal works by Kurt Weyland (1999, 2001, 2003) and Kenneth Roberts (1995) are obvious. These scholars were among the first to demonstrate that left-wing redistributive economic policies were not defining features of populism since there emerged many populist leaders and governments in Latin America in the 1980s and 1990s embracing strict neoliberal economic policies. Such contributions led many researchers, including the adherents of ideational and political-strategic approaches to populism, to exclude policy preferences, and particularly policy preferences in economy, from the definition of populism. Hence, for example, Hawkins, in his detailed analysis of social policy in Venezuela, argues that "definitions of populism emphasizing economic policy put the cart before the horse, failing to appreciate the underlying ideas that drive policy preferences. Statist redistributive policies such as the Missions are understandable consequences of a populist worldview in a material context of poverty and inequality" (2010, 195–196). In short, Hawkins insists that populist policy practice is purely the unfolding of populist ideas.

But what this perspective misses in the analysis of populist policy practice is that populism is not really only about initial intentions in the formal design of pro-poor policies. As I have demonstrated so far with reference to economic policy in Venezuela, it is also regarding how these policies are put in effect and implemented and how discursive populist pledges to universality (such as the discourse of "21st-century populism" and "endogenous development") are intermingled with short-term concerns (such as winning elections), informality (such as bypassing procedures and institutions), particularism/clientelism (such as targeting your own constituencies in social services and aid, see Penfold-Becerra 2007), responsiveness and corruption. If populist policy was a simple outcome of pro-poor and anti-elite worldview, one would expect a much better economic performance from the Chavez governments and the following Maduro governments in terms of diversifying the Venezuelan economy and creating a more sustainable system with more robust agricultural and industrial sectors akin to some of the socialist development models in the 20th century (Schincariol 2020, 105). In other words, if populism (especially in power as a governmental practice) was simply a reflection of an ideology, one would expect its adherents to be more loyal to their ideas and less compromising in the

150 Case studies

face of short-term pressures. (Here, it is important to reassert that, during the initial years of the Chavez governments between 1999 and 2003, Venezuela embraced pretty orthodox economic policies; see Corrales & Penfold 2011, 54.)

But populism, as a governmental practice, is not simply an ideology. It is not even a thin ideology. As asserted in the previous theoretical parts of this book, populism is a spontaneous, pragmatic, and tactical practice that responds to the immediate expectations, interests, and tastes of supportive majorities. As such, populism does not simply belong to the sphere of ideas. As a practice, it stems from the interaction between ideas and concrete political and social pressures as well as the political culture and economic structure of a country, as we see in Venezuela. What we see in Venezuela in the sphere of economic and social policy is not the unfolding of an abstract populist worldview. In fact, as demonstrated so far, what we see in the sphere of economy is an orientation and practice guided by previous oil-based redistributive proclivities in economy, culture of paternalism widespread among the citizenry that renders them extremely demanding from the state, culture of *"facilismo"* and immediate electoral pressures that led the political elite to swift, easy and short-term solutions. Coupled with already existing clientelistic and nepotistic arrangements within the state bureaucracy, Venezuela's fully populist practice in the sphere of economy ended up with an economic and social catastrophe.

In this respect, populism is indeed, as the analysts of classical populism highlight (Dornbusch & Edwards 1991), characterized by imprudent, short-sighted, and short-term policies. Because, as a political-governmental practice, the distinguishing feature of populism is personalism, immediacy and responsiveness that is anathema to long-term, well-planned, institutional solutions. Understanding populism simply as an idea/ideology/discourse constructed around the distinction between people and elite misses the point that populism – especially as a governmental practice – is a fundamentally temporal, relational, and dynamic phenomenon, mostly conditioned by electoral concerns and pressures, with concrete implications in policy implementation (beyond policy design). Populism, as a political/governmental practice, is in favour of being "now and here" for the constituency, usually at the expense of the future. The last couple of decades in Venezuela have been an extreme and bleak example of this dynamic in populist practice.

Notes

1 https://www.aljazeera.com/news/2022/8/31/over-6-8-million-have-left-venezuela-since-2014-and-exodus-grows, accessed: 24.11.2022.
2 https://www.reuters.com/world/americas/extreme-poverty-venezuela-rises-766-study-2021-09-29/, accessed: 25.11.2022.

References

Bajpai, P. (2018). "The impact of Venezuela's Bolivar exchange rates", online essay, *Investopedia*, October 25, 2018. https://www.investopedia.com/articles/forex/022415/impact-venezuelas-bolivar-exchange-rates.asp, accessed: 25.11.2022.

Barracca, S. (2007). Military coups in the post-Cold War era: Pakistan, Ecuador and Venezuela. *Third World Quarterly*, 28(1), 137–154.

Block, E. & R. Negrine (2017). The populist communication style: Toward a critical framework. *International Journal of Communication Systems*, 11, 178–197.

Boratav, K. (1983). Türkiye'de popülizm: 1962–76 dönemi üzerine bazı notlar. *Yapıt*, 1, 7–18.

Brading, R. (2013). *Populism in Venezuela*. London: Routledge.

Buxton, J. (2003). Economic policy and the rise of Hugo Chavez. In S. Ellner & D. Hellinger (Eds.), *Venezuelan Politics in the Chavez Era* (pp. 113–130). Boulder, CO and London: Lynne Rienner Publishers.

Coronil, F. (1997). *The Magical State – Nature, Money and Modernity in Venezuela*. Chicago, IL: The University of Chicago Press.

Corrales, J. & M. Penfold (2011). *Dragon in the Tropics – Hugo Chávez and the Political Economy of Revolution in Venezuela*. Washington, DC: Brooking Institution Press.

Dornbusch, R. & S. Edwards (Eds.). (1991). *The Macroeconomics of Populism in Latin America*. Chicago, IL: Chicago University Press.

Ellner, S. (2003). Introduction: The search of explanations. In S. Ellner & D. Hellinger (Eds.), *Venezuelan Politics in the Chavez Era* (pp. 7–26). Boulder, CO and London: Lynne Rienner Publishers.

Ellner, S. (2005). Revolutionary and non-revolutionary paths of radical populism: Directions of the "Chavista" movement in Venezuela. *Science & Society*, 69(2), 160–190.

Ellner, S. (2008). *Rethinking Venezuelan Politics*. Boulder, CO and London: Lynne Rienner Publishers.

Handlin, S. (2016). Mass organization and the durability of competitive authoritarian regimes: Evidence from Venezuela. *Comparative Political Studies*, 49(9), 1238–1269.

Hawkins, K. A. (2010). *Venezuela's Chavismo and Populism in Comparative Perspective*. Cambridge: Cambridge University Press.

Keyder, Ç. (2003). *Türkiye'de Devlet ve Sınıflar*. İstanbul: İletişim.

Kurmanaev, A. (2019). "Venezuela's collapse is the worst outside of war in decades, economists say", online news report, *The New York Times*, May 17, 2019. https://www.nytimes.com/2019/05/17/world/americas/venezuela-economy.html, accessed: 25.11.2022.

Lupu, N. (2010). Who votes for "Chavismo"? Class voting in Hugo Chávez's Venezuela. *Latin American Research Review*, 45, 7–32.

Marquez, P. (2003). The Hugo Chavez phenomenon: What do "the people" think?. In S. Ellner & D. Hellinger (Eds.), *Venezuelan Politics in the Chavez Era* (pp. 197–214). Boulder, CO and London: Lynne Rienner Publishers.

Maya, M. L. (2018). Populism, 21st century socialism and corruption in Venezuela. *Thesis Eleven*, 149(1), 67–83.

152 Case studies

Mommer, B. (2003). Subversive oil. In S. Ellner & D. Hellinger (Eds.), *Venezuelan Politics in the Chavez Era* (pp. 131–146). Boulder, CO and London: Lynne Rienner Publishers.

Monaldi, F., R. A. Gonzalez de Pacheco, R. Obuchi & M. Penfold (2006). *Political Institutions, Policymaking Processes, and Policy Outcomes in Venezuela.* Inter-American Development Bank: Research Network Working Paper #R-507.

Naim, M. & F. Toro (2016). "Venezuela is falling apart", online essay, *The Atlantic,* May 12, 2016. https://www.theatlantic.com/international/archive/2016/05/venezuela-is-falling-apart/481755/, accessed: 25.11.2022.

Ostiguy, P. (2017). Populism: A socio-cultural approach. In C. R. Kaltwasser, P. Taggart, P. O. Espejo & P. Ostiguy (Eds.), *The Oxford Handbook of Populism* (pp. 73–97). Oxford: Oxford University Press.

Penfold-Becerra, M. (2007). Clientelism and social funds: Evidence from Chavez's Misiones. *Latin American Politics and Society, 49*(4), 63–84.

Pittaluga, G. B., E. Seghezza & P. Morelli (2021). The political economy of hyperinflation in Venezuela. *Public Choice, 186*(3), 337–350.

Rita, G. (1994). Bureaucracy and agricultural policy implementation in Venezuela (1958–1991). In A. Farazmand (Ed.), *Handbook of Bureaucracy* (pp. 501–516). New York, NY: Marcel Dekker, Inc.

Roberts, K. M. (1995). Neoliberalism and the transformation of populism in Latin America: The Peruvian case. *World Politics, 48*(1), 82–116.

Roberts, K. M. (2003). Social polarization and the populist resurgence in Venezuela. In S. Ellner & D. Hellinger (Eds.), *Venezuelan Politics in the Chavez Era* (pp. 55–72). Boulder, CO and London: Lynne Rienner Publishers.

Roberts, K. M. (2012). Populism and democracy in Venezuela under Hugo Chavez. In C. Mudde & C. Rovira Kaltwasser (Eds.), *Populism in Europe and Americas* (pp. 136–159). Cambridge: Cambridge University Press.

Salas, M. T. (2015). *Venezuela: What Everyone Needs to Know.* Oxford: Oxford University Press.

Schincariol, V. E. (2020). *Society and Economy in Venezuela – An Overview of the Bolivarian Period (1998–2018).* Cham: Springer.

Sutherland, M. (2018). La ruina de Venezuela no se debe al "socialismo" ni a la "revolución". *Nueva Sociedad, 274*, 142–151.

Toro, F. & D. Kronick (2015). "Venezuela's currency circus", online commentary, March 6, 2015, *The New York Times.* https://www.nytimes.com/2015/03/07/opinion/francisco-toro-dorothy-kronick-venezuelas-currency-circus.html, accessed: 25.11.2022.

Vera, L. (2015). Venezuela 1999–2014 – Macro-policy, oil governance and economic performance. *Comparative Economic Studies, 57*(3), 539–568.

Weisbrot, M. & L. Sandoval (2007). *The Venezuelan Economy in the Chávez Years.* Washington, DC: Center for Economic and Policy Research.

Weisbrot, M., L. Sandoval & D. Rosnick (2006). Poverty rates in Venezuela: Getting the numbers right. *International Journal of Health Services, 36*(4), 813–823.

Weyland, K. (1999). Neoliberal populism in Latin America and Eastern Europe. *Comparative Politics, 31*(4), 379–401.

Weyland, K. (2001). Clarifying a contested concept: Populism in the study of Latin American politics. *Comparative Politics, 34*(1), 1–22.

Weyland, K. (2003). Neopopulism and neoliberalism in Latin America: How much affinity? *Third World Quarterly, 24*(6), 1095–1115.

7

BUREAUCRACY DURING GREECE'S POPULIST DEMOCRACY

The PASOK practice

The PASOK and the rise of a "populist democracy"

Modern Greece emerged out of the Ottoman imperial order in the 1820s. For Greeks of the Balkan Peninsula, the Ottoman imperial state had been by no means an entity that they could trust although Greeks of İstanbul/Constantinople had a long-lasting loyalty to the "Sublime Porte" (*Bab-ı Âli*), a loyalty that extended to a period after Greek gained her independence. This legacy of lack of trust between the imperial state and local Greek communities kept shaping the state-society relations in Greece. Even after the independence of Greece and the establishment of the modern central Greek state, Greeks remained suspicious of central authorities and more trusting of local elites and power holders as well as immediate kin and family. Combined with the fact that modern Greece remained mainly as a rural country for a long period of time throughout the 19th and 20th centuries, this legacy of distrust towards the central state fostered widespread, persistent, and complicated patronage relations in Greek society. Greece's political development in the 19th and 20th centuries certainly witnessed a lot of formal institutional change and political turmoil. But the prevalence of patronage relations and their impact on the country's politics never changed although the way these particularistic relations are organized has changed remarkably, especially in the 1980s.

Following a long and tumultuous parliamentarian political experiment under the impact of various local oligarchies and monarchs, a bitter disappointment in irredentist adventures in Anatolia in the 1920s, an occupation in World War II by German forces, a civil war and a military dictatorship, Greece managed to make a transition to a more stable democracy only in the mid-1970s. The military dictatorship between 1967 and 1974 was certainly

DOI: 10.4324/9781003294627-10

154 Case studies

one of the factors that defined the democratic development and party-state-society relations in Greece since the 1970s. One of the legacies of the military dictatorship, apart from its rampant cruelty, was closing the ranks of the bureaucracy, particularly to the recruitment of left-wing sectors of society under the guise of a meritocratic administration. The conservative colonization of the state throughout the military junta rule deepened the already existing suspicion of large segments of Greek society towards the state and bureaucracy.

In 1974, Greece managed to make a transition to democracy amidst domestic and international political turmoil and a crisis with Turkey over the Cyprus issue. Most notably, the ruthless crushing of the Polytechnic uprising and the Turkish intervention to Cyprus as a response to the military coup by the Greek junta accelerated the fissures within the dictatorship and paved the way to its fall (Clogg 1997, 167–168). Konstantin Karamanlis, a prominent right-wing politician of the pre-authoritarian period, led the transition to democracy. Karamanlis aimed to create a moderately plural party system ideally consisting of two parties in the political realm and national economic growth through an interventionist state in the economic sphere. During the Karamanlis rule, apart from taking control of major sectors of the economy, the government deployed substantial subsidies and made direct investments to encourage economic growth. This was especially crucial when both foreign and domestic capital showed reluctance in making direct investments in Greece (Pappas 2014, 17–18). Thus, a state and public sector that was ripe for widespread patronage practices already started to emerge during the New Democracy (ND) government under Karamanlis. Another major development during the Karamanlis period was Greece's accession to the European Union which certainly consolidated the democracy in the country.

But the liberal and moderate democratic regime Karamanlis had in mind and that he tried to initiate in the second half of the 1970s was immediately challenged. The main challenger was Andreas Papandreou's Panhellenic Socialist Party (PASOK). While the party officially defined itself as a socialist entity, as will be revealed below, the defining discursive and practical inclinations for PASOK was "populism". Pappas succinctly puts the difference between Karamanlis's ND and Papandreou's PASOK: "We have seen that Karamanlis's program emphasized constitutional legality, formal procedural rules, mainstream party politics, political moderation, deliberation, compromise, and gradual political change. In sharp contrast, Papandreou favored extrainstitutional and rather informal politics, mass plebiscitary mobilization, adversarial tactics, and breaking with existing realities with a redemptive intent" (2014, 22).

Papandreou, at the most basic discursive level, embraced a deeply populist stance and presented politics to his followers as a struggle between good and evil, right and wrong. As Lyrintzis puts "a catch-all strategy which presented

Greek society as one split by the fundamental division between an all-embracing 'non-privileged' majority and a tiny 'privileged' oligarchy representing foreign interests and domestic 'monopolies'" (1987, 668) was one of the main factors explaining the rise of PASOK to power at the beginning of 1980s. As Stavrakakis notes, "PASOK not only addressed 'the people' [...], but also attempted to simplify the social topography according to a logic of equivalence, stressing the antagonism between them (the dominant sectors, the power-bloc) and us (the underdog, the oppressed and dominated sectors)" (2005, 248). A quotation from one of Papandreou's speeches is emblematic in this respect: "Our national independence will be guaranteed for us by the non-privileged Greeks, the workers, the farmers, the craftsmen, the salaried workers, the small-business professionals and the youth" (Papandreou 2014, 20–21). Papandreou juxtaposed this "cross-class under-dog alliance" against "the bourgeoisie, the big industrialists and entrepreneurs" and "the established oligarchic forces" (*Papandreou quoted in* Pappas 2014, 25).

One notable quality of PASOK in opposition, which will later impact the way the party ruled Greece, was its organization. As Papandreou argued in skilful rhetoric, "PASOK was a movement that arose from the 'guts of the people'" (Papandreou 2014, 21). Throughout its time as an opposition force, PASOK built a massive organization since Papandreou himself was in the opinion that they needed to "create [...] a massive popular base—[consisting of] the majority of Greeks who are both oppressed and denied the privileges of the economic oligarchy" (Papandreou 2014, 19). In August 1975 in a speech in Corfu, Papandreou was urging PASOK members to organize: "We must organize. We need a broad-based organization in all facets of the movement. Local organizations. Labor organizations in every facet of public political life" (Papandreou 2014, 19). It seems that throughout its years in opposition PASOK achieved a remarkable degree of organizational density and coherence. Between 1975 and 1977, when PASOK was in opposition, it appeared to be a mass party with routinized activities. Large masses were quite active at the party's grassroots, and the party activity at the local level had a remarkably ideological content. The party also had regular relations between the local branches and the centre (Ustaoğlu 2021, 654). In the period from 1977 to 1980, PASOK experienced a remarkable expansion in its organizational structure, accompanied by a consistent increase in the party's popularity among the voters (Lyrintzis 1982, 309). While entering the 1981 elections, the number of PASOK members was around 110,000, and the party headquarters also had the power to supervise both the local branches and the party in the parliament (Ustaoğlu 2021, 655–656). Membership numbers of PASOK doubled in a few years after the party came to power in 1981 (Moschonas 1999, 113). As Moschonas noted, "the expectations of 'individual gains' seem to have influenced this 'invasion' of new members to a significant degree, while the huge public sector was recruiting

156 Case studies

exclusively from within the movement's ranks" (Moschonas 1999, 113). But, as Lyrintzis implied in an early study on PASOK, the party was a novel force with regards to clientelistic operations, too, since it largely relied upon a new stratum of elites and, from the very beginning, had a tendency towards novel, more centralized forms of clientelism that had the potential to circumvent traditional local political elites of Greece (Lyrintzis 1984).

Nevertheless, the predominance of Papandreou over the PASOK was far from contested. Despite its very active organization, the leader was the determining force in PASOK (Spourdalakis 1985, 251; Lyrintzis 1987, 668–671). This certainly had something to do with the cross-class base of the PASOK and its populist discourse and practice that left so little room for a more ideologically driven and institutionalized organization (in terms of value fusion). As Moschonas noted, the personalistic leadership provided the PASOK, in classic populist fashion, with "greater tactical and strategic flexibility" that helped the party to "adjust better to new conjunctures" (1999, 115). Hence, as Lyrintzis asserts, PASOK was more "popular" than being "socialist" in a strictly doctrinaire sense of the term (1987, 672).

As soon as PASOK came into power in 1981, its populist orientation started to inform the party's way of ruling the country. PASOK initiated comprehensive redistributive strategies by deploying state resources and transforming the patterns of public employment and policy. These changes were based on a kind of revised Keynesian economics with profoundly redistributive inclinations (Spourdalakis 1985, 251; Moschonas 1999, 120). Such drastic changes in the public sector were only possible by a polarizing discourse that were condemning towards the ND in particular and the right in general (Pappas 2014, 29). As will be elaborated below, PASOK engaged in large-scale colonization of the state with its members, nationalization of private enterprises, and enlarging the public sector as a whole. As Mavrogordatos highlights, such massive changes were only possible and legitimate when the PASOK government was able to present the so-called previous meritocratic system in the public sector as an authoritarian fraud (1997, 18–19). But it should also be noted that PASOK governments had some real accomplishments in favour of the unprivileged segments of the Greek society ranging from raising the status of women to improving the conditions of poor, from enlarging the educational system for underprivileged sectors to establishing a free national health service (Spourdalakis 1985, 256). Such improvements were certainly the main pillar of the electoral appeal of the early PASOK years.

With the rise of PASOK rule, nothing remained the same in the Greek political system. As Pappas convincingly shows, PASOK's populist discourse and practice started to shape ND's strategies and way of ruling the country as well. After regaining power at the beginning of the 1990s, the ND faced a serious strategic choice between "liberalism" and "vote-catching populism". Thus, ND engaged in polarizing discourse as well as short-term,

Bureaucracy during Greece's populist democracy **157**

redistributive strategies in order to compete with the PASOK. In the 1990s, two major forces of the Greek party system started a race of overpromising in order to win a majority in elections. In an emblematic example, for instance, the ND leader promised the electorate a 152,000 drachmae minimum pension while PASOK was offering 150,000 (Pappas 2014, 34–35). Thus, populism, at a practical level, started to shape the entire Greek political system and transformed it into a "populist democracy", "a democratic subtype in which the party in government and (at least) the major opposition party are both populist" (Pappas 2014, 36).

No doubt that, during the so-called period of "populist democracy", Greek governments formally introduced many seemingly prudent policies requiring fiscal restraint and meritocratic recruitment and appointment in the bureaucracy. But, as will be demonstrated below, all of these policies were accompanied by formal and informal populist practices that juxtaposed or undermined the formal technocratic propensity. Thus, it would be fair to argue that a decisively populist logic and practice characterized the Greek politics after the rise of PASOK to power.[1] This "populist democracy", as will be discussed in length in the following parts of this chapter, was unsustainable in many respects and came to a bitter end starting with the 2008 economic crisis. The economic crisis led the PASOK and ND reluctantly to acknowledge the need for reform as a result of pressure from the EU. In a political system comprising constituencies who were used to a populist democracy, such drastic turn to neoliberal reform was unacceptable. This mainly paved the way to the rise of new, and more radical populist forces in Greece in the 2010s, both on the right and left, such as SYRIZA and ANEL.

State and bureaucracy in modern Greece

One of the historical legacies informed the relationship between Greek citizens and the bureaucratic institutions is the long Ottoman rule over Greece that lasted until the Greek War of Independence in 1820s. The relationship between Ottoman authorities and Greek populations was by no means smooth and shaped the view of Greek people towards any bureaucratic authority, even after they established their own state. Danopoulos and Danopoulos highlight a very important consequence of the Ottoman imperial legacy: "Subject people distrusted authority and instead sought the protection of local primates and chieftains—practices that continued in the decades following independence" (2001, 954).

At the beginning, the centralized administrative organization of the Greek state was not compatible at all with the highly rural and parochial Greek society of the 19th century (Danopoulos & Danopoulos 2001, 954–955). Because Greek modernizers, as Legg and Roberts (1997) argue, were in the opinion that a centralized bureaucracy was necessary in order to curb the

158 Case studies

autonomy of oligarchs and notables in the province. So, the attempts at constructing a centralized bureaucratic administration in Greece have always been in contradistinction with parochial forces such as notable families. Yet, the Greek state could gradually emerge as a centralized entity throughout the decades stretching from the 19th century to the 20th century (Legg & Roberts 1997, 72). Meanwhile, however, until at least the mid-20th century, large rural populations in Greece trusted powerful provincial notable families and "patrons" due to their accessibility and responsiveness more than the distant central bureaucratic authorities (Legg & Roberts 1997, 74).

One should, however, also note that this process of bureaucratic development was accompanied by an early oligarchic parliamentarian democracy that emerged at a very early stage following the independence of Greece (Sotiropoulos 1996, 17–18; Mouzelis 1986). This early parliamentarianism emerged in the mid-19th century and preceded the industrialization and the formation of sizeable urban industrial classes, and most notably, a well-organized working class. In the absence of the struggle between modern industrial classes, the state bureaucracy and resources in Greece have become the main arena of contestation and consensus between competing political forces in an oligarchic democracy (Sotiropoulos 1996, 18). Since these competing political forces were nothing more than personal patronage networks of powerful families and notables (Mouzelis 1985) patron-client relations deeply shaped the Greek bureaucracy from the beginning of its development onwards. Thus, the competition between various factions of the political class in this early parliamentarian regime, for a long time, had been over the distribution of the spoils of the state.

Therefore, the Greek bureaucracy, from its very beginning, has been a deeply politicized entity (Sotiropoulos 1996, 17). The form of this politicization changed, but essentially, it remained intact throughout decades of political development. One should also note here that this politicization is not akin to, for example, highly politicized and ideological worldview of the Kemalist bureaucracy in Turkey, which contained a kind of bureaucratic ethos. This politicization was largely about the clientelistic competition between the factions of the political class. Thus, Greek bureaucracy was always seen as a centralized but highly clientelistic entity providing employment to politically protected and supported personnel. In fact, clientelism through state resources has emerged as the main method of the political incorporation of the masses in Greece's modern competitive political system.

As a consequence, the Greek public administration and bureaucracy have many maladies repeated in many different accounts. Legg and Roberts vividly articulate these different ills of the Greek administration, which started to emerge in the 19th century such as the constant expansion of bureaucracy, overstaffing, underemployment, inefficiency, and political patronage under the auspices of local oligarchies (1997, 167). Nevertheless, one should also note the conservative character of the political elite that controlled the Greek bureaucracy and public administration at least until the rise of PASOK. As Sotiropoulos (1996) convincingly demonstrates, the patronage enjoyed by Greek public employees was provided by powerful conservative patrons until 1981. After the Civil War and with the rise of the Colonel's dictatorship, this conservative character of the patronage provided by the Greek political class only deepened (Sotiropoulos 1996, 30–32) despite the junta's "meritocratic claims".[2]

Ultimately, this structural relationship between the Greek public administration and the Greek political class created a kind of populist propensity – a tendency both in the political class and the ordinary people towards meeting material and symbolic expectations quickly and informally – even before the rise of PASOK. The Greek bureaucracy, for example, hardly possessed the necessary and reliable information (Legg & Roberts 1997, 171) that is *sine quo non* for a modern governmentality. "Short-termism", it seems that, has been the primary hallmark of the Greek bureaucracy in an obvious populist fashion since the major concern of the political "patrons" of Greek bureaucracy has always been winning elections more than public service. As a result, for example, problems like inflation and unemployment turned into permanent ills of government in Greece. The Greek state has also been very inefficient in terms of tax collection and the citizens have been usually prone to tax evasion (Legg & Roberts 1997, 173). There have always been so many people that were dependent on the state through patronage networks. Thus, it has been impossible to reduce the public employment in Greece. In a classic populist fashion, pay increases for public servants and pensioners and releasing new subsidies and public work projects before general elections have been common in Greek politics (Legg & Roberts 1997, 174–175). As Legg and Roberts argue, "one character of social policy is acceptance and implementation without reference to financial costs" (1997, 164).

Before moving to discussing the impact of PASOK on this fundamentally populist system of politics one should perhaps highlight the fact that populism, as a practice, is always "a game of two". For example, in the mid-20th century:

> For those arriving in Athens without capital, the standard practice was to construct illegal dwellings on the periphery of the city. Illegality itself assisted in the integration of such people into the political system. High land values reinforced the desirability of home or apartment ownership. Construction, as well as services such as water, electricity, and roads, and facilities such as schools required the support of a political patron. The suburbs of Athens and Piraeus were places where entrepreneurial politicians and the organizations of the left could mobilize votes. Over time, these new urbanites came to experience social mobility and saw continued

160 Case studies

population growth, and economic development increased the values of their homes and shops. Unfortunately, the continued growth of Athens and the economic and political advantages that ensued for some sectors of the population ultimately produced serious environmental and transportation problems. As the population grew and construction was done without much governmental planning, investments in public works such as parks and schools lagged.

(Legg & Roberts 1997, 80)

This is a pattern that is very similar to the urban development elaborated in Turkey in previous chapters. Ultimately, in populist practice, what we see is always a kind of collusion (or complicity) between sizeable groups of underprivileged people and a populist political class providing particularistic benefits. Thus, again, as Legg and Roberts argue, "it is in the nature of political discourse in Greece for political leaders to promise voters everything. Popular demands are translated into rights that require immediate satisfaction. Since support for mainstream parties could be found across class and occupational lines, this is not surprising" (1997, 176). The PASOK rule in this respect, was more typical compared to other periods of modern Greek political history due to several factors elaborated below.

Practices in public administration and public sector recruitment during the PASOK rule: Unbridled populist practice

The public administration in Greece had its ills before the rise of PASOK populism and the "populist democracy of Greece" – as termed by Pappas (2014) – that lasted until the 2010s. As researchers of modern Greek politics and state highlight, even before the rise of PASOK populism, Greek bureaucracy was not a meritocratic system at all (Sotiropoulos 1996; Spanou 2020). But there was a structural change with the rise of PASOK in the clientelistic practices directly related to state bureaucracy. One of the sources of this change was the discourse and organization PASOK embraced. Before the rise of PASOK, clientelistic practices in Greek politics and state were overwhelmingly under the control of prominent families and notables with oligarchic tendencies. But with the rise of PASOK's more deep-rooted populism with discursive and organizational implications "traditional clientelistic politics" became quickly outdated. As Mavrogordatos argued, "PASOK's accession to power in 1981 brought with it a quantum leap in party patronage, and the transformation of traditional clientelism into machine politics" (1997, 1). While traditional patronage was based on interpersonal patron-client relations, with the rise of PASOK, an "impersonal party machine" started to run clientelistic practices at a massive level in line with partisan affiliations (Mavrogordatos 1997, 17). There were mainly two consequences of this

The politicization of the bureaucracy

While patronage in public bureaucracy was rampant even before the rise of PASOK, as emphasized so far, the logic and mechanisms behind patronage recruitment by then were mostly particularistic and personal. The relationship between individual politicians, notables, and families was more important than partisan affiliation. With the rise of PASOK, the party membership became the main criterion of such patronage appointments in the public sector, and local, regional and national party organizations started to play important roles in clientelistic recruitments (Sotiropoulos 2020, 42). It seems that the weak state bureaucracy in Greece was easily subordinated by the powerful PASOK organization and this tradition of seeking total political control of the state was inherited by the ND governments after PASOK. The political landscape maintained a competitive nature where the dominant party reaped most of the benefits. However, as parties increasingly embraced clientelistic approaches and populism, the process of democratic learning suffered from a lack of consensus-building. This process involved the total political control of the administration by the so-called "underprivileged" segments affiliated with PASOK. During this process, many competent bureaucrats at top executive positions were replaced with politicized PASOK appointees (Spanou 2020, 174).

This dynamic, at some point, started to define almost every policy realm in Greece throughout the era of populist democracy. In public schools, telecommunications, the national bank, and enterprises, political appointments became the norm. In public secondary education, for example, "party clientelism operated freely when it came to the selection of school counsellors and administrators" (Mavrogordatos 1997, 7). In the public telecommunications institution, too, PASOK's accession to power brought with it widespread "partisan temporary appointments" (Mavrogordatos 1997, 7). In public National Bank, too, the public sector was not immune to populist politicization. According to Mavrogordatos, the National Bank in Greece had the reputation of being one of the most meritocratic institutions in contemporary Greece relying on "highly competitive examinations" in hiring new personnel (1997, 9). With the rise of PASOK this structure changed dramatically "due to operation of strictly partisan clientelism, mostly through the hiring of superfluous auxillary or temporary personnel, which was then massively promoted to higher and permanent status" (Mavrogordatos 1997, 10).

In his analysis, Mavrogordatos gives a dramatic example of PASOK's influence on the National Bank. Between 1982 and 1989, and later from 1993 onward, a particular deputy personnel manager played a pivotal

162 Case studies

role in facilitating PASOK's clientelism within the bank's personnel department. Initially employed by the bank in an unskilled position, his rapid advancement can be entirely attributed to his influence and authority within the party apparatus. Consequently, he exemplified the extreme impact of PASOK's practices on the careers of National Bank employees (Mavrogordatos 1997, 11). The same pattern, as a matter of fact, was valid for public industrial enterprises. In the Piraiki-Patraiki Cotton Manufacturing Company, the PASOK rule brought radical changes in recruitment from the mid-1980s onwards. The limited job openings within the company's management were exclusively occupied by individuals from the PASOK government who were affiliated with the party. Simultaneously, the PASOK party organization within the trade unions (PASKE) effectively took control of power within the company (Mavrogordatos 1997, 12).

The populist expansion

The increasing populist politicization of the bureaucracy was also accompanied by the expansion of the public sector in Greece. One of the sources of this expansion was the nationalization of previously private industries under the PASOK rule. During the PASOK rule, for example, Piraiki-Patraiki Cotton Manufacturing Company was taken over by the state and its personnel numbers increased in line with a clientelistic logic. The government hired 1,000 new workers in 1985 (Pappas 2014, 41–42). In fact, there were a lot of state-owned enterprises in Greece (Sotiropoulos 2020, 44). And during the PASOK rule, the number of employees in these enterprises increased dramatically. By the mid-1990s, the Greek public enterprise sector alone employed about 130,000 individuals, or the equivalent to 6 percent "of wage earners, whose operations were often inefficient, the quality of service generally unsatisfactory with repercussions on other sectors, and [all in all] an extensive drain on the public purse" (Pappas 2014, 47).

But the major changes in this respect emerged in the already existing public sector and administration. In fact, even before the rise of PASOK, the Greek public administration was already overstaffed and inefficient. The percentage of employees in the total population was remarkably high although this high proportion of public employees never improved the quality of public services. But with the rise of PASOK there were dramatic increases in the public sector employment. As Pappas (2014) notes, at the beginning of the 1980s, the Greek public sector was employing slightly more than 500,000 personnel. In 1990 this figure was 786,200 employees, "an increase of over 50 per cent in a single decade" (Pappas 2014, 47). In 2009, this figure was above 1 million which corresponded to the "22 per cent of the country's active workforce" (Pappas 2014, 47). Thus, "for three decades, each of Greece's major parties had striven to outbid the other with promises to society of state-related entitlements" (Pappas 2014, 45).

The enlargement of higher education is another solid evidence of the practical populist logic at work in the public sector. As Lyrintzis (1987) notes, in a society where higher education has always been viewed as a pathway to achieve upward social mobility and where every lower and middle-class family aspires to have their children admitted to university, the PASOK government opted to announce ambitious initiatives. These included plans to establish new universities and gradually increase student enrolment rather than addressing fundamental issues. In the PASOK period, however, the value of university degrees diminished, leading to high unemployment rates among various categories of university graduates. Instead of tackling these challenges, PASOK succumbed to popular demands for more higher education by creating new universities, exacerbating existing problems. By expanding these universities and establishing new ones in the Aegean and Ionian islands, PASOK aimed to present itself as a champion of the people's right to education. However, this approach neglected investments in existing institutions for consolidation and modernization, and overlooked the social and economic needs of Greek society (Lyrintzis 1987, 680–681).

As Lyrintzis (1987) asserts, the enlargement of higher education in Greece perfectly reflects the populist logic. This was the case because of two interrelated respects. This enlargement did not only render the access to higher education easier for masses, but it must have created new opportunities for clientelistic employment in the rapidly enlarged higher education sector for PASOK supporters, thus contributing to the enlargement of the public sector in general. But, as Lyrintzis (1987) notes, the "short-termism" of populism is evident in this realm of public sector and policy, too, as is the case with the imprudent and inefficient expansion of the public sector employment in general. The populist logic behind the politicization of the public bureaucracy and the expansion of the public sector is evident. But how these consequences emerged, how populism operated in practice to create the politicization and expansion of the public sector is still missing in this story. In the following part of this chapter, I address the operational nature of populism and its "tactical" orientation aiming at satisfying the immediate needs of supportive masses.

Populist "tactics" satisfying the immediate needs of supportive "underprivileged" segments

While the Greek bureaucracy was not a perfect embodiment of Weberian legal-rational authority, it nevertheless, throughout decades, developed views attaching importance to the rational and meritocratic recruitment patterns (Sotiropoulos 1996, 17–34). Ironically, these views were put into action in

164 Case studies

the realm of public recruitment by PASOK governments through various laws aiming at a more meritocratic system starting in 1983 (Sotiropoulos 1996, 85–96). Especially in 1994, the Greek government decided to introduce a central authority to administer tenure-track public employment in order to curb the impact of clientelism. But as already noted, in the 1990s and 2000s, the number of public employees kept increasing. So, how was it possible for the populist PASOK and ND to increase the number of public employees under pressure to reform the public sector? The answer demonstrates the majoritarian and tactical nature of populism that subtly circumvents procedures with political cunning. One of the major methods of increasing the number of public employees in a clientelistic manner under the strain of meritocratic reforms was abusing short-term contracts. As Sotiropoulos notes, "further on, after completing several [...] temporary job contracts, public employees mobilized to demand the change of their job status from temporary to permanent. With the help of either PASOK or ND governments temporary employees were eventually successful in this endeavour" (2020, 42).

In this case, what we see is that populist supply and demand in practice meets and enlarges the public employment in contradistinction to a long-term rationality. This happens, first, through the supply of public sector jobs by populist politicians via short-term contracts. This is followed by the demand of populist constituencies for more entrenched benefits, which is ultimately being realized with the granting of permanent positions to the beneficiaries of clientelistic practices. As Spanou (Spanou 2020) highlights, there was a notable increase in the practice of employing individuals on short-term contracts, primarily based on partisan considerations, with the implicit commitment to grant them permanent positions later on. These discretionary short-term appointments circumvented the official hiring protocols, and a substantial number of tenure requests were granted during electoral periods. This approach undermined the concept of human resources planning in both qualitative and quantitative aspects. Consequently, the resulting misallocation of resources became an ongoing problem, while an emphasis on a labour-intensive administrative approach rendered the imperative for technological and operational modernization weaker (Spanou 2020, 174).

The populist practice emerged out of populist supply and demand in the realm of public bureaucracy was not only related to recruitment. It was also related to payment and retirement patterns. High increases in salaries with the rise of PASOK were no doubt related to the fact that salaried employees had remarkably low levels of income, and there was a remarkable degree of inflation in the Greek economy before 1981. But as Pappas (2014) notes, public employees in the mid-1990s were receiving wages twice the amount in the private sector. Powerful public sector trade unions organized in public enterprises related to key services and goods were forming the populist demand in this respect. When these trade unions thought it was necessary, they did not shy away from using their "power to hold the country hostage to their demands" (Pappas 2014, 47). The expansionary populist logic in the Greek public bureaucracy was also evident in the social security arrangements. In the early 1980s, "pensions were increased, coverage was extended to new groups of [the] population and the level of minimum pensions provided by IKA [Greece's major pension fund for private wage earners] was fixed at 20 times the minimum wage of unskilled workers" (Pappas 2014, 48). Not surprisingly, the most privileged strata of pension receivers were public enterprise employees. Staggeringly, such pensioners could receive wages more than the amount they were earning as active workers. It should also be noted that, in a classic populist fashion, although the official retirement age in Greece was 65 throughout most of the 1990s (Featherstone & Papadimitriou 2008, 90), "early retirement was widespread", which no doubt, in many instances, required the bending of rules (Pappas 2014, 48).

The populist practice in Greece also unfolded in ignoring many other widespread illegal practices benefitting ordinary majorities. As Pappas and Aslanidis relate, in addition to "tangibles" such as public employment, high wages, and pensions, many intangible benefits were also associated with the populist democracy of Greece "ranging from the selective protection by the state to several professions against market hazards to widespread impunity from violating the law (as in the cases of tax evasion, illegal construction or squatting on state property)" (2015, 184). Although the Greek state has never been successful in tax collection, this problem became more acute during the era of "populist democracy". On the one hand, the large informal sector escaped the record, and on the other hand, populist sensitivities rendered effective tax collection a liability. All these dynamics together made it really difficult for the Greek state to collect taxes. Especially in election periods, the Greek state has been very reluctant to "punish evaders" and chase the "tax" debt (Pappas 2014, 49). A very similar pattern of populist impunity can be seen in "illegal construction": "It has been estimated that as many as one million homes and other dwellings have been built illegally in Greece in recent decades. In a fashion resembling their response to rampant tax evasion, successive cash-strapped Greek governments have periodically promised to legalize illegally built dwellings for a fee, but not with any significant success" (Pappas 2014, 50). It is not hard to imagine that pragmatic amnesties for such illegal constructions have been widespread before elections, as was the case in Turkey regarding slum houses (*gecekondular*).

Such a flawed public administration and policy certainly invited discussions of reform in Greece. In the 1990s, 2000s, and 2010s, administrative reform was at the top of the agenda. But the historical legacies "subordinating welfare functions to clientelistic and corporatist pressures" outlined so far were major hindrances to these reforms (Spanou 2020, 173). More important than this, the mindset of Greek majorities was accustomed to populist

166 Case studies

practice and supply. Large majorities gained materially from this informal social contract with very little effort and they were very reluctant to support reform minded politicians (Pappas 2014, 66).

All these structural problems generated by populist governmental practice accumulated in an unprecedented economic and political crisis in Greece in the 2010s. In 2010, the Greek state had to ask for foreign loans from the IMF, and foreign lenders imposed a strict austerity program on the Greek government. In fact, the Greek system of populist democracy was already crumbling towards the end of the 2000s. Austerity measures implemented by main actors of this populist democracy including decreasing the number of public jobs, diminishing role of state in economy, and the increasingly more pro-private business environment curbing labour rights, were by no means popular among populist constituencies. On the contrary, these measures' "implementation was stalled due to society's lack of cooperation" (Pappas 2014, 74–75). The result was widespread social unrest following the economic crisis and the fall of the party system dominated by PASOK and the ND starting with the 2012 general elections (for a vivid and concise review of the period after 2010, see Pappas 2014, especially chapters 9 to 13).

Concluding discussion: The practical and tactical nature of populism

The interaction between public bureaucracy and competitive politics, particularly in the era that started with the rise of PASOK rule, provides ample evidence for understanding populism as a governmental practice. First, the oligarchic democracy preceding industrialization and bureaucracy formation, and then the introduction of systematic mass clientelism by PASOK governments, created the basis of a remarkably developed form of a populist governmental practice in Greece. The predominance of notables and powerful patrons in politics subjugated the Greek bureaucracy to the country's conservative political class in the absence of an industrialized and urbanized society well before the rise of *metapolitefsi*. Thus, patron-client relations accompanying an oligarchic competitive politics turned the Greek bureaucracy and public employment into a large-scale patronage resource for the competing elites. This legacy of an early parliamentarian regime in Greece facilitated a certain "tacit agreement", "virtual consensus" or "informal social contract" between Greek citizens/voters and the political elite. In this agreement, political elites had the obligation to provide jobs, privileges, licences, guidance, and room for avoidance from "unpopular" legal measures to their clientele and the clientele has the obligation to provide the patrons with demanded political support in forms of votes and mobilization. In a competitive political system, these mutual obligations gradually became prevalent at the mass and elite levels over the decades. Thus, politicians' particularistic responsiveness started to be seen as part and parcel of usual democratic politics.

With the rise of PASOK based on a massive organization, the previous system of personal patronage was replaced with systematic mass clientelism and a more marked populism with discursive features. The PASOK, with its superior organization and populist worldview, challenged the oligarchic political class and their personal patronage networks in Greek democracy and replaced this with mass clientelism recruiting from underprivileged sectors of Greek society. The PASOK, in a sense, re-colonized the Greek bureaucracy (which was already colonized by conservative clients of the oligarchic political class) in line with a populist ethos and with "new men". Thus, the populist practice and the clientelistic nature of the Greek political system did not change entirely with the rise of PASOK. But PASOK's deeply populist discourse, worldview and practice, was much more evident compared to the previous eras and kept defining Greek politics even after its demise. As Pappas (2014) demonstrated, PASOK's populism transformed the liberal ND into a populist actor and drove it towards populist and clientelistic competition of imprudent overpromising to citizens.

To a certain extent, however, one can argue that the populist practice in Greek politics stretching from the oligarchic period to the PASOK rule and beyond was successful in several respects. It incorporated Greek people to a new state and political system skilfully throughout a prolonged period starting with Greece's independence. Especially in the PASOK period, it consolidated the democratic experience and incorporated left-wing citizens through systematic mass clientelism who were excluded from the political system after the Civil War. The *metis* embedded in populist practice helped the Greek political system to incorporate its own periphery into national politics, first through local patrons and notables, then through the parties of the *metapolitefsi* based on full-fledged populism. And this is done through allowing the material demands of the masses – regardless of the fact that they were rightful or not – to reach to the top and responded by the elites.

The problem with this particularistic responsiveness of the Greek political system, however, was its short-term perspective, which ultimately culminated in an unprecedented economic crisis in the 2010s. Large numbers of public employees (recruited through short-term contracts tactically and later on promoted to permanent positions), widespread tax evasion ignored by a populist ruling class and an incapacitated bureaucracy, generous pay increases to public servants and pensioners before elections, disregard for formal rules when the issue was popular demands, etc. culminated into an economic, political and social crisis in Greece. In short, populist practices that were targeting to satisfy the immediate needs of large chunks of voters/clienteles in a competitive system were actually not sustainable at all. From a more general point of view, the problem with populist practice and its tactical

168 Case studies

nature, immediacy, informality, and over-responsiveness is also about its disregard for institutional rationality and the importance of such rationality for sustainability. But these anti-institutional tendencies are essential to a populist logic: "As Papandreou himself once famously declared during a widely televised party rally: 'There are no institutions - only the people rule in this country.'" (Pappas 2014, 28).

This again brings us to the theory of populism. It is not surprising that, with such a rich repertoire of populist discourses and practices, Greek scholars have always been at the forefront of discussions on populism from Mouzelis (1985, 1986) to Lyrintzis (1987) and Sotiropoulos (1996), and from Pappas (2014) to Stavrakakis and Katsambekis (2014). But, from the perspective developed in this book, it should be acknowledged that the earlier generation of Greek scholars writing on the PASOK practice in power –when PASOK was still a powerful actor in Greek politics – had a much deeper understanding of the practical and material dimension of the phenomenon of populism. Therefore, they had a more materialist conception of populism than what we observe today in the populism scholarship. For example, in his seminal work on PASOK populism, Sotiropoulos strongly asserts the populist character of PASOK, and unlike Mouzelis (1985, 1986), he does not think that the PASOK was populist only because of the party's discourse or particular way of organization and mobilization of constituencies. Sotiropoulos argues that "it is important to characterize PASOK as a typical populist party rather than any other type of party or hybrid party, because its populist character explains to a large degree its behaviour while in power, and this kind of behaviour, in turn, justifies attaching the label 'populist' to PASOK" (1996, 46–47). But it was another author, writing on PASOK in the mid-1980s, who was clearer on the practical nature of the phenomenon of populism. According to Christos Lyrintzis, what is more important regarding the phenomenon of populism is not ideology, discourse, or worldview but political practice:

> Populism, though defined in terms of ideology and approached as a specific logic constructing its own discourse, is by no means restricted at the level of discourse. Populism has direct implications for political practice. The relationship between state and civil society is affected by populist logic which transforms all kinds of demands into legitimate rights of the people that require immediate satisfaction. It is in this sense that one can speak of populist policies.
>
> *(1987, 682)*

Finally, it should be reasserted that populism, as a practice, is a game of two. At times, it appears as paternalistic supply for the material demands of underprivileged majorities. In this respect, it is a beneficial collusion between

Bureaucracy during Greece's populist democracy **169**

the populist elite and their underprivileged supporters. But at other times, it takes the form of complicity, satisfaction of unrightfully demanded mass privileges by a political elite lacking a long-term horizon. Both the bright and the dark faces of populism as a political-governmental practice can be clearly seen in the case of Greece and particularly in the populist conduct of bureaucracy under PASOK rule.

Notes

1 I would like to thank Dimitri Sotiropoulos for drawing my attention to this point of controversy.
2 Mavrogordatos highlights how the colonel's junta in Greece used the clientelistic character of the Greek political system and presented it as a "corrupt parliamentary regime" as a pretext for the military intervention (1997, 2).

References

Clogg, R. (1997). *A Concise History of Greece*. Cambridge: Cambridge University Press.
Danopoulos, C. P. & A. C. Danopoulos (2001). Greek bureaucracy and public administration. In A. Farazmand (Ed.), *Handbook of Comparative and Development Public Administration* (pp. 953–961). New York and Basel: Marcel Dekker, Inc.
Featherstone, K. & D. Papadimitriou (2008). *The Limits of Europeanization – Reform Capacity and Policy Conflict in Greece*. New York: Palgrave MacMillan.
Legg, K. R. & J. M. Roberts (1997). *Modern Greece – a Civilization on the Periphery*. London: Routledge.
Lyrintzis, C. (1982) The rise of Pasok: The Greek election of 1981. *West European Politics*, 5(3), 308–313.
Lyrintzis, C. (1984). Political parties in post-junta Greece: A case of "bureaucratic clientelism"?. *West European Politics*, 7(2), 99–118.
Lyrintzis, C. (1987). The power of populism: The Greek case. *European Journal of Political Research*, 15(6), 667–686.
Mavrogordatos, G. T. (1997). From traditional clientelism to machine politics: The impact of PASOK populism in Greece. *South European Society and Politics*, 2(3), 1–26.
Moschonas, G. (1999). The Panhellenic Socialist Movement. In R. Ladrech & P. Marliere (Eds.), *Social Democratic Parties in the European Union – History, Organization, Policies* (pp. 110–122). London: MacMillan.
Mouzelis, N. (1985). On the concept of populism: Populist and clientelist modes of incorporation in semiperipheral polities. *Politics & Society*, 14(3), 329–348.
Mouzelis, N. P. (1986). *Politics in the Semi-Periphery*. New York: Macmillan.
Papandreou, N. (2014). "Life in the First Person and the Art of Political Storytelling: The Rhetoric of Andreas Papandreou". Greece Paper no. 85. London: The Hellenic Observatory, The London School of Economics.
Pappas, T. (2014). *Populism and Crisis Politics in Greece*. New York: Palgrave Macmillan.
Pappas, T. & A. Aslanidis (2015). Greek populism: A political drama in five acts. In H. Kriesi and T. S. Pappas (Eds.), *European Populism in the Shadow of the Great Recession* (pp. 181–196). Colchester: ECPR Press.

170 Case studies

Sotiropoulos, D. A. (1996). *Populism and Bureaucracy: The Case of Greece under PASOK, 1981–1989*. Notre Dame and London: University of Notre Dame Press.

Sotiropoulos, D. A. (2020). State-society relations in Greece. In K. Featherstone & D. A. Sotiropoulos (Eds.), *The Oxford Handbook of Modern Greece* (pp. 38–53). Oxford: Oxford University Press.

Spanou, C. (2020). Public administration. In K. Featherstone & D. A. Sotiropoulos (Eds.), *The Oxford Handbook of Modern Greece* (pp. 171–186). Oxford: Oxford University Press.

Spourdalakis, M. (1985). The Greek experience. *Socialist Register, 22,* 249–267.

Stavrakakis, Y. (2005). Religion and populism in contemporary Greece. In F. Panizza (Ed.), *Populism and the Mirror of Democracy* (pp. 224–249). London and New York: Verso.

Stavrakakis, Y. & G. Katsambekis (2014). Left-wing populism in the European periphery: The case of SYRIZA. *Journal of Political Ideologies, 19*(2), 119–142.

Ustaoğlu, B. (2021). Yunanistan'da Panhellenik Sosyalist Hareket'in (PASOK) kuruluşu ve iktidara yükselişi (1974–1981). *Balkan Araştırma Enstitüsü Dergisi, 10*(2), 635–681.

8

POPULIST JUDICIAL PRACTICE IN INDIA UNDER BJP RULE

Challenging secularism via judicial tactics

Two modes of populism in India

Well before the term became popular in Western political science literature, various episodes of contemporary Indian political history since the independence have been identified with the term populism by its students. There have been two different understandings of populism with reference to modern Indian politics that emerged after the independence. One of these understandings pertains to the realm of "politics as usual", which relies upon deploying a repertoire of redistributive measures consisting of various patronage and social policy-based means to appeal to the underprivileged segments of the society. Such redistributive practices targeting selected individuals and constituencies close to national and regional parties incrementally gained a pejorative meaning, and, therefore, populism in the Indian context started to connote irresponsible pledges and policies of political parties.

The second understanding of populism with reference to post-independence India is more compatible with current predominant approaches to populism in the scholarly literature. Such understandings, first, in line with an ideational and discursive approach, underline the discourse of various political leaders appealing to unprivileged majorities by highlighting the corruption of elites. These mainstream understandings of Indian populism also emphasize the direct, plebiscitary bond between personalistic leaders and ordinary majorities that circumvent organizational or clientelistic intermediation. Particularly, the rule of Indira Gandhi in the 1970s and the rule of Modi from the 2010s onwards are seen as examples of such political populism in India.

DOI: 10.4324/9781003294627-11

172 Case studies

While, today, the understanding of populism as a redistributive strategy is heavily criticized by the predominant approaches in the scholarly literature, it is, in fact, exactly such practical aspects of "populism" in contemporary India that shapes the nexus between leaders, parties and the voters. It can even be argued that such practical implementation provides flesh and bone to the recent right-wing populist discourses, ideas, and mobilization in India, as will be revealed in the parts regarding the populist judicial/legislative practice in this chapter. It should also be noted at the beginning that the populist practice in the judicial realm in India was not really about the ideational content of judicial verdicts – as emphasized by conceptual propositions on judicial populism[1] – but more about majoritarian and tactical uses of judicial instruments by populists in line with the general theoretical arguments of this book. In the following parts of the chapter, however, first, I would like to briefly demonstrate the origins of populism in India and then demonstrate the two modes of populist politics and the intersection between these modes: Populist redistributive practice and ideational/mobilizational populism.

Factors facilitating the growth of populism in India

There have been several factors that rendered populism relevant for understanding the case of India. First of all, the nation's colonial past and the humiliation this past inflicted upon various groups in India, and particularly upon the Hindu majority, was one of the factors that should be taken into account in the growth of populism in India. The major legacy of the tight colonial bond between India and Britain has been ironically the control of a Westernized elite over the independence struggle against Britain run by the Indian National Congress. In the 1980s, for example, Charan Singh, a former Congress member, representing an agrarian populism, was depicting the Nehru family as an "Ox-bridge educated elite" who were distant to the harsh realities of poor rural Indian populations (Jaffrelot & Tillin 2017, 183). The other legacy of the Congress rule after the independence facilitating populism in India has been its liberal secularist orientation that was prone to protect Muslim minorities and lower castes across India. Such strict secular ethos of modern India under the progressive rule of the Indian National Congress gradually triggered populism in the form of Hindu nationalism. As Jaffrelot and Tillin highlight, for the Hindu nationalists, "enemies are not the establishment defined in socio-economic terms, but an establishment defined in cultural terms, a group made of English speaking, Westernized-up-rooted elites who defend secularism at the expense of the authentic, Hindu identity of the nation. [...] they complain about the appeasement of Muslim minorities by 'pseudo-secular' Congress governments" (2017, 184).

One should also acknowledge the sheer size and ethnic and regional diversity of modern India laying the ground for regional populist reactions in various Indian states and particularly in the Southern states. Despite its federal structure, there has always been a centralizing tendency in the post-Independence India. But the nation building processes provoked populist ethno-nationalisms as early as the 1960s, as it is well documented by the work of Narendra Subramanian (1999). For example, "[the Tamil political identity] developed a popular appeal more through its association with 'plebian' cultural modes than as an anti-outsider platform. It was associated with non-Sanskritic cultural traditions that were strongest among intermediate and lower castes; with those who spoke Tamil more than English; and was opposed to national political elites who sought the imposition of Hindi as a national language" (Jaffrelot & Tillin 2017, 190).

Besides its cultural diversity and the tension between centralizing and regional forces, rigid socio-economic and socio-cultural hierarchies apparently created another kind of populism in the form of personalistic national political leadership in India. India's rigidly layered society on the basis of caste and class differences created a kind of hierarchical "patronage democracy" populated by various brokers-patrons between ordinary people and national elites (Kenny 2017, especially see chapter 4). While this system worked very well for a long time after the independence, and especially throughout the Nehru period, in the 1970s it started to crumble and paved the way to the rise of the personalistic populism of Indira Gandhi that was directly appealing to ordinary people over the heads of regional and local bosses (Kenny 2017, especially chapters 5 and 6). No doubt that this patronage system was also prone to corruption and this rendered challenges to it by strong populists like Gandhi possible. In the 2010s, this time, it was Modi who "sidelined the Bharatiya Janata Party (BJP) organization, appealed directly to the Indian public through sophisticated use of technology including simulcast speeches by 3D holograms of himself, and fostered state of permanent mobilization that seeks to bypass intermediaries" (Jaffrelot & Tillin 2017, 180). Modi and BJP also never missed the opportunity to depict the Congress rule as the domination of corrupt secularist elites (Chacko 2018, 553; Chakrabarti & Bandyopadhyay 2021, 100–102). Another factor that should certainly be taken into account as the basis of populist politics in modern India has been the widespread poverty in the sub-continent. This, as the part below will scrutinize, created redistributive populist practices all over the political spectrum to respond quickly to the immediate needs of unprivileged majorities in India.

Redistributive populism

Even the most mainstream approaches to populism in India acknowledge the prevalence of redistributive practices in Indian politics. According to Jaffrelot and Tillin, for example, populist movements and parties in South

174 Case studies

India usually engage with various redistributive practices appealing to poor people (2017, 189). In South India what is called "paternalistic populism" has always been based on strategies such as distributing food to poor schoolchildren (Jaffrelot & Tillin 2017, 190). Chakrabarti and Bandyopadhyay (2021) provide an excellent account of such redistributive populist practices in India, which certainly was not confined to the period of rule by Indira Gandhi and Narendra Modi. As Chakrabarti and Bandyopadhyay highlight, "populism in popular parlance in India is used to refer to virtually any policy that is redistributive in nature instead of being purely growth oriented. This is particularly true when such a policy is announced before impending elections" (2021, 98). While such redistributive strategies can be expected of regional and local social democratic and communist forces, one can come across the implementation of such strategies by almost every political actor in India. This fact makes it possible to think certain types of redistributive strategies independent from the left-wing ideological proclivities.[2] As Chakrabarti and Bandyopadhyay further note, according to this conception of populism, employment assurance programs, food security legislation (ensuring a certain quantity of subsidized food grains), and elderly pension initiatives established in various states are all considered "populist" measures. The same applies to periodic debt waiving initiatives for farmers and, indeed, all the different forms of occasional subsidies. All of these can be categorized as part of the overarching theme of "populism". Thus, in line with the argument in this book, Chakrabarti and Bandyopadhyay explicitly state that it is important to focus on the "practice of populism" (2021, 98–99).

Chakrabarti and Bandyopadhyay (2021) also assert that the media in India has typically employed the term "populism" to describe the irregular allocation of public resources for distributing goods to voters. Due to these associations with politics aimed at pleasing the masses, populism has acquired a negative connotation. Politicians embracing populist strategies are often accused of providing "freebies" or "sops" and appealing to the less noble impulses of the electorate. It is presumed that populist leaders govern in irrational and imprudent manners, potentially endangering fiscal stability through their generosity (Chakrabarti & Bandyopadhyay 2021, 99–100). While it is important to approach this common sense understanding with caution, there is no doubt that the Indian case provides ample evidence that populism is something more than mere words. According to Chakrabarti and Bandyopadhyay, many political parties believe that offering individual and group benefits is the most effective strategy for winning the support of voters, particularly to those who are economically disadvantaged. Therefore, it can be asserted that populist measures served as the means by which politicians secured votes and attained power in India (Chakrabarti & Bandyopadhyay 2021, 104).

Thus, in various parts of India, it is possible to see redistributive populist implementations such as distributing highly subsidized food to the poor in Tamil Nadu and free laptops for students in Uttar Pradesh (Chakrabarti & Bandyopadhyay 2021, 107–111). While these populist measures found solutions to immediate problems of poverty, as Chakrabarti and Bandyopadhyay (2021) argue, their cost has usually been the sacrifice of long-term development and investment. While subsidized food restaurants in Tamil Nadu brought corruption and state inefficiency regarding long-term solutions to poverty (Chakrabarti & Bandyopadhyay 2021, 108), in Uttar Pradesh, in order to address the problems within the education system with cutting-edge technology, the state government overlooked the fact that the majority of schools in this state lacked access to electricity, let alone desktop computers. In the specific context of Uttar Pradesh, allocating resources to construct schools or purchase books for the school library could have a lasting positive impact, benefitting multiple generations of students and remaining accessible to all within the school community. Nevertheless, when a government chooses to distribute laptops to individual students, it essentially transforms public resources into private possessions (Chakrabarti & Bandyopadhyay 2021, 111). Yet, from the perspective of the populist audiences, importance of such benefits should not be overlooked.

Ideational/mobilizational populism

In the scholarly literature, however, what is deemed especially populist in the context of post-independence India has been the personalistic rule of two national leaders, respectively: Indira Gandhi from the Congress Party and Narendra Modi from the BJP. No need to say that such approaches to populism in India embrace ideational/discursive or mobilizational perspectives and adopt the approaches by Mudde (2004) and Weyland (2001), respectively, or a combination of these two different approaches. From this mainstream perspectives, Jaffrelot and Tillin (2017) underline the prevalence of personalistic and populist leadership in contemporary India. According to these authors, both Gandhi and Modi "in different ways, saturated the public sphere with images of their person and governed in a way that sought both to embody the 'people', variously depicted, and to reach to them over the heads of political intermediaries" (Jaffrelot & Tillin 2017, 179). Therefore, Jaffrelot and Tillin see Modi's populism as directly related to his success at circumventing the BJP organization and intermediaries through the use of sophisticated technology to appeal to broad masses (2017, 180). In a similar vein, Kenny (2017) depicts the populism of Indira Gandhi in the 1970s as a struggle against Congress bosses and brokers. According to this particular account, it was only after the demise of the broker autonomy in the National Congress that Gandhi's direct appeal to

176 Case studies

the Congress electorate through a populist discourse has been possible. So, according to Kenny (2017), populism has been the result of the crisis of patronage democracies.

One should, however, also note that ideational and leader-centred mobilizational approaches to populism also draw attention to the anti-elite and anti-corruption discourses of these populist leaders. Hence, they combine discursive/ideational and mobilizational/strategic approaches to the phenomenon of populism in India. For example, Gandhi's populism was not only about her circumvention of the Congress bosses and highlighting her own persona. But it was also about a discourse that accused patronage-oriented Congress politics and appealed very well to ordinary people and poor (Kenny 2017, 112). Similarly, Modi's – and many other BJP leaders' – discourse shows clear evidence for a discursive and performative kind of populism. Modi always depicted himself as an ordinary Hindu in front of the masses: "Modi's populism in office has largely manifested in his continued self-promotion as a 'common man', fighting a corrupt system from the inside. Hence, in his first Independence Day speech after taking office in 2014, he told the crowd: 'I come from a poor family', and 'I am an outsider for Delhi ... I have been quite isolated from the elite class of this place'" (McDonnell & Cabrera 2019, 492). As the work of McDonnell and Cabrera (2019) convincingly demonstrates, most of the BJP elite deploy a similar mind set and discourse. For, the BJP elites described a variety of social segments and institutions representing elites including prestigious universities and their students, some judges, and most notably the Congress Party as their enemies. Especially the Congress was depicted as a "party of rich elites that was very distant from the people and utterly centred on the Gandhi family, which itself was not really Indian (and hence not of the people)" in the interviews conducted by McDonnell and Cabrera with BJP elites (2019, 489).

What brings these two faces of populism – the redistributive practice and the ideational/mobilizational dimension built around personalistic leadership-together has been that both of these populisms shared an anti-institutional and anti-procedural logic that was highly sensitive to practical and immediate majoritarian expectations. Thus, Chakrabarti and Bandyopadhyay raise an important point when arguing that "populists, due to their plebiscitary view on democracy, inevitably end up being motivated by public opinion and mood, and therefore populist decisions can become more responsive and at the same time more irresponsible. In favoring quick decisions over patient negotiations, they diminish the quality of the decision-making process" (Chakrabarti & Bandyopadhyay 2021, 119). This is certainly the outcome in the judicial/legislative realm, as the evidence from India below in the following parts demonstrates.

State, politics, and judiciary in modern India

While the British colonial legacy was key to the development of state, bureaucracy, and judiciary in modern India, it is important to acknowledge the impact of pre-colonial and pre-modern legacy of South Asia in these institutions' formation. Before the British colonial rule, the South Asian sub-continent was a melting pot for various foreign invaders and native rulers. For example, while the Muslim Mughal rule was keen to articulate the native elites to the administrative system, they also introduced the "mansabdari system"[3] (Bose & Jalal 2004, 30). Thus, even before the modern era, there was a built-in tension between centralizing and decentralizing proclivities in the formation of administrative and judicial apparatuses in the Indian sub-continent simply due to its territorial vastness and astounding social, cultural, and ethnic heterogeneity. The result was a highly syncretic administrative and judicial structure mixing the legal systems of foreign invaders and that of native elites.

With the introduction of British colonial rule in the mid-18th century – first in the form of company rule, then in the form of direct colonial rule by the British crown – these tensions did not change considerably and remained intact. For example, the company rule in the 19th century, at least formally, acknowledged the status of local elites and their judicial traditions. While English judicial practices were gradually introduced into the civil and criminal law domains, certain fundamental aspects of the Mughal legal system were retained. The officials of the East India Company did not only seek the counsel of Mughal law experts, including qazis, muftis, and pandits, but also respected and implemented their judgments as long as they aligned with principles of justice, fairness, and moral conscience. This pragmatic approach was adopted by the colonial power with the explicit aim of reducing the risk of social backlash. In line with this strategy, significant efforts were made to avoid offending the sensibilities of colonial subjects by refraining from making provoking changes to Muslim and Hindu personal laws (Bose & Jalal 2004, 58).

Nevertheless, the continuity with the pre-colonial past in the Indian legal sphere during the colonial period should not be exaggerated. There were profound changes to the legal system of India introduced by the colonial rule.[4] The British rule created many new inequalities and social groups and identities within the Indian sub-continent (Bose & Jalal 2004, 79), and all of these new identities/groups found a position in the colonial legal system. As Bose and Jalal (2004) notes, "the depressed classes" and the "Indian Muslims" were some of these identity constructions turning into legal entities. Thus, "British social engineering through censuses helped create supra-local caste and religious categories to whom the colonial state could distribute

178 Case studies

differential patronage" (Bose & Jalal 2004, 84). This was certainly a logical outcome of the British colonial empire's "divide and rule" strategy. As Jalal argues, the colonial rule in Indian sub-continent skilfully manipulated local elites through delicate engagements while subtly extending the control of colonial state apparatuses (2002, 12).

Nevertheless, after the independence, India inherited a pretty robust central administration from the British Colonial rule (Bose & Jalal 2004, 169). This legacy, as Jalal (2002) argues from a sub-continental comparative perspective, was critical in the growth of democracy in India after the independence compared to Pakistan (2002, 18). Yet, in India, too, centrifugal tendencies have always been vibrant and it would be misleading to think that the central apparatuses as almighty and overwhelming to the periphery (Jalal 2002, 157–158). As Jalal (2002) notes, India's diverse landscape, characterized by numerous languages, dialects, and a rich tapestry of religious and cultural differences, made the establishment of a federal system not just a political option but a pressing necessity. However, rather than crafting a truly federal structure, India's early leaders were primarily focused on consolidating central authority to align with their vision of a unified and integrated nation (Jalal 2002, 161). These concerns deeply shaped the democratic experience in India. The party system dominated by the Indian National Congress immediately after the independence was a reflection of worries the national elites had against potential centrifugal tendencies based on class, caste, or religion.

In fact, even before the independence, the Congress had already turned into a "classical patronage party, in which those who could mobilize vote banks came to occupy pivotal and profitable roles as brokers between the people and the state" (Kenny 2017, 68). Despite the emphasis on socialism, Nehru's Congress was a coalition of central and local elites extending its patronage to poor local constituencies and the party was by no means a reflection of the representation of a particular social segment (Jalal 2002, 41). The democratic processes in India, which also shaped the post-independence Indian polity in administrative and judicial terms, were deeply defined by the vertical solidarity of elites positioned at different levels stretching from localities to the national leadership. Kenny (2017) identifies this political system emerged after the independence as a "patronage democracy". The Congress Party was located in the centre of this patronage democracy. This political arrangement was also deeply shaping the administrative system and the state-level politicians had a considerable control over how the administrative machinery ran at the local level (Kenny 2018, 72–73).[5] As stated above, even under the tight control of the centre during the Indira Gandhi period, local politics in India retained its patron-client dynamics.

Indeed, a closer ethnographic look at the workings of local administrations demonstrates that looking at Indian politics with a presumption of a powerful and well-coordinated central state penetrating into the local society is, to say the least, deeply misleading. Akil Gupta's critical work demonstrates the blurred boundaries between state and society, particularly at the local level, which facilitated a populist governmental practice – mixed with corruption and politics of expediency – in its widest sense. Through his ethnographic field research in an Indian village, Gupta demonstrates that, state, as a well-coordinated and coherent reality – as it is presented by political elites – is not existing at all in the localities. Instead, what the local society experienced was "discrete and fragmentary: land records officials, VDWs, the Electricity Board, headmen, the police, the Block Development Office, and so forth" (Gupta 2012, 90). Gupta's analysis of local administration and bureaucrats also reveals the fact that they blurred the boundaries between the public and the private and the legal and the illegal. For example, local state personnel may use their own private properties or other private public spaces such as coffee houses for conducting bureaucratic affairs (Gupta 2012, 90). They are also, as many incidents related by Gupta demonstrate, into bribery and corruption that was linked to a wider system of patronage stretching from local officials to national political elites (2012, 91). Top level politicians, in the Indian patronage democracy, rely on top level bureaucrats and these bureaucrats also rely on lower-level bureaucrats for supporting the political class financially. The lower-level bureaucrats extract resources from local communities and this is why the local administrations in India seem very corrupt although corruption is endemic and encompasses every level of the polity (Gupta 2012, 91). As Gupta quotes, a particular businessman in India argues that "without corruption there is no politics" (2012, 92).

Nevertheless, there are signs that this system of patronage and corruption that is blurring the boundaries between public and the private, and formal and the informal, is seen as some sort of shortcut between state and society that renders India's administration more effective or responsive in the eyes of some of its researchers: "there has been a revisionist streak in the scholarly literature that points to the positive impact of corruption on economic development as it enables the bypassing of inefficient government mechanisms and lets the market work more efficiently. As for its impact on the poor specifically, […] 'in general the literature on corruption often overlooks the distributional implications of corruption'" (Gupta 2012, 80). In sum, the realities of day-to-day government in India have been extremely complex and barely correspond to a governmental practice that is in line with Weberian legal-rational authority. Instead, what we see are spontaneous populist practices – mixed with corruption, bribery, politics of expediency, and personal interests – that are circumventing the legal order and rational implementations for finding short-term and tactical solutions to structural problems. Gupta provides a solid example in this regard about how the censuses are conducted in rural India. In contrast to an accurate counting of every inhabitant in an accurate procedural manner, census officials responsible for the counting in

180 Case studies

rural India go to particular houses in villages and ask the inhabitants that how many people live in the village (Gupta 2012, 42–43). What does such populist practice provide is obviously not a reliable statistical knowledge that is required by an effective biopolitics. Instead, it is an example of a populist practice and its tactical orientation and propensity to "acting as if" (Wedeen 1998) there is an effective modern state machinery. Populism, in such examples, unfolds as a representation of modern administrative state in practice by "politics of expediency".

Such populist undercurrents in the administrative practice of India also surfaced in the legal realm after the pretty strict implementation of secularism since the foundation of modern India with the independence. As noted above, India, since it emerged as an independent polity, had to counterbalance its own social, cultural, and regional diversity and its centrifugal forces. Hence, many legal and political arrangements in post-Independence India have been conducive towards consolidating the centre *vis-à-vis* centrifugal regional, ethnic, and sectarian forces. In this respect secular Indian nationalism was key and another factor that was explaining the puzzling resilience of democracy in India compared to other sub-continental polities such as Pakistan and Bangladesh (Jalal 2002, 207). Yet, Hindu communalism remained as a potent force throughout the post-colonial period, especially since the 1990s. It also started to undermine the secularist tendencies of the Indian judiciary, as will be elaborated in the following part.

The populist judicial practice

Since the foundation of modern Indian democracy, secularism has been seen as a key to India's democratic unity despite its deep ethnic, religious, sectarian, and communal diversities. At least until the 1990s, the Indian judiciary has been perceived as the guardian of secularism and democracy (Mehta 2007, 70). It also seems that, for a very long time, the Indian judiciary, with its higher and lower courts, has been able to protect its autonomy from the executive and could undertake its role as the guardian of the democratic and secular order to a considerable extent (Singh 1999).[6] Nevertheless, in the 1990s, and parallel to the rise of Hindu nationalism, clear signs of divergence from a secular orientation emerged in the Indian judiciary. Not surprisingly, this divergence, implicitly or explicitly, appeared in the form of a majoritarian Hindu nationalism. Especially in the 1990s, several rulings of Indian high courts reveal this tendency.

The dispute over the demolition of Babri Mosque

The tendencies of the Supreme Court in India towards a majoritarian view of secularism became evident, especially after the demolition of the Babri

Mosque in Ayodhya. The existence of a mosque at this particular spot in Ayodhya has been an issue of contestation for decades and right-wing Hindu nationalists were claiming that the centuries old mosque was built over a Hindu temple. Mobilized by radical right-wing organizations, on December 6, 1992, a rally attended by more than 150,000 people at the Babri Mosque surroundings turned violent. The mob attacked the historical mosque and destroyed the ancient structure made of pretty soft material with axes, hammers, etc.. A wave of communal violence across India followed the demolition, and at least 2,000 people died, mainly Muslims.[7] Adding insult to injury, right-wing nationalists in India kept pushing for the construction of a Hindu temple at the very spot of Babri Mosque. These enterprises started with the claim of "right to religious ritual" by Hindus at the site of demolition and, later on, a push for the construction of a Hindu temple at the very spot of the tragic incident.

The initial decision of India's Supreme Court regarding the area of demolition was appropriating the site as a public property and planning the construction of a facility consisting of a Hindu temple, a mosque, amenities for pilgrims, a library and museum (Saxena 2018, 383). Not surprisingly, this decision encountered a resistance in a legal case initiated by a Muslim, Ismail Faruqui, claiming that the decision was anti-secular, in favour of the Hindu majority and legitimated the demolition of the ancient mosque, which was apparently a criminal act (Kapur 2019, 365). The decision in Ismail Faruqui's case was subtle, but it is hard to miss the populist proclivity appealing to the majoritarian expectations. As Saxena argues, the Supreme Court's decision to insist on building a multi-religious facility on the demolition site was clearly ignoring the role of the organized right-wing forces, including the BJP, behind the demolition and accused only a few "miscreants" for the incident (Saxena 2018, 383). This was the case, despite the BJP, in a 1993 manifesto, presented the events as the will and desire of the people (*decision quoted in* Saxena 2018, 383).

As Kapur (2019) notes, the majority of the judges rejected the argument that the land acquisition violated the constitutional principle of secularism. The majority opinion commended the principle of religious tolerance found in Hindu scriptures. They also concluded that a mosque was not an indispensable aspect of practicing the Islamic faith, asserting that Muslims could offer prayers anywhere. The court ruled that the land acquisition did not infringe upon the religious freedom of Muslims. In this case, the court supported an interpretation of secularism rooted primarily in Hindu scriptures and acknowledged the notion that secularism in India was largely based on the religious tolerance found in these scriptures (Kapur 2019, 365). Nielsen and Nilsen (2022) are also in line with Kapur when considering the Supreme Court judgement on Ayodhya dispute in 2019. As Nilsen and Nielsen quotes from one of the experts on the Indian Supreme Court, with the rise of the

182 Case studies

BJP in recent decades and particularly Modi's ascendancy to power, there emerged "'the complete capitulation of the Supreme Court to the majoritarian rule of Prime Minister Narendra Modi'", reducing it to "'a cheerleader for the Modi government's agenda'" (Nielsen & Nilsen 2022, 96).

Secularising "Hindutva"

Towards the end of the 1980s, India's high courts produced other judgements appealing to the majority tastes and expectations. In rulings knowns as "Hindutva judgements", the court paved the way to the free use of exclusionary and majoritarian religious discourses in electoral campaigns despite the principle of secularism in the constitution. Before the elections for the Maharashtra State Assembly, candidates from BJP and Shiv Sena deployed obvious exclusionary religious discourse. One of the winners of these elections, Yashwant Prabhu, for example, appealed directly to Hindu religious sentiments with a deeply exclusionary language towards Muslims in one of his campaign speeches despite the secular constraints in the constitution, as quoted in Saxena (2018, 384). As Saxena notes, the high court in Bombay declared the election of Prabhu invalid since he ignored the constitutional arrangement that "the use of religion [in elections] was a corrupt practice" (Saxena 2018, 384). Prabhu's appeal to the Supreme Court was also dismissed. However, as Saxena highlights, the court was inclined to separate Hinduism and Hindutva and tempted to attach a secular meaning to the latter in its verdict (Saxena 2018, 385). In another case, with a similar majoritarian interpretation, the court made the decision that another right-wing candidates' expression of the desire to build a "Hindu state" in his electoral campaigns was not problematic. The court deemed this candidate's election valid (Saxena 2018, 385). What was seen in all of these cases was that the high courts in India, in a shy and subtle manner, responded very well to majoritarian expectations and redefined the Hindutva as a secular ideology, "a way of life of the people in the sub-continent".

"Cow protection" vigilantism

Hindu courts' proclivity to appeal majoritarian sentiment became even stronger during the BJP governments. As a committed Hindu, it is known that Modi has always been in favour of a national ban on cow slaughter. It seems that the BJP has been able to implement a cow protection law in states where the party has the upper hand. For example, in Gujarat, there are laws that punish the violations of cow protection laws with life-long prison sentences (Nielsen & Nilsen 2022, 96). The judicial populist practice in India under Modi rule also extended to a level that reaches penal populism. For example, "the Adityanath government is also known to publish the name and photograph of people accused of breaking the state Cow Slaughter Act if they try to evade the law enforcement agencies" (Nielsen & Nilsen 2022, 97). While appealing to the Hindu majority, such legal restrictions inflicted considerable damage economically to Muslim and Dalit minorities (Nielsen & Nilsen 2022, 97). Lower courts in India frequently heavily penalize practices against cow protection laws. In a recent incident, for example, the judge of a provincial court sentenced a cow smuggler to life imprisonment.[8] What is more striking in this case is that the judge in this particular lower court did not shy away from explicitly underlining the importance of cows for Hinduism with allegedly scientific evidence, as well as through a highly religious-ideological discourse.[9]

In addition, many state legislatures in India try to respond to Hindu religious sentiments by constraining the transportation of cattle even if they do not implement a complete ban on cow slaughter. According to a news report, for example, the Assam state assembly introduced a cow protection bill in order to more tightly control the illegal transportation of cattle.[10] No doubt that, in such cases, state legislature and lower courts in India responded to the majoritarian expectations without adequate consideration to minority rights. In the case of cow protection, permissive attitudes towards "cow protection vigilantism" is another aspect of judicial populist practice in India. In a particular case, for example, suspects of a cow vigilantism incident leading to murder have been on trial on bail.[11] It also seems that some cow vigilantes are working with police and enjoy some sort of informal protection when they are engaged in violence.[12]

"The love jihad"

The populist judicial practice in India also takes the form of a struggle against inter-religious marriages and love, or what is called "the love jihad" by right-wing Hindu groups. As Nielsen and Nilsen demonstrate, the use of legal instruments and judiciary for appealing to right-wing populist expectations also extends to the private realm and inter-religious sexual affairs:

> "Love jihad" is an Islamophobic conspiracy theory centred on the false claim that Muslim men marry Hindu women in order to force them to convert to Islam. [...] Much like the case of cow protection laws, the Uttar Pradesh legislation against "love jihad" illustrates the proximity between Hindu nationalist statecraft and extra-legal majoritarian violence. The policing of interfaith relationships has been a staple activity among Hindu nationalist vigilante groups under Modi – indeed [...] in promulgating this law, the BJP-controlled state apparatus is picking up the baton from these vigilante groups.

> *(2022, 97)*

184 Case studies

In a particular case related by Saxena, for example, the conversion of a young Hindu woman to Islam has been subject of inquiry by the Supreme Court on the allegation that "the young and vulnerable girls are identified and trapped by coercion or fraud marriages, indoctrinated and used for the purpose of propagating terrorist and anti-national activities of Jihad" (2018, 392). In this particular case, throughout the probe, Hadiya, the Hindu woman who converted to Islam after her marriage, remained in her parent's home (Kapur 2019, 361). After Hadiya insisted on the fact that his marriage was genuine and consensual, the court allowed her to continue her medical studies but deprived her of the possibility of living with her husband or alone (Kapur 2019, 361). While ultimately, the Supreme Court accepted the validity of Hadiya's marriage and her autonomy to choose her religion, it is plausible to think that the entire judgement process was triggered by bottom-up populist pressures and has created a populist judicial practice at least in the lower court judgements against secular principles.

It seems that such majoritarian bottom-up pressures transforming the legislative and judicial practices in India are pretty common. According to a recent news report, for example, a massive protest march took place in Dadar, Mumbai, organized by Hindu groups to voice concerns about "love jihad" and to call for the implementation of anti-conversion laws in Maharashtra. Notably, this marked the occurrence of approximately 30 similar rallies held throughout Maharashtra thus far, according to the news report on *India Today*.[13] Such pressure also leads state legislatures in India to design laws against inter-religious marriages and relationships. According to another news report, for example, the Maharashtra government has revealed its intention to examine bills and laws from other states pertaining to "love jihad" and subsequently make a suitable decision.[14] It should be noted that such regulations have already been introduced in BJP strongholds such as Uttar Pradesh[15] and Madhya Pradesh.[16] What is important to note in such cases is that the executive and the judiciary embrace the position of populist vigilantes, and, in fact, they learn new tactics from them. Here, we see another aspect of populist governmental practice: It is indeed the colonization of modern governmentalities from below. Another point that is needed to be asserted in the context of "love jihad" is that populist governmental practice effectively blurs the distinction between public and private through subtle judicial tactics.

Use of ordinances, colonial legislation, and impunity as populist tactics

No doubt that the Modi regime deployed new legal codes to undermine secularism and create a more majoritarian state structure in India through legal means (Nielsen & Nilsen 2022, 92). But there were also other subtler ways of manipulating legal order in India under the populist BJP rule. One of these methods in the legal realm, which could be seen as populist judicial practice in the context of Modi rule, is the use of ordinances and obsolete colonial legislation to pursue a majoritarian direction and to respond to the immediate expectations of the Hindu majority without waiting for lengthy legislative procedures. For example, demonetization during the Modi rule by withdrawing 1,000 and 500 rupees from the economy in order to protect the Indian economy from so-called corruption and manipulative and exploitative financial interventions of "elites" was introduced by ordinances. As Chacko (2018) notes, this was done through ordinances to circumvent the parliamentary approval. Interestingly, the Modi government has employed ordinances at a much higher frequency than the previous government (Chacko 2018, 558–559).

As Blom Hansen asserts, alongside ordinances, the BJP government also used colonial legislation to curtail freedoms in line with a majoritarian logic and, time to time, avoid using new legislation (2019, 23). It is important to note that, in addition to active use and tactical deployment of laws for the majoritarian causes, it is also the non-application of law, the widespread indifference of police, especially in crimes against minorities, and ultimately, the impunity for the Hindu majority, that constitutes one of the important dimensions of the populist governmental practice in India in the judicial realm. For example, as Blom Hansen notes, "the active complicity of the Bombay police force in targeting Muslims while protecting Shiv Sena activists during the riots in 1992–93 was assiduously documented by the Srikrishna Commission" (2019, 39). Indifference in crimes against minorities and the following impunity for perpetrators is a pattern in India's populist judicial practice that reappeared, for example, in cases such as the Naroda Gam and Gujarat riots and intercommunal violence in 2002. According to a news report, one of the provokers in the Naroda Gam riots, Maya Kodnani, found guilty by the Supreme Court but was able to remain on bail.[17] Thus, impunity in the form of police indifference and complicity towards Hindu nationalist activism and crimes by lower courts as well as tolerance of courts towards crimes committed in the name of "people", constituted the rather subtler dimension of the judicial populist practice in India.

Concluding discussion: "Judicial populism" or "judicial populist practice"?

Populism has many faces in India. While conventionally, it has been seen as a concept describing various redistributive practices, in figures like Indira Gandhi and Narendra Modi, the term gained a connotation that is exclusively implying the direct political bond between these personalistic leaders and their followers circumventing organizational or patronage-based

186 Case studies

mediation. In these exclusively "political" interpretations of populism in India, researchers also focus on the discourse of these populist figures. For example, many accounts on Modi and the BJP tended to focus on how Modi presented himself as the champion of unprivileged segments of India *vis-à-vis* the so-called corrupt elite rule of the Congress. However, from the theoretical perspective adopted in this book, populism as governmental/political practice has much deeper roots in modern India. As a responsive governmental practice appealing to immediate needs and concerns of unprivileged and poor majorities in India, populism has always been a strong undercurrent in Indian politics that has provided food and shelter to the poor, solved problems of voters, and appealed to majoritarian cultural and moral concerns.

With the rise of the populist BJP under the leadership of Modi, however, just like Turkey, this undercurrent in Indian democracy – which appeared in the form of widespread redistributive and majoritarian-religious measures – fully unfolded as a national political phenomenon. While this populism certainly has an ideational and socio-cultural content appealing to a populist mind set by constructing the people and flaunting the native and the popular, it also perfectly reveals itself as a form of governmental/political practice in the judicial realm. On the one hand, as demonstrated so far, populism emerges as a majoritarian proclivity in the judicial considerations and verdicts of the Supreme Court as well as other high courts and lower courts, especially in cases where the issue at stake is related to the concerns of Hindu majorities. In addition, new legislation undermining the liberal secularism in India should also be considered a part of judicial populist practice such as "cow protection" regulations. On the other hand, however, one can notice a subtler populist dimension in judicial/legal practice in India that complements the populist practice: In contemporary India, Modi's populist rule also deployed ordinances and obsolete colonial legislation to circumvent lengthy legislative procedures in order to quickly appealing majoritarian expectations. At lower levels, populist tactics in the judicial realm also emerged as "non-activity": Police indifference to crimes against minorities and widespread impunity for people who committed crimes in the name of Hindu religious cause. These tactical and manipulative orientations in the realm of judicial practices have also certainly been facilitated by widespread proclivities in the administrative system of contemporary India towards informality, personalism and patronage critically demonstrated by Gupta (2012). No doubt that, like other cases examined in this book, the short-term gains through populist judicial practice have been undermining communal harmony in India more than ever. The rise of populist judicial practice and the decline of the secular system protected by the Congress' predominance resulted in unprecedented rise in communal violence in India in recent decades, and particularly throughout the Modi era (Werleman 2021).

Finally, it is important to discuss all these evidences from a more theoretical perspective. What we see in India as the implication of the rise of populism in recent decades is not simply a political discourse that is pitting "people" against a so-called secular "elite". And in judicial verdicts and legislative regulations, it is really hard to identify a kind of "judicial populism", as defined by Bernstein and Staszewski (2021), in line with an ideational approach. Populist ideational and discursive themes might or might not be found in the cases of judicial populist practices. But what is always there is a formal or informal proclivity to protect majorities and solve problems in their favour without any consideration to long-term consequences for social harmony. Thus, in the judicial realm too, populism as a governmental practice has concrete and direct consequences for everyday lives of millions of people, and populism does not remain in the realm of political discourses. Thus, populism does not only pertain to the realm of political discourses and mobilization, or it is not simply the penetration of ideologies and political discourses to judicial rhetoric. It is a practice that has concrete implications in the judicial realm. In short, it is also a judicial populist practice.

Notes

1 For an ideational perspective on populism in the judicial realm, see Bernstein and Staszewski (2021).
2 By the term "redistribution", I do not only refer to universal and formal distribution of wealth but also to more particularistic forms such as patronage, clientelism, and pork-barrel politics. Both of these forms of redistribution can be populist as long as they reveal the operational and temporal characteristics of populism discussed in Chapters 2 and 3: short-sighted and poorly planned social policies as well as less coercive forms of mass clientelism working for the benefit of majorities could be considered populist. Also, see the discussion in Chapter 2 under the subtitle "Clientelism and personalism as responsive governmental practices".
3 During the reign of Akbar, mansabdari system was introduced by the Mughal Empire in order to provide the state with a solid hierarchy. Akbar organized the elites of the empire by associating them with numbers and distributed authorities and responsibilities in proportion to these numbers. As the associated numbers increased, the authority, responsibility, and the renumeration that elites can secure increased. See Chandra (2007).
4 For the continuities and discontinuities in the legal realm in India under the late colonial rule with a particular emphasis on economic relations, see Birla (2009).
5 For the ongoing importance of patron-client relations in local and regional politics in India on the basis of ethnic favouritism also see Chandra (2004). Chandra defined India as a "patronage democracy" well before Kenny (2017).
6 No doubt that the Indian judiciary's acceptance of the authoritarian emergency regime under the rule of Indira Gandhi should be noted. I would like to thank Narendra Subramanian for drawing my attention to this and other important points in this chapter.
7 https://en.wikipedia.org/wiki/Demolition_of_the_Babri_Masjid, accessed: 23.2. 2023.

188 Case studies

8 https://timesofindia.indiatimes.com/city/surat/atomic-radiation-cannot-affect-cow-dung-houses/articleshow/97295770.cms, accessed: 24.2.2023.

9 Ibid.

10 https://www.indiatoday.in/india-today-insight/story/why-assam-is-introducing-a-cow-protection-bill-1806786-2021-05-25, accessed: 24.2.2023.

11 https://indianexpress.com/article/cities/jaipur/five-years-later-fresh-ghatmika-killings-open-old-wounds-of-a-family-8452216/, accessed: 24.2.2023.

12 https://timesofindia.indiatimes.com/india/how-cow-vigilantism-thrives-here-with-police-help/articleshow/98144950.cms, accessed: 24.2.2023.

13 https://www.indiatoday.in/cities/mumbai/story/hindu-outfits-march-against-love-jihad-mumbai-demand-anti-conversion-laws-2328067-2023-01-30, accessed: 24.2.2023.

14 https://www.indiatoday.in/news-analysis/story/maharashtra-pushing-join-states-law-against-love-jihad-2312610-2022-12-23, accessed: 24.2.2023.

15 https://economictimes.indiatimes.com/news/politics-and-nation/uttar-pradesh-cracks-down-on-interfaith-marriages-sparks-fear-of-further-polarisation/articleshow/79684768.cms, accessed: 13.12.2023.

16 https://www.outlookindia.com/national/anti-conversion-law-sc-agrees-to-hear-mp-govt-s-plea-against-hc-order-news-250486, accessed: 13.12.2023.

17 https://indianexpress.com/article/what-is/what-is-naroda-gam-riot-case-maya-kodnani-amit-shah-bjp-kar-sevaks-godra-gujarat-4849345/, accessed: 26.2.2023.

References

Bernstein, A. & G. Staszewski (2021). Judicial populism. *Minnesota Law Review*, *106*, 283.

Birla, R. (2009). *Stages of Capital – Law, Culture, and Market Governance in Late Colonial India*. Durham and London: Duke University Press.

Blom Hansen, T. (2019). Democracy against the law – reflection on India's illiberal democracy. In A. P. Chatterji, T. B. Hansen & C. Jaffrelot (Eds.), *Majoritarian State – How Hindu Nationalism is Changing India* (pp. 19–39). Oxford: Oxford University Press.

Bose, S. & A. Jalal (2004). *Modern South Asia: History, Culture, Political Economy*. London: Routledge.

Chacko, P. (2018). The right turn in India: Authoritarianism, populism and neoliberalisation. *Journal of Contemporary Asia*, 48(4), 541–565.

Chakrabarti, K. & K. K. Bandyopadhyay (2021). Populism in contemporary Indian politics. In S. J. Lee, C. Wu & K. K. Bandyopadhyay (Eds.), *Populism in Asian Democracies – Features, Structures, and Impacts* (pp. 97–120). Leiden: Brill.

Chandra, K. (2004). *Why Ethnic Parties Succeed? Patronage and Ethnic Head Counts in India*. Cambridge: Cambridge University Press.

Chandra, S. (2007). *History of Medieval India (800–1700)*. Hyderabad: Orient Blackswan.

Gupta, A. (2012). *Red Tape – Bureaucracy, Structural Violence, and Poverty in India*. Durham and London: Duke University Press.

Jaffrelot, C. & L. Tillin (2017). Populism in India. In C. R. Kaltwasser, P. Taggart, P. O. Espejo & P. Ostiguy (Eds.), *The Oxford Handbook of Populism* (pp. 179–194). Oxford: Oxford University Press.

Jalal, A. (2002). *Democracy and Authoritarianism in South Asia – a Comparative and Historical Perspective*. Cambridge: Cambridge University Press.

Kapur, R. (2019). "Belief" in the rule of law and the Hindu nation and the rule of law. In A. P. Chatterji, T. B. Hansen & C. Jaffrelot (Eds.), *Majoritarian State – How Hindu Nationalism is Changing India* (pp. 353–371). Oxford: Oxford University Press.

Kenny, P. (2017). *Populism and Patronage – Why Populists Win Elections in India, Asia and Beyond*. Cambridge: Cambridge University Press.

McDonnell, D. & Cabrera, L. (2019). The right-wing populism of India's Bharatiya Janata Party (and why comparativists should care). *Democratization*, 26(3), 484–501.

Mehta, P. B. (2007). India's unlikely democracy: The rise of judicial sovereignty. *Journal of Democracy*, 18(2), 70–83.

Mudde, C. (2004). The populist zeitgeist. *Government and Opposition*, 39(4), 542–563.

Nielsen, K. B. & A. G. Nilsen (2022). Hindu nationalist statecraft and Modi's authoritarian populism. In S. Widmalm (Ed.), *Routledge Handbook of Autocratization in South Asia* (pp. 92–100). London: Routledge.

Saxena, S. (2018). 'Court'ing Hindu nationalism: Law and the rise of modern Hindutva. *Contemporary South Asia*, 26(4), 378–399.

Singh, M. P. (1999). Securing the independence of the judiciary – the Indian experience. *Indiana International & Comparative Law Review*, 10, 245.

Subramanian, N. (1999). *Ethnicity and Populist Mobilization – Political Parties, Citizens and Democracy in South India*. Delhi: Oxford University Press.

Wedeen, L. (1998). Acting "as if": Symbolic politics and social control in Syria. *Comparative Studies in Society and History*, 40(3), 503–523.

Werleman, C. J. (2021). Rising violence against Muslims in India under Modi and BJP rule. *Insight Turkey*, 23(2), 39–50.

Weyland, K. (2001). Clarifying a contested concept: Populism in the study of Latin American politics. *Comparative Politics*, 34(1), 1–22.

9

DUTERTE'S PENAL POPULISM IN PHILIPPINES

Populism in modern Philippines: The tradition of violent/transgressive patrons

Before Spanish colonialism, there was no meaningful central authority in the massive archipelago that is known as the Philippines today. Prior to Spanish rule that started in the mid-16th century, inhabitants of the Philippines were under the control of various smaller traditional polities spread across the archipelago. This certainly exacerbated the impact of colonialism on the Philippines. Colonial authorities in the Philippines created a central administration from scratch by subordinating the native population. But during the 19th century, a mestizo landed elite with Chinese origin has started to dominate the Philippine politics in collaboration with colonial powers. Following the Spanish colonialism, the United States forcefully imposed its domination in the islands as a colonial force through a long and bloody war at the beginning of the 20th century. In the absence of a robust, centralized state machinery with powerful security apparatuses and industrial development, the landed elite in the Philippines turned into "armed oligarchies". Nevertheless, this "oligarchy" has usually collaborated with the colonial powers, first with the Spanish and then with the American colonial authorities, and embraced a Westernized lifestyle despite their authoritarian predispositions in domestic politics.

Thus, various historical factors in the Philippines facilitated populist governmental practice and "strong man personalism" at the local and national level as part and parcel of the phenomenon of populism in modern Philippine politics. Memories of colonialism have been one of the root causes of populist currents in Modern Philippine politics. But the collaboration of local

DOI: 10.4324/9781003294627-12

oligarchies with colonial authorities has also corroborated especially the national level populism of strong men like Marcos and Duterte. Thus, Webb and Curato, for example, emphasize that in the Philippines, "the down/ up antagonism is not only framed as a large powerless group, 'the people' against a small and powerful 'elite', but the Filipino nation itself has also been framed as an underdog, which is then the subject of elite abuse, whether by colonial authorities, interfering foreign powers, or the local oligarchy. Populist claims have often been framed as attempts to subvert this old hierarchy and establish a new set of power relations" (2019, 52). Populism's enemies in Philippines, therefore, "were not only the Spanish, then American colonial authorities, but also a Filipino *ilustrado* elite—Europe-educated, suit-wearing, reformist intellectuals—who actively collaborated with foreign powers" (Webb & Curato 2019, 53). As a result, populism in Philippines usually revealed itself in the form of a "strong man rule" against colonial powers and dispersed local elite domination. Thus, from Quezon to Duterte, the populist "strong men" in the Philippines, while presenting themselves as the tribune of people/nation against domestic and international elites, also responded to the "popular need for order" (McCoy 2017, 12) in the absence of a robust and penetrating security apparatus.

Especially during the first Marcos era, local oligarchies/elites have been the target of a national level populist discourse and various "strong man" practices in the Philippines. Marcos usually presented himself as someone who is fighting to centralize the state for the people and against fellow local oligarchs (Webb & Curato 2019, 54). More importantly, even before the notorious measures of Duterte in his "war on drugs" (which will be delineated in the following parts), these personalistic strong men deployed a populist practice in the fight against petty crime as well as unleashing an "incumbent terror" upon an increasingly alienated populist audience in the mid-1980s. As McCoy (2017) relates, towards the end of the Marcos era, the Marcos regime, which once prided itself on its "constitutional authoritarianism", orchestrated a display of unlawful violence. During the later years of martial law, Marcos deployed his internal security forces to instil fear in the population, resulting in approximately 77 percent, or 2,520 out of 3,257 extra-judicial killings that occurred during martial law. These unlawful killings, referred to as "salvagings", involved disposing of the victims' remains, marked with signs of torture, in public areas to communicate a message of terror through the visible wounds. In the capital city, where only around four thousand police officers were responsible for six million residents, the metropolitan government authorized hundreds of "secret marshals" to shoot petty criminals on sight. This initiative led to more than thirty fatalities within the program's inaugural month in May 1985 (McCoy 2017, 34).

192 Case studies

After the fall of Marcos dictatorship, the Philippines opted for a sort of "elite democracy" in which local oligarchies restored power and found considerable room for manoeuvre and "manipulate formal democratic procedures to their liking" (Webb & Curato 2019, 55). The period after Marcos, despite the absence of a national-level strong man against local oligarchies, generated national populist elites like former film star Joseph Estrada with a deeply populist style in politics that was highly appealing especially for the lower classes. But the pre-Duterte liberal-reformist period in the Philippines remained unsatisfactory for the majority in terms of economic development and security concerns (Thompson 2019). This dissatisfaction certainly facilitated the rise of a new populist strong man in the Philippines with the election of Duterte as president in the 2016 general elections. It was not only Duterte's fierce and transgressive populist rhetoric and discourse that rendered him a populist. It was also his transgressive style which ironically recalling the practices of "armed oligarchies" (like every strong man preceding him) in order to find short-cut, fast solutions to problems of "order and security" that were appealing to the "common sense" of people that rendered him a populist in the context of Philippines. Therefore, in the Philippines, populism always had a practical component related to a sort of functional/strategic violence appealing to the taste and needs of majorities that surpassed the rhetoric and the transgressive style (like scandalous objections to international order and human rights discourses by Duterte). Thus, besides rhetoric and performance, populism in the Philippines has always been a governmental practice. This phenomenon, like other cases examined in previous chapters, has certainly been related to the historical development of the administrative apparatuses of the Philippines and its relationship with the political class and society.

Politics, state, and populist policing practices in modern Philippines

Modern Philippine politics has always been notoriously inclined to personalistic leadership in localities and at the national level. While widespread patronage relations and electoral violence created armed patronage networks based on family ties in rural Philippines since the end of American colonialism (McCoy 1993), the vertical solidarity between "patrons" and "clients" created the phenomenon of "bossism" in urbanizing Philippines (Sidel 1997; Kimura 2018, 23). Competitive politics with violent proclivities also created "strong men" in Philippine politics at the national level from Quezon to Duterte. Such a strong propensity to personalistic politics has been the main pillar of Philippine populism and has its roots in the colonial period and, especially, in political institutions created by American colonialism.

Before colonialism, people living on territories of modern Philippines had no developed centralized state machinery to counter-balance the Spanish "*conquistadores*". There were only scattered animist communities and weak traditional local polities all over the islands, which were gradually converted to Christianity after the Spanish occupation (Anderson 1988, 8). But in the 19th century a mestizo landed elite with Chinese origins started to form more rigid hierarchies among the domestic populations of the Islands. Modern social class hierarchies also started to become more visible during the 19th century (Mojares 1991). The first modern centralized administrative institutions in the Philippines had been the creation of Spanish colonialism, but these institutions remained weak and predatory/extractive/exclusionary in character (Constantino 1975, 129–145; Agoncillo 1990, 80–101; Quilop 2006, 5). After Spanish colonialism came to an end, the Philippines had its own independent government, but it remained as a short-lived experience. American colonialism destroyed this short experience of self-rule and provided the Philippines with more elaborate political and administrative structures (Quilop 2006, 5). However, "local autonomy was encouraged apparently as a result of an agreement among the American administrators and Filipino leaders to establish a strong and independent local government system" (Quilop 2006, 5). Nevertheless, this autonomy granted to Filipino leaders had its own limits defined by the colonial power and could extend only to a boundary where American interests were not undermined (Webb 2022, especially chs. 1 and 2). As Anderson notes, the political and administrative system left by the Americans in the Philippines in the first half of the 20th century mainly emulated the patronage-ridden characteristics of the American system and its weak central bureaucratic institutions at that time and ultimately created notorious local dynasties in the Philippines as the main power foci (1988, 11–12).

Thus, the modern administrative institutions in the Philippines, from the very beginning, developed in the context of colonial dependency relations of Philippine elite. And the institutional legacy of Spanish and American colonialism, for example, has been much weaker than what was left behind by the British colonialism in India. When this is coupled with the socio-economic underdevelopment, it is hard to identify the Philippine civil service as a "Weberian legal-rational bureaucracy". Two of the major problems of the Philippines' civil service have been corruption and politicization. The extensive local autonomy of "*cacique* oligarchies" and their challenge to the "monopoly of violence" of the Philippine state have always undermined the development of a more robust central state structure in the Philippines (Anderson 1988). Thus, arbitrary behaviour of executive authorities has been a common tendency in Philippine politics at local and national levels. Anderson highlights the fact that, in fact, the Marcos dictatorship, despite its objection to the local *cacique* oligarchies, was the logical outcome of *cacique* democracy with its propensity to spectacular political and electoral violence (1988, 20–21). In the Philippines, the prevalence of electoral and political

194 Case studies

violence stretched to such an extent that, in the 1987 elections, for example, when 124 people were killed during the elections (much fewer than the casualties in previous competitive elections), authorities described the election process ironically as "peaceful" (Anderson 1988, 30).

Hence, the political system in the Philippines during the competitive periods has relied upon widespread clientelistic networks and a kind of "oligopoly of violence". Since Lande's (1965; 1968) crucial and influential works, clientelism and patronage have been the main concepts deployed in understanding competitive politics in the Philippines. When the Philippines was more rural and less developed, *cacique* family oligarchies and the patronage networks they established around themselves were the main sources of political power. As Kimura notes, these patronage systems were composed of "vertical dyads" which had "multi-layered structures" (2018, 19). In these multi-layered structures, the immediate followers of the leader have their own set of followers, who, in turn, possess their followers, forming multiple layers which are not really tightly connected to the higher level of the pyramid (Kimura 2018, 19). Hence, the Philippine competitive political system has been extremely weak in terms of institutionalization and reveals a strong propensity to "personalistic politics" in the absence of stable and institutionalized programmatic parties (Webb & Curato 2019, 53).

But one should here also note that, with social change, and more particularly with the penetration of market relations in rural Philippines and with the increasing urbanization, the character of Philippine politics based on "*cacique* family oligarchies" and traditional "patron-client" relations changed. As revealed by Machado (1974), local oligarchic family predominance started to leave its place to "machine politics" and more "transactional relations" under the control of "new men" in the Philippines, especially in and around big city centres like Manila, starting with the 1970s. In another important study, however, Sidel (1997) underlines the fact that the power of traditional *cacique* oligarchies in the Philippines did not disappear immediately with the rise of the "machine politics". Especially in the contexts far from the capital of the Philippines, such as Cebu, the "dynastic families", who transferred their savings from agriculture to sectors such as tourism and construction, continued their political dominance. In these contexts, these dynastic families held power and local authority for a very long time by deploying methods beyond patronage such as electoral fraud, vote buying, and violence. For example, a family in this region was able to hold on the municipality with different generations from 1937 to the end of the 1990s. While these notable families were seen as generous bosses, on the one hand, they were also able to use all kinds of bullying and intimidation to win elections (Sidel 1997, 953–954). But, as Machado (1974) and Sidel (1997) highlight, alongside these traditional family oligarchies, at least since the 1970s, a specific form of more impersonal clientelistic "machine politics" became widespread, especially in major urban centres in the Philippines.

The civil service

The prevalence of local oligarchies and political machines, albeit with differing forms, had a uniform impact on the Philippine state. They have effectively undermined the administrative capacity of the Philippine state and created many "defects" that were filled by "populist practices", "local patrons", and "national strong men" throughout the tumultuous competitive political experience of the Philippines. As Hodder highlights, for example, shaping of the civil service by legislative elites and presidents has been a widespread problem in the Philippines which was either done for personal enrichment or political patronage (2018, 75). Thus, politicians in the Philippines are deeply involved in the formation of the civil service. Due to insufficient payment, bureaucrats and civil servants also heavily tended to dodge and circumvent procedures. Corruption has also been widespread in Philippine bureaucracy and civil servants followed a logic of over-conformity in their practices (Hodder 2018, 76–78). All these problems with the Philippine civil service have ironically entailed the proliferation of the bureaucracy because "the quickest path to the implementation of a few high-profile initiatives may be to create a new office regardless of what already exists in an agency" (Hodder 2018, 79). But, as Hodder notes, the defects of this bureaucracy also created some "constructive informal practices", which form the basis of "populist practices" in the realm of many different policy spheres including those related to "order and security" in the Philippines. Hodder (2018) notes that such informal behaviour within the bureaucracy also created the space and environment in which creative thinking, discussions, and decisions can flourish, and the deficiencies inherent in highly formalized arrangements and acts could be compensated, especially when establishing open and effective counter-procedures is politically unfeasible. Ultimately, even the involvement of populist politicians may sometimes contribute to better services to people, as Hodder (2018, 80–81) asserts.

The Philippine police

These "defects" as well as "constructive informal practices" in Philippine administrative apparatuses have been all too evident in the police institution. The development of police institutions in the Philippines has also been deeply affected by the colonial system of administration left by the Americans. As Varona (2010) highlights, the Philippine "constabulary", the institutional ancestor of the national police in the Philippines, established for – and formed the core of the instruments deployed by – American colonial repression. The constabulary was also the vehicle of the Philippine landed elite, which was in collaboration with American colonialism. Especially

196 Case studies

throughout the Marcos era, the corruption intensified and the police turned into an instrument of political repression. Even after the Marcos era, despite waves of reform attempts, the politicization of the police remained intact (Varona 2010, 103–105), like other branches of the public bureaucracy delineated above. Patronage has been rampant in the Philippine police, both between political "patrons" and their proteges within the police institution and between higher and lower ranked officers inside the institution (Varona 2010, 105–109).

One of the major problems with the police institution, that also facilitated "penal populism" as populist political practice, has been the overwhelming influence of local power holders on the institution, which rendered violent populist governmental practices legitimate and, more importantly, provided those who exercised it with a remarkable degree of impunity. As Varona (2010) notes, the law that established the Philippine National Police stipulates that local government officials, such as provincial governors and city or municipal mayors, are granted the authority to exercise operational supervision and control over police personnel assigned to their respective areas. Operational supervision and control encompass the power to direct, oversee, supervise, and inspect police units or forces. This also permits local political leaders to utilize or deploy the police forces assigned to them as they deem necessary to uphold local law and order. In essence, this grants local executives a degree of authority akin to that of the president concerning policing matters (2010, 108–109).

According to Varona (2010), the police institution is also notoriously underfunded and under-equipped that many police officers often find themselves in the position of having to buy their own uniforms, equipment, firearms, and ammunition due to meagre salaries. This can lead to officers purchasing cheaper but inadequate or subpar ammunition and gear. During Varona's interviews, police officers have revealed that the combination of low pay and an institution that fails to provide them with essential professional supplies has sometimes pushed them towards engaging in corrupt practices, including extortion and bribery. These issues, along with patronage politics, have been widespread within the entire Philippine criminal justice system. Especially in the Philippine National Police internal corruption is particularly prominent in the recruitment and logistics procurement processes, as well as in the allocation of funds and resources. Furthermore, some police officers have been implicated in criminal activities such as drug trafficking, kidnapping, car theft, and, even murder. Bribes have been offered to police officers to manipulate evidence and obstruct criminal investigations (Varona 2010, 109–110). This context of "underdevelopment" should certainly be seen as the framework in which populist governmental practices could emerge in "corrupt" as well as "constructive informal" forms.

"Diskarte" by the police and the policed

Accompanying the widespread problem of political violence in the Philippines, the Philippine National Police itself has usually been seen as a source of arbitrary violence, and even murders, to an extent that there is a special expression in the Philippines to describe "extra-judicial" killings: "salvaging". As Hapal and Jensen notes, even before the Duterte's war on drugs, extra-judicial killings, or "salvaging" by police was a common practice in the Philippines (2017, 40) alongside corruption and rampant patronage in the police institution. But, as Hapal and Jensen do, one should ask how police officers in the Philippines legitimized such "vices" in order to understand the tacit approval of such practices within the institution and by the broader public. As Hapal and Jensen note, "[m]ost analyses of police violence and police corruption point to fragile institutional frameworks and impunity coupled with low pay and low prestige in policing. While police officers, to some extent, second these explanations, not least the low salaries, there is also strong emphasis on what the police officers call *tulong* or *ayuda* (help). This is what, with Olivier de Sardan, we could call the moral economy of corruption" (2017, 40).

The bottom-up view of the police practices in the Philippines by Hapal and Jensen (2017) provided us with a framework for understanding the interactions in the realm of order and security and how a particular "moral economy" legitimized many problematic practices in the eyes of police and the policed. Hapal and Jensen's excellent bottom-up and ethnographic study of police practices in the Philippines provides compelling evidence regarding the complicity between police, policed, and victims in the emergence of what I call "populist governmental practice" in this book in the realm of "order and security". In their important work, Hapal and Jensen relate the story of a mother whose child was taken into custody and how this woman was able to save his child from the prison with a "reduced bribe" through the use of tactics, or "*diskarte*" as called in the Philippines, or through "*metis*" as called by Scott. This, and similar tendencies related by Hapal and Jensen's study, demonstrates that populist governmental practices are usually products of widespread proclivities among ordinary majorities towards a tactical orientation in their dealings with public bureaucracies and similarly tactical responses of street bureaucrats to unprivileged citizens under the circumstances of material and organizational deprivation. While this is "*diskarte*" in the Philippines, it is, for example, "*kurnazlık*" in Turkey. But the essence of the practical moral inclinations of majorities remains the same: Circumventing the procedures and responsibilities in encounters between public authorities and ordinary citizens. While ordinary citizens are inclined to embrace such practices and seek "easy ways out" from their troubles with the public authorities, public authorities themselves, and in this case, the personnel of the

198 Case studies

police institution, are prone to bypass procedures through tactics in order to reduce the workload for themselves and for the entire criminal justice system.

In another incident that they related in their study, Hapal and Jensen describe the story of a driver who was involved in a traffic accident resulted in the injury of a child. In this incident, while the driver wanted to avail a judicial procedure and police violence and deployed *"diskarte"* in order to achieve this goal, the local police that was taking care of this incident was also not that keen to send the driver to the court. Ultimately, in return for a bribe, the police officers convinced the injured child's mother – in return for the driver's payment of hospital expenses – and released the driver after several hours that he spent in the local police station. Even in this particular case, one can distinguish the defining features of a populist governmental practice such as responsiveness of the police officers, informality of the processes that took place in the police station, and the complicity among the parties (police officers, driver, and the injured child's mother) involved in the interaction at the public arena. Thus, populist governmental practice is a mode of administrative practice in which public authorities (including politicians as well as politicized public personnel) and ordinary citizens struck deals that, to a certain extent, benefit every party.

"Tulong" vs. "ganid"

Thus, Hapal and Jensen also convincingly document how such *"diskarte"* has been legitimized by the public authorities by identifying most of them as *"tulong"* or *"ayuda"* against more self-interested *"ganid"*/greed in the Philippines. Hapal and Jensen, therefore, note that "at least some corrupt acts by the police, in light of an inefficient criminal justice system, form part of a parallel –albeit informal– means of administering justice and punishment that is to the advantage of the citizens they police, not the opposite" (2017, 57). But certainly, in populist practices, there is a particular threshold that, when that is transgressed, things can turn into "corruption" for the parties involved in these practices. When practices that were initially "populist" start to target only self-enrichment and become personal greed, or *"ganid"*, populist practices disappear and left its place to more clear corrupt practices. But usually, as Hapal and Jensen notes, populist governmental practices are ways that compensate and solve the problems of dysfunctional bureaucratic systems under the circumstances of underdevelopment. Therefore, it is very typical to see the claim to "public responsibility" that civil servants (in this case, police officers) think that they are undertaking through populist governmental practice under the circumstances of a judicial and bureaucratic incapacity.

In a particular case that Hapal and Jensen (2017) observed regarding the handling of domestic violence in urban Philippines, this "moral economy" embedded in populist governmental practice becomes evident. In the example of the practice of a pretty popular police officer examined by Hapal and Jensen, people accused of domestic violence were rarely referred to the judicial system but penalized by the local police officers: Either through a long counselling, or through a "*piyansa*" (an unofficial bail) or, in some cases that requires more drastic measures, through beating ups by the police. As Hapal and Jensen relate, parties with public authority involved in such practices legitimized their way of handling the issue of domestic violence with a clear populist logic: "According to PO [police officer] Carol, if they were to prosecute all of the cases in Bagong Silang, especially cases of domestic violence, the city jails and courts would overflow. She also said that counselling is better than detaining husbands. Incarcerating fathers destroys families by depriving them of the breadwinner. PO Carol was proud of this form of 'assistance' and claimed it as one of the achievements of their office" (2017, 57).

Populist political practice as penal populism: Duterte's "war on drugs"

Duterte's "war on drugs" should be seen in the context of a long tradition of extra-judicial violence in the Philippines exerted by local war lords as well as a weak security apparatus in the absence of a proper "monopoly of violence" constructed by the central state (Webb & Curato 2019, 62). In fact, Duterte belongs to a plethora of mayors who used very similar tactics in their combat against crime. As Thompson (2019, 50) notes, several mayors in the Philippines have adopted similar strategies of "eliminating" criminals through extra-judicial killings. Their rationale usually extended beyond crime deterrence, as they also sought to gain popularity that bolstered their chances of re-election. In an environment marked by lawlessness and weak institutions, a strong man who positions himself as a protector of the common people against criminal elements not only justified his ruthless methods but also secured a long-lasting grip on power. During his tenure as mayor, Duterte cultivated a tough-guy (*siga*) persona, presenting himself as the saviour of Davao, a city allegedly infiltrated by communists and plagued by crime. This image-building effort predated his national prominence and was a key element of his mayoralty in Davao City. Duterte himself, in fact, can be fairly described as a "war lord" (Thompson 2019, 50). Not surprisingly, Duterte opted for taking the excessive rates of crime and violence in Davao City under control through "death squads". It seems that Duterte did not only deploy these "death squads" for fighting with crime and violence but also turned this capacity into an instrument of political dominance by using these death squads against his opponents as a means of repression (McCoy 2017, 38). Thus, extra-legal violence – which is by no means a practice that is unfamiliar for ordinary majorities in the Philippines – has also been part and parcel of Duterte's rise as a national political figure.

200 Case studies

Nonetheless, Duterte's time as mayor has been presented as a success story in terms of sustaining order and security as a part of his political image building (Webb & Curato 2019, 61). It should also be seen in the context of failures of the "liberal reformist" period in the Philippines before Duterte. As Thompson (2019) notes, throughout this period, the Philippine economy grew considerably, but inequalities also increased dramatically, which eventually facilitated the rise of Dutertismo. The failures of the Aquino regime – and liberal reformism, therefore – preceding the Duterte rule became all too evident in administrative terms when the government failed to respond properly in the aftermath of the devastating super typhoon "Haiyan" in 2013 (Thompson 2019, 43). Hence, in general, Aquino rule was ineffective in administrative terms. It is also the failures of the justice system that paved the way to the rise of a "penal populism" under Duterte rule. The perceived shortcomings in the justice system and the alleged neglect of addressing criminality and drug abuse during the Aquino administration created a room for Duterte to make promises and subsequently implement a brutal anti-drug campaign (Thompson 2019, 47).

As Webb and Curato highlight, Duterte's populism "restores the esteem of many who have felt beaten up for decades" (2019, 62). Although Duterte's appeal was very strong for the middle classes, it also seems that Duterte's political style appealed to underprivileged, less educated sectors of Philippine society too and touched upon a socio-cultural divide in the country between high and low-brow cultures (Ostiguy 2017). As Curato notes, opponents of Duterte call his supporters as "Dutertards" with a word play clearly alluding to the expression "retards" (Curato 2016, 92). Duterte was also a very transgressive figure (Webb & Curato 2019, 59) who did not shy away from swearing and making "rape jokes" in public. As Curato notes, his machismo was part and parcel of his populist style (2016, 95). But, no doubt, the Duterte rule was more than populist flamboyance.

When Duterte came to power, "extra-judicial killings" were rapidly unleashed over the so-called "dangerous other" by "death squads" under his control. According to McCoy (2017), in the initial six months of his presidency, before a temporary suspension following the police killing of a South Korean national, Duterte's anti-drug campaign resulted in around 7,000 bodies being found on the streets. Often, these victims were accompanied by crude cardboard signs declaring *"Pusher ako"* (I am a pusher). Disturbingly, many victims had their faces wrapped in brown packaging tape, a grim signature reminiscent of the DDS (Davao Death Squad). After restarting the anti-drug campaign in March 2017, Duterte dismissed concerns about human rights abuses and even went so far as to tell the police that if they killed those who accused them, "I will pardon you". To justify these extreme measures, Duterte made exaggerated claims that the Philippines was on the brink of becoming a "narco-state" with 3.7 million drug addicts. Official figures, however, indicated only 1.8 million users, resulting in a relatively modest drug abuse rate of 1.69 percent (compared to a global average of 5.2 percent). Nonetheless, Filipino voters still identified illegal drugs, along with low wages, as their top concerns (McCoy 2017, 39).

One should, however, note that, as Curato (2016) asserts by relying on her first-hand observations in Manila's slums, drug-related problems are really central to the harsh living conditions of the inhabitants of these parts of the city. And the drug problem had already become a "national issue" in the Philippines before the rise of Duterte (Curato 2016, 100). Under the conditions of a weak judicial system and an incapable security apparatus, Duterte's appeal, which pledged to solve the problem of drugs through extra-judicial killings, became more attractive to the masses than promising to solve the problem through long-term social policy measures (Thompson 2019, 48). As Curato emphasizes, Duterte's promises were simple: "Crisis can be averted. Drugs, crime and corruption can be eliminated. All of this comes with a price, and that price can be liberal rights. He would close down Congress if it threatened to impeach him. He would declare martial law if the Supreme Court interfered. His reign would be bloody and many would die, but his way is the only way to salvation" (2016, 98). In other words, a "populist practice" or a "populist policy implementation" appealing to "populist common sense" trumped legal-rational policies and administration with the rise of Duterte.

The rationale of support for Duterte, however, should be elaborated. As Curato (2016) rightly points out, when evaluated in context, Duterte supporters had a point. When Duterte promised to solve the problem in a bloody manner, this resonated very well with his supporters' worldviews and concerns in Philippine's slums:

> Such moral judgement – considering violent talk as "just right" – does not represent the case of a respondent with poor ethical calculations. Part of the populist public support for aggressive rhetoric is the promise of justice that comes with it. Citizens who often find themselves hassled by petty thieves and addicts envision a sense of finality, a sense that their everyday tormentors will be put in their place, even if it happens at the expense of due process. After all, what use is due process if it entails taking part in the slow and inefficient process of the criminal justice system?
>
> *(Curato 2016, 101)*

Thus, as Curato notes, "a strong leader evoking a sense of control resonated to communities who wished to reclaim stability in an otherwise fragile context" (2016, 101). In addition, especially his performance in helping the survivors of the super typhoon in 2013 was never erased from the public memory (Curato 2016, 102). There was this very deep belief among the

202 Case studies

Philippine poor that "Duterte treated [them] like human beings" (Curato 2016, 103). Under these circumstances the pledges by Duterte to solve administrative problems in a quick and decisive manner resonated very well with the underprivileged sectors of Philippine society (Curato 2016, 105). When he came to power, Duterte had no chance but to fulfil his promise of "populist practice" or "policy implementation". He really bypassed the bureaucratic and judicial procedures, especially when the issue was related to law, order, and security. Thus, the important thing was not really Duterte's "populist" pledges and promises or his fierce rhetoric of solving the problems in a quick, violent, and decisive manner. What made Duterte's appeal, especially after his ascent to power, very powerful and thoroughly populist was his deeds, his "populist practice" as the new strong man of the nation.

Having said all of these, the negative consequences of populist governmental practice are especially obvious when it reveals itself in the form of "penal populism". As already stated, death squads related to Duterte rule killed thousands of people without due process in their so-called "war on drugs". There were serious doubts and criticism regarding these methods against so-called "pushers" and drug users. When the issue of "human rights" was raised by critiques of the Duterte regime he replied critiques in a blunt and shameless way: "forget the laws on human rights" (Thompson 2019, 51). It also seems that there was a remarkable degree of "*diskarte*" and tactics involved in these extra-judicial killings when it was hard to prove that the killed people were really guilty. As Thompson notes, "investigation also revealed that the murders are staged to make them seem like legitimate police operations, as evidence is planted and reports falsified" (2019, 51).

The more uncomfortable and ironic aspect of the entire Duterte episode was that "most victims of police and vigilante 'hits' are poor and defenceless people, making the war against the drugs appear more like a war against the poor" (Thompson 2019, 51). All these extra-judicial killings intensified the corrupt practices in the judicial and security bureaucracies in the Philippines besides claiming the lives of many innocent people (Thompson 2019, 52). Today, Duterte's "war on drugs" has become under much stronger scrutiny by international organizations. As a news report in *Manila Times* relates, although Duterte is no longer in office, he enjoys substantial support in his legal confrontation with the International Criminal Court (ICC) regarding the deaths of numerous drug suspects during his aggressive anti-drug campaign.[1] More concerningly, as Curato notes, "the punitive foundations of the politics of fear limits the public's imagination for measured and systematic responses to the drug problem. Instead, it promotes spectacular short-term solutions to complex problems at the expense of human rights" (2016, 106). The negative consequences of populist practice in the realm of order and security as a result of its "short-term and restricted horizon of time" is really evident in the case of Duterte rule in the Philippines.

Concluding discussion: Populist policing as penal populism

The administrative legacy of colonialism in the Philippines has been a weak central state and assertive local power holders (initially a landed elite, then new men as "bosses" in urban contexts who were incorporated into the capitalist market economy) with a very strong propensity to patronage politics based mainly on armed followers. As the popular expression claims, Philippine politics has always been about "guns, goons, and gold" and relied upon notoriously personalistic politics lacking a stable party system and institutionalized parties. This setting also means that the Philippines in the post-colonial period has been characterized by an "oligopoly of violence", "war lordism", assertive local bosses as well as a series of strong men at the national level from Quezon to Duterte. This setting has consequences with regard to institutions and policies pertaining to the realm of law, order, and security under the circumstances of underdevelopment and poverty. The police institution in the Philippines has always been weak and ill-equipped and remained under the impact of local oligarchies and powerful national politicians, most notably the presidents. Patronage and corruption were not only problems of the Philippine political system but they also had implications for the Philippine civil service in general and the national police institution in particular.

Extra-judicial violence has been part and parcel of politics as well as policing practices in the Philippines alongside corruption and patronage politics. This should be seen as the reflection of lack of an institutional capacity. Especially the corrupt practices in the police institution could also be seen as innovative methods of its personnel for compensating positions that are underpaid and ill-equipped for the job. A moral economy perspective on the Philippine police institution, as developed by Hapal and Jensen (2017), also demonstrates that, under the circumstances of poverty and institutional incapacity, some of the "corrupt" practices in the police institution have become populist ways of solving problems in a financially and institutionally incapacitated public administration realm. Thus, "*diskarte*" and "*tulong*" circumventing the judicial procedures – most of the time for the immediate benefits of victims, perpetrators, and the institutions of law and order – in the Philippines could be seen as reflections of a populist policing practice.

Duterte's "war on drugs" as penal populism, thus, should be seen in the context of these more common practices of populist policing in the Philippines. It should also be located in a culture of "war lordism" and "oligopoly of violence" emerged throughout the history of modern Philippines. Extra-judicial killings or "salvaging" had become part and parcel of Philippine politics and policing well before the rise of Duterte. But Duterte decisively exerted this common practice in the Philippines with a clearly transgressive populist discourse and style, and this is why extra-judicial killings have

204 Case studies

become the hallmark of his rule for many commentators. Works on contemporary Philippine politics also show that drugs are a real problem, especially for poor people and slums, and this is why Duterte's "tough" attitude on crime as well as his proposal of a populist "quick fix" to this problem appealed very well to underprivileged majorities in the Philippines.

In fact, his "war on drugs" based on "extra-judicial killings" and "death squads", as researchers of contemporary Philippines asserts (especially see Curato 2016), could be seen as a flawless reflection of "penal populism". In this respect, populist policing practices in the Philippines in the form of extra-judicial violence and killings unleashed upon drug sellers and users are indeed in line with textbook definitions of "penal populism" (Pratt 2007, 12). But penal populism should also be seen as a specific form of broader populist governmental practice in which populism is not only about appealing to ideas and "intuitions" of the public discursively but solving real problems of administration (and, in this case, in the realm of "law, order and security") through practices based on "*discarte*" or "*metis*". Duterte's law on drugs based on extra-judicial killings and death squads did not only appeal to the sentiments and expectations but also dealt with a real public security problem in a practical way based on a unique moral and administrative economy: In order to solve this problem of public security – quickly and responsively – the populist practice blurred the boundaries between legal and the illegal, formal and the informal, as well as the state and the society.

But as a populist practice *par excellence*, the problems entailed by "populist policing" and "penal populism" in the Philippines are evident. Even the less violent and more benign forms of populist practices in the realm of law, order, and security in police stations across the Philippines, despite the shortcuts and the "economy" it provided in the short-term, inevitably brought corruption in the long run. Because when it comes to policing, usually, the boundaries between "*tulong*"/help and "*ganid*"/greed blur quickly. The use of "*metis*" in the realm of public administration and policy may quickly turn into an instrument of personal gain and domination that escapes the control of a fair Weberian legal-rational order. The consequences in the case of "extra-judicial killings" and "death squads" for combatting public security problems in a populist manner are evidently graver. As documented so far, and which has been subject to international scrutiny, Duterte's war on drugs based on extra-judicial killings claimed the lives of thousands including many innocent citizens without due process. Duterte's populist handling of the drug problem, therefore, may have created more serious human rights problems than the drug problem itself. Thus, populist practices in the realm of law and order can easily descend into thoughtless and uncalculated cruelty since they ignore the very important legal-rational procedures rendering public security measures just and moral. Therefore, populist practices appealing to the "gut feelings" (Taggart 2022, 71) of majorities are usually devoid of a longer time horizon as well as a wider understanding of a moral and effective criminal justice system. While its responsiveness and quick fixes satisfy the immediate feelings and grievances of the masses, populist practices usually cause more problems in the long run than they claim to have solved in the short term.

Note

1 https://www.manilatimes.net/2023/04/03/opinion/columns/a-chorus-of-disinformation-vs-icc/1885491, accessed: 9.4.2023.

References

Agoncillo, T. A. (1990). *History of the Filipino People*. Quezon City: R. P. Garcia.

Anderson, B. (1988). Cacique democracy and the Philippines: Origins and dreams. *New Left Review*, 169, 3–31.

Constantino, R. (1975). *A History of the Philippines: From the Spanish Colonization to the Second World War*. New York and London: Monthly Review Press.

Curato, N. (2016). Politics of anxiety, politics of hope: Penal populism and Duterte's rise to power. *Journal of Current Southeast Asian Affairs*, 35(3), 91–109.

Hapal, K. & S. Jensen (2017). The morality of corruption: A view from the police in Philippines. In S. Jensen & M. K. Andersen (Eds.), *Corruption and Torture – Violent Exchange and the Policing of the Urban Poor* (pp. 39–68). Aalborg: Aalborg University Press.

Hodder, R. (2018). The civil service: Weaknesses and constructive informal practices. In M. R. Thompson & E. V. C. Batalla (Eds.), *Routledge Handbook of Contemporary Philippines* (pp. 73–84). London: Routledge.

Kimura, M. (2018). Clientelism revisited. In M. R. Thompson & E. V. C. Batalla (Eds.), *Routledge Handbook of Contemporary Philippines* (pp. 17–25). London: Routledge.

Lande, C. H. (1965). *Leaders, Factions, and Parties – the Structure of Philippine Politics*. New Haven: Yale University.

Lande, C. H. (1968). Parties and politics in the Philippines. *Asian Survey*, 8(9), 725–747.

Machado, K. G. (1974). From traditional faction to machine: Changing patterns of political leadership and organization in the rural Philippines. *The Journal of Asian Studies*, 33(4), 523–547.

McCoy, A. W. (Eds.). (1993). *An Anarchy of Families – State and Family in the Philippines*. Madison, WI: University of Wisconsin.

McCoy, A. W. (2017). Global Populism: A lineage of Filipino strongmen from Quezon to Marcos and Duterte. *Kasarinlan: Philippine Journal of Third World Studies*, 32(1–2), 7–54.

Mojares, R. B. (1991). The formation of a city: Trade and politics in nineteenth-century Cebu. *Philippine Quarterly of Culture and Society*, 19(4), 288–295.

Ostiguy, P. (2017). Populism: A socio-cultural approach. In C. R. Kaltwasser, P. Taggart, P. O. Espejo & P. Ostiguy (Eds.), *The Oxford Handbook of Populism* (pp. 73–97). Oxford: Oxford University Press.

Pratt, J. (2007). *Penal Populism*. London: Routledge.

Quilop, R. J. G. (2006). Nation-state formation in the Philippines. In N. N. Morada & T. S. Encarnacion Tadem (Eds.), *Philippine Politics and Governance* (pp. 1–12). Quezon City: University of the Philippines.

Sidel, J. T. (1997). Philippine politics in town, district, and province: Bossism in Cavite and Cebu. *The Journal of Asian Studies*, 56(4), 947–966.

Taggart, P. (2022). Populism vs politics. In L. Manucci (Ed.), *The Populism Interviews – a Dialogue with Leading Experts* (pp. 70–72). London: Routledge.

Thompson, R. (2019). The rise of illiberal democracy in the Philippines: Duterte's early presidency. In I. Deinla & B. Dressel (Eds.), *From Aquino to Duterte (2010–2018)* (pp. 39–61). Singapore: ISEAS Yusof Ishak Institute.

Varona, G. (2010). Politics and policing in the Philippines: Challenges to police reform. *Flinders Journal of History and Politics*, 26, 101–125.

Webb, A. (2022). *Chasing Freedom – the Philippines' Long Journey to Democratic Ambivalence*. Brighton: Sussex Academic Press.

Webb, A. & N. Curato (2019). Populism in the Philippines. In D. Stockemer (Ed.), *Populism Around the World* (pp. 49–66). Cham: Springer.

10

NASSER'S SOCIO-ECONOMIC AND EDUCATION POLICIES IN EGYPT

Virtues and ills of "populist social contract"

Populism in Nasser's Egypt: The "populist social contract"

From the 1930s to 1980s, a series of regimes in Latin America, Middle East, Asia, and Africa were called populist (Worsley 1970; Allcock 1971; Di Tella 1997, especially ch. 4). This was not simply because of domination exerted over these regimes by popular and personalistic leaders but also because of socio-economic policies those leaders embraced, which were based on effective redistribution of wealth to popular sectors in order to retain their support and obedience (Hinnebusch 2020). Especially in the Middle East and Africa, these regimes gained a specifically nationalistic orientation since they objected to colonial domination. Most of these "populist regimes" based on effective redistribution were also "post-colonial" in character that recently got rid of exploitative foreign domination. In some cases – as we can see in Egypt at the beginning of the 1950s – this exploitative colonial impact was intermingled with monarchical rule too, which tended to make exploitation only subtler and deeper.

The almost bloodless coup led by Gamal Abd-al Nasser, in this respect, was a reaction to a kind of double exploitative system: A colonial as well as a monarchical one. Nasser's populism in the 1950s and 1960s was very much based on an antagonism between underdog Egyptian nation and a westernized-alienated elite – including the monarchy – emerged throughout the period marked by British control. As Johnson (1972) notes, in 1952, prior to the Free Officers assuming authority, Egypt was on the brink of a revolution. The British military occupation's excessive actions, the blatant meddling of the British embassy in the nation's political matters, King Farouk's erratic behaviour, a succession of ineffective governments, foreign

DOI: 10.4324/9781003294627-13

208 Case studies

conquerors' oppressive control over land, foreigners dominating commerce, and the Egyptian army's defeat in Palestine a few years earlier had collectively incited people from all social strata, except the elite, to take charge of their own future (Johnson 1972, 3). In this respect, it is important to note a structural change in the socio-economic and socio-cultural characteristics of the army officers in Egypt starting with the 1930s. These transformations created the cohort of the Nasser era that was mostly coming from Egyptian middle classes who were more prone to populist policies compared to previous generations of officer corps with more aristocratic/traditional elite backgrounds (Halpern 1965, 257–261; Perlmutter 1974, 113; Abdalla 1988, 1452–1453).

After Free Officers seized the power, Nasser consolidated his position within the revolutionary "junta" that he was already leading. Nasser's populism, in the most conventional meanings of the term, helped him become prominent. This conventional populism was related to his style, as well as his discourse and way of building mobilizational rapport with the masses. As Tignor (2010, 260) notes, Nasser was a "modest", "inspiring figure", who became remarkably more successful in oratorical skills by the time. In many respects, he was "the right man at the time for the task" (Tignor 2010, 260). It is clear that it was not only his lifestyle but also his ideas towards Egyptian elites, especially the landed power holders and party politics before the 1952 revolution, were making him a populist in the conventional sense of the term. As Vatikiotis notes, "he saw himself as a plebeian autocratic reformer, a benevolent despot, who insisted on monopolising the initiative for changes" (1978, 190). Therefore, in the Weylandian sense of the term, Nasser tended to denounce party politics and underlined his direct emotional rapport with the people. As Vatikiotis highlights, "Nasser's rejection of parties was complemented by a constant appeal to his special relationship with the masses" as his own words demonstrate (1978, 191): "I feel unlimited gratitude to the masses of our great struggling nation, hoping each day to satisfy them; something that is beyond my capacity to do because I possess nothing beside my work and life" (*Nasser quoted in* Vatikiotis 1978, 191). Nasser was also worried about a strike back by – or the return of – a privileged elite, even among the ranks of the National Union,[1] which he reluctantly had to establish as a political vehicle of his populist-authoritarian rule: "I am with the people. ... We must at all costs prevent the emergence of a new class, that believes privilege is their due inheritance from the old ruling class" (*Nasser quoted in* Vatikiotis 1978, 191).

But these qualities and discursive and mobilizational proclivities of Nasser were only surface reflections of a deeper and genuine populist conviction that revealed itself in the form of a "populist governmental practice" *par excellence*. Nasser himself was well aware of the fact that "words" had their limits when it came to establish stable rapports between his rule and the masses.[2] Immediately after the "revolution", Nasser wanted to implement a series of radical reforms – such as land reform, nationalizations, and subsidies for vital goods and services – that could improve the conditions of underprivileged segments of the population *vis-a-vis* traditional notables as well as more urban elites. It was in this sense, too, the Nasser regime was populist, as noted by Bayat (1993, 65). In a similar fashion, Hinnebusch (2020) calls such regimes as polities based on a "populist social contract" in which even authoritarian leaders found themselves required to supply some basic goods and services to unprivileged masses to acquire and sustain legitimate authority. (This is a point that I will turn back in the following parts). This "populist governmental practice" based on the understanding of a "social contract" between populist rulers and their audiences in the Middle East, was expressed through the notion of "Arab Socialism" during the time of Nasser. As Roussillon (1998) notes, however, "Arab Socialism" was not "socialism" in a strict sense, and it was actually a corporatist-statist ideology rejecting stricter Marxist-Leninist interpretations. Following this line of reasoning, "socialism" can be encapsulated as the rejection of exploitation and the establishment of economic balance among citizens to enable the attainment of justice. It entailed providing equal opportunities for everyone and safeguarding national unity. This is characterized by democratic collaboration among various segments of the working population, including peasants, labourers, soldiers, intellectuals, and the national capital. The Arab Socialist Union positioned itself as the guardian of this concept (Roussillon 1998, 347). Thus, unlike other more doctrinaire socialist experiences of the era, Arab Socialism was not against private property and it was deeply pragmatic and flexible.

As Blaydes notes, the economic policies of the Nasser era were characterized by extensive state control and nationalizations as well as partially successful assaults on large landowners (2010, 29). But what provided the Nasser era with a decisively populist orientation was its proclivities and implementations in the realm of social and educational policies including generous subsidies and free-of-charge public education under the circumstances of a rapidly expanding public sector (Blaydes 2010, 29). In this regard, it is also important to note that, Gamal Abd-al Nasser was by no means an ordinary Middle East strong man obsessed with power and coercion. As the evidence below will testify, he deserves to be called a "populist revolutionary" with a genuine concern for the poor who achieved considerable success in uplifting popular sectors in Egypt. Nasser achieved this goal without inciting violent social and elite reactions by avoiding a full-fledged confrontation with the *status quo*. But his project of "populist developmentalism" also inflicted some chronic problems upon the Egyptian nation, which is a perfect example of pitfalls of populist governmental practice.

210 Case studies

Populist socio-economic and educational policies: Trade-offs of responsive political practice

National developmentalism

The Egypt inherited by the Free Officers rule was characterized by two inter-related social problems, which, as El Shakry (2007) highlighted, defined the social scientific imagination as well. These were the problems of "peasants" and "population growth" (2007, 198). The intersection of these common problems, predating the Nasser rule, was poverty of large parts of the Egyptian population as well as low levels of productivity in Egyptian economy and agriculture. In order to deal with these problems, Nasser rule expanded the already existing "etatist" traditions in Egypt. This "social welfare mode of regulation" (El Shakry 2007, 198) was based on comprehensive interventions of the state not only to economy but also to other realms of social and political life in order to reduce poverty and inhibit any radical kind of mass movement by absorbing the dissent of masses through redistribution. Yet, during the Nasser era, the etatist traditions of Egypt gained a new and more comprehensive form than ever.

As Shehata (2018) notes, during the 1950s and 1960s, the government expanded its control over various sectors of the economy. In 1956, it nationalized all foreign-owned assets, and by 1961, a majority of assets owned by the Egyptian private sector were also nationalized in line with socialist decrees of July 1961. Additionally, the regime initiated an ambitious industrialization effort, overseeing the establishment of numerous new factories. The Nasser regime took on extensive social and welfare responsibilities. For instance, it mandated the state employment of all university and technical institute graduates in 1964. This led to a significant transformation in the Egyptian labour force, with the civil service and public sector becoming predominant in both urban and, to a lesser extent, rural job markets. Furthermore, in 1963, the government enacted a new law that made higher education free for all secondary school graduates. Consequently, the number of university and technical university students tripled, and the number of technical university students increased sixfold between 1952 and 1969. The regime also provided subsidies for various essential goods and services, including housing, transportation, and healthcare (Shehata 2018, 102). In short, "Nasser instituted a populist distributive regime that relied on welfare and populist reforms" (Shehata 2018, 109).

These reforms were populist in character as the term defined here due to a couple of respects. First of all, regardless of the eventual accomplishments, they targeted large parts of popular sectors and genuinely strived to improve their conditions. Thus, nationalizations in Egypt during the Nasser rule was not really a consequence of a fanatical socialist commitment but a result of a genuine and immediate concern regarding the situation of poor masses under intellectual and political circumstances of the Nasser's age, which were largely influenced by the achievements of the Soviet economy. When the fact that the Nasser regime tried to appeal to a "national bourgeoisie" and carefully wanted to distinguish itself from Marxist-Leninist interpretations of socialism in its initial years is taken into account, pragmatism of the Nasser's rule is understood better (Joya 2020, 39–40). One should also note that the expansion of the public sector in Egypt started with the nationalization of foreign companies and enterprises, which is all too understandable given the anti-colonial orientation of the new regime. But, as Mansfield notes, nationalizations of foreign industries and enterprises incrementally turned into expropriation of Egyptian companies around the beginning of the 1960s (1973, 680–681). At a certain moment, Nasser's regime initiated more aggressive state interventions to the private sector, including assets of foreign companies such as the Suez Canal. This created a long list of sectors in public ownership ranging from banking and insurance to textile and food-processing plants, from urban retail trade to hotels, cinemas, and theatres, from newspapers to major construction companies. One of the reasons that led Egyptian political elites of the time to such strict measures – aside from consolidating their power – was the conviction that the private sector and the national bourgeoisie did not play its role in the development plan and they did not undertake the distributive role they were expected of (Waterbury 1983, 76–77).

Another reflection of the populist orientation of Nasser's regime in the realm of socio-economic policies was the "land reform" or the "agrarian reform". In fact, Nasser, and the Free Officers that he was leading, came to power in a struggle, not only with monarchy but also with large landowners. As Shehata notes, "Nasser overthrew the old oligarchic regime made up of the monarchy, the landed elite, and the foreign-born bourgeoisie. In its place, he created a nationalist, socialist-populist, authoritarian regime supported by the military, the state bureaucracy, the salaried middle class, and the lower classes" (2018, 101). Thus, a land reform aiming at a relatively more equal distribution of wealth was not surprising at all, and it was one of the first measures the new regime implemented after seizing power (Roussillon 1998, 338). The new Egyptian regime confiscated the land concentrated in the hands of already small circle of large landowners and foreign companies and distributed these to landless peasants in order to solve deeply exploitative landowner-tenant relationships in rural Egypt (Joya 2020, 43–46). As Joya (2020) notes, the agrarian reform had three key components. First, it established a land ownership limit of 200 feddans in 1952, which was further reduced to 100 feddans in 1961. The second aspect of the reform aimed to regulate lease terms to mitigate the exploitative relationships between landlords and tenants. The third dimension of the reform focused on

212 Case studies

structuring the redistributed lands through the establishment of agricultural cooperatives (2020, 44). The agrarian reform had a major effect on Egyptian society since it remarkably reduced rural inequality and poverty in Egypt (Joya 2020, 46–47).

The "developmentalist" urge of the new Egyptian regime was perhaps not more visible in any other case than the construction of a huge dam on the Nile, which is known as the "High Dam" or the "Aswan Dam". The Nasser regime was willing to turn Egypt into an industrializing nation and this required more productive agriculture as well as better electricity supplies. Not only the aspiration to become an industrial nation but the perennial problems of population expansion and poverty led the Egypt's leadership to such an investment even under very dire financial conditions. The populist Egyptian elite of the time, by building this huge dam, strived to achieve an expansion of the land suitable for agriculture, and a new source of energy for industrial development, which, together, expected to raise the life standards of underprivileged Egyptians (Little 1965, 39–40). Even before the construction of the dam, however, the hazards this may entail were obvious. As Tignor (2010, 262–264) notes, there were a few serious shortcomings that will threaten Egypt's ancient heritage, ordinary Egyptians' life and health as well as the ecology of the Nile basin. Because collecting Nile's water in a huge artificial lake behind the dam was certainly going to leave some ancient statues in the region under water, the silt that was going to remain at the bottom of this lake would no longer enrich the soil in the lower parts of the Nile (a problem that was expected and planned to be solved through industrial fertilizers) and finally, it was almost certain that the canals that will remain full with water year-round would increase the threat of bilharzia for the peasant populations. But, not surprisingly, more immediate material needs guided the choices of populist-developmentalist Egyptian leadership and, in a clearly populist fashion, they disregarded the archaeological, ecological, and public health risks. Ultimately, the High Dam of Egypt, with its impressive scale, was complemented in 1970 with heavy borrowings from foreign landers, most notably the USSR (Mansfield 1973, 682).

But the construction of the dam, not unexpectedly, brought with it the hazards that were predicted: "The silt-free water flowing through the High Dam has virtually eliminated marine life in the Nile River, from Aswan to the Mediterranean Sea, 600 miles away" (Rubinstein 1972, 8). The Dam also slowed down the flow of the Nile causing a fertile breeding ground for snails and increased the incidence of bilharzia among Egyptian peasants, a disease that causes fatigue. And providing the fertilizers that was required for the increasingly poorer soil of the lower Nile basin were proved to be harder and costlier than initially expected. Yet, there was no doubt that the dam brought some immediate benefits that were expected by the populist leadership (Rubinstein 1972, 8). For example, the dam provided electricity to 90 percent of villages in Egypt which used to lack this comfort beforehand (Mansfield 1973, 682). In a more recent study, economic and social benefits of the Aswan Dam such as the remarkably increased agricultural production, the increasing electrification of rural Egypt, the enabling of feeding a much larger population as well as the dam's regulatory impact that helped the authorities to save the Nile from unexpected floods and drought have been confirmed (Robinson *et al.* 2008, 239–241). In this regard, it is important to note again the immediate material benefits of the dam as a response to pressing needs of the Egyptian population. For populist-developmentalist leaderships, such benefits certainly outweigh the evident risks and threats for archaeological and long-term ecological hazards posed by such policies. In populist governmental practice, it is not the administrative prudence and a long-term horizon but responsiveness and immediacy shape decisions.

Feeding the nation: Subsidies for the basics

The immediacy and responsiveness of the populist rule during the Nasser era unfolded in responding to the rather more hand-to-mouth existence of ordinary Egyptians as well. As Shehata notes, "the regime [...] subsidized many basic foods and services including housing, transportation, and healthcare" (2018, 102). In fact, "since the 1940s, Egypt's government has operated a system of food subsidies. After having expanded in the 1970s, the food subsidy system in 1980–81 covered more than a dozen items, representing 14 percent of total government spending and 13 percent of total private consumption" (Löfgren & El-Said 2001, 66). As Gutner (2002) notes, during the 1960s and 1970s, the food subsidy system expanded and became part of a broader range of consumer welfare programs. These encompassed subsidies for transportation, housing, energy, as well as consumer goods like soap and cigarettes. These policies played a crucial role in maintaining stable prices amidst urbanization and rapid population growth (Gutner 2002, 461).

Nevertheless, the hazards of the food subsidy system were already known during the Nasser era. As Roussillon noted, the system caused "unjustified increase in consumption", "waste", "black market" and, at times, benefitted the rich instead of the poor (1998, 362). Yet, due to the populist social contract, it was almost impossible to completely abandon this policy because, even some reforms in this realm caused unprecedented reaction. For example, during the Sadat era and the *infitah* (economic liberalization) process, Egyptian governments attempted to remove subsidies from some basic consumer goods but this was not possible. It immediately provoked violent protests in Cairo and Alexandria (Roussillon 1998, 362–363). The country-wide violent "bread riots" could only be suppressed with a curfew and by revoking the price rises for basic goods by the Sadat administration (Soliman 2021, 25–26).

214 Case studies

Not only food subsidies but also subsidies for housing and health for Egyptians were introduced during the Nasser era. As Joya notes, during the Nasser era, for urban workers, "the provision of public housing and the implementation of rent control policies significantly lowered their costs of living" (2020, 47). In the realm of health too, populist interventions brought a lot of benefits, as Mansfield (1973) noted. Addressing health issues among the rural population, known as the *fellahin*, has been a challenging and costly endeavour, similar to the efforts to eradicate illiteracy. Nevertheless, the populist regime achieved some notable improvements in this regard. By 1965, the number of doctors had increased two and a half times compared to 1952. Numerous new hospitals had been constructed, and significant progress had been made in establishing a network of health centres across rural areas. One of the most significant accomplishments has been the provision of clean drinking water to all villages. Diseases such as tuberculosis and ophthalmic ailments saw substantial reductions, and there was a promising outlook for the complete eradication of malaria, which had previously been a severe and widespread problem (Mansfield 1973, 685).

Expansion of education, and especially the higher education

The most visible realm for the populist governmental practice in the Nasser era was education. A brief historical evaluation of education in modern Egypt suffices to reveal deeply rooted problems in this realm before the rise of the Nasser regime. Like many developing countries, attempts to modernize education in Egypt started during a period of colonialist aggression. In its early stages, the inception of modern secular education can be attributed directly to military requirements. This process can be traced back to a period of defensive modernization when the emerging and ambitious ruling elite of Egypt (especially the Mehmet Ali Pasha of Kavala), facing significant external and internal challenges, recognized the need to revitalize the military establishment. Consequently, they focused their efforts on strengthening the armed forces by establishing new schools that followed European models designed to educate officers in modern European methods of warfare. Under this initiative, Mehmet Ali Pasha initiated the development of an extensive military school system aimed at providing the armed forces with engineers, doctors, pharmacists, and veterinarians. Additional schools were also established to provide the civilian sector with individuals trained in basic administration, technical subjects, and foreign languages, catering to the broader needs of the society beyond the military (Faksh 1976, 235). Later on, modern primary and secondary education systems started to develop, but the colonial rule of Britain effectively impeded the improvement in the educational realm through budget cuts lest a nationalist anti-colonial movement develops in Egypt (Faksh 1976, 237).

The 1952 Revolution represents a watershed moment in the development of education in Egypt. There were severe problems in the realm of education when the Free Officers seized the power despite the attempts of nationalist forces for expanding the educational system during the period between 1922 and 1952. These included the low levels of literacy, the inadequacy of higher education institutions, and the number of students enrolled in these institutions. These problems continued even after the Nasser era reforms. As Rubinstein (1972) noted at the beginning of the 1970s, government statistics indicated that approximately 65 percent of the population was illiterate. This was primarily attributed to the fact that not all eligible children were covered by primary education, with around 20 percent being left out. Furthermore, graduates of primary schools struggled to find suitable reading materials, leading to a recurrence of illiteracy. Additionally, there was a severe shortage of teachers, as college graduates were reluctant to accept positions in rural areas due to the lack of urban amenities (Rubinstein 1972, 9).

Yet, it is difficult to underestimate the efforts of the Nasser regime in this realm. The education system in Egypt remarkably expanded with the rise of Nasser (Faksh 1976, 239; Richards 1992, i). As Faksh notes, especially primary school and higher education expanded dramatically during the Nasser era, and both of them became overwhelmingly free (1976, 240). As Richards (1992) highlights, Nasser's concern for education stemmed from two interrelated objectives: As a true populist, he actually committed to equity. But he was also aiming at providing a social basis for an industrialized state and society (Richards 1992, 7–8).[3] The expansion of primary education was rapid, increasing from around one million students in 1952 to nearly 3.5 million in 1965/66, representing an annual enrolment growth rate of just under 9 percent. Other educational sectors saw even more rapid expansion: Preparatory school enrolments surged sixfold in just five years, going from 8,000 to 42,000 between 1956 and 1961, while secondary school enrolments more than tripled during the same period, going from 22,000 to 75,000 students.

This surge in primary and secondary school enrolments laid the foundation for a significant increase in the number of students entering higher education in the late 1960s and 1970s, known as the "Nasser years cohort". The abolition of fees, implemented into law in 1963, further stimulated university enrolment. With the combination of free higher education and the promise of employment, there was a strong demand for university education. As a result, university enrolments surged from just over 50,000 in 1952/53 to over 160,000 in 1969/70. Initially, these students were accommodated within the existing universities of Cairo, Alexandria, and Ain Shams. Subsequently, "local branches" of these existing universities were established, and eventually, these branches evolved into autonomous

216 Case studies

universities. Although this process began with the creation of Asyut University in 1957 during the Nasser government, it reached its peak with a wave of establishment of new universities in the first half of the 1970s (Richards 1992, 8).

But this populist expansion in the realm of education, and especially in the realm of higher education, came with some serious shortcomings with regard to the quality of the education. As Richard underlined, "inevitably, educational quality crumbled before the quantitative flood" (1992, 8). The dramatic expansion of education in primary and secondary schools also corroborated the structural problems of education such as being relied overwhelmingly on "memorization" and "inadequately trained teachers" (Richards 1992, 8). The picture of higher education was not different. Rapid quantitative expansion of higher education institutions by the populist regime and the dramatic increase in the number of students resulted in serious problems of educational infrastructure, quality of teaching personnel and education methods. Richards provides a vivid depiction of these problems, apparently based on some on-site observations of the educational realm in Egypt. These problems vary from lack of adequate teaching material to an education based on memorization, from crowded classrooms to deficiencies of libraries due to inadequate budgets, from lack of labs for science students to underpaid professors who did not fulfil their teaching responsibilities properly due to pressing needs of earning their living via other occupations (Richards 1992, 13–14).

But the particularly populist aspect of the policies in the educational realm during the Nasser era was not really its rapid expansion. It is, in fact, how the Nasser regime connected the expansion of higher education to public employment. As Richards (1992) notes, in 1964, the government made a commitment to provide employment to any university graduate who couldn't secure a job in the private sector. This assurance essentially transformed obtaining a university degree into a guarantee of a relatively stable, though modest, life-long income. As a result, the individual advantages of pursuing a university education greatly expanded while the elimination of fees significantly reduced the personal financial burden. This combination of increased benefits and reduced costs led to a sharp increase in the demand for higher education, which was already substantial due to societal factors (Richards 1992, 9). This deeply populist approach to higher education and the public sector typically reveals the short-term virtues of populist governmental practices that are creating long-term ills. Egyptian public sector and bureaucracy, therefore, needs a closer scrutiny since it has been the embodiment of populist socio-economic and educational policies started in the Nasser era. The next part will focus on the notorious Egyptian bureaucracy created by the "populist social contract" established during the Nasser era.

A bureaucracy created by a modern "populist social contract"

As Hinnebusch (2020) notes in a very important article, many Middle Eastern regimes between the 1930s and 1980s embraced substantially distributive policies in order to absorb the reactions of the masses. In those decades, global redistributive currents were coupled with the traditions of the region inherited from the Ottoman past and created, what Hinnebusch aptly called, a "populist social contract" in which underprivileged masses had considerable expectations of livelihood from the ruling elites. In return, the ruling elites – even in non-democratic regimes – felt obliged to respond to these demands through highly distributive measures, such as food subsidies exemplified above, for their legitimacy. The "populist social contract" for countries like Egypt, which made remarkable progress in terms of economic and political modernization compared to, for example, Gulf monarchies, gained the form of a modern redistributive regime deploying more than material subsidies. As noted above, Nasser's populist developmentalist regime provided the "populist social contract" with a new dimension by expanding the education at every level and making it free for underprivileged populations. Again, as a somewhat logical extension of the "populist social contract" in a modernizing polity, the Nasser regime promised the graduates of recently expanded universities a public sector job if they cannot find a job in the private sector. This has been exactly the most persistent legacy of the populist rule in Egypt by creating a colossal bureaucracy with numerous ills.

As Ayubi (1982) notes, following the 1952 Revolution, the expansion of the public bureaucracy in Egypt accelerated significantly, primarily driven by the government's policies aimed at expanding industrial activities, enhancing welfare services, and providing free education. These measures encompassed extensive nationalizations of industries, trade, and financial sectors, increased worker involvement in management and profit-sharing, and the introduction of comprehensive programs for social services and insurance. Between 1952 and 1970, the number of civil servants in Egypt increased from 350,000 to 1,200,000. As Ayubi (1982) draws attention, the legacy of the populist Nasser rule had been persistent, and, as a consequence, the public bureaucracy kept growing even during the liberalization process initiated by Anwar Sadat in the 1970s. In 1978, it was estimated that the Egyptian bureaucracy was employing 3,200,000 civil servants, including those in state companies. No doubt that such excessive number of civil servants created a problem of "excess manpower" in the Egyptian bureaucracy which amounted to 50 percent of all employees (Ayubi 1982, 286–289).

In fact, overstaffing and budget difficulties were the inevitable outcomes of the populist policy of expanding the higher education in Egypt. Because the expansion of higher education also entailed the potential risks of unemployment of the educated such as political radicalization and social

218 Case studies

unrest (Ayubi 1982, 289). This is why, as Ayubi (1982) noted, even in a period of relative liberalization under Sadat and Mubarak rules, the Egyptian state felt obliged to keep employing university graduates. The problem was, apparently, solved by employing excess graduates in the state bureaucracy in "organizationally unnecessary and professionally unsatisfying" jobs with "low salaries". This huge bureaucracy was not efficient at all and showed an extremely poor performance. Ayubi (1982), evidently based on first-hand observations, provides vivid details regarding the consequence of the bureaucratic growth in Egypt as a result of populist policies of the Nasser era. These consequences involve poor physical conditions of government offices, lack of order and cleanliness, lack of discipline among the majority of the civil servants and an appalling disregard for working hours – which ironically reduces congestions in Cairo's traffic-, overstaffing including thousands of unqualified personnel such as messengers and cleaners and surprising levels of inefficiency (1982, 292–293).[4]

Ironically enough, Ayubi also notes the problems of Egyptian bureaucracy which emerged as a result of populist practices and policies but which were, at the same time, anathema to a populist logic. These included "the idolization of papers and documents, signatures and seals, 'routine and red tape', and the complexities and repetitiveness of a large number of formalities and procedures, all of which inevitably lead to bottle-necks and delay. Serious carelessness and negligence are also among the most dangerous of Egyptian bureaupathologies" (1982, 295). The Mogamma building, in this respect, represented all the pathologies of the Egyptian bureaucracy originally generated by the populist social contract of the Nasser era. With its colossal structure, maze-like, loud interior, and irresponsive and arrogant employees who, as a contemporary Egyptian journalist, Khaled Diab notes, made the citizens "to metamorphose from a proud human into a shrinking, trembling, deferential insect".[5] Thus, an excessive proclivity to populist governmental practice in the long run, ironically created, what, initially seems something anathema to a populist logic: A colossal, irresponsive, and dominant bureaucracy. Which, later, overcome only through various bottom-up popular practices ranging from "connections" to "bribes" as Diab notes:

> Despite the dominant and often traumatic role bureaucracy plays in Egyptian life, there is surprisingly no widely circulated local word for it, with Egyptians appropriating the English word 'routine' to describe it. However, there is an abundance of words used to describe ways to circumvent it, including '*wasta*' (connections), '*mahsoubiya*' (favouritism) and '*kousa*' (courgette) to describe string pulling, or '*halawa*' (halva), '*shai*' (tea) or even '*bakshish*' (tip) to describe bribery.[6]

Concluding discussion

From a long-term, bottom-up, and broader perspective, populism cannot be simply seen as a discursive, mobilizational, or performative phenomenon pertaining to the realm of electoral power politics. It is also a phenomenon of policy practice and implementation, especially in the rule of politicians with strong populist proclivities. This perspective renders the Nasser era and its long-term consequences an important case of populist governmental practice. The Nasser era was not populist simply due to Nasser's down-to-earth character and his highly populist worldview and discourse. It was also a perfect example of populist regimes which were based on a "populist social contract" (Hinnebusch 2020) with decisive implications in the realm of socio-economic and education policies. In other words, the Nasser era populism was not simply about words or political performance on the stage of elite politics but it was also based on complex relations of material and symbolic reciprocity with broad underprivileged masses.

These relations of reciprocity provided Egyptian popular sectors with unprecedented gains from the 1950s to 1970s ranging from land distribution, food and housing subsidies to free education at every level. The populist proclivity was also evident in the developmental policies of the Nasser era as the construction of "High Dam", a concrete infrastructural investment with direct and immediate material benefits, testified. The dam contributed a lot to increasing the welfare of Egyptian citizens and Egypt's industrialization. As Mansfield noted, "there are elements of truth in all [...] criticisms but they must be set against the positive achievements" ranging from "high rates of growth" to a "shift of income to the working class", from the reduction of "rural poverty" to remarkable progress in "industrialization", from the expansion of social services and aid to enlargement of the education and remarkable improvements in the basic indicators of health in the Nasser's Egypt (1973, 684–685).

Despite immediate benefits, however, all of these achievements came with a price as a result of the short-termism and pragmatism of the populist governmental practice. For example, as Roussillon (1998, 338) notes, land distribution was not implemented decisively, so it left a powerful landed class behind. In general, as El Shakry notes, with a profoundly populist logic, the Egyptian Revolution of 1952, in fact, turned into a "passive revolution" and "rather than inaugurate either a national bourgeois revolution or the radical socialist transformation it espoused, effected what amounts to piecemeal, molecular, legal and reformist revisions of the previous political-economic order, without radically dismantling class relations and power structures" (2007, 202). The Aswan Dam too created a lot of economic and ecological problems in the long run, as elaborated above. Even the most benign forms of populist practice entailed problems such as the issue of waste and

220 Case studies

corruption brought by comprehensive food subsidies. The populist social contract between the Egyptian masses and the Nasser regime gained such a comprehensive form in the 1960s that the Egyptian state decided to provide public sector jobs to every graduate from the expanded higher education system if they were unable to find jobs elsewhere. This, however, left a lasting legacy and ironically gradually created a colossal, irresponsive, and inefficient bureaucracy. One of the lessons that can be derived from the case of Egypt is that populism as a governmental practice has a long-lasting and persistent impact that cannot be undone under a new government, as the impact of populist socio-economic and education policies had on Egyptian bureaucracy testified. Thus, when the populist governmental practice is extended to its limits, it has the potential to create its very opposite in the long run. Thus, the case of Egyptian populism perfectly captures the virtues and vices of populist governmental practice.

Notes

1 More than a "party" and channel of participation for the masses, the "National Union" – later became the Socialist Union – established by Nasser, as Binder (1966) notes, was a means to control the masses and absorb their appetite for political participation. It was a mechanism to suppress other avenues of political participation for the masses (Binder 1966, 227).
2 "We make a mistake in our definition of power. Power is not merely shouting aloud. Power is to act positively with all the components of power" (Nasser 1963, 66).
3 The following data comes from Richard's (1992) study.
4 In this very colourful and vivid part of his study including many interesting details of a routine day in an Egyptian public service office, Ayubi notes that "on average, the Egyptian civil servant was estimated to 'work' solidly only for a period of between twenty minutes and two hours every working day" (1982, 293).
5 https://www.aljazeera.com/opinions/2016/1/18/mogamma-egypts-other-great-pyramid, accessed: 24.6.2023.
6 Ibid.

References

Abdalla, A. (1988). The armed forces and the democratic process in Egypt. *Third World Quarterly*, *10*(4), 1452–1466.
Allcock, J. B. (1971). "Populism": A brief biography. *Sociology*, *5*(3), 371–387.
Ayubi, N. N. (1982). Bureaucratic inflation and administrative inefficiency – the deadlock in Egyptian administration. *Middle Eastern Studies*, *18*(3), 286–299.
Bayat, A. (1993). Populism, liberalization and popular participation – industrial democracy in Egypt. *Economic and Industrial Democracy*, *14*(1), 65–87.
Binder, L. (1966). Political recruitment and participation in Egypt. In J. L. Palombara and M. Weiner (Eds.), *Political Parties and Political Development* (pp. 217–240). Princeton, NJ: Princeton University Press.

Blaydes, L. (2010). *Elections and Distributive Politics in Mubarak's Egypt.* Cambridge: Cambridge University Press.

Di Tella, T. S. (1997). Populism into the twenty-first century. *Government and opposition, 32*(2), 187–200.

El Shakry, O. (2007). *The Great Social Laboratory – Subjects of Knowledge in Colonial and Post-Colonial Egypt.* Stanford, CA: Stanford University Press.

Faksh, M. A. (1976). An historical survey of the educational system in Egypt. *International Review of Education, 22*(2), 234–244.

Gutner, T. (2002). The political economy of food subsidy reform: the case of Egypt. *Food Policy, 27*(5–6), 455–476.

Halpern, M. (1965). *The Politics of Social Change in the Middle East and North Africa.* Princeton, NJ: Princeton University Press.

Hinnebusch, R. (2020). The rise and decline of the populist social contract in the Arab world. *World Development, 129.* https://doi.org/10.1016/j.worlddev.2019.104661.

Johnson, P. (1972). Egypt under Nasser. *Merip Reports, 10,* 3–14.

Joya, A. (2020). *The Roots of Revolt – A Political Economy of Egypt from Nasser to Mubarak.* Cambridge: Cambridge University Press.

Little, T. (1965). *The High Dam at Aswan – the Subjugation of the Nile.* New York: The John Day Company.

Löfgren, H. & M. El-Said (2001). Food subsidies in Egypt: Reform options, distribution and welfare. *Food Policy, 26*(1), 65–83.

Mansfield, P. (1973). Nasser and Nasserism. *International Journal, 28*(4), 670–688.

Nasser, G. A. (1963). *The Philosophy of the Revolution-Book 1.* Cairo: Mondiale Press.

Perlmutter, A. (1974). *Egypt - the Praetorian State.* New Brunswick: Transaction Books.

Richards, A. (1992). "Higher Education in Egypt". World Bank Working Paper Series 862, Population and Human Resources Department, The World Bank, https://documents1.worldbank.org/curated/en/163341468770080097/pdf/multi-page.pdf, accessed: 8.3.2024.

Robinson, S., K. Strzepek, M. El-Said & H. Lofgren. (2008). The High Dam at Aswan. In R. Bhatia, R. Cestti, M. Scatasta & R. P. S. Malik (Eds.), *Indirect Economic Impacts of Dams – Case Studies from India, Egypt and Brazil* (pp. 227–274). New Delhi: Academic Foundation.

Roussillon, A. (1998). Republican Egypt interpreted - revolution and beyond. In C. F. Petry & M. V. Daly (Eds.), *The Cambridge History of Egypt, 2* (pp. 334–393). Cambridge: Cambridge University Press.

Rubinstein, A. Z. (1972). Egypt since Nasser. *Current History, 62*(365), 6–13.

Shehata, D. (2018). Sixty years of Egyptian politics – what has changed? *The Cairo Review of Global Affairs, 29,* 101–109.

Soliman, N. A. (2021). Remembering the 1977 Bread Riots in Suez: Fragments and ghosts of resistance. *International Review of Social History, 66*(S29), 23–40.

Tignor, R. L. (2010). *Egypt – a Short History.* Princeton, NJ: Princeton University Press.

Vatikiotis, P. J. (1978). *Nasser and His Generation.* London: Croom Helm.

Waterbury, J. (1983). *The Egypt of Nasser and Sadat – the Political Economy of Two Regimes.* Princeton, NJ: Princeton University Press.

Worsley, P. (1970). *Third World.* Chicago: The University of Chicago Press.

11

THE POPULIST FOREIGN POLICY CONDUCT DURING TRUMP'S PRESIDENCY IN THE UNITED STATES

Populism in the United States: A deep-rooted tradition of politics

Any generalizing account of populism with a historical perspective would start by citing the original populist movement in the United States that emerged in the last decades of the 19th century. Alongside Russian Narodnism, American populism in general, and the history of the People's Party in particular, have always been considered the prototypical examples of populist experiences preceding the populist currents in the 20th and 21st centuries. Unlike European political systems – which, until the rise of populist parties in recent decades, have been considered immune to populism – populist politics in various forms has been part and parcel of American politics. And it has not been really only about the impact of the People's Party towards the end of the 19th century, but it has also been about figures who dominated regional politics, especially in the American South, like Huey Long and George Wallace in the 20th century. In addition, some Republican presidents in the second half of the 20th century, such as Nixon and Reagan, have been considered populists in certain respects. Today, at various wings of the American political spectrum, various authors identify populist politicians like Bernie Sanders, Sarah Palin, and Donald Trump. This is certainly not only due to the notorious conceptual ambiguity of populism. It is rather about strong proclivities of American politics towards populist discourses, ideas, mobilizational strategies, styles, and practices in politics. The emergence of such populist figures and actors finds their roots in the historical and social conditions of America that have facilitated populism since the rise of the United States as an independent political entity.

DOI: 10.4324/9781003294627-14

The populist foreign policy conduct during Trump's presidency **223**

The American proclivity to populist politics: From democratic conviction to "machine politics" and Trumpism

Regardless of the definition one embraces about populism, one could find typical examples of the phenomenon in US political history. Populism in the United States comes in the form of ideas, styles, and strategies as well as solid political/governmental practices. As a kind of undercurrent, populism has always been present in US politics (Green & White 2019). There are several historical, political, social, economic, cultural, and geographical conditions that have facilitated the remarkable presence of populism in the US political history. First of all, one should underline the fact that the United States emerged as a country of colonization based mainly on immigration from protestant Europe. The United States, from the very beginning, lacked an aristocracy and traditional social hierarchies in general, which created profoundly egalitarian propensities and expectations among its inhabitants. Later, the struggle with a monarchy for independence and objection to traditional social hierarchies consolidated the American elites almost *en bloc* propensity to democratic politics and popular sovereignty, except enclaves in the Southern United States based on an underdeveloped rural economy relying upon slave labour. The land abundance and the enlargement of the small propertied social segments in the United States – as the "frontier" (Turner 2008) of the polity expanded gradually towards the West – have deepened the egalitarian attitudes in American society to such an extent that, at some point, Tocqueville was worried that the American society would prefer "equality" over "liberty" (Green & White 2019, 109–110).

In combination with these social attitudes, early democratization and the introduction of universal suffrage before the industrialization processes undermined the rise of class politics in the United States (Scarrow 2006). The lack of a class-based mass party might have opened room for the rise of populism in US politics, while European continental politics was dominated by strictly ideological mass parties of the right and left. It is also important to note that industrialization of the United States under the circumstances of universal suffrage paved the way to populist "machine politics" in urban contexts in the absence of left-wing mass parties. Hence, the US electorate's propensity to populist political practice was not only ideological and mobilizational, it was also a practical one. Notorious urban machine politics in the United States, in several respects, has been deeply populist. The swift arrival of new immigrant populations who strongly identified with their families and ethnic backgrounds, along with the allocation of significant exclusive privileges like control over transportation, electricity, power, and similar areas, as well as access to government employment, created a fertile environment that encouraged the development of political party machines based on material exchange between powerful patrons and poor constituencies (Scott 1969, 1145). In Scott's seminal article on machine politics, one can see the intermingling of populist rhetoric and clientelistic practices as the basis of populist governmental practice in the United States since

> the vaguely populist image of the machine party was based less on its pronouncements of general policy (which are rare) than on a myriad of acts that symbolized its accessibility, helpfulness, and desire to work for the "little man". For the rank and file, the machine boss represented a patron of those at the bottom of the social pyramid, and while the court system with its rational justice may have favored property interests, the boss typified for them an empirical justice "that works more consistently in the interests of the poor, for attention is focused upon their concrete needs and deprivations". Hints of municipal corruption and graft were winked at, even applauded, by the machine clientele as the social banditry of an urban Robin Hood in spite of their long-run costs to the city.
>
> *(Scott 1969, 1144)*

As Scott demonstrates in this crucial article, machine politics in the United States was deeply clientelistic. But at the same time it was also deeply populist in its practical orientation, exactly in a manner that is testifying the blurred boundaries between clientelism and populist governmental practice. The importance of machine politics in the United States is that it perfectly captures the extra-linguistic dimension of populism and shows that its practitioners did not settle with populist rhetoric at all. Thus, it can be assumed that there has always been a propensity and, even a tradition of, populist governmental practice in the United States as a resilient undercurrent.

These dynamics of US politics have also been accompanied by a widely shared egalitarian ethos that is deeply sceptical about privileges enjoyed by political elites and "government" (especially the federal government and bureaucracy). The expansion of this bureaucracy over time and the highly intricate and mediated form it assumed throughout decades also fed a nativist/populist sentiment among the American public. Thus, the reaction against government regulation and interference usually took the form of populist politics in ideational (populist movements and views) and practical respects (pragmatic and informal politics such as "machine politics"). This scepticism has always been fed by the geographical immensity of the United States putting huge distances between provincial regions and the political and economic power centres of the country too (Green & White 2019, 111).[1]

Today, the rise of Trumpism in the United States is also explained by a theory of "cultural backlash", which describes a reaction to the "silent revolution" in Western societies starting with the 1960s that has rendered them more cosmopolitan, multicultural, and pluralist. As Norris and Inglehart

The populist foreign policy conduct during Trump's presidency **225**

(2019) demonstrate, longitudinal surveys provide compelling evidence that, over time, the public in Western societies has generally embraced more progressive social viewpoints on a range of issues. However, it is unsurprising that certain groups, such as the interwar generation, those who haven't pursued higher education, working class individuals, white Europeans, deeply religious individuals, men, and residents of rural communities, continue to uphold traditional and conservative values. Consequently, these particular groups are more likely to feel estranged from the ongoing societal shift towards progressive social and moral values, as they vehemently oppose these cultural changes (Norris & Inglehart 2019, 15–16). In countries like the United States "the spread of post-materialist and other socially progressive policies stimulated a reaction on the part of social conservatives" (Norris & Inglehart 2019, 44). In the United States too, therefore, alongside the historical propensity of the United States to populist politics, there have been more conjectural developments facilitating the contemporary populism in the form of Trumpism such as the reaction to "post-materialist" values, ever increasing plurality of American society due to immigration and processes of deindustrialization (Rosenberg & Boyle 2019) debasing the economic privileges of white American workers.

The original populists: The People's Party

The American propensity to populist politics can be seen in the rise of grassroots populist movements and practices as well as the People's Party that challenged the two party system in America in the last decade of the 19th century. As Taggart (2004, 38) notes, the Civil War in the United States left a legacy of underdeveloped South relying on specific values and culture while the victorious North kept enjoying the privileges of the industrial, cultural, and economic power centres that concentrated in this part of the country. Before the rise of the People's Party, there were, however, various grassroots movements defending the rights and interests of the small farmers in the United States (Taggart 2000, 43). At the beginning of the 1890s, these grassroots movements turned into a political party, the People's Party, with clear populist themes that could be identified in the rhetoric of its leaders. The populist ideas and rhetoric, the division of the society into "elites" and ordinary "people", and the moral depiction of this struggle, is crystal clear in speeches by leaders of the People's Party.[2]

At an ideational level, American populists' views were embodied in a "producerist" ideology claiming that "the production of material goods by farmers and workers was the economic and moral basis of the social and political order" (Frank 2017, 637). As Frank (2017) asserts, American populists held the belief that individuals who accumulated wealth through means other than direct production – such as those involved in shaping markets,

226 Case studies

facilitating exchanges, or engaging in banking – were seen as exploiting the productive capabilities of the nation. This perspective was rooted not only in economic theory but also in a broader distrust of abstract concepts and delegation of authority. In line with this producerist ideology, the view among common Southerners in the United States was that the wealth should remain primarily in the hands of those who physically created it. Similarly, there was also the conviction that personal independence and that of one's local community should not be compromised by impersonal market forces or by decisions made by distant and unaccountable bureaucrats in both the economic and political spheres (Frank 2017, 637).

It is important to reassert here that American populism, from its very inception, has been more than political ideas and rhetoric. It contains a vivid practical element pertaining to the realm of policy that is hard to miss. And this practical element was not really only about egalitarian and redistributive economic policy proposals devoted to the protection of "ordinary man" such as the introduction of a graduated progressive taxation and the nationalization of railway networks (Taggart 2004, 44). As Jason Frank's account on "populism and praxis" demonstrates, early American populism was populist *in practice* as well even before its policies became a part of a party manifesto in the Omaha Platform declaration. Based largely on Lawrence Goodwyn's seminal historical work on populist agrarian movements, Frank argues that "the farmers' exprerimentation with new democratic forms and their sustained collective effort to understand and act on the impoverished conditions of their lives -to generate cooperative democratic power outside the established institutions of governance- defines American Populism's radical democratic realism" (2017, 635). In order to overcome a perceived system of economic and political injustice American populists, well before the rise of the People's Party, engaged in developing "cooperative economic organizations" in order to circumvent "structural and impersonal forces practically undermining their republican ideals of independence and equality" (Frank 2017, 636). Thus, populism in its original American form was, first and foremost, a practical and pragmatic endeavour in economic realm targeting the empowerment of ordinary people that it strived to protect. Many historically nuanced analyses of early American populism demonstrate this practical dimension of populism that was proved empowering for ordinary people, which uplifted them as economic, social, and political subjects.[3]

Southern politics as populist political practice

The experience of the People's Party did not last long and the party dissolved into two mainstream parties of the United States as early as the first decade of the 20th century. But the impact of populism in the United States has continued. The agenda of populism did not only shape some of the Progressive

The populist foreign policy conduct during Trump's presidency **227**

Era reforms but also penetrated into the "New Deal" program introduced by Roosevelt (Taggart 2004, 49). More importantly, the impact of populism in the United States has been more direct at the state level, especially in the Southern politics, through figures like James Vardaman, Huey Long, and George Wallace. As Green and White note, Vardaman's populist style was so spectacular that he did not shy away from "bringing to one public event an ox that was decorated with flags emblazoned with pejorative words like 'redneck' and 'low-down'" (2019, 113). Vardamana tried to "associate himself with poor white voters" and believed to said that "democracy, no matter how dirty, belonged to 'the people'" (Green & White 2019, 113).

The more spectacular figure in this respect was Huey Long from Louisiana who was elected as the governor in 1928 (Vergari 2017, 244). Long was decisively populist in his ideas, style, and rhetoric. From the very beginning of his career, he was against the concentration of wealth in specific hands and the inequalities in education. As Taggart notes, "throughout his political life Long cultivated a folksy image, entreating voters to call him by his first name, ignoring the rules of decorum in the Senate [...]. His dress was as colourful as his language, and it can be little surprise that he provoked threats of physical violence from senators as much as from less austere opponents" (Taggart 2000, 39). Having said all of these, like other Southern populists, Long was by no means a progressive when it came to the issue of "race" and time to time he did not shy away from flaunting the white supremacist sentiment among his constituencies (Taggart 2000, 50). But Long's bombastic style and racist proclivities should not lead to overlook the practical aspects of populism in his rule that had concrete policy implications. V. O. Key, in his seminal work *Southern Politics* (1949), vividly demonstrates how Long's rule benefitted his poor constituencies and how it was deeply populist –that is to say that a governmental practice based on tactics, informality, complicity as well as conflict and strategic use of violence – in operational terms:

> In the maintenance of its power and in the execution of its program, the Long organization used all the techniques of reward and reprisal that political organizations have employed from time immemorial: patronage, in all its forms, deprivation of perquisites, economic pressure, political coercion in one form or another, and now and then outright thuggery. Beyond these short-range tactics, Long commanded the intense loyalties of a substantial proportion of the population. The schoolbooks, roads, bridges, and hospitals were something more than campaign oratory. The people came to believe that here was a man with a genuine concern for their welfare, not one of the gentlemanly do-nothing governors who had ruled the state for many decades.
>
> *(Key 1949, 162)*

228 Case studies

In the 1950s, populism in the political arena of Southern states reappeared with the rise of George Wallace in Alabama. With regard to the issue of race, Wallace embraced a deeply reactionary position to appeal to the white supremacist sentiment and defended the segregationist measures (Taggart 2004, 51). As Judis notes, Wallace presented his pro-segregationist stance as a requisite of representing the "average man" (2016, ch. 1). In addition, he also clearly divided the society between "average citizen" and "multibillionaires" (Judis 2016, ch. 1). When it came to his style, Wallace was thoroughly populist. As Taggart highlights, "Wallace's style, as befitting an ex-boxer, was pugnacious and bombastic. He cultivated an image of ordinariness. He dressed in cheap suits, slicked his hair back and professed his predilection for *country* music and 'ketchup on everything'" (2000, 39).

But besides his racist propensity against the civil rights movement and his "bombastic" style, Wallace was also sincerely interested in improving the lives of his supporters at a practical level. In other words, his populism has never been only about ideas, rhetoric and style but also about policies appealing to the poor and the underprivileged. As Judis asserts Wallace, "in his campaign brochure in 1968, [...] boasted that in Alabama, he had increased spending on education, welfare, roads, and agriculture" (2016, ch. 1). As Kazin strongly emphasizes in his seminal book on the topic, Wallace "as a post-FDR Democrat and the governor of a poor state, [...] explicitly favored a government that aided the common folk - as long as it stayed out of their schools, their unions, and their family lives" (1998, 236).

The bureaucracy, foreign policy establishment and the tradition of "populist" objection in the United States

The rise of American bureaucracy and the "populist" scepticism

American bureaucracy, especially at the federal level, has been shaped under the reaction of deeply populist values of the American public delineated so far. As McKay notes "unlike the citizens of most West European states – and indeed of America's immediate neighbours, Mexico and Canada– Americans have always mistrusted the very idea of *big* government. Low taxes and limited public spending have been populist rallying cries since the beginning of the Republic" (2013, 2). Nevertheless, in time, the American bureaucracy and government have become the biggest administrative apparatuses that the world has ever seen with its federal, state, and regional/local levels in order to cope with the immense size of the country itself and its increasing global impact and hegemony, especially throughout the 20th century. Yet, while the number of state and local bureaucrats increased dramatically throughout the decades, the number of federal bureaucrats remained mostly stable (McKay 2013, 263). However, this does not change the fact that, today, the American bureaucratic apparatus is colossal with any standard, containing over 22 million public employees (Bernstein & Shannon 2022, 369).

Combined with the bureaucracy's massive size, the American propensity to populism has entailed claims arguing that "government workers are elitist who are distant from the public or care only about the wellbeing of their city at the expense of the nation at large" (Green & White 2019, 111). In addition, as McKay notes, in the "public folklore" the figure of bureaucrat in the United States is usually depicted as someone who is overpaid, inefficient, and wasteful as well as in the service of private interests immersed in corruption (2013, 257). There is indeed a problem of control, efficiency, and accountability, when especially it comes to the federal bureaucracy, as some classics on American public administration assert (Wilson 2000, ch. 17). Nevertheless, as McKay contends, some of these problems that are being espoused frequently should be approached with scepticism since these views were largely shaped by the American public's prejudices towards "big government" (2013, 265). A series of Republican presidents stretching from Reagan to Bush, encouraged by widespread populist attitudes, dramatically politicized the government and diminished the reputation of the federal civil servants (McKay 2013, 271–274).

An exclusive and elitist institution in the middle of foreign policy activity: The State Department

It is hard to decouple the economic might of the United States from its international standing. As the United States got more and more involved in global politics as a result of two world wars, and especially after World War II, its foreign policy establishment has grown considerably in size and complexity. The United States' presence in the international realm has not only been through culture and economy but also through military presence. This fact rendered foreign policy realm a very delicate field for American decision and policymakers since the issue at stake has been the lives of American citizens. As Rosati and Scott (2011) underline, the US government allocates more than 700$ billion annually towards military expenditures and a scientific-industrial framework that serves the military. These investments have significant effects on both the economy and the quality of life for individuals within the military as well as across American society (Rosati & Scott 2011, 3).

Especially after the September 11 attacks on American soil, the foreign policy-related issues turned into a matter of internal security for the American establishment. It is impossible to delineate the gradual expansion of the American foreign policy bureaucracy here, but it is important to note that, throughout the 20th and first decades of the 21st century, the foreign policy-related departments in the US administration grew dramatically in size, personnel number and complexity as globalization intensified and America's global role expanded. As Rosati and Scott highlight, the dramatic change in the budget and personnel number figures of the State Department as the core component of American foreign policy establishment, alongside the Department of Defence and National Security Council, demonstrates this overall dramatic transformation of the American foreign policy bureaucracy. The State Department had its origins in 1789, initially staffed by just six individuals with a modest budget of 7.961$ and two diplomatic missions. However, by 2010, its budget had grown significantly, surpassing 16$ billion, and it had expanded to operate more than 250 diplomatic missions, spanning nearly every country and numerous international organizations. This transformation has made the State Department a highly intricate entity, owing to its global reach and the fact that a majority of its foreign service officers work abroad. In fact, due to its extensive geographic coverage and the distinct foreign service culture, the State Department functions as a large bureaucratic organization both domestically and internationally (Rosati & Scott 2011, 132–133). Thus, the presidents' influence on foreign policy in the United States incrementally diminished as the size and complexity of the foreign policy bureaucracy increased, especially after the Vietnam War (Rosati & Scott 2011, 6).

Nevertheless, American presidents and elected elites have always strived to effectively influence the foreign policy realm in the United States. Hence, the two important features of the American foreign policy realm have been identified as its complexity and its political orientation (Rosati & Scott 2011, 5). This sketch regarding the foreign policy institutions in the United States, in fact, implies a strong propensity for conflict in this particular realm when a populist incumbent rises. Because, on the one hand, the American foreign policy establishment, and most notably the State Department, tend to be highly complex, technocratic, and elitist. But on the other hand, powerful politicians, and most notably the powerful presidents, have always strived to personalize the foreign policymaking processes. Thus, the foreign policy establishment in the United States has always been a battleground between populist and anti-populist or elitist tendencies. As soon as a markedly populist government takes shape, these struggles become more visible within the US foreign policy establishment.

Yet, the presidents' position in the United States *vis-à-vis* the foreign policy bureaucracy became more and more complicated due to its size, complexity, and historical development. Most notably, the Cold War and, afterwards, the September 11 attacks enlarged the foreign policy bureaucracy and rendered foreign policymaking and implementation an extremely complicated process. In addition, under the conditions of increasing globalization, domestic and foreign policy in the United States intermingled more tightly than ever by providing an "international component" to almost every department in the executive branch (Rosati & Scott 2011, 96). Nevertheless, American

The populist foreign policy conduct during Trump's presidency **231**

presidents have always had an impact on this large and complex bureaucracy through the appointment of top-level bureaucrats to critical positions such as National Security Council (NSC) adviser, Secretary of State, Secretary of Defence, Central Intelligence Agency (CIA) director, and Secretary of Treasury at the expense of policy continuity and stability (Rosati & Scott 2011, 100–103). As the American foreign policymaking and implementation processes got more complicated, the American presidents developed a propensity to increasingly rely on the NSC staff (Rosati & Scott 2011, 110). Richard Nixon's presidency is emblematic in this respect.[4] As a politician, Nixon had very low levels of trust in the bureaucracy and tried to bypass foreign policy establishment whenever it was possible. It is not surprising that "Henry Kissinger, and thus the office of national security adviser, reached a pinnacle of power under President Nixon that no single policymaker had experienced before or since" (Rosati & Scott 2011, 114).

Thus, there has always been a struggle between foreign policy establishment and American presidents with populist and personalistic inclinations. This conflict becomes more visible when the issue at stake is the role of the professional foreign policy bureaucracy, in other words, the State Department. The State Department is the most important institution in the making and implementation of American foreign policy. Yet, the State Department's role has declined throughout the historical process of rising American power and globalization due to reasons outlined by Rosati and Scott: "(1) the growing importance of international affairs for the United States; (2) the growing power of the United States in the world; (3) the global communications revolution; (4) the rise in the use of force as an instrument in U.S. foreign policy; and (5) the increasing importance of international economics" (2011, 129).

Despite its relative decline *vis-à-vis* the Department of Defence, the NSC, and the presidency, the State Department remained as the main channel of communication between the world and the United States. As a huge channel of communication with a massive HQ (the "Foggy Bottom") and hundreds of embassy and consulate workers at home and abroad, the State Department is a huge bureaucracy. As such a bureaucracy consisting of thousands of meritocratic personnel, the State Department has always been a target of populist political actors in US political history. Because, as Rosati and Scott note, the foreign service office in the US tradition of foreign policy, by definition, relies upon an elitist and cosmopolitanist tradition, both in cultural and social respects (2011, 144).

It is known that the foreign service in the United States is very elitist and the recruitment is the outcome of a series of highly challenging exams. As a result, most of the personnel recruited by the foreign service come from Ivy League graduates from wealthy WASP families (Rosati & Scott 2011, 145). As Rosati and Scott note, despite the relative "democratization" of the institution in recent decades, "the key [to entrance to the Foreign Service has

232 Case studies

been] an individual's 'pedigree' -family, background, education- and his connections. This exclusiveness resulted in an air of superiority among foreign service officers relative to other government employees, especially as other foreign policy bureaucracies expanded during World War II and the cold war" (2011, 145). Today, despite a degree of change, "the foreign service continues to be dominated by white men from affluent segments of society" (Rosati & Scott 2011, 145).

Another quality that makes foreign policy officers a suitable target for populist leaderships and their audiences is that some of them abroad, at times, seen more willing to protect the interests of countries they are resided on behalf of the United States more than the interests of the United States (Rosati & Scott 2011, 145). In addition, in an increasingly "hard power" orientation in international relations throughout the post-September 11 era, the emphasis on the role of "diplomacy" must be rendering the foreign policy service a target to politicians with populist orientations. No surprise that American presidents have always seen the foreign policy service from a negative perspective: "From a presidential perspective, six complaints are often voiced about the State Department's performance: 1. Inefficient and slow, 2. Poor staff work, 3. Unresponsive, 4. Resistant to change, 5. Incapable of putting its house in order, and 6. Unable to lead" (Rosati & Scott 2011, 149). No doubt that such accusations and evaluations can become rather rampant with the rise of profoundly populist presidencies in the United States. This is what happened throughout Trump's presidency, as will be delineated below.

The rise of Trump: Populist foreign policy practice in a highly institutionalized environment

The rise of Trumpism in historical perspective: The "cultural backlash" against the "silent revolution"

The "cultural backlash" theory, as explained previously, draws attention to the role of frustration created by post-materialist values attaching importance to multiculturalism, gender equality, and environmental protection in the rise of populism. As Norris and Inglehart (2019) highlight, this is especially the case behind the phenomenon of Trump in the United States: "The revolution in *education*, with rapidly growing access to college-level education, has also had a profound impact on Western cultures, helping shift attitudes in a more socially liberal direction" (2019, 38). In addition, "urbanization, combined with growing ethnic diversity in major cities, has reinforced a long-standing center–periphery cultural cleavage" (Norris & Inglehart 2019, 39). The result is that "the lifestyles and values of younger populations in multiethnic conurbations differ sharply from those of older, less-educated, and more homogeneous populations in declining small towns" (Norris & Inglehart 2019,

The populist foreign policy conduct during Trump's presidency **233**

39). As Norris and Inglehart point out, "from the start, the spread of post-materialist and other socially progressive policies stimulated a reaction on the part of social conservatives" (2019, 44). And these views usually have been in contradistinction to "politically correct" orientations, explaining Trump's blunt approach to ethnic and racial differences and women (Norris & Inglehart 2019, 47).

It seems that, under the conditions of increasing globalization accompanying neoliberalism, especially the insecurities of white working classes found a place of refuge in Trump's appeal. One should note that immigration, especially the illegal forms of it, amplified Trump's appeal to white working classes, as can be seen in some of his speeches (Judis 2016, ch. 3). As Kazin (2016) notes, Trump's appeal should also be seen in connection with long term trends facilitating and accompanying particular reactionary forms of politics in the United States such as xenophobia and racism. But there were also profound economic hardships combined with the crisis of a political project that is called "progressive neoliberalism" by Nancy Fraser (2019) – which refers to the alliance between social segments with progressive cultural and identity-based views and values and the most dynamic and globalized sectors of American capitalism such as tech, finance, and entertainment – that boosted the support for the Trump. Because, as Fraser (2019) noted, "these policies hollowed out working-class and middle-class living standards while transferring wealth and value upward – chiefly to the 1 percent, of course, but also to the upper reaches of the professional-managerial classes". This was exactly the practical material reason why Trump's populist discourse has been dominated by motives pertaining to the realm of foreign policy and trade. But before moving to Trump's foreign policy practice as a populist governmentality, I would like to briefly demonstrate the populism of Trump in discursive, stylistic, and practical levels in realms other than foreign policy in the United States.

The Trump phenomenon as a case of populist discourse, style, and practice

From a discursive point of view, there is abundant evidence demonstrating the populism of Trump in the United States. As Norris and Inglehart quote, during his campaigns and rule, Trump presented himself as the representative of the underprivileged, wronged constituencies he strived to re-empower (2019, 4). In other occasions, Trump did not shy away from accusing his opponents in his campaigns as powerful elites trying to stop him as the tribune of people: "The establishment, the media, the special interest, the lobbyists, the donors, they're all against me. I'm self-funding my campaign. I don't owe anybody anything. I only owe it to the American people to do a great job. They are really trying to stop me" (*Trump quoted in* Judis 2016, ch. 3).

234 Case studies

Trump's discursive populism has been demonstrated by other more systematic research on discourse and content analysis. In a systematic analysis of his speeches, Staufer demonstrates that "Donald Trump's speeches and his book reflect a discursive logic in which incompetence and ineptitude have run the United States into the ground and a rich businessman is the one to reinstate its 'greatness'" (2021, 231). Also, Hawkins and Rovira Kaltwasser (2018) demonstrate the populism in the discourse produced by Trump during his election campaign processes (2018, 241).

Having said these, probably the thing that was making him a "populist" in the eyes of many was more about his style and transgressive performance than his words, as revealed in detail by Ostiguy and Roberts (2016). As they demonstrate, despite his wealth, Trump has been seen as the representative of "common people": "The Reverend Jerry Falwell Jr. expressed this notion well at the Republican Convention when he called Trump 'America's blue-collar billionaire' and 'a champion of the common man'" (Ostiguy & Roberts 2016, 43). Trump himself too repeatedly highlighted his affinity to ordinary people and the mission he is willing to undertake on their behalf by arguing that he "joined the political arena so that the powerful can no longer beat up on people that cannot defend themselves. Nobody knows the system better than me, which is why I alone can fix it … My pledge reads, 'I'm with you, the American people.' I am your voice … I am with you, I will fight for you, and I will win for you" (Ostiguy & Roberts 2016, 43). Trump's appeal, as Ostiguy and Roberts illustrate, was not only about his discourse but how he was embedded in the American popular culture and the plebeian tastes inherent to it, in themes ranging from reality TV to casinos and beauty pageants, from NASCAR to WrestleMania (2016, 43–44). Thus, his populist discourse was complemented by a populist style and socio-cultural proclivity that is flaunting the "low", a term that Ostiguy (2017) deployed to refer to the low-brow, popular, and native values and tastes.

But populism also impacted Trump's rule and was not only about rhetoric and style or about the presentation of his political self in the public arena. From the enmity to bureaucracy (Lowndes 2021, 123–124) and the established political class (Green & White 2019, 115) to scepticism regarding immigration (Judis 2016) and objections to the allegedly "unfavourable" regulations in international trade and economics (Green & White 2019, 115),[5] Trump's populism had concrete implications in the domain of policy and administration. For example, as Lowndes asserts, Trump's populism brought with itself a serious "norm defiance" effecting the shape and structure of American administration based on the belief that "the norms he disrupts are either elitist, insincere, or corrupted forms of bureaucracy and expertise that work against common sense" (2021, 123). Trump administration also fired hundreds of civil servants who were seen unsuitable from their populist perspective (Lowndes 2021, 123–124).

The populist foreign policy conduct during Trump's presidency **235**

This was also valid in the realm of foreign policy. As Lowndes demonstrates, the populist practice in the Trump era resulted in "defying established diplomatic protocol, engaging in everything from informality to open rudeness toward other world leaders, performs a populist 'America First' politics by exemplifying the masculine social norms of the 'common people' while suggesting that other countries and their leaders simply are not all that important" (2021, 128). It is important to note here that these views and approaches in foreign policy realm also complemented by the practical engagement highlighting the role of Trump as the allegedly skilful "deal-maker". In the following part, I demonstrate the populist practice in the realm of foreign policy during the Trump rule in more detail.

Trump's impact on the foreign policy realm: The populist practice

Even before his time in office, Trump's election campaign in 2016 was heavily dominated by his views regarding America's international standing. His famous campaign slogan, "make America great again", for example, implied a relative decline in America's standing at the international stage and pledged the voters a restoration of an imagined "greatness" in the past. Wojczewski highlights the predominance of foreign policy-related themes in Trump's campaign rhetoric while demonstrating the populist discourse of the sensational leader through using evidence from his speeches: "In his election campaign, Trump contested the bipartisan consensus on American internationalism that has guided US foreign policy since World War II: he called NATO obsolete, accused US allies of ripping the United States off through unfair trade practices and defense burden-sharing, and suggested that the promotion of the liberal international order is not in America's interest" (2020, 2).

When it comes to the policy content, Trump's campaign revealed a clearly protectionist and nationalist proclivity. As Drezner (2019) notes, foreign policy proposals occupied an important position in Trump's election campaigns, and he argued that liberal international economic relations have harmed the United States in the past. As a result, Trump advocated more protectionist international economic relations as revealed by the frequently used slogan "America first" (Drezner 2019, 724). This protectionist nationalist policy stance expressed with more blunt words by members of the Trump administration: "Somewhat more crudely, a senior White House official told Goldberg, 'The Trump Doctrine is 'We're America, Bitch.' That's the Trump Doctrine'" (Drezner 2019, 725). Nevertheless, what rendered the Trump administration's foreign policymaking and implementation "populist" in practical terms have not been its policy content. Because, as experts on the topic highlight, there was no consistent "Trump doctrine", and "unpredictability" dominated the foreign policy realm during Trump's tenure (Bentley & David

236 Case studies

2021). "The inconsistent and erratic character of Trump's foreign policy", in fact, "endure[d] well into his presidency" (Macdonald 2018, 434).

The populism in Trump's foreign policy was evident more in formal and informal implementation and practice. First of all, the populist practice in Trump's presidency was a continuation of the general scepticism of the office of the president towards the "institutions" and, more precisely, towards the "administrative state". As a highly "elitist and exclusive" part of this "administrative state", the State Department hazily became a target for the Trump administration, as Drezner noted (2019, 728). In order to undermine the power of foreign policy establishments, the Trump administration used various formal and informal methods ranging from budget cuts to cadre denials and even to mobbing of experienced personnel. As a career diplomat effected by the Trump administration's populist practice relates, "complete and utter disdain for [their] expertise" among Trump's political appointees were common (Drezner 2019, 727). As a result of these tactics, the morale among the diplomatic personnel declined dramatically during the Trump presidency (Drezner 2019, 727).

Besides anti-institutionalism undermining foreign policy bureaucracy, populist practice in the Trump administration was evident in the personalization of the foreign policy realm. "When asked in the fall of 2017 about the dearth of State Department appointees, Trump replied, 'Let me tell you, the one that matters is me. I'm the only one that matters, because when it comes to it, that's what the policy is going to be'" (Drezner 2019, 728). However, the personalization of foreign policy realm was not only about the personal bravado of Trump but also his attempts to solve profound international problems through his personal initiatives, as the case was with his meeting with the North Korean autocrat and frequent telephone connections with presidents like Putin and Erdoğan in which Trump attempted to present himself as a tough "deal-maker" able to cope with strong men across the globe. But as some evidence suggest, Trump was probably not as successful as he thought in these deals. According to information deriving from the US bureaucracy, in his direct deal making efforts with seasoned executives like Putin and Erdoğan via phone calls, for example, expert informants are in the opinion that, despite his public bravado,[6] Trump was "consistently unprepared for discussion of serious issues, so often outplayed in his conversations with powerful leaders like Russian President Vladimir Putin and Turkish President Recep Erdogan".[7] It seems that the frequency of calls with Erdoğan had become especially concerning for the foreign policy advisors and experts around Trump, to the degree that they thought "Erdoğan took [Trump] to the cleaners" in these informal and personal "deal making" efforts regarding critical foreign policy problems such as the Syrian conflict.[8]

It should also be added that some of his close relatives such as his son-in-law Jared Kushner as well as personal acquaintances such as Jason Greenblatt

The populist foreign policy conduct during Trump's presidency **237**

and David Friedman started to play important roles in critical foreign policy issues such as the one pertaining to Israel-Palestine conflict (Siniver & Featherstone 2020, 5–6). This "plutocratic populism" was another aspect of the personalization of the foreign policy realm during the Trump era as part and parcel of this particular administration's populist practice. It also entailed what one can describe as a simplification of the foreign policymaking and implementation and reduction of complex diplomatic issues to financial calculations: "At the heart of this low-level conceptual complexity is a plutocratic worldview which frames foreign policy situations through an economic-transactional prism which often supersedes a more nuanced calculation of political, diplomatic and national security interests" (Siniver & Featherstone 2020, 5).

The anti-institutional, anti-technocratic, and personalistic inclinations of Trump's foreign policy practice as "populist practice" resulted in a more "unpredictable and erratic" foreign policy "that often oscillates between a very hawkish and confrontational rhetoric and a willingness to accommodate America's rivals and enemies through direct dialogue. Not only Trump's approach to North Korea has followed this pattern, but also his Russia policy" (Wojczewski 2020, 26–27). As Wojczewski notes, "the personalization, simplification, emotionalization, and acts of transgression as populist markers of Trump's foreign policy are articulated in opposition to 'conventional' foreign policy and diplomacy with its greater emphasis on formal procedures, institutions, and often lengthy, incremental, and expert-driven politics of deliberation and negotiation" (2020, 28–29). But, the case of Trump's foreign policy practice also reveals that, in a highly institutionalized context, the impact of populism as a governmental practice could be contained. As Drezner (2019) notes, the Trump administration has struggled to effectively integrate its foreign policy concepts into established or emerging foreign policy structures. But Trump's form of populism has had more success in undermining established institutions devoted to liberal internationalism than in establishing populist alternatives (Drezner 2019, 723–724).

Concluding discussion: Populist practices and liberal institutional resistance

While, in the 20th century, populism was seen as a phenomenon belonging to the developing world, in fact, the United States, towards the end of the 19th century, had already produced prototypical examples of populism with the rise of the People's Party and provided a name to a universal phenomenon in an emerging age of mass democracy. American politics and society, with its various traits such as a strong proclivity to equality (in the sense of rejecting aristocratic and traditional claims of superiority and entitlement) and scepticism towards "big government" and "administrative state", has always

238 Case studies

facilitated different reflections of populism in a long period stretching from the presidency of Jackson to that of Trump. Meanwhile, the United States gradually became an industrial and financial world power with dramatic territorial, economic, and social inequalities. The egalitarian spirit emerged during the foundation of the United States was challenged by increasingly unequal relations between industrialized, financialized metropolitans (especially clustered in the Northwest) and the overwhelmingly rural rest of the country. These experiences of inequality, first, paved the way for the populist objection of various farmer alliances and, eventually, the People's Party, which defended the interests of "common man" against an increasing financial domination.

In the 20th century, populism re-emerged in Southern politics with controversial regional political elites such as Huey Long and George Wallace. This time, albeit with some racist tendencies, these figures had also the stylistic inclination to populism with their low-brow tastes and behaviour. But from the People's Party to Long and Wallace, populism in the United States shared a common sensitivity towards the problems of the "underprivileged" populations and genuinely tried to find practical solutions to their grievances and necessities. While this, for example, gained the form of cooperation building in the era of the People's Party, in the 20th century, it took the shape of patronage and "machine politics", especially in the South. The populist logic and practice are crystal clear in the classical machine politics in the United States, as revealed, for example, by the speeches of infamous George Washington Plunkitt, as a populist patron, who drew attention to the restricted effect of "words" and the impact of "deeds" and a close touch with the poor with material incentives in local politics.[9] It is precisely these attempts of politicians to solve the "practical" problems of their constituencies with a genuine affection to the concerns of the "common people" have usually transformed populism in the United States into what is called "populist governmental practice" in this book. Because, populism in the United States, as elsewhere, has never been only about ideas, discourses or style. It has also been about the way politicians "do politics" and a particular manner in the making and implementation of public policy prioritizing responsiveness and immediacy.

The foreign policy realm was not an exception to this pattern. Alongside the economic, political and social change of the United States inciting a populist reaction, there was the dramatic growth of the "administrative state", especially throughout the 20th century, that started to challenge the proclivity of the American public towards small and restricted government. As the United States gained a superpower status after the world wars, the foreign policy administration, alongside the military, gained a new importance within the US administrative state in a context of rapid globalization which blurred the boundaries between domestic and international politics

The populist foreign policy conduct during Trump's presidency **239**

in the realms of economy, culture, and domestic security especially since the 1970s. Under these conditions, the foreign policy administration expanded and turned into a sizeable technocratic bureaucracy, especially after the end of World War II and throughout the Cold War. Thus, including Republican presidents like Nixon and Bush in particular, the populist scepticism regarding the administrative state usually targeted the foreign policy establishment and, more precisely, the permanent foreign policy bureaucracy, namely the State Department. Thus, there was always a sort of "populist" reaction to foreign policy establishment resulted in the concentration of power in the White House for the foreign policymaking processes with the rising importance of the National Security Advisor.

However, with the rise of Trump, these populist undercurrents against the administrative state, and especially the form it took in the realm of foreign policy, transformed into outright populist governmental practice since Trump was, as various studies on him from the mainstream perspectives acknowledge, profoundly populist in his discourse and style. The implications of this more visible populism in the Trump era for the foreign policy realm were rather dramatic. During the Trump era, not only the discourses of Trump reflected a thoroughly populist worldview and logic in the understanding of international relations, but the conduct of foreign policy realm reflected a populist governmental practice in action. First of all, Trump inherited the deeply entrenched scepticism towards the foreign policy bureaucracy from its right-wing predecessors. But he deepened the assaults on foreign policy bureaucracy, and especially the State Department, by budget and personnel cuts, believing in the bureaucratic inefficiency of the institution and despising the expertise of seasoned foreign policy personnel. Alongside an anti-institutional and anti-technocratic logic, a simplistic and reductionist approach to foreign policy issues defined Trump's practice, viewing complex international and diplomatic problems from the perspective of financial and economic gains or losses. Trump also personalized American foreign policy to an unprecedented level by appointing his relatives and fellow plutocrats to critical positions in the domain of foreign policymaking and implementation. He also presented himself, as someone coming from a business background, as a skilful "deal-maker" who will secure America's economic and security-related interests personally. All these qualities of the populist foreign policy conduct during the Trump era required circumventing and weakening of the procedures and established institutions of foreign policy in the United States.

No doubt that this approach and the promise to "make America great again" with "good deals" has been very appealing for the domestic populist audience.[10] But this "responsive" foreign policy practice rendered entire foreign policymaking and implementation in the United States throughout the Trump era very erratic and, at times, unsuccessful. Yet, as Drezner argues (2019), Trump was unable to left a kind of "institutional" heritage,

240 Case studies

although he undermined the foreign policy institutions to a certain extent. Thus, it is safe to argue that populism's impact in the realm of critical policymaking and implementation, especially under the circumstances of high levels of institutionalization, seems temporary and contained to a very large extent. This finding should also be seen in congruence with the arguments of a recent volume by Weyland and Madrid (2019) highlighting the built-in institutional resistance and strength in the American political system against populist conduct and assaults on liberal check and balance mechanisms. This consequence, in other words, populism's inability to leave an institutional legacy after a long exercise of executive power – in line with the theoretical argument of this book – should have something to do with the essentially practical nature of populism and its orientation towards unfolding itself in deeds more than words and ideas. As a result, populism has a strong proclivity to shy away from doctrinaire embodiments that can facilitate a sort of "populist institutionalization".

Notes

1 The movie *Hillbilly Elegy* based on the memoir by J. D. Vance is an elegant demonstration of the socio-cultural rift this distance opened up between the rural-provincial United States and the powerful "civilized" metropoles.
2 For a particularly eloquent example reflecting a genuine concern for the poor by populists, see the speech by Lorenzo D. Lewelling, one of the leaders of the People's Party in Kansas in 1894 in Tindall (1976, 159).
3 For the rather brighter practical dimensions of early American populism, see works by Goodwyn (1976), Kazin (1998), Postel (2007), Judis (2016), Perkins (2017), and Critchlow (2020). Also, see works by Stavrakakis (2017) and Jäger (2017, 2019) for how this early experience of American populism started to be seen under a profoundly negative light after the work of historian Richard Hofstadter (1996) in the 1950s and the introduction of theories of political modernization and development after the World War II.
4 It is not surprising to see that some researchers of American politics tend to describe Nixon as a "populist". See Lowndes (2016), Bonikowski and Gidron (2016), and Patenaude III (2019).
5 See Trump quoted in Green and White for his populist concerns regarding economy: "I have visited the laid-off factory workers, and the communities crushed by our horrible and unfair trade deals. These are the forgotten men and women of our country, and they are forgotten, but they will not be forgotten long. These are the people who work hard but no longer have a voice. I am your voice" (2019, 115).
6 For an example, see Trump's letter to President Erdoğan after Turkish incursion into Northern Syria: "Donald Trump warned his counterpart Recep Tayyip Erdoğan 'don't be a fool' and said history risked branding him a 'devil' in an extraordinary letter sent the day Turkey launched its incursion into north-eastern Syria. The letter, first obtained by a Fox Business reporter, was shorn of diplomatic niceties and began with an outright threat. 'Let's work out a good deal!' Trump wrote in the letter dated 9 October, whose authenticity was confirmed to various news outlets by the White House. Days after appearing to greenlight an invasion by pulling US troops from the Kurdish-dominated region, Trump told the Turkish

The populist foreign policy conduct during Trump's presidency **241**

president he would wreck Ankara's economy if the invasion went too far. 'You don't want to be responsible for slaughtering thousands of people, and I don't want to be responsible for destroying the Turkish economy – and I will,' he wrote. 'History will look upon you favorably if you get this done the right and humane way,' Trump continued. 'It will look upon you forever as the devil if good things don't happen.' 'Don't be a tough guy. Don't be a fool!' he finished, adding: 'I will call you later.'" See https://www.theguardian.com/us-news/2019/oct/16/trump-letter-erdogan-turkey-invasion, accessed: 23.5.2023.

7 See the CNN news report based on sources inside the White House: https://edition.cnn.com/2020/06/29/politics/trump-phone-calls-national-security-concerns/index.html, accessed: 23.5.2023.

8 Ibid.

9 See one of Plunkitt's extraordinary speeches vividly describing the populist practice of patrons of local machines in the United States at the beginning of the 20th century in Riordon (1995).

10 Some comments to the news report on PBS regarding Trump's threatening letter to Erdoğan concerning the incursion to Syria testifies the appeal of Trump's style and practice to the populist audience: "It's a fair appeal, a measured threat. Sanctions don't work, but the cancellation of favors, funded by the US taxpayer, may. Trump did well". "I love how the credentialist wokeness boys don't like this letter because it is direct and to the point. The coastal diplomatic elites have 'norms' of diplospeak gobblygook and high falutin' blather because it makes them seem more important and impressive than they really are". See https://www.pbs.org/newshour/world/read-trumps-full-letter-to-turkeys-erdogan-dont-be-a-tough-guy-dont-be-a-fool, accessed: 23.5.2023.

References

Bentley, M. & M. David (2021). Unpredictability as doctrine: Reconceptualising foreign policy strategy in the Trump era. *Cambridge Review of International Affairs*, 34(3), 383–406.

Bernstein, J. L. & A. C. Shannon (2022). *Vital Statistics on American Politics – 2017–2020*. London: Sage.

Bonikowski, B. & N. Gidron (2016). The populist style in American politics: Presidential campaign discourse, 1952–1996. *Social Forces*, 94(4), 1593–1621.

Critchlow, D. T. (2020). *In Defense of Populism – Protest and American Democracy*. Philadelphia, PA: University of Pennsylvania Press.

Drezner, D. W. (2019). Present at the destruction: The Trump administration and the foreign policy bureaucracy. *The Journal of Politics*, 81(2), 723–730.

Frank, J. (2017). Populism and praxis. In C. R. Kaltwasser, P. Taggart, P. O. Espejo & P. Ostiguy (Eds.), *The Oxford Handbook of Populism* (pp. 629–643). Oxford: Oxford University Press.

Fraser, N. (2019). *The Old Is Dying and the New Cannot Be Born – from Progressive Neoliberalism to Trump and Beyond*. London and New York: Verso.

Goodwyn, L. (1976). *Democratic Promise – the Populist Moment in America*. Oxford: Oxford University Press.

Green, M. & J. K. White (2019). Populism in the United States. In D. Stockemer (Ed.), *Populism Around the World* (pp. 109–122). Cham: Springer.

Hawkins, K. A. & C. Rovira Kaltwasser (2018). Measuring populist discourse in the United States and beyond. *Nature Human Behaviour*, 2(4), 241–242.

242 Case studies

Hofstadter, R. (1996). *The Paranoid Style in American Politics and Other Essays.* Cambridge, MA: Harvard University Press.

Jäger, A. (2017). The semantic drift: Images of populism in post-war American historiography and their relevance for (European) political science. *Constellations,* 24(3), 310–323.

Jäger, A. (2019). The past and present of American populism. In M. Oswald (Ed.), *The Palgrave Handbook of Populism* (pp. 31–47). New York: Palgrave Macmillan.

Judis, J. B. (2016). *The Populist Explosion – How the Great Recession Transformed American and European Politics.* New York: Columbia Global Reports.

Kazin, M. (1998). *The Populist Persuasion – An American History.* Ithaca, NY and London: Cornell University Press.

Kazin, M. (2016). Trump and American populism: Old whine, new bottles. *Foreign Affairs,* 95 (6), 17–24.

Key, V. O. Jr. (1949). *Southern Politics in State and Nation.* New York: Vintage Books.

Lowndes, J. E. (2016). White Populism and the transformation of the silent majority. *The Forum,* 14(1), 25–37.

Lowndes, J. E. (2021). Trump and the populist presidency. In P. Ostiguy, F. Panizza & B. Moffitt (Eds.), *Populism in Global Perspective – a Performative and Discursive Approach* (pp. 118–135). London: Routledge.

Macdonald, P. K. (2018). America first? Explaining continuity and change in Trump's foreign policy. *Political Science Quarterly,* 133(3), 401–434.

McKay, D. (2013). *American Politics and Society.* Chichester: Wiley-Blackwell.

Norris, P. & R. Inglehart (2019). *Cultural Backlash – Trump, Brexit, and Authoritarian Populism.* Cambridge: Cambridge University Press.

Ostiguy, P. (2017). Populism: A socio-cultural approach. In C. R. Kaltwasser, P. Taggart, P. O. Espejo & P. Ostiguy (Eds.), *The Oxford Handbook of Populism* (pp. 73–97). Oxford: Oxford University Press.

Ostiguy, P. & K. M. Roberts (2016). Putting Trump in comparative perspective: Populism and the politicization of the sociocultural law. *Brown Journal of World Affairs,* 23(1), 25–50.

Patenaude III, W. (2019). Modern American populism: Analyzing the economics behind the "silent majority," the Tea Party, and Trumpism. *American Journal of Economics and Sociology,* 78(3), 787–834.

Perkins, J. B. (2017). *Hillbilly Hellraisers – Federal Power and Populist Defiance in the Ozarks.* Urbana, IL, Chicago, IL, and Springfield: University of Illinois Press.

Postel, C. (2007). *The Populist Vision.* Oxford: Oxford University Press.

Riordon, W. L. (1995). *Plunkitt of Tammany Hall – a Series of Very Plain Talks on Very Practical Politics, Delivered by Senator George Washington Plunkitt, the Tammany Philosopher, From His Rostrum – The New York County Court House Bootblack Stand.* New York: Signet Classics.

Rosati, J. A. & J. M. Scott (2011). *The Politics of United States Foreign Policy.* Boston, MA: Wadsworth.

Rosenberg, J. & C. Boyle (2019). Understanding 2016: China, Brexit and Trump in the history of uneven and combined development. *Journal of Historical Sociology,* 32(1), e32–e58.

Scarrow, S. (2006). The nineteenth-century origins of modern political parties: The unwanted emergence of party-based politics. In R. Katz & W. Crotty (Eds.), *Handbook of Party Politics* (pp. 16–24). London: Sage.

Scott, J. C. (1969). Corruption, machine politics, and political change. *American Political Science Review*, 63(4), 1142–1158.

Siniver, A. & C. Featherstone (2020). Low-conceptual complexity and Trump's foreign policy. *Global Affairs*, 6(1), 71–85.

Staufer, S. J. (2021). Donald Trump, Bernie Sanders and the question of populism. *Journal of Political Ideologies*, 26(2), 220–238.

Stavrakakis, Y. (2017). *How did "populism" become a pejorative concept? And why is this important today? A genealogy of double hermeneutics*. Thessaloniki: POPULISMUS Working Papers, 6, 1–23. https://ikee.lib.auth.gr/record/313933/files/stavrakakis-populismus-wp-6-upload.pdf, accessed: 9.3.2024.

Taggart, P. (2000). *Populism*. Buckingham: Open University Press.

Taggart, P. (2004). *Popülizm* (B. Yıldırım, Trans.). İstanbul: Bilgi Üniversitesi Yayınları.

Tindall, G. B. (Ed.). (1976). *A Populist Reader: Selections from the Works of American Populist Leaders*. New York: Harper Torchbooks.

Turner, F. J. (2008). *The Significance of the Frontier in American History*. London: Penguin.

Vergari, S. (2017). Contemporary populism in the United States. In R. C. Heinisch, C. Holtz-Bacha & O. Mazzoleni (Eds.), *Political Populism – a Handbook* (pp. 241–254). Baden-Baden: Nomos Verlagsgesellschaft.

Weyland, K. & R. L. Madrid (Eds.). (2019). *When Democracy Trumps Populism*. Cambridge: Cambridge University Press.

Wilson, J. Q. (2000). *Bureaucracy – What Government Agencies Do and Why They Do It?* New York: Basic Books.

Wojczewski, T. (2020). Trump, populism, and American foreign policy. *Foreign Policy Analysis*, 16(3), 292–311.

SECTION IV
Conclusion

12

ENLARGING THE SCOPE OF "POLITICS"

Dynamics and consequences of populist governmental practice and some methodological and theoretical implications

Populism is by no means a silent phenomenon. In fact, today, thanks to the help of traditional as well as new media, populists tend to be very loud, even noisy actors of contemporary mass politics. They produce words on words and provide the masses, the media, and the researchers with endless fiery speeches. Thus, it becomes understandable that a lot of researchers today are inclined to focus on the discursive content produced by populists and their strategic and ideational/ideological implications (Mudde 2004; Laclau 2005). Populism is not only talkative and noisy, but it is also extremely visual and showy, even to the extent that it transgresses what is considered "proper" liberal consensual politics – even in cases when populists strive to be seen as modest actors in contradistinction to rich and powerful political elites. Hence, researchers (Moffitt 2016; Ostiguy 2017) also skilfully explored populisms' visual and stylistic features in the public realm or in the theatrical stage of politics in very different corners of the world (Panizza *et al.* 2021). In addition to these, populism today is also a phenomenon of powerful mass mobilization, a "winning electoral strategy" relying on a particular economy of organization. Thus, researchers also focus on its mobilizational dynamics, which, most of the time, revolves around a personalistic leadership with a special direct bond with large masses through words and images conveyed via media, mass rallies, etc. (Weyland 2017; 2021; Barr 2019; Kenny 2023). In fact, researchers problematizing these rather louder and more visible aspects of the phenomenon of populism are doing this for plausible reasons and the theoretical-conceptual studies reviewed in this book so far provided us very valuable tools to understand, to use Taggart's term, a "chameolonic" (2000, 4) reality.

DOI: 10.4324/9781003294627-16

248 Conclusion

Having said all of these, in this account, I tried to demonstrate that populism, especially as a governmental practice, has always been more than words, stage performances and a strategy of mass mobilization. No doubt that a convincing discourse and performance separating "people" from the "elite" and flaunting the culture and tastes of "popular sectors" is central to the phenomenon of populism and these dimensions indeed appeal to large, unprivileged constituencies. Personalistic leadership, a "strong man", and his direct relationship with his supporters surpassing organizational mediation, the identification with, and trust to, this leader too should be acknowledged as a source of the enormous electoral impact of populism today. But, for researchers who are living in contexts like Turkey (or in clear cases of "populism in power") and doing research on party politics through "ethnographically sensitive" (Schatz 2009) qualitative methods requiring field research in localities (Baykan 2018; Baykan & Somer 2022), the numerous symbolic and material transactions underlying and facilitating the stage of electoral politics, public discourses, performances and strategies pursued on the national "elite level" by populists are hard to miss. When combined with a critical review of the existing literature, such a bottom-up perspective also requires to interrogate some of the presumptions in the existing literature, such as attributing exclusive importance to discourses, images, and leaderships of populist movements and parties. I am not arguing that these are not important, but from a bottom-up perspective, in this book, I just wanted to demonstrate that what comprises populism is also a very rich repertoire of praxis, especially in government, consisting of many macro and micro tactics and gestures ranging from redistribution to pork-barrel politics, from clientelistic relations to warm local interactions consisting of visits to households of sick, attention to weddings, participation to funerals, etc.

In addition, populism's appeal also stems from its pragmatic and practical orientation, its tendency to being tactical and informal, its swiftness and responsiveness in localities and at the national level for addressing immediate symbolic (e.g., expectations of direct personal concern from someone with political authority) and material (ranging from the expectations of food or fuel or help in hospitals by individual supporters of populists to demands of infrastructural investment by certain local communities) needs of majorities mostly without adequate long-term considerations. Thus, my impression as someone closely witnessing an experiment of a clear case of populism in power and as someone doing research on the practical forms that politics takes on the ground and in localities, has been that, as the English idiom goes, populists speak louder through actions than their words. And these actions usually include a marked material dimension, and not purely confined to the "stage of performance". For the constituency of populism, especially in the developing world, who are prone to value concrete and visual over abstract and ideational, it can be misleading to expect that they are primarily moved

Enlarging the scope of "politics" **249**

by discourses, let alone words juxtaposing "people" against the "elite". It is equally misleading to expect that it is only the leader which mobilizes populist constituencies. In fact, it is the practices of loyal populist functionaries and brokers at the local level, it is their delivery of particularistic symbolic and material benefits, it is their protection of poor constituencies, their attention to their problems and their efforts to solve these problems, and their pace and tempo in these efforts which have always been more appealing to populist constituencies. At the national level too, it is also the "concrete achievements" of populist governments, their appeal to concrete material interests of majorities, which have been so appealing for populist constituencies – at least, as equally appealing as populist "thin ideologies" (Mudde 2004), antagonistic discourses (Laclau 2005), "populist scripts and appeals" (Ostiguy 2017), performances (Moffitt 2016), and personalistic leadership (Weyland 2001).

Dynamics of populism as a particular mode of political and governmental conduct

Thus, in this book, I proposed a broader and a more complex understanding of populism as a governmental practice that may help researchers to take the very rich praxis of populism into account in their analyses. In order to do this, first of all, I proposed to have a broader understanding of politics in populism research. Thus, I made a distinction between "politics proper" and "micro politics" in Chapter 2. While the first of these concepts refers to conventional electoral politics and struggles for executive authority, the second concept refers to more diffuse power relations which have implications for local as well as national level, collective as well as individual interests. Thus, while proclivities in the realm of public administration and policy generate real implications for "micro politics", there are also more informal practices that could be seen in the context of "micro politics" such as personalism, clientelism and various tactics circumventing procedural liberal legal-rational politics and administration. I assert in this account that it is the mastery of populism in the realm of "micro politics" that provides the phenomenon with its vitality and strength as a mode of politics and governmental practice.

Relying on this enlarged understanding of politics including the realm of administration, policy, and informal relations and institutions, I elaborated on the dynamics of populism in Chapter 3 from a theoretical perspective. In this chapter too, in a dialogue with the current discussions on social and political theory and populism, I proposed a broader understanding of politics. But this time, I also elaborated on different components of this broader understanding of politics: *Spatial, operational,* and *temporal* dimensions. In this chapter, I drew attention to the spatial, operational, and temporal

250 Conclusion

dynamics of populist governmental practice in comparison with the dynamics of non-populist politics (most notably formally institutionalized liberal democracy) as well as in comparison to other more conventional understandings of populism. As a result of this analysis, I propose to understand populism as a dynamic governmental phenomenon that is (a) blurring the boundaries between public and the private in spatial terms with consequences for local and national politics, (b) embracing mainly informal and tactical modes of action in operational terms, and (c) adapting responsiveness and swiftness with a short horizon of time with regards to temporal dynamics of politics.

In short, in this chapter, I argued that "populism as a governmental practice" should be understood as a mode of political practice that is penetrating, comprehensive, and pragmatic, adapting a rich repertoire of informal and tactical methods in order to be responsive and swift in addressing majority demands. Thus, populism is a pragmatic, responsive, and practical majoritarianism as a mode of political and governmental conduct. It should also be noted that not every form of pragmatism and flexibility is populism. Only those forms of pragmatism which avoid pure personal gain and benefit majorities and ordinary citizens in a given polity or political system at national and/or local levels should be considered as such. In Chapter 3, I also draw attention to the fact that populism is usually deployed by incumbents and political contenders who find themselves required to function and exercise authority under circumstances of marked material and organizational deprivation. In this respect, populism, as a mode of governmental conduct, can be defined as *the practical proclivity of weak authorities and political contenders to personalism, informality, tactics and responsiveness (in spatial, operational and temporal terms) that is appealing to the short-term material and symbolic expectations, interests and tastes of supporting unprivileged majorities. In short, as a praxis, populism is a practical and pragmatic majoritarianism.*

Such an approach to populism also has implications for governmentality and public administration and policy. In this book, I argued that the impact of electoral politics, especially in developing nations, had some important consequences for the formation of modern governmental rationalities. Modern governmentalities designed and set for conducting individual (bodies) and collective (populations) lives of the governed in line with a scientific, long-term rationality have frequently been interrupted by another rationality, the rationality of electoral politics, in which popular sectors started to play a major role as mass suffrage expanded. In this respect, populism, as the unfolding of electoral democracy, especially in the developing world, is in sharp contradistinction with long-term prudent rationality in spheres of administration and policy, and most notably in the realm of economic policy (Brittan 1975).

Enlarging the scope of "politics" **251**

I assert in Chapter 3 that populism, in a certain respect, amounts to the colonization of modern governmentalities from below due to the complicities/cooperations between populist authorities and popular sectors such as the informal permissions by authorities to the use of public land by the poor in return of political support, connivance towards tax evasion and petty crime for not provoking a backlash from the voters, overlooking government failures by citizens as long as it does not intervene into the livelihood of the governed, etc.. This is also to say that, populism, as a governmental practice, has implications for legal-rational authority structures and its Weberian bureaucratic form. It is, in fact, in contradistinction to Weberian bureaucracy, as some recent studies on the relationship between populist incumbents and bureaucracy highlighted (Peters & Pierre 2019).

Yet, I also argued that the relationship between bureaucracy, public administration practice, public policy, and populism is more complex and not confined to the external interactions between bureaucratic institutions and processes and populist political elites. In fact, as Bartha *et al.* (2020) rightly point out, there are some intrinsically populist proclivities in the conduct of public administration and policy under populist rule. The impact of populism on bureaucracy is not really only on the policy content and institutional structure, but as a way of doing politics, populism reshapes procedural aspects of public administration and policy. It undermines institutional procedures, circumvents experts, and ignores prudence, but, at the same time, populist governmental practice transforms bureaucratic conduct –at least initially and in the short run – into a responsive and majoritarian political activity. Personalism, particularism, and informality appear as key drivers of this process, but the dynamic reflection of public administration under populist rule is a very pragmatic, responsive, and swift mode of action.

In the empirical part of the book, in numerous examples from several cases, I demonstrated these propensities of populist governmental practice. Turkey was a key case in this respect, and in Chapters 4 and 5, I focused on the historical and contemporary dynamics of populism in this particular case. In Chapter 4, I located the populist governmental practice into the background of the historical transformation of state-society relations in the late Ottoman and early Republican periods and highlighted the importance of "politics of expediency", in other words, a politics of "impression management" that was appealing to the rising "public opinion" of the middle classes as the precursor of the later populist practices. As the Ottoman Empire modernized and as the middle class intelligentsia became more and more sensitive regarding the governmental functions of the state and its biopolitical and disciplinary agency, the ruling elite in the late Ottoman Empire started to take public opinion more carefully into account. Even in cases in which these elites could not provide the citizenry with an effective public administration and policy, they strived hard to appear as if they were ruling a civilized and

252 Conclusion

modern administration by deploying various tactics. With the transition to a multi-party regime, this sensitivity to appear as an effective modern state that is capable of regulating the society through "politics of expediency" turned into a fully populist governmental practice. Because with the transition to multi-party politics, political elites in Turkey needed to take into account not just the public opinion but the direct impact of masses as electoral agents. With this transition, for example, political elites turned a blind eye to the formation of slums on public land in metropoles across Turkey in the 1960s, 1970s, and 1980s and, as an obligation of the "informal social contract" between elites and the masses, political elites granted formal rights to occupiers of public land in a series of electoral cycles in Turkey stretching from 1950s to 2000s. With the transition to multi-party politics in Turkey, therefore, patronage, clientelism, and populism intermingled, and political elites strived really hard to respond symbolic and material demands of poor majorities.

In Chapter 5, I focused on the more contemporary unfolding of the populist governmental practice in Turkey throughout the *Adalet ve Kalkınma Partisi* (AKP – The Justice and Development Party) rule. The AKP rule continued the tradition of populist governmental practice in Turkish competitive mass politics. But it also perfected it to such an extent that its populist rule started to curtail the competitive aspects of Turkish party politics. The AKP was not only remarkably more populist than a series of right-wing ruling parties preceding it in the history of Turkish politics in ideational, mobilizational, discursive, and socio-cultural respects but, during its long tenure stretching from 2002 to the present, it fully engaged in populist practice in numerous domains of public administration and policy. In realms of policy as different as economy, bureaucratic conduct, judicial politics, order and security, social policy, education, and foreign policy, the AKP always opted for short-term and short-cut solutions for fundamental problems of administration and policy in Turkey in order to appeal to immediate material and symbolic needs of majorities. This took the shape of, for example, opting for economic growth through low-tech sectors such as construction that has the potential to finance politics and provide poor majorities with employment in the short term at the expense of more substantial and sustainable economic development and growth in the long run. In the realm of social policy, too, the AKP governments preferred to deploy formal and informal methods of redistribution instead of empowering poor populations and providing them with a kind of long-term agency. This only rendered poverty sustainable in Turkey without eliminating it. In many other policy fields, the short-termism, responsiveness, and immediacy of populist governmental practice led the AKP governments to mix various formal and informal methods to appeal to their electorate and manage day-to-day administration and policy implementation responsively while ignoring the long-term prudence that would have been sustained in a liberal democratic regime with more robust check and

Enlarging the scope of "politics" **253**

balance mechanisms. This proclivity to responsiveness, immediacy, and informality in the conduct of public policy and administration usually resulted in the preference of "easy ways out" in the face of fundamental problems in Turkish society and politics. While such populist governmental practices increased the welfare of citizens in the short run, they, without exception, resulted in major long-term problems that diminished the welfare of citizens. This, as the other cases analysed in this book demonstrate, is an inevitable consequence of extended rule by populists and prolonged implementation of markedly populist governmental practice.

In Chapter 6, I focused on the economic policies in Venezuela, and in this case too, one can clearly see the long-term detrimental impacts of "short-termism", "responsiveness", and "immediacy" intrinsic to the populist governmental practice. In order to solve the acute problem of poverty in Venezuela, the Chavez administration, instead of transforming the Venezuelan economy into a more diversified and productive system, opted for redistribution of the oil wealth through various formal and informal mechanisms at the cost of a dramatic economic crisis in the long run with tragic consequences.

In Chapter 7, I analysed the populist democracy in Greece in the 1980s and 1990s, which was shaped under the impact of Panhellenic Socialist Movement (PASOK) rule, and particularly due to its impact on bureaucracy. Throughout the PASOK rule, in order to respond quickly to mass clientelistic demands, PASOK, and later New Democracy, two protagonists of the "populist democracy" in Greece, opted for unprecedented enlargement of the public bureaucracy resulting in serious economic and social problems that culminated in the economic crisis of the 2010s.

Very similarly, in Chapter 8, I demonstrated that in India under Modi and Bharatiya Janta Party (BJP) rule, the judicial policies started to give in to the symbolic expectations of the Hindu majority, and, through various formal and informal mechanisms, populist rule started to shape public and private lives of Indian citizens. These effects can be seen in various cases concerning "cow protection" vigilantism or in the reactions against so-called "love jihad". Especially in the case of India, it has become clear that populist governmental practice in the judicial realm is shaped by bottom-up pressures and, to a certain extent, follows and learns from the tactics and initiatives initiated by populist constituencies at the local and regional levels.

In Chapter 9, I examined the impact of populist governmental practice in the realm of order and security through the case of Duterte rule in the Philippines. In this example, too, populist governmental practice reveals its tendency to responsive, short-cut, and short-term solutions for appealing to the immediate symbolic and material expectations of the majorities. This tendency in the Philippines to solve issues of order and security through informal and tactical measures resulted in widespread corruption and violation of human rights. While the negative consequences of populist

254 Conclusion

governmental practice in the realm of order and security have taken the shape of allegedly beneficial petty corruption in police stations across the Philippines, under Duterte rule, it took the form of death squads, execution of alleged drug dealers without due process and, eventually, serious human rights violations.

A very similar dynamic can be seen in the populist developmentalist rule of Nasser in Egypt in the 1950s and 1960s in the realm of socio-economic and educational policies. Nasser rule in Egypt not only engaged in massive levels of redistribution in order to cope with poverty but it also expanded the education opportunities, and especially the higher education opportunities, for all Egyptians to unprecedented levels. Moreover, Nasser rule promised a public job to all university graduates. This populist practice in the realm of education and public employment, like the consequences in Greece, incrementally resulted in a huge and ineffective bureaucracy and major economic problems in the long run.

Thus, these cases of robust populist rule demonstrate that, ironically, the short-termism of populism eventually results in the opposite of what populist rule promises at the beginning; the promise that the problems of administration and policy would be swiftly solved, the distance between government and the citizenry would be reduced and the welfare of the citizens would be improved. In fact, in many cases of emblematic populist rule, the consequence has been the opposite: Short-term, swift, and poorly calculated solutions (such as swift responses to poverty via formal and informal, redistributive and clientelistic means including the expansion of public employment, etc.) for really complicated and complex problems of administration and policy ironically cumulated into bureaucratization and ineffectiveness as the populist rule extends over time.[1]

Such consequences of populist rule can only be averted if there are serious institutional constraints over populist incumbents. What we see in the case of the Trump rule in the United States examined in Chapter 11 and its impact on the domain of foreign policy was exactly this. Although the Trump administration made a real impact on the foreign policy bureaucracy by undermining the resources of the State Department, sidelining career diplomats and experts, and personalizing many foreign policy-related issues, it could not dissolve and transform the robust administrative apparatuses of the foreign policy conduct in the United States. But, in this case too, the personal, short-cut, and tactical solutions embraced by Trump in the realm of foreign policy did not always turn into concrete gains for the United States as he promised despite the momentary celebration of his machismo and bravado by his audience. On the contrary, Trump's bravado and excessive self-confidence accompanying his lack of information and expertise in many global affairs resulted in weaknesses in his personal "deal making" efforts with seasoned leaders such as Putin and Erdoğan.

Despite many idiosyncrasies revealed by these cases, I believe I have been able to demonstrate that, with its certain features, populist governmental practice is an almost universal phenomenon (perhaps more universal than modern liberal and formal institutional governmentality) and unfolds even in settings with very robust liberal and institutional check and balance mechanisms (such as the United States). But especially for the developing world with mass suffrage and a more or less competitive politics, populism, in fact, is the central *modus operandi* in the political and governmental realm. Because, as a governmental practice, populism is the democratic response of weak authorities and elites to material, symbolic, and organizational deprivation. Hence, populism, as a mode of politics, can also be considered a measured response to a constant emergency. Populism is, in fact, a mode of action embraced under the circumstances of a routinized "state of exception" (Agamben 2005; Schmitt 2018). Thus, populists' discursive and temporal emphasis on the moment of crisis (Lazar 2022) and their propensity to personalistic conduct, and even to "dictatorship" (Vergara 2020), should be seen in light of these circumstances of material and symbolic deprivation. But focusing on the top executive authority and the "crisis" and "emergency" that is brought to the fore in the phenomenon of populism should not divert researchers' attention from its diffuse practice. In fact, while at the temporal level, populists discursively highlight the ruptures and crisis moments, in practical terms, they tend to see the time consisting of a continuous flow of individual and collective, minor and major, particular and universal demands by popular constituencies. While practitioners of populism perceive time as a continuous flow of requests, their distinguishing response to this perception is not a kind of paralysis and postponement/suspension but swift action and responsiveness. Thus, in temporal terms, populists' pace of action tends to be hasty, as Hermet (2001) emphasizes in his seminal work. This is another dynamic of populism that renders it an effective strategy for a "routinized" emergency rule.

Consequences of populism as a governmental practice

Majority of the researchers focusing on the phenomenon of populism problematized its impact on democracy. This is understandable since most of these researchers had a conventional view of politics and constrained their analyses with the exploration of electoral politics. Most of the time, the discussion regarding the impact of populism on democracy (and more precisely on its liberal institutional component), on its formal procedures and institutions, diverts researchers' attention from its direct impact on citizens. But from the broader perspective that I developed in this book on politics, populisms' impact on administration and policy, and more importantly, its impact on the welfare of individuals and collectivities becomes more important.

256 Conclusion

As the analyses of very different cases in this book reveal, populist governmental practice, and especially its majoritarian tendency, usually led populists to particularistic and universal forms of redistribution. Populists are involved in these redistributive measures pretty hastily, "here and now", for their constituencies. Because the problem of poverty has usually been one of the gravest issues for experiences of populist rule across the globe. In cases as different as Turkey, Venezuela, Greece, India, and Egypt, populism, at least initially, increased the material welfare of citizens through informal means such as "systematic mass clientelism" as well as via formal universal methods of social policy such as direct social assistance to poor, unemployment payments, subsidies for the basic consumption goods, free of charge education and health services, etc.. Yet, the "systematic mass clientelism" exerted by populists in a competitive political system under the auspices of a national populist personalistic leadership and his "patrimonial" domination usually extends to such range and encompasses such broad sectors of underprivileged constituencies that it ceases to appear particularistic for the majority of citizens and perceived as the "paternalism" stemming from an affectionate and responsive rule.

In addition, populists' efforts to solve problems in realms ranging from economy to order and security, from education to foreign policy quickly, and their accessibility and responsiveness in their engagement with these realms usually provided governments with a "popular legitimacy" that non-populist governments are critically lacking in these contexts. One should also add here the "sweet gestures of populism" improvised by local populist functionaries such as visits to households with sick inhabitants, participation in weddings with small presents, and support for constituencies in funerals, etc., in localities and in very remote corners of countries into the picture. Such practices, too, improved the popular legitimacy of populists and the political systems they seized and started to dominate.

Populism, in the current scholarly literature, is usually associated with instability. But from a wider perspective, populist governmental practice can in fact be seen as a mode of politics that is providing stability to otherwise extremely unstable and fragile polities. Populist governmental practice as a *metis* (Scott 1999), in fact, finds solutions to irresponsive procedural governmental conduct, especially under the conditions of material and organizational deprivation. Here it is also important to remind Chatterjee's (2011, 2018, 2020) contention in his various works that the exercise of power shaped by the demands of "political society", and the "governmentality in the East" or "populist governmentality", in fact, could be seen as a form of permanent "passive revolution".[2] Populism as a governmental and political practice transforms modes of executive action, changes the pace of political conduct, and expands the locus of government in such a way that it starts to penetrate into the daily lives of citizens more effectively than non-populist

Enlarging the scope of "politics" **257**

forms of rule. It certainly challenges the old ways of "doing politics", it polarizes the society, and it is prone to conflict in the electoral and discursive realm. But, at the same time, populism, as a form of "passive revolution" – as Gramsci (1992, 137) conceptualizes – leaves many just and unjust hierarchies and social distinctions, and most notably, the *status quo* intact. Populism is not a totalitarian project of state and societal transformation. Populism as a governmental practice, its pragmatism, flexibility, and adaptability, in this respect, is in contradistinction to what is genuinely "revolutionary". And in most of the genuinely revolutionary processes, humanitarian costs are undeniable regardless of our sympathies to these major events.

Populism, as a form of passive revolution, in fact, saves polities from destabilizing revolutionary processes and turmoils of states of "dual power" by diverting and channelling dissent from radicalism to electoral politics as well as towards cooperations and complicities between authorities and the governed. Thus, while undermining the legal-rational legitimacies of polities, populism provides political systems with a "popular legitimacy" based on the cooperations and complicities between popular sectors and populist governments. When this "absorption" is lacking, when populism, as a mode of action, loses the consensual orientation and falls into full revolutionary polarization, when it becomes purely particularistic, or when radical ideologies start to dominate populist governments, this usually results in destabilization of polities and, more critically, violent dissent. But when this happens, this also means that populism disappears as a governmental phenomenon that is in congruence with competitive electoral politics. Thus, most of the time, not the populism *per se*, but its dissolution, its corruption into something non-populist running against short or long-term majority interest that is generating really serious practical problems for the masses. What we have witnessed in Venezuela after the passing of Chavez is an emblematic example in this respect (Maya 2018). And also what we witness in many African countries devastated by civil war can be seen as the outcome of the absence of a national populist governmental practice or the deterioration of such a rule towards exclusionary and particularistic ethnic identity politics.[3]

In other words, for many polities on the globe, in the absence of a genuine possibility to build a functioning liberal democracy, populist governmental practice may be the best way to sustain the survival of large parts of populations and a decent degree of order and security through a *pragmatic, flexible and –more or less – tolerant majoritarianism*. In other words, with a broader perspective on politics as well as history that is taking the experiences in the Global South seriously into account, populism's reputation should be restored, and populist elites' and audiences' role in sustaining more or less functioning polities under very adverse conditions should be appreciated. Here, one can raise the question that how this view of populism can be conciled with the reality of profoundly exclusionary and repressive measures in terms

258 Conclusion

of identity pursued by some of the populists today, such as Modi rule in India and Erdoğan rule in Turkey. In fact, exclusionary and repressive dynamics in these examples are more of a result of their right-wing ideational proclivities than their "populist governmental practice". It can even be argued that what tames these exclusionary and repressive dynamics, especially in the realm of identity politics in such examples, is, in fact, populism as governmental practice with its pragmatic and flexible orientation.

But the discussion so far regarding the "merits" of populism should not divert researchers' attention from the "dark sides" of populist governmental practice. As a lot of examples explored in this account demonstrate, populism as a governmental practice, as a mode of rule, brings considerable costs to societies and polities in which populist mode of government is predominant. Leaving the discussion regarding the impact of populism in power on democracy aside, for now (I will turn this point soon), perhaps it is important to see the impact of populism on administrative capacity, and through this impact, populism's effect on citizen welfare in the long run. As many accounts of populism in power (Müller 2016; Pappas 2019) and the relationship between populism and the state (i.e., public administration and bureaucracy) (Peters & Pierre 2019; Bauer & Becker 2020) reveal, populism undermines some of the pillars of the modern administrative state. While appealing to the common sense and immediate material and symbolic interests of their constituencies, populists usually disregard expertise, prudence, and institutional procedures. It is not only a result of populists' ideational/ ideological predisposition towards anti-institutionalism or their hostility to experts and bureaucratic elites. No doubt these ideational motives play their part. But, the analysis in this book also implies that populist actors' proclivity to disregard expertise and procedures usually stems from their urge to move swiftly and quickly to satisfy the immediate demands of populist constituencies. Thus, the temporal dynamics of populism is the fundamental underlying factor in populism's disregard for scientific and bureaucratic expertise and long-term prudence.

No example other than the expansion of higher education under populist rule (in Turkey and Egypt as well as in Greece) examined in certain parts of this book can better represent this tendency: While populists strive to address their constituencies' demands quickly, they usually do this hastily and, inevitably, in a manner that sacrifices quality. In other domains of policy, too, responsiveness embraced by populism entails conscious negligences and disregards that cumulate as "human-made catastrophes" in the long run. I cannot think of a more telling example in this respect than the earthquake that hit Southeast Turkey on February 6, 2023, that I briefly analysed at the very beginning of this book. What we have seen in this example was diffused complicities/cooperations between populist incumbents and populist constituencies, populist authorities' intentional disregard for expertise and prudence

Enlarging the scope of "politics" **259**

to appeal to the "common sense" of people and ultimately attracting their votes. Such tendencies –no doubt going back to pre-AKP periods – year by year prepared a catastrophe as populist incumbents turned a blind eye to irregular constructions and as citizens materially benefited from looser controls over construction processes. Such examples, in which natural disasters turn into human-made catastrophes, are abundant and can be found in this book and in the practices of populist incumbents in other parts of the world. I am sure the readers of this book can now recall similar incidents in contexts they know well, contexts other than the cases examined in this book.

This discussion also brings us to the problematic relationship between populism and corruption.[4] While in opposition, "anti-corruption" language is a fundamental aspect of populist discourses, in power, populist conduct itself produces corruption. But as Mendilow (2021) notes, the subjective interpretations of populist audiences gain a crucial weight in this respect. As long as majorities think that "defensive" or "collective" forms of corruption work in the benefit of "ordinary people", populist incumbents keep enjoying a popular legitimacy and they can even enjoy the veneration by the public for their cunning. But this does not eradicate the massive problem of accountability in cases of populist governmental practice. This is a logical consequence of populist governmental practice since it has a marked proclivity to blur the boundaries between the public and the private. For example, the boundary between corruption allegedly benefitting and protecting majorities and enriching populist incumbents individually can be really thin, as the case of a populist Brazilian governor related in Mendilow's account demonstrates:

> The former governor [of Rio de Janeiro], Sérgio Cabral Filho, was found guilty of diverting some 4 million $ from public budgets to his own account in a scheme that involved a bribe rate of 5 percent of all administrative contracts between the state administration and private companies. Resorting to a populist rhetoric, his defense was that all elites are corrupt. As the representative of the "pure" people, it was his function to ensure that their interests would be served. To do so, he ensured the best price and, in a combination of "compensatory corruption" and "group oriented corruption", deposited the kickback in his account because no one else could have ensured that it would return to the people.
>
> *(2021, 23)*

One of the consequences of all of these dynamics is that "administrative states" under populist rule lose prestige and authority in the long run. More importantly, under populist rule, long-term security and welfare of citizens are traded with short-term material and symbolic gains. Thus, in the previous parts, I drew attention to the capacity of populist governmental practice to improve citizens' welfare in the short run. But in the long run, in terms

260 Conclusion

of citizen welfare, populism, in the best-case scenario, only brings a standstill (as we experience in Turkey) or, worse, a serious backsliding after an initial improvement of some of the basic indicators of welfare (as we see in Venezuela).

One of the side effects worth mentioning here is that prolonged exercise of populist governmental practice, sooner or later, brings incremental but continuous migration of qualified populations that are fed up with polarizing and particularistic inclinations of populist rule. Combined with progressive loss of income and purchasing power, well-educated middle and upper-middle classes tend to leave countries ruled by populist governments.[5] In cases like Hungary, this, so to say, "bleeding" or "hemorrhage" in terms of qualified human resources extends to institutions, as the case of Central European University testifies, which migrated to Austria after continuous attacks from the Orban government. In worse cases, migration takes new and massive forms and expands to less better-off segments of society, as the case of Venezuela demonstrates. The consequence in the long-term is obvious: Prolonged exercise of "untamed" populist governmental practice results in the loss of relatively more skilled, productive, and innovative segments of nations' human resources. This, in turn, undermines the current as well as future welfare of societies under populist rule: Some of the best academics, physicians, engineers, artists, and professionals, all these segments with – as called by Norris and Inglehart (2019) – "post-materialist" values migrate and populist regimes are usually confined to unproductive and non-innovative agricultural, industrial and service-based economies or natural resources. Thus, the "brain drain" becomes one of the consequences of prolonged populist governmental practice. This is certainly no good news for the long-term prospects of societies under populist rule.

Here, it is important to note the dynamics of institutional decay under populist rule as well as some potential consequences this may entail. As noted so far, the main temporal dynamic of populism is its propensity to move quickly, its urge to respond social demands as quickly as possible. This is one of the significant factors that leads to increasing "personalization" (Rahat & Kenig 2018) or "presidentialization" (Poguntke & Webb 2007) of executive authority in cases of populism in power. But what differentiates "personalization" or "presidentialization" of executive power in populist regimes is that, unlike personalization counterbalanced by robust administrative states, personalization in populist regimes results in an executive authority structure in which personalistic national leadership becomes a "key stone" in the middle of many intersecting arches of administrative institutions. And for the sake of responsiveness – through informal methods circumventing legal constraints and procedures – the personalistic leadership in populism starts to substitute administrative institutions. This process can be called as "focalization" of executive authority that is distinct from "centralization". Process of

Enlarging the scope of "politics" **261**

"centralization" leaves administrative branches under control as functioning state apparatuses. But in the process of "focalization" of executive authority, populist leaders suck the ability to function from these diverse set of administrative institutions and render themselves indispensable to the administrative apparatuses. In short, "focalization" is the process that populist leaderships substitute themselves and their loyal personnel in places of institutions. As long as diligent national populist leaders keep their position at the helm (like Chavez and Erdoğan), consequences of "focalization" remain latent. But the fall of such diligent and popular populist leaders paves the way to marked turmoil afterwards due to the decay of functioning administrative institutions during their populist rule. Here again, we see a strategy which works initially and in the short term but later turns into something deeply hazardous for society and the polity in the long run.

One of the important puzzles here is related to a set of simple questions: Why do populists engage in practices and policies that are evidently detrimental to the welfare of citizens in the long run, including their own constituencies? Why do populists, most of the time, opt for responsiveness over responsibility and prudence? Do not populist leaders and elites foresee the ultimately detrimental consequences of practices and policies they embrace? Why do populist actors, who are, in fact, usually much more cunning and smarter than researchers working on populism and populist practices, cannot see the consequences that can be seen by researchers as well as parts of the citizenry with an average intelligence? I think better responses to these questions lie beyond the simple explanation that is underlining the populist leaders' alleged hunger for power. This may be playing its part alongside populists' cognitive, socio-cultural, and practical propensity to concrete achievements "here and now". The proclivity of populists to "short-term gains", in fact, should be seen as a result of a "bounded rationality" that is shaped by a set of contextual dynamics that are constraining the choices for populist incumbents. This set of dynamics contains

a incentives created by mass politics (i.e., regular elections for office or potentials for effective protest that is prone to violence);
b urgency of the material (widespread poverty as well as administrative and financial incapacity of the state) and symbolic (such as the sense of alienation felt by large chunks of citizenry from the national polity that is undermining political legitimacy) deprivation that requires swift action by populists;
c hostile oligarchic and establishment reactions (anti-populism in the form of non-electoral pressures by elite groups in the media and in state machinery, which can even take the form of a military coup) to populism requiring constant support and preparedness to mobilization maintained through particularistic means and methods; and

262 Conclusion

d frequently, the lack of institutionalized organizations that are based on programmes and ideas backing populist incumbents due to the personalistic nature of the phenomenon of populism and due to the need to keep diverse clusters of supporters together through performative and particularistic means.

Under these adverse circumstances, swiftness and short-term gains, most of the time, could be perceived by populists as the best option in cases that are subject to strategic political decisions. In short, populist authorities are, in many respects, "weak authorities" with a markedly restricted control over time. Thus, despite the knowledge of other more "prudent" options, populist incumbents are usually attracted to short-term solutions by a bounded rationality defined under the circumstances of a highly restrictive competitive political context.

Consequences of populism for democracy have been more competently demonstrated in other accounts (Mudde & Kaltwasser 2012), but in relation with populist governmental practice, I would like to touch upon this aspect too. There is now a consensus on the fact that prolonged exercise of power by populists is detrimental for democracy (Mudde & Kaltwasser 2012; Müller 2016; Pappas 2019; Urbinati 2019). With the terminology generated by comparativists, it seems that populism drives electoral democracies towards "competitive authoritarianism" (Levitsky & Loxton 2013). But it is usually not only because of majoritarian and alleged "anti-pluralist"[6] views of populism. Relying on the analysis in this book, I contend that the drive towards competitive authoritarianism is more of a product of populism's praxis than its alleged ideational core. For example, populism's tendency to create polarization should also be seen more of a consequence of its propensity to material redistribution than a result of its blind pursuit of any strict ideological conviction. As a form of virtual/implicit "emergency rule" run by personalistic leaderships and, as a *metis* implemented by "weak authorities", populism tends to disregard liberal institutional check and balance mechanisms. Thus, undemocratic consequences of populism are more a result of its praxis, and as such, the danger posed by populism for democracy can be seen as a threat that is being exaggerated by the scholarly community and journalists since populism, as a practice, is not really the unfolding of a radically transformative worldview or strictly adhered and square ideology. Populism as a governmental practice is not a genuinely transformative revolutionary phenomenon. And the personalistic leadership that we observe in the populism of our age should not be conflated with genuinely transformative charismatic leadership of previous centuries. Thus, populism as a governmental practice may not be posing such a grave threat to democracy compared to the totalitarian and/or charismatic and deeply ideological politics did in the past century (such as Nazism, Fascism, and Stalinism).

Enlarging the scope of "politics" **263**

But this is not to deny that populist governmental practice is dangerous. Although experiences of populism do not bring spectacular breakdowns of democracy, they erode it incrementally and progressively in an extended period of time in remarkably different corners of the world. This makes the literature on the struggle against populism really crucial, a topic that is drawing more attention only recently.[7] From the perspective developed in this book, however, one of the major criticisms that can be raised against this mostly "anti-populist" literature is that there is no way to eradicate populism, especially as a governmental practice, completely from the scene of politics. Populism as *metis*, as a responsive governmental practice relying on tactics, informality, and improvisations for providing the support of majorities, will remain intact in the realm of "micro politics" and activities of local politicians and their interactions with their supporters even in the case that liberal institutional politics manages to purge populist ideas, discourses, strategies and mobilization from the public realm. Populism as a governmental practice can only be eradicated from politics at the cost of democracy and freedom. This was done in the form of totalitarianism in the 20th century. And currently, this is the dystopia of "surveillance capitalism", which aims to subjugate social relations and individual lives under the total control of "instrumentarian power" and eradicate contingency (Zuboff 2018). Thus, populism should be seen as an ally instead of an enemy in the struggles of liberal democracy in the 21st century.

Thus, I think, the better question regarding the relationship between populism and democracy is not really "how to combat with populism". The question, with respect to the reality of populism as a governmental practice, should be "how to tame populist governmental practice" and eradicate its excesses posing threats to democracy and welfare of citizens. To put it in empirical and more concrete terms, the dilemma here can be expressed as follows: How would it be possible to keep populisms' responsiveness and swiftness alive while curbing down its potential long-term hazards to citizen welfare and democracy? For example, how would it be possible to make populism work through "petty corruption" in solving the problem of housing for urban poor through complicities/cooperations with popular sectors without long-term negligence that turns these buildings into potential graves in cases of natural disasters? In this regard, it is clear that a return to unresponsive and highly mediated institutional liberal democracy is not a remedy for majority of the world nations since populism today is a response to these unresponsive systems and the representation crisis they fostered.

In this respect, Chantal Mouffe (1993, 2000, 2005, 2013, 2018) and Camila Vergara (2020) provide some important insights. It is really important to introduce and impose "agonism" as a shared ground of democratic politics – while retaining and containing the conflictual nature of populism within the democratic systems – via a diligent struggle of hegemony in

264 Conclusion

intellectual and political domains and save populism from being hijacked by exclusionary identity politics, as proposed by Mouffe. A more particular recommendation in this respect comes from Vergara who highlights the importance of containing excesses of "personalistic leadership" in populist practice. While "personalistic leadership" as a legal and legitimate "dictatorship by election", as Vergara notes, can work in favour of the unprivileged sectors ranging from working classes to oppressed women and defend "society" against oligarchies, it is important to define the limits of populism as an "emergency rule" and "crisis government" in order to save the "society" from the "populist saviours". As Vergara notes, there should be clear limits to the room of manoeuvre for the "plebeian dictator" (Vergara 2020, 217). What Vergara implies in his work, for example, as a solution to this problem by following the work of political theorist John McCormick, is a kind of "institutionalized plebeian power" like "people's tribunate" within the constitutional structure of liberal democracies. Solutions can vary, but it is really important to make liberal democracies able to hear the voices of the materially and symbolically oppressed and the excluded. This cannot be done by eradicating populism from the public sphere but by taming it through various innovative mechanisms of representation and participation for the *demos*.

The issue of taming populism is also problematic at the level of day-to-day government and administration due to the problem of populisms' propensity to responsiveness, which frequently turns into beneficial "petty corruption", especially in the form of negligences towards the survival tactics of the urban poor, and, its radical aversion from "accountability". Rather the more problematic issue here is impeding the transformation of these "petty corruption" into genuinely corrupt practices serving only the benefit of the few that is undermining equality for and welfare of the majority. Thus, populism as a governmental practice, its pragmatism and flexibility compensating the unease caused by strict proceduralism, should be kept under control. Studies on how to struggle with corruption through legal and other means may contain lessons for taming populist governmental practice, in other words, keeping it away from corruption that is only serving private interests. Thus, students of populism should also put some thought on new methods and instruments of accountability which does not suffocate the innovativeness and creativity of populist governmental practice.

Methodological and theoretical implications

This study embraced a diffused and comprehensive understanding of politics and proposed to focus on the realms stretching beyond the boundaries of electoral politics for populism research. By diverging from currently predominant approaches to populism and their focus on the conventional realms of electoral politics such as ideas, ideologies, discursive and mobilizational strategies, as well as media-oriented public performances, this study highlighted the importance of focusing on domains of administration and policy too which have implications for local communities as well as interpersonal relations and individual lives of citizens, in order to fully grasp the phenomenon of populism in power. Such a comprehensive understanding of politics has implications in populism research with regards to its scope: Populism, as a governmental practice, is not necessarily a national phenomenon but is also a local phenomenon that is shaping the practice of local politicians and authorities. It is also a phenomenon that is generating implications stretching from the public realm to private realm with marked propensities to informality. Hence, populism is a phenomenon of "micro politics" which consists of personalistic, particularistic, clientelistic, and tactical relations at the local and national levels, as much as it is a phenomenon of "macro politics" or "politics proper" consisting of conventional dimensions of politics such as parties, leaders, ideas, strategies, mobilization efforts, discourses, etc.

Thus, relying on a more diffused and comprehensive understanding of "the political", this study has certain implications regarding the study of populism – and other important phenomena of electoral politics and government – in spatial, operational, and temporal terms. When populism is seen as a diffused governmental practice with consequences at national and regime levels as well as local, and even, at individual levels, some presumptions regarding spatial boundaries in many comparative politics research become problematic. As the examination of populism in this study shows, today, relevant political phenomena, not just populism but other fundamental phenomena of politics such as democracy, authoritarianism, state capacity, etc., too should be seen as surpassing the boundaries between public and private, national and local.

The second and interrelated implication of a diffused and more comprehensive understanding of politics in this study is that the operational dynamics that the researchers focus on should not be confined to the public, formal, official, and procedural practices. Researchers should also take unofficial, informal, and tactical dimensions of the phenomenon under investigation into account as much as possible.[8] No doubt, it is never easy to have reliable knowledge and opinions on more informal and tactical aspects of politics, but there are always some publicly available data and information that could shed some light on these aspects of contemporary mass politics, with a well-thought process of interpretation.

And finally, this research also has implications regarding the role of "temporality" in contemporary mass politics and its various examinations. In this study on populism, I strived to demonstrate the temporal dynamics of populism as a governmental practice. Temporality is not simply about

266 Conclusion

how various forms of politics conceive time and discursively articulate this perception (Lazar 2022), but it is also about the actual pace and tempo embraced by political actors adapting different forms of doing politics. In cases of populism, the pace and tempo is hasty and swift. But in other phenomena, scholars may discover many different variations of political actors' practical relationship to temporality. This is important because power, a fundamental concept of politics, itself, is a temporally bounded phenomenon. What makes actors and relations "powerful" or "power-less", as de Certeau (2002) contends, is usually about their control (or lack of it) over time, timing, speed, and pace. Fundamental concepts of comparative politics directly related to the phenomenon of power, such as populism, democracy, authoritarianism, etc., should all be subject to a systematic consideration of temporal dimensions of politics, as Grzymala-Busse (2011) proposes.

From a much broader methodological and theoretical perspective, this re-search, in its entirety, can be seen as an exercise in social research in favour of a more interdisciplinary approach to the socio-political phenomenon instead of a disciplinary specialization. Positivistic-behaviouralistic trends and research agendas in comparative politics (and on populism) imposing specialization in certain aspects and verticality in perspective and methods should be complemented by more horizontal perspectives discovering and diagnosing connections between different sub-disciplines of social and po-litical sciences such as comparative politics, political theory, public admin-istration and policy, political economy as well as political sociology and political anthropology. Today, on populism, and related political phenom-enon, while more robust part of existing body of research is specialistic and disciplinary, more interdisciplinary approaches to critical political phe-nomena of our age, including populism, are still limited in terms of quality and quantity. I have undertaken this research with the contention that we need more interdisciplinary research with bottom-up perspectives that strive to understand rationalities and meanings attributed to their actions by ac-tors of politics through an interpretive approach. Especially in the study of populism, we see the development of such interpretive endeavours (Panizza *et al.* 2021) using bottom-up qualitative and ethnographic methods (Auy-ero 2001; Garrido 2017; Mazarella 2019; Meade 2020; Venizelos 2022) devoted to understanding the frameworks of meaning attributed to their ac-tions by actors embedded in populist interactions and social relations. Con-ducting research with "ethnographic sensibilities" (and, even better, with "ethnographic methods") and open-minded interdisciplinary and interpre-tive approaches have enormous potential to contribute to our understand-ing of the critical political phenomena of our age and their fundamentally relational and diffuse nature.

Notes

1 This finding is compatible with Weyland's (2013) analysis of the social policy record of populist incumbents in Latin America.
2 I would like to note here that, not surprisingly, Erdoğan's AKP in Turkey defined the "transformation" it achieved in the realms of "democracy" and "social and economic development" as a "silent revolution" in a book documenting the party's progress in 2014. See https://www.akparti.org.tr/haberler/sessiz-devrim/, accessed: 22.8.2023.
3 For a comprehensive analysis of contemporary populism in Africa, see Makulilo (2013). The author notes that when populists use "ethnic identity" to protect their interests, this strategy usually leads to civil wars (Makulilo 2013, 198).
4 Populist governmental practice is not necessarily associated with corruption. Non-populist, bureaucratic rules may very well be immersed into corruption. But when the personalistic, particularistic, and non-bureaucratic logic of populism unfolds in the governmental practice for immediate solutions and responsiveness for supporters, this usually bypasses procedures and creates privileges for certain segments of citizens (as service providing entrepreneurs and service users). This is why there is a selective affinity between populist governmental practice and corruption.
5 For an illustrative news report relying on interviews with tens of highly educated middle class migrants from Turkey documenting the "brain drain" under populist rule see: https://www.youtube.com/watch?v=FvaCY6qeVqY&ab_channel=medyascope, accessed: 21.8.2023.
6 The attribution of "anti-pluralism" to populism has been subject to compelling criticism. See Ostiguy (2017) and Katsambekis (2022).
7 For some recent works problematizing how to struggle with populism, see Kaltwasser and Taggart (2016), Baykan *et al.* (2021), Gamboa (2022), and Bourne and Olsen (2023).
8 For such an approach to the phenomenon of authoritarianism with a comprehensive, bottom-up view, see Balderacchi's (2022) work problematizing local, informal, and tactical sources of a "latent" authoritarianism in a cluster of Latin American countries with allegedly competitive politics.

References

Agamben, G. (2005). *State of Exception* (K. Attell, Trans.). Chicago: The University of Chicago Press.

Auyero, J. (2001). *Poor People's Politics*. Durham, NC and London: Duke University Press.

Balderacchi, C. (2022). Overlooked forms of non-democracy? Insights from hybrid regimes. *Third World Quarterly, 43*(6), 1441–1459.

Barr, R. R. (2019). Populism as a political strategy. In C. de la Torre (Ed.), *Routledge Handbook of Global Populism* (pp. 44–56). London: Routledge.

Bartha, A., Z. Boda & D. Szikra (2020). When populist leaders govern – conceptualising populism in policy making. *Politics and Governance, 8*(3), 71–81.

Bauer, M. W. & S. Becker (2020). Democratic backsliding, populism, and public administration. *Perspectives on Public Management and Governance, 3*(1), 19–31.

Baykan, T. S. (2018). *The Justice and Development Party in Turkey – Populism, Personalism, Organization*. Cambridge: Cambridge University Press.

268 Conclusion

Baykan, T. S., Y. Gürsoy & P. Ostiguy (2021). Anti-populist coups d'état in the twenty-first century: Reasons, dynamics and consequences. *Third World Quarterly*, 42(4), 793–811.

Baykan, T. S. & M. Somer. (2022). Politics of notables versus national machine: Social, political and state transformations, party organizations and clientelism during AKP governments. *European Journal of Turkish Studies*, 34. https://journals.openedition.org/ejts/8111, accessed: 18.8.2023.

Bourne, A. & T. V. Olsen (2023). Tolerant and intolerant responses to populist parties: Who does what, when and why?. *Comparative European Politics*. https://doi.org/10.1057/s41295-023-00335-7, accessed: 15.5.2023.

Brittan, S. (1975). The economic contradictions of democracy. *British Journal of Political Science*, 5(2), 129–159.

Chatterjee, P. (2011). *Lineages of Political Society – Studies on Postcolonial Democracy*. New York: Columbia University Press.

Chatterjee, P. (2018). Governmentality in the East. In S. Legg & D. Heath (Eds.), *South Asian Governmentalities – Michel Foucault and the Question of Postcolonial Orderings* (pp. 37–57). Cambridge: Cambridge University Press.

Chatterjee, P. (2020). *I am the People – Reflection on Popular Sovereignty Today*. New York: Columbia University Press.

de Certeau, M. (2002). *The Practice of Everyday Life* (S. Rendall, Trans.). Berkeley, CA: University of California Press.

Gamboa, L. (2022). *Opposition at the Margins*. Cambridge: Cambridge University Press.

Garrido, M. (2017). Why the poor support populism: The politics of sincerity in Metro Manila. *American Journal of Sociology*, 123(3), 647–685.

Gramsci, A. (1992). *Prison Notebooks – Volume I* (Joseph A. Buttigieg, Trans. & Ed.). New York: Columbia University Press.

Grzymala-Busse, A. (2011). Time will tell? Temporality and the analysis of causal mechanisms and processes. *Comparative Political Studies*, 44(9), 1267–1297.

Hermet, G. (2001). *Les Populismes dans le Monde*. Paris: Fayard.

Kaltwasser, C. R. & P. Taggart (2016). Dealing with populists in government: A framework for analysis. *Democratization*, 23(2), 201–220.

Katsambekis, G. (2022). Constructing "the people" of populism: A critique of the ideational approach from a discursive perspective. *Journal of Political Ideologies*, 27(1), 53–74.

Kenny, P. (2023). *Why Populism – Political Strategy from Ancient Greece to the Present*. Cambridge: Cambridge University Press.

Laclau, E. (2005). *On Populist Reason*. London and New York: Verso.

Lazar, N. C. (2022). Populism and time. In L. Manucci (Ed.), *The Populism Interviews – a Dialogue with Leading Experts* (pp. 159–163). London: Routledge.

Levitsky, S. & J. Loxton (2013). Populism and competitive authoritarianism in the Andes. *Democratization*, 20(1), 107–136.

Makulilo, A. B. (2013). Populism and democracy in Africa. In S. Gherghina, S. Mişcoiu & S. Soare (Eds.), *Contemporary Populism: A Controversial Concept and Its Diverse Forms* (pp. 167–202). New Castle upon Tyne: Cambridge Scholars Publishing.

Maya, M. L. (2018). Populism, 21st-century socialism and corruption in Venezuela. *Thesis Eleven*, 149(1), 67–83.

Mazarella, W. (2019). The anthropology of populism: Beyond the liberal settlement. *Annual Review of Anthropology, 48*, 45–60.

Meade, R. (2020). Populism from the bottom up – ethnography from Trump's U.S. and Kirchner's Argentina. In A. Ron & M. Nadesan (Eds.), *Mapping Populism – Approaches and Methods* (pp. 248–258). London: Routledge.

Mendilow, J. (2021). Introduction to populism and corruption. In J. Mendilow & E. Phelippeau (Eds.), *Populism and Corruption – the Other Side of the Coin* (pp. 1–35). Cheltenham: Edward Elgar Publishing.

Moffitt, B. (2016). *The Global Rise of Populism*. Stanford, CA: Stanford University Press.

Mouffe, C. (1993). *The Return of the Political*. London: Verso.

Mouffe, C. (2000). *The Democratic Paradox*. London: Verso.

Mouffe, C. (2005). *On the Political*. London: Routledge.

Mouffe, C. (2013). *Agonistics – Thinking the World Politically*. London: Verso.

Mouffe, C. (2018). *For a Left Populism*. London: Verso.

Mudde, C. (2004). The populist Zeitgeist. *Government and Opposition, 39*(4), 542–563.

Mudde, C. & C. Rovira Kaltwasser (Eds.). (2012). *Populism in Europe and Americas – Threat or Corrective for Democracy*. Cambridge: Cambridge University Press.

Müller, J. W. (2016). *What Is Populism?*. Philadelphia, PA: University of Pennsylvania Press.

Norris, P. & R. Inglehart (2019). *Cultural Backlash – Trump, Brexit, and Authoritarian Populism*. Cambridge: Cambridge University Press.

Ostiguy, P. (2017). Populism: A socio-cultural approach. In C. R. Kaltwasser, P. Taggart, P. O. Espejo & P. Ostiguy (Eds.), *The Oxford Handbook of Populism* (pp. 73–97). Oxford: Oxford University Press.

Panizza, F., P. Ostiguy & B. Moffitt (Eds.). (2021). *Populism in Global Perspective: A Performative and Discursive Approach*. London: Routledge.

Pappas, T. S. (2019). Populists in power. *Journal of Democracy, 30*(2), 70–84.

Peters, B. G. & J. Pierre (2019). Populism and public administration: Confronting the administrative state. *Administration & Society, 51*(10), 1521–1545.

Poguntke, T. & P. Webb (Eds.). (2007). *The Presidentialization of Politics*. Oxford: Oxford University Press.

Rahat, H. & O. Kenig (2018). *From Party Politics to Personalized Politics*. Oxford: Oxford University Press.

Schatz, E. (Ed.). (2009). *Political Ethnography*. Chicago and London: The University of Chicago Press.

Schmitt, C. (2018). *Siyasal Kavramı* (E. Göztepe, Trans.). İstanbul: Metis.

Scott, J. C. (1999). *Seeing Like a State: How Certain Schemes to Improve the Human Condition Have Failed*. New Haven, CT and London: Yale University Press.

Taggart, P. (2000). *Populism*. Buckingham: Open University Press.

Urbinati, N. (2019). *Me the People*. Cambridge and London: Harvard University Press.

Venizelos, G. (2022). Populism in power. In L. Manucci (Ed.), *The Populism Interviews – a Dialogue with Leading Experts* (pp. 112–117). London: Routledge.

Vergara, C. (2020). Crisis government – the populist as plebeian dictator. In A. Ron & M. Nadesan (Eds.), *Mapping Populism – Approaches and Methods* (pp. 210–220). London: Routledge.

Weyland, K. (2001). Clarifying a contested concept: Populism in the study of Latin American politics. *Comparative Politics, 34* (1), 1–22.

Weyland, K. (2013). Populism and social policy in Latin America. In C. J. Arnson & C. de la Torre (Eds.), *Latin American Populism in the Twenty First Century* (pp. 117–145). Washington: Woodrow Wilson Center Press/Johns Hopkins University Press.

Weyland, K. (2017). Populism: A political-strategic approach. In C. R. Kaltwasser, P. Taggart, P. O. Espejo & P. Ostiguy (Eds.), *The Oxford Handbook of Populism* (pp. 48–72). Oxford: Oxford University Press.

Weyland, K. (2021). Populism as a political strategy: An approach's enduring – and increasing advantages. *Political Studies, 69*(2), 185–189.

Zuboff, S. (2018). *The Age of Surveillance Capitalism.* New York: Public Affairs.

INDEX

Note: Page numbers in bold denote tables, page numbers in italics denote figures. Page numbers of the form XnY denote footnote Y on page X.

accountability 229, 259, 264
administrative capacity 195, 258
administrative incapacity (of populists) 11
administrative state 12–13, 65, 72, 78, 180, 236–239, 258–260
agonism 263
AKP (*Adalet ve Kalkınma Partisi* – the Justice and Development Party) xiii, xvi–xvii, 3, 14, 17, 19, 22, 87, 94–96, 100, 103–105, 107–129, 139, 252, 259
Alabama 228
American colonialism 192–193, 195
amnesty 117–118, 129
anti-pluralism 13, 73, 267n6
anti-populism 261
anti-populist 17, 70, 105, 139, 230, 263
Aquino, B. 200
Arab Socialism 209
Arab Socialist Union 208–209, 220n1
Assam 183
Aswan Dam 212–213, 219
Atatürk, M. K. 90
authoritarianism 10, 42, 44, 120, 191, 211, 265, 266
Ayubi, N. N. 217–218, 220n4
ayuda 197–198

Babri Mosque 180–181
Betz, H-G. 79n10
big government 228–229, 237
biopolitics 34, 65–66, 89, 93, 180
BJP (Bharatiya Janata Party) 22, 171, 173, 175–176, 181–186, 253
boligarchs 147
bossism 192
bounded rationality 261–262
brain drain 260
bread riots 213
bribe 197–198, 259
bribery 179, 196, 218
Britain 172, 214
British colonial rule 177–178
bureaucratic clientelism 41, **42**
bureaucratization 254
Bush, G. H. W. 229, 239

cacique democracy 193
cacique oligarchies 193–194
Canovan, M. 6, 32
Caracazo 141, 143
charisma 33, 76, 80n12, 142
charismatic authority 75
charismatic leadership 76, 262
Chatterjee, P. 67–68, 256
Chavez, H. 22, 138–139, 141–150, 253, 257, 261

272 Index

CHP (*Cumhuriyet Halk Partisi* – the Republican People's Party) 90, 92–94, 99
CİMER (*Cumhurbaşkanlığı İletişim Merkezi* – the Presidential Communication Centre) 111–112, 128
clientelism 37–49
coercion 41, 44–45, 64, 184, 209, 227
Cold War 230, 232, 239
common sense 48, 50n15, 76, 125, 174, 192, 201, 234, 258–259
competitive authoritarian regimes 44, 76, 115
competitive authoritarianism 76, 262
complicities 4–5, 70, 78, 251, 257–258, 263; *see also* complicity; informal consensuses; informal social contract; populist social contract; tacit agreement; tacit consensus; virtual consensus
complicity 60, 62–63, 64, 70, 77, 91, 128–129, 141, 160, 169, 185, 197–198, 227; *see also* complicities; informal consensuses; informal social contract; populist social contract; tacit agreement; tacit consensus; virtual consensus
Congress 172–173, 175–176, 178, 186
Constitutional Court (in Turkey) 114–115
constructive informal practices 195–196
contingency 56, 58, 263
corporatist welfare regime 118
cow protection 182–183, 186, 253
cronyism 142
cultural backlash 224, 232

de Certeau, M. 6, 20, 34, 69–71, 266
de la Torre, C. xv, 6, 8–10, 33
deindustrialization 225
Demirel, S. 92–93
dirty institutionality 6, 35, 47, 49n3
discipline 64–66
discourse-theoretical approach (to populism) 7–8, 37, 56–57, 103–105
diskarte 197–198, 202–203
Duterte, R. 22, 190, 191–192, 197, 199–205, 253–254
dynastic families 194

Ecevit, B. 99
e-governance 111
e-government 111

Egypt xvi, 6, 23, 44, 113, 130, 207–220, 254, 256, 258
electoral democracies 70, 78, 91, 93
emergency rule 255, 262, 264
enchufados 147
Erdoğan, R. T. xiii, 22, 40, 42, 95–96, 100, 103–106, 108, 116, 122, 124–128, 236, 254, 258, 261
Estrada, J. 43, 192
ethnographic sensibility 18, 266
EU (European Union) 126, 154, 157
executive prerogative 116

facilismo 141, 146, 150
favouritism 22, 107–108, 123, 128, 218
federal bureaucracy 229
fellahin 214
Foggy Bottom 231
food subsidies 213–214, 217, 220
Foucault, M. 6, 20, 21, 34, 64–69
Fraser, N. 233
Free Officers 207–208, 210–211, 215
Fujimori, A. 73

Gandhi, I. 171, 173–176, 178, 185
ganid 198, 204
Global South xviii, 20, 47, 257
globalization 107, 229–231, 233, 238
governmentality 6, 16–17, 21, 34, 36, 49, 59, 62, 64–69, 93, 159, 250, 255–256
governmentalization 66–67, 92
Greece xvi, 6, 22, 46, 73, 113, 126, 130, 153–163, 165–167, 169, 253–254, 256, 258
Gujarat 182, 185
Gülen Community 114, 126, 131n20
Gülenists 115
Gupta, A. 179–180, 186

hegemonic party 41–42, 44
hegemony 34, 35, 87, 99, 111, 228, 263
Hermet, G. 61–62, 255
High Dam *see* Aswan Dam
Hillbilly Elegy 240n1
Hindu communalism 180
Hindu nationalism 172, 180
Hinduism 182–183
Hindutva judgements 182
Hinnebusch, R. 209, 217
Hofstadter, R. 240n3
Hungary 73, 75, 260
hybrid regimes 44, 76
hyperinflation 147–148

ideational approach (to populism) 7–8, 32, 104, 124–125, 187
import substitution 37
impunity 70, 117, 165, 184–186, 196–197
India xvi, 6, 22, 45, 67–68, 130, 171–187, 193, 253, 256, 258
Indian National Congress *see* Congress
infitah 213
informal consensuses 4; *see also* complicities; complicity; informal social contract; populist social contract; tacit agreement; tacit consensus; virtual consensus
informal social contract 60, **63**, *64*, 68, 76, 78, 91, 166, 252; *see also* complicities; complicity; informal consensuses; populist social contract; tacit agreement; tacit consensus; virtual consensus
informality 21, 33, 36, 44, 58, 60, 62–63, 68, 72, 77–78, 91, 110, 112, 127, 129, 149, 168, 186, 198, 227, 235, 250–251, 253, 263, 265
Inglehart, R. 224, 232–233, 260
İnönü, İ. 92
instrumentarian power 263
Ivy League 231

Jackson, A. 238
Jimenez, M. P. 140
judicial activism 114
judicial populism 185, 187
judiciary 22, 107, 111, 114–117, 130, 177, 180, 183–184

Karamanlis, K. 154
Key, V. O. 227
Keynesian economics 156
King Farouk 207
Kissinger, H. 231
kurnazlık 197

Laclau, E. 6–8, 31–32, 34–35, 56–57
Lande, C. H. 194
latent authoritarianism 267n8
legal-rational authority 76, 163, 251
legitimate domination 75
local dynasties 193
Long, H. 222, 227, 238
Louisiana 227
love jihad 183–184, 253

machine politics 37–38, 160, 194, 223–224, 238
Mair, P. 58
majoritarianism 13, 72, 116, 180–186, 250, 257
mansabdari system 177, 187n3
Marcos, F. 191–193, 196
mass party 155, 223
Mehmet Ali Pasha 214
metapolitefsi 166–167
metis 21, 55, 70–72, 76, 78, 124, 127, 167, 197, 204, 256, 262–263
micro politics 16, 20–21, 31, 34–35, 36–37, 46–49, 88, 92, 94, 96–99, 249, 263, 265
military coup 144, 154, 261
misiones 144–147
Modi, N. 22, 171, 173–176, 182–186, 253, 258
Moffitt, B. 19, 31–33, 105
Mogamma 218
moral economy 77, 92, 197–198, 203
Mouffe, C. 56–57, 263–264
Mouzelis, N. 39–40, 168
Mubarak, H. 218
Mudde, C. 6–9, 14, 31–32, 56, 175

Narodnism 222
Nasser, G. A. 23, 207–220, 254
National Security Council (NSC) 230–231
National Union *see* Arab Socialist Union
ND (New Democracy) 154, 156–157, 161, 164, 166–167, 253
Nehru, J. 173, 178
neoliberal governmentality 66, 75
neoliberal policies 106–107, 110, 120, 141–142
neoliberal populism 14, 108, 128
neoliberalism 45, 233
nepotism 142
New Deal 227
New Public Management (NPM) 75
Nile 212–213
Nixon, R. 222, 231, 239
Norris, P. 224, 232–233, 260

oligarchies 40, 42, 158, 190–192, 194–195, 203, 264
oligarchy 110, 155, 190–191
Ombudsmanship 111–112, 128
oral culture 50n15, 70
Orban, V. 73, 75, 260

274 Index

Ostiguy, P. xv, 6–8, 31–33, 47, 105, 234
Ostrogorski, M. 50n7
Ottoman Empire 88, 100, 115, 251

Papandreou, A. 154–156, 168
partidocracia 142
party-voter linkages 17, 34, 41
PASOK (Panhellenic Socialist Party)
  xvi, 40, 46, 73, 153–157, 159–164,
  166–169, 253
passive revolution 90, 219, 256–257
pastoral power 65
paternalism 141, 150, 256
paternalistic authority 40
paternalistic populism 174
patrimonial clientelism **42**, 43, 47
patrimonial domination 43, 256
patronage 12–14, 35, 37–**42**, 45–46
patronage democracy 173, 178–179
PDVSA (*Petróleos de Venezuela, S.A.*)
  141, 144–146
penal populism 118, 182, 190, 196,
  200, 202–204
People's Party 222, 225–226, 237–238
performance legitimacy 80n14
performative and socio-cultural
  approach (to populism) 7–8, 14, 17,
  35, 37, 56–57, 59
Peronism 46, 49
Personalism 7, 22, 31, 33, 35, **36**–37,
  43–44, 47, 49, 105, 125, 141, 150,
  186, 190, 249–251
personalistic leaders 171, 207
personalistic leadership 32, 35, **36**–37,
  43, 47, 49, 72, 105, 125, 141, 150,
  186, 190, 249, 250
personalization 72, 125, 127,
  236–237, 260
Peru 73
petty corruption 5, 35, 45, 35, 77, 254,
  263–264
Philippine Constabulary 195
Philippine National Police 196–197;
  see also Philippine Constabulary
Philippines xvi, 6, 11, 22, 41, 43, 130,
  190–195, 197–204, 253–254
piyansa 199
Plunkitt, G. W. 238, 241n9
police 116–117, 126, 183, 185–186,
  195–200, 202–204
political style 7, 19, 33, 35, 37, 98, 200
political-strategic approach (to
  populism) 7–8, 32, 37, 40–41, 56–57,
  59, 149

politics of amnesty 117
politics of expediency 21, 87–94, 96,
  100, 116, 179–180, 251–252
politics proper 10, 20–21, 31, **36**,
  34–37, 48–49, 97–98, 249, 265
popular legitimacy 75–76, 78,
  256–257, 259
populist audience 24n11, 70, 126, 129,
  191, 239
populist governmentality 5, 16, 18, 68,
  70, 78, 127, 233, 256
populist social contract 23, 207,
  209, 213, 216, 217–220; *see also*
  complicities; complicity; informal
  consensuses; informal social contract;
  tacit agreement; tacit consensus;
  virtual consensus
pork-barrel politics 14, 40, 45, 248
post-materialist 225, 232, 260
power bloc 7, 155
presidentialization 260
private sector 119, 164, 210–211,
  216–217
probation 118, 129
producerist 225–226
productive consumption 24n11
Progressive Era 226–227
progressive neoliberalism 233
public employment 75, 156, 159,
  164–166, 216, 254
public opinion 21, 88–89, 92–93,
  251–252
public procurement 108–109
public sector 22, 41, 140, 146,
  154–156, 160–164, 209–211,
  216–217, 220
Punto Fijo 138, 140, 142

Quezon, M. 191–192, 203

Ranciere, J. 57
Reagan, R. 222, 229
redneck 227
religiously motivated associations 120
resistance 6, 16, 17, 34, 36, 49, 55, 59,
  68–69, 74
Roberts, K. 32, 234
Roosevelt, F. D. 227
Rose, N. 66
rule of law 116

Sadat, A. 213, 217
salvaging 191, 197, 203
Sanders, B. 222

Schmitt, C. 57
Scott, J. C. 6, 20, 34, 38, 70–71, 197, 224
Secularism 180–181, 184, 186
silent revolution 224, 232
slumhouses (*gecekondular*) 4, 98
social aid 118–119
social assistance 119–120, 122, 129, 256
Socialist Union *see* Arab Socialist Union
sovereignty 64–66
Spanish colonialism 190, 193
state capacity 265
State Department 229–232, 236, 239, 254
state of exception 115
Stavrakakis, Y. 8, 155, 168
strategic legalism 116
strategic use of violence 227
strategic violence 192
strategy 69
Supreme Court (in India) 180–182,
184–186, 201
surveillance capitalism 58, 263
systematic mass clientelism 40–41, **42**,
43, 46–47, 166–167, 256

tacit agreement 166; *see also*
complicities; complicity; informal
consensuses; informal social contract;
populist social contract; tacit
consensus; virtual consensus
tacit consensus 91; *see also* complicities;
complicity; informal consensuses;
informal social contract; populist
social contract; tacit agreement;
virtual consensus
tactics 21, 31, 34, 35–37, 44, 49,
62, **63**, 64, 65, 67, 69, 70–72, 76,
78, 114, 154, 163, 171, 184, 186,
197–199, 202, 227, 236, 248–250,
252–253, 263–264

Taggart, P. xii, 225–228, 247
Tamil Nadu 175
TBMM (*Türkiye Büyük Millet
Meclisi* – Grand National Assembly of
Turkey) 87, 90
thick description 18
Tocqueville, A. 223
Trump, D. 23, 73, 125–127, 222,
232–239, 254
tulong 197–198, 203–204
Turkey xii–xiii, xv–xvii, 3–4, 6, 11,
14–15, 17–19, 21–22, 35, 42, 77,
87–88, 90–100, 103–130, 154, 158,
160, 165, 186, 197, 248, 251–252,
256, 258, 260

United Kingdom xiii, xv, 37
United States (US) 6, 23, 37, 72,
126–127, 130, 138, 190, 222–235,
237–239, 254–255
USPV (United Socialist Party of
Venezuela) 139
Uttar Pradesh 175, 183

Vardaman, J. 227
Venezuela xvi, 6, 11, 22, 73, 113, 130,
138–150, 253, 256–257, 260
virtual consensus 15, 60, 77, 166;
see also complicities; complicity;
informal consensuses; informal social
contract; populist social contract; tacit
agreement; tacit consensus

Wallace, G. 222, 227–228, 238
WASP families 231
Weber, M. 75–76
Weyland, K. 7–9, 14, 31–32, 34, 40, 43,
56, 105, 149, 175, 240
World War II 153, 229, 232, 235, 239

Printed in the United States
by Baker & Taylor Publisher Services